The MIT Encyclopedia of
the Japanese Economy

The MIT Encyclopedia of the Japanese Economy

Robert C. Hsu

The MIT Press
Cambridge, Massachusetts
London, England

This book was set in Palatino by Asco Trade Typesetting Ltd., Hong Kong and
was printed and bound in the United States of America.

Library of Congress Cataloging-in-Publication Data

Hsu, Robert C.
   The MIT encyclopedia of the Japanese economy / Robert C. Hsu.
      p.   cm.
   Includes bibliographical references.
   ISBN 0-262-08227-6
   1. Japan—Economic conditions—1945–   —Dictionaries. 2. Japan—
   Economic policy—1945–   —Dictionaries. I. Title.
   HC462.9.H73   1994
   330.952′003—dc20   93-34556
                                                                CIP

to my family—Sharon, Nancy, and Steven

Contents

Tables

Preface

The purpose of this book is to explain concisely the essentials of a large number of important topics on the contemporary Japanese economy, from A to Z, thereby filling a gap in the literature. The book contains 159 topical essays and more than 200 short definitional entries, all listed alphabetically. All **bold-lettered** terms in the text are the topics of separate essays. Definitional entries have cross references to indicate that they are also discussed in one or more essays in a larger context.

The essays vary greatly in length, depending on the importance of the topic. Each essay contains the definition and descriptions of the topic, discussions of important issues, some statistical information or tables, cross-references, addresses of relevant organizations where appropriate, and references in English for further reading.

Japanese government fiscal year (FY) begins on April 1 of each year and ends on March 31 of the following year. A lot of government and business publications and statistics are published on fiscal-year basis. However, some are published on both fiscal-year and calendar-year bases or just on calendar-year basis. Where statistics are based on the fiscal year, it is so indicated in the book.

With the exception of international trade and investment, economic figures such as income, production, sales, profits, and wages are given in yen (¥). This is because the yen–dollar exchange rate has fluctuated so much over the years, due to various factors, that it is not always meaningful to use it to translate yen figures into dollar equivalents. In particular, because of Japan's chronic trade surplus, the yen–dollar exchange rates do not reflect the real purchasing power of the two currencies in their respective countries. Readers interested in converting the yen figures into dollars can use the exchange rates of the relevant years given in the essay on **yen–dollar exchange rates** (table Y.1).

Because of the wide range of topics discussed in the book, errors are no doubt inevitable. I would be grateful if knowledgable readers would inform me of the errors so that they can be corrected in the next edition.

Acknowledgments

This book is an outgrowth of a course on the Japanese and Chinese economies that I have been teaching at Clark University for many years. My first intellectual debt therefore goes to my students in the course whose interests have stimulated my teaching and research.

In writing this book, I had the privilege of visiting the following private organizations and companies in Japan: American Chamber of Commerce in Japan, Anelva Corp., Central Union of Agricultural Cooperatives (Zenchu), Federation of Economic Organizations (Keidanren), General Summit Enterprise Co., Japan Economic Research Center, Japan Federation of Employers' Association (Nikkeiren), Japan Iron and Steel Federation, Japan Trade Union Confederation (JTUC-RENGO), Matsumi Sangyo Co., Mitsubishi Heavy Industries, NEC Corp., Nissan Motor, Nihon Keizai Shimbun, Inc., Nomura Research Institute, Sony Corp., Toyo Keizai, Tokyo Stock Exchange, and Toyota Motor. To the organizations, companies, and the many individuals who hosted my visits and spent much time with me, I am deeply grateful.

I also had the honor of visiting the following ministries and agencies of the Japanese government: Bank of Japan, Economic Planning Agency, Fair Trade Commission, Institute of Developing Economies, Land Agency, Ministry of Agriculture, Forestry and Fisheries, Ministry of Finance, Ministry of International Trade and Industry (MITI), Patent Office, and Yokohama City Hall. All these government organizations arranged for me to interview their senior officials and provided me with their latest publications and statistics. I want to thank, in particular, the Bank of Japan and MITI, which I visited several times over the years; I have benefited greatly from lengthy discussions with their senior economists in their research/statistics departments.

The following companies and private organizations provided me with timely materials: Federation of Bankers Association of Japan, Itochu Corp.,

Japan Automobile Manufacturers Association, Japan Economic Institute (in Washington, DC), Japan Economic Research Institute, Japan Securities Dealers Association, Japan Shipbuilders Association, Keizai Koho Center, Mitsubishi Corp., Mitsubishi Economic Research Institute, Mitsui and Co., NEC Corp., Sharp Corp., and Sumitomo Corp.

The following Japanese government ministries and agencies responded generously to my requests for materials: the Japan Institute of Labor, Management and Coordination Agency, Ministry of Health and Welfare, Ministry of Labor, Ministry of Posts and Telecommunications, Nagoya Municipal Government, National Tax Administration Agency, Osaka Municipal Government, the Prime Minister's Office, the Small and Medium Enterprise Agency, and Tokyo Metropolitan Government. The American Embassy in Tokyo also provided useful materials.

I am indebted to the following professors and experts who gave generously their time and advice during interviews: James Abegglen of Sophia University and chairman of Gemini Consulting (Japan); Robert Ballon of Sophia University; Elaine Crepeau, formerly of Sophia University; Yujiro Hayami of Aoyama Gakuin University; Ken-ichi Imai of Stanford Japan Center; Kanji Ishizumi of Chiyoda Kokusai Law Office; Nobuo Kodama of Meisei University; Ryutaro Komiya of Aoyama Gakuin University and the Research Institute of MITI; Tamao Tokuhisa of Aoyama Gakuin University; and Masu Uekusa of Tokyo University. I would like to thank in particular Elaine Crepeau and Nobuo Kodama, who have helped me in Japan in many ways over the years.

The following individuals read portions or all of the manuscript and gave valuable comments for improvement: Michiko Aoki, Akinari Horii, Yukiko Oda, Jon Sigurdson, Aleta Thielmeyer, Fujio Uryu, Adis Vila, and anonymous reviewers. Gail Skamarack of Goddard Library, Clark University, was extremely helpful in making available some essential serials on the Japanese economy. The staff at the following libraries was also very helpful to me: Harvard-Yenching Library of Harvard University, the library of the International House of Japan, and the library of the Ministry of International Trade and Industry. I also received competent research assistance from Steffanie Fewerestein at Clark University and Tsunemasa Hinoki in Tokyo. To all these individuals go my sincere thanks. Naturally all remaining errors are my responsibility alone.

Research for this book was supported by grants from Clark University's faculty development fund, a Takahashi grant administered by Clark University, a sabbatical leave from Clark University during the fall semester of 1991, and a Fulbright research grant under the *Japan Today* program during the summer of 1992. The Japan–United States Educational Commission (Fulbright Program) assisted me in arranging for some interviews in the summer of 1992.

I am grateful to Nihon Keizai Shimbun Inc., the publisher of Japan's leading business daily (see **Economic/Business Research and Publications**) for giving me permission to adapt some tables published in *The Nikkei Weekly* for use in the book.

Finally, my family—Sharon, Nancy, and Steven—was always supportive and understanding despite the countless hours during which I had to be away. I deeply appreciate such support and understanding.

Worcester, Massachusetts
July 1993

A

administrative guidance   Administrative guidance (*gyosei shido*) refers to the suggestions or "unwritten orders" given by Japanese bureaucrats to firms to implement official policies. It is based on the broad discretionary power of the bureaucracy rather than on specific laws. Administrative guidance is important in Japan because it gives the bureaucrats much flexibility in implementing policies. Hence it is freqently used in lieu of government regulations by bureaucrats to steer the private sector.

Compliance with the guidance is not mandatory. However, to maintain good working relationships with the bureaucrats, business managers usually find it advantageous to follow this practice, for fear that the latter may frustrate them in business operations. The high respect that the Japanese public traditionally accords elite bureaucrats and the close working relationship between bureaucrats and business managers are other factors that induce compliance with administrative guidance.

All government ministries and agencies practice administrative guidance in their interactions with the private sector. The **Ministry of International Trade and Industry** (MITI) and the **Ministry of Finance**, however, are particularly active in its use because of their wide scope of jurisdiction. In its actual practice administrative guidance has been applied to a wide range of business activities. For example, in the early 1960s MITI advised firms in the steel and auto industries to merge into fewer firms in order to compete with foreign producers. In 1985 it urged the Japan Automobile Manufacturers Association to send an auto-parts buying mission to the United States to help reduce Japan's trade surplus and alleviate U.S. protectionist sentiment. It also pressured a minor service station to withdraw its application for importing gasoline from Singapore. In 1991 it called on Japanese automakers to sell American-made cars in Japan through their sales networks.

Administrative guidance, however, is rarely a one-sided top-down government measure imposed on unwilling business managers. Prior consultations with business managers usually take place before a guidance is given in order to ensure maximum cooperation. Oftentimes administrative guidance is given in response to industry's requests for government's guidelines (Eads and Yamamura 1987: 433). Since compliance with administrative guidance is voluntary, it is not always assured. This is because government bureaucrats can and have made errors of judgment and their suggestions may contradict the interests of those to be guided. For example, the automobile industry did not follow MITI's suggestion of mergers in the early 1960s, and it managed to become internationally competitive in spite of its relatively large number of firms.

In the wake of the securities industry's scandals as revealed in 1991, and in light of the failure of the Ministry of Finance to prevent them, Japanese mass media has severely criticized administrative guidance as having protected big businesses at the expense of market competition. In addition, because administrative guidance is often vague and secretive, it is also criticized as having left the public uninformed while fostering an environment of collusion between the Ministry of Finance and big business. It is said to have caused businesses to cultivate smooth relations with authorities as the top priority.

As a result of these criticisms, it is expected that an administrative procedures bill will be enacted soon, replacing administrative guidance with written directives.

See also **industrial policy**.

References

Bureauractic "guidance" is unwanted, unwarranted. *Nikkei Weekly* editorial, Aug. 24, 1991: 6.

Eads, George C., and Kozo Yamamura. 1987. The future of industrial policy. In *The Political Economy of Japan*, vol. 1: *The Domestic Transformation*, ed. by Kozo Yamamura and Yasukichi Yasuba. Stanford: Stanford University Press.

Gyosei shido: Inside Japanese bureaucracy. *Tokyo Business Today*, Jan. 1986: 34–37.

Johnson, Chalmers. 1982. *MITI and the Japanese Miracle*. Stanford: Stanford University Press. Ch. 7.

Koh, B. C. 1989. *Japan's Administrative Elite*. Berkeley: University of California Press.

Okimoto, Daniel I. 1989. *MITI and the Market*. Stanford: Stanford University Press. Ch. 2.

Agricultural Basic Law, 1961   A law enacted to support agriculture and to reduce the disparity in productivity and standard of living between the agricultural and nonagricultural sectors.

See **agricultural policy**.

agricultural cooperatives   Japan has an extensive and well-organized system of agricultural cooperatives (*nokyo*, or *nogyo kyodo kumiai*). It promotes farming and farmers' interests in Japan under the political leadership of Zenchu (Central Union of Agricultural Cooperatives), the nation's most powerful farm lobby group. It has a politically active membership of eight million, of which six million are farmers. The cooperatives are politically powerful and are closely involved in various facets of rural lives.

Agricultural cooperatives are organized into three tiers:

1. *Primary agricultural cooperatives*. These are organized at the city, town, and village levels. They are classified into two types: (a) Multipurpose agricultural cooperatives (*sogo nokyo*, 3,223 at the end of 1992) are engaged in marketing members' agricultural products and in providing them with agricultural inputs, banking, credit, insurance, welfare, and educational services, and so forth. They serve as grass roots credit institutions in rural areas. They accept deposits from members and lend funds to members and the farming community. At the end of 1992, agricultural cooperatives had ¥63.9 trillion in deposits and ¥17.1 trillion in loans. Virutally all farm households are members. (b) Single-purpose agricultural cooperatives (*senmonren nokyo*, 4,097 in 1990) are organized in specific sectors—such as fruits and vegetables, sericulture and livestock raising—to market their products. Almost all of their members are concurrently members of multipurpose cooperatives.

2. *Prefectural federations and unions*. At the prefectural level two types of federations are organized. (a) Federations that are composed of multipurpose agricultural cooperatives as members such as prefectural economic federations (*keizairen*), prefectural credit federations (*kenshinren*), prefectural mutual-insurance federations (*kyosairen*), and prefectural welfare federations (*koreiren*). These federations provide the cooperatives with services in their respective areas. For example, the prefectural credit federations accept deposits from, and make loans to, agricultural cooperatives, assist them in their credit operations, and smooth regional surpluses and deficits among the cooperatives. They are also involved in various investment activities. At the end of 1992, they had a total of ¥48.2 trillion in deposits and ¥10.1

trillion in loans. (b) Federations that are composed of single-purpose agricultural cooperatives as members such as dairy cooperative federations, sericultural cooperative federations, and horticultural cooperative federations.

Each of the 47 prefectures has a prefectural union of agricultural cooperatives. Their members are primary cooperatives and prefectural federations. They are engaged in guidance, coordination, and research, and they represent the interests of the cooperatives in each prefecture.

3. *National level organizations.* All prefectural federations have their counterparts organized at the national level such as the National Federation of Agricultural Cooperative Associations (Zennoh), Central Cooperative Bank for Agriculture and Forestry (Norinchukin Bank), National Mutual-Insurance Federation of Agricultural Cooperatives, National Fedederation of Dairy Cooperatives, and National Federation of Livestock Cooperatives. The Central Cooperative Bank for Agriculture and Forestry is one of Japan's largest banks. At the end of 1992, it had ¥27.6 trillion in deposits and ¥14.8 trillion in loans. Finally, there is the Central Union of Agricultural Cooperatives (Zenchu), the political leadership of Japan's agricultural cooperative movement. Its members are primary agricultural cooperatives, prefectural federations, prefectural unions, and various national federations. Zenchu is not only involved in services such as guidance, coordination, education, and information, but it also conducts political campaigns to promote farmers' interests. Its president is the spokesperson for agricultural cooperatives and the farming community's top negotiator with the government bureaucracy and business organizations.

Administratively the agricultural cooperative also serves as a government agent in the agricultural sector. It performs a number of semiofficial duties under various agriculture-related laws—the Food Control Law, the Livestock Price Stabilization Law, the Feed Demand and Supply Stabilization Law, the Dairy Farming Promotion Law—to assist farmers. For example, it is in charge of the collection and shipment of rice that is not sold to the government ("independent distribution rice") and charges commissions as rice passes through it. As a government agent it receives commissions and subsidies from the government, and its activities are monitored by government administrators.

Structural changes are in store for the agricultural cooperatives. Because of financial deregualtion, Zenchu plans to reduce the number of the credit federations of agricultural cooperatives to make them more competitive with other financial institutions. The number of agricultural cooperatives will also be reduced to about 1,000 by the year 2000. The number had already declined from 8,273 at the end of 1965 to 3,223 at the end of 1992.

See also **agricultural policy, banking system, rice production and distribution**.

Addresses

Central Union of Agricultural Cooperatives
8-3, Otemachi 1-chome, Chiyoda-ku, Tokyo 100
Tel: (03) 3245-7565   Fax: 3242-1581

National Federation of Agricultural Cooperative Associations
8-3, Otemachi 1-chome, Chiyoda-ku, Tokyo 100
Tel: (03) 3245-7035   Fax: 3245-7442

Norinchukin Bank
8-3, Ohtemachi 1-chome, Chiyoda-ku, Tokyo 100
Tel: (03) 3279-0111

References

Central Union of Agricultural Cooperatives. 1991. *Agricultural Cooperative Movement in Japan.*

Cheng, Peter P. 1990. Japanese interest group politics. *Asian Survey* 30, 3: 251–265.

Moore, Richard M. 1990. *Japanese Agriculture: Patterns of Rural Development.* Boulder, CO: Westview. Ch. 8.

Rothacher, Albrecht. 1989. *Japan's Agro-Food Sector: The Politics and Economics of Excess Protection.* London: Macmillan Press.

The power politics of rice. *Tokyo Business Today*, Oct. 1990: 26–35.

Shida, Tomio. Farm co-ops seek spot to sow huge cash harvest. *Japan Economic Journal*, Apr. 1, 1989: 2.

Taro, Yayama. 1987. Cooperatives, the curse of Japanese agriculture. *Japan Echo* 14, 1: 7–8.

agricultural policy   In the postwar period the Japanese government had to deal with various agriculture-related issues: to increase food supply in the immediate postwar period, to support farmers' income as the agricultural sector declined in the economy, and to protect the domestic agricultural market from foreign producers as the latter clamored to enter the Japanese market. The relative importance of these issues changes over time and helps to shape the focus of Japan's agricultural policy in any particular time period.

In the immediate postwar period the main objectives of the agricultural policy were to ensure adequate food supplies and to implement the agricultural land reform program as mandated by the U.S. occupation in its effort to democratize the society. These objectives were achieved as planned.

By the mid-1950s the Japanese economy had recovered from the devastation of the war and its industry developed very rapidly thereafter, causing an outflow of labor from agriculture to industry. In addition productivity in industry rose much more rapidly than in agriculture, causing a growing disparity between industrial wages and farm income. To deal with these problems of structural changes in the economy, the Agricultural Basic Law was enacted in 1961. It authorized the government to protect and support agriculture and farmers' income. This became the focus of Japan's agricultural policy from early 1960s to the late 1980s. Various instruments were used to attain the objective. Through government purchase of rice at high prices—eventually as high as four times the world price level—the government supports the income of farm households. The government purchase price is set annually on the basis of production costs including the imputed cost of farmers' own labor, which is calculated on the basis of industrial wages (see **pricing practices**). The import of rice is banned.

The production of selective agricultural products is promoted and protected. With rising income, Japanese households are changing their diets; they are consuming more meat, dairy products, fruits, and so on, and less rice. The government therefore has taken measures to promote the production of livestock, fruits, and vegetables. Import restrictions in the form of quotas are imposed on beef, fruits (particularly oranges), dairy products, flour, beans, fish, shellfish, and processed foods.

The general strategy of agricultural import protection is to give high protection (i.e., low quotas) to final consumer agricultural goods to encourage their domestic production or processing and to permit the imports of needed raw materials or products by giving them low protection. Examples of the latter are feed grains for livestock, wheat for flour and flour products, and soybeans for soy products. As a result of this strategy, Japan's self-sufficiency rate for agricultural products used as food decreased from 90% in 1960 to 72% in 1980 and about 67% in 1990. The rate for rice has remained 100% in 1990 and that for dairy products was 85% in 1985 but declined to 78% in 1990. There was rice surplus at times as high government purchase prices encouraged excessive production; the self-sufficiency rate of rice was 110% in 1975 and 107% in 1985.

Subsidies over and above the subsidy on rice prices are also given to agriculture. They amounted to 49% of total agricultural budget in 1960, 61% in 1980, and 66% in 1991. They are paid to growers of a large number of agricultural items. Thus a large number of small farmers benefit from these payments; this is politically important to the ruling Liberal Democratic Party. With the subsidy on rice prices (which appear in the agricultural budget as a transfer from the general account to the food control special account) the ratio of subsidy to total agricultural budget can be as high as 80% (Hayami 1988: 57).

The protection program outlined above has expanded rapidly since the mid-1960s for two reasons: the increased demand for protection coming from the politically powerful farm block organized under the **agricultural cooperatives** and the decline in domestic countervailing power against agricultural protection. Since the Japanese have become more affluent and the share of food in their total consumption expenditures has declined, they have become more tolerant of high food prices. Consumers, trade unions, and business leaders have seldom protested government protection policies (Hayami 1988; author's interview, July 2, 1992).

There are constraints, however, on the government's protection policies that come from both domestic and external sources. Domestically, high rice prices have stimulated overproduction and strained the government's budget. Externally, foreign food-exporting countries, particularly the United States, have protested Japan's import quotas. Much of the agricultural imports come from the United States. In fact Japan has become the largest importer of agricultural products from the United States, and the United States has become the largest food supplier to Japan. However, as Japan–U.S. trade imbalance grew in the 1980s and as Japan enjoys open markets for its manufactured goods in the United States, Japan's remaining restrictions on food imports has become a major source of Japan–U.S. trade frictions. Washington has demanded greater access to Japan's agricultural market.

The products of particular interests to Washington have been beef, oranges, and rice. Beef and oranges were protected by Japan with quotas. In 1978 Washington negotiated with Tokyo to increase quotas gradually wthout disrupting Japanese domestic production. In 1988, after several years of hard bargaining, the **Beef-Citrus Agreement** was reached— quotas would be increased during 1988–90 but replaced by tariffs in 1991.

Washington's demand for the liberalization of rice imports has not yet been achieved because of very strong domestic opposition to it in Japan. It has become part of the agricultural issues at the Uruguay Round of GATT negotiations. As Europe and other countries also protect their agriculture, the resolution of the rice issue will depend on the outcome of the Uruguary Round negotiations. Observers expect Tokyo to accept tariffication in place of quotas if the Uruguay Round reaches a successful agreement on the liberalization of agricultural trade.

See also **agricultural cooperatives, pricing practices, rice production and distribution**.

References

Hayami, Yujiro. 1988. *Japanese Agriculture under Siege: The Political Economy of Agricultural Policies*. London: Macmillan.

Hayami, Yujiro, and Saburo Yamada. 1991. *The Agricultural Development of Japan: A Century's Perspective*. Tokyo: University of Tokyo Press.

Moore, Richard M. 1990. *Japanese Agriculture: Patterns of Rural Development*. Boulder, CO: Westview.

Reich, Michael, Yasuo Endo, and C. Peter Timmer. 1986. Agriculture: The political economy of structural change. In *American versus Japan*, ed. by Thomas K. McCraw. Boston: Harvard Business School Press.

airline industry   Japan has three major airlines, all privately owned— Japan Airlines Co. (JAL), All Nippon Airways Co. (ANA), and Japan Air System Co. (JAS). JAL and ANA are by far the largest two. JAS is a member of the Tokyu Group, a large family-controlled conglomerate. There are also some other smaller regional airlines.

Japan Airlines, the national flag carrier and one of the world's largest, is engaged in both domestic and international operations. In FY 1991 it derived 51% of its revenues from international passenger service, 23% from domestic passengers, and 16% from cargo operations. It has the largest number of Japan's international routes but is expanding its domestic services. Because it was only privatized in November 1987, it is still in the process of restructuring. It is known for quality service but is reportedly still suffering from the heritage of high operating costs, particularly personnel costs, and inefficient management. In FY 1990 and 1991 it had operating revenues of ¥1,119 billion and ¥1,115 billion, respectively, but its pretax profit was only ¥27.3 billion in FY 1990, which declined to a loss of ¥13 billion in FY 1991.

All Nippon Airways is Japan's second largest airline. The bulk of its operations is in domestic passenger service (89% of revenues in FY 1991).

It started international flights in 1986 when industry liberalization encouraged open competition among airlines and has been actively expanding its international routes ever since. It also operates hotels. In FY 1990 and 1991 it had sales of ¥733 billion and ¥799 billion, respectively, and pretax profits of ¥25.3 billion and ¥39.2 billion.

Japan Air System, the third largest airline, is currently limited to domestic routes but is attempting to break into international passenger service. It derived 93% of its revenues in FY 1991 from domestic passenagers and 3% from air cargoes. As of September 1991, 25.5% of its shares were held by Tokyu Corp. because of its membership in the Tokyu Group. In FY 1990 it had operating revenues of ¥243.5 billion and pretax profits of ¥6.5 billion.

Japan's airline industry enjoyed rapid growth in the 1980s. The Gulf War of 1991 and Japan's recession during 1991–92 adversely affected international air travel and industry profits. Nevertheless, in FY 1991 Japanese airlines carried a record 68.7 million passengers on regularly scheduled domestic flights and 11.3 million passengers on regularly scheduled international flights, an increase of 5.3% and 7%, respectively, over the previous year. Analysts expect the airline industry to remain healthy in the long run because of the strong travel industry in Japan. Continual economic growth and shorter working hours in Japan will increase the demand for leisure services, including air travel. In addition Japanese companies are increasingly globalized, necessitaing more business travel overseas. A total of 12 million Japanese traveled abroad in 1992, and the number is expected to increase further.

The industry has a severe and unique problem—namely the major airports have reached their capacity limits. Tokyo Narita Airport, the nation's major international airport, has only one runway; it handles 122,000 flights annually, 10% more than initially planned. Tokyo Haneda Airport, the main airport for domestic flights, has two runways. It handles 180,000 flights annually, and more than 42 million passengers use it annually, about double that of Narita. As a result it is extremely difficult to increase the number of flights or to open new routes out of these two largest airports. In recent years the airlines have expanded the use of regional airports for international flights. The major regional airports are located in Sapporo and Nagoya. Also JAL and ANA each set up a subsidiary in 1990 that specializes in charter flights out of regional airports.

This airport constraint will ease somewhat in the mid-1990s. The new Kansai International Airport, under construction on a human-made island in Osaka Bay, is scheduled to open in the summer of 1994. Haneda Airport will have three new runways completed in 1995. The Ministry of Transport plans to build two new runways at Narita Airport, but it will take many more years for the government to acquire the land and initiate construction, although a new second terminal was opened in late 1992.

See also **railway companies**.

Addresses

All Nippon Airways
2-5, Kasumigaseki 3-chome, Chiyoda-ku, Tokyo 100
Tel: (03) 3592-3065   Fax: (03) 3592-3039

Japan Air System
5-1, Toranomon 3-chome, Minato-ku, Tokyo 105
Tel: (03) 5473-4100

Japan Airlines
7-3, Marunouchi 2-chome, Chiyoda-ku, Tokyo 100
Tel: (03) 3284-2511   Fax: (03) 3284-2529

References

Airlines. In *Japan Economic Almanac*, various years. Tokyo: Nihon Keizai Shimbun.

Hasegawa, Mina. 1993. JAL restructuring: Will it fly? *Nikkei Weekly*, Mar. 8: 1.

Is JAL losing its wing. *Tokyo Business Today*, Sept. 1992: 56–58.

Japan Company Handbook. Autumn 1992. Tokyo: Toyo Keizai.

All Nippon Airways Co. (ANA)   Japan's second largest airline with its bulk of business in domestic flights.

See **airline industry**.

amakudari   Literally "descent from heaven," *amakudari* refers to the time-honored practice of Japanese officials, upon early retirement, to move to high positions in an industry with which they had worked closely during their government service. This had its origin in the early Meiji period when the government set up industrial and commercial undertakings to provide jobs for functionless *samurai*.

Between 1974 and the mid-1980s, the **Ministry of International Trade and Industry** had the largest number of *amakudari* of all government agencies (Blumenthal 1985). In more recent years the **Ministry of Finance** has been in the lead. According to the National Personnel Authority, in 1988, 3,043 government officials resigned or retired at the average age of

55.2. About 10% of them took new jobs at companies with close relationships to their previous offices. Among the ministries the Ministry of Finance topped the list with 50 *amakudari* officials, followed by the Ministry of Posts and Telecommunications (28), the Ministry of Agriculture, Forestry and Fisheries (27), the Ministry of Construction (21), the Ministry of International Trade and Industry (19), the Ministry of Education (18), and the Ministry of Transport (18).

Japanese companies reportedly like the practice of *amakudari* for various reasons. It provides them with fresh blood, expertise, and seasoned leaders, and it provides them with connections with government bureaucrats, thereby improving communication between the two. Caldor (1989) contends that this is particularly useful for medium-sized, less-established firms that normally cannot attrack top college graduates. However, Aoki (1988: 266) maintains that ministries push to expand *amakudari* opportunities as rewards to retiring bureaucrats and as a means to extend their influence. Other critics charge that the practice leads to conflicts of interests and abuses of power. Government officials may curry favor with companies for possible postretirement jobs. Ministries may use *amakudari* bureaucrats in the companies to monitor company activities. Some companies do not like the pressure on them to hire retired government officials, nor do they think that ex-bureaucrats have enough business sense. On the other hand, defenders of the practice such as Okimoto (1990) have argued that government ministries have been careful not to abuse their connections with *amakudari* officials lest the latter's careers be compromised.

In order to minimize possible abuses, Japan's National Public Service Law stipulates that government employees are not allowed to join private companies for two years after retirement if they had close relationships with the companies within five years before retirement; in these cases special approval from the National Personnel Authority is needed. The National Personnel Authority approved 232 such cases in 1988 and 246 cases in 1989.

In the wake of securities companies scandals in 1991, the Ministry of Finance has been criticized as having a collusive relationship with the securities industry. Consequently the ministry adopted a policy of voluntary restraint regarding the hiring of retired bureaucrats by securities companies. The policy, however, is not expected to last long.

In addition to private companies, public corporations and other government-related nonprofit institutions have been the recipients of *amakudari*. It is rare, however, for retiring officials to teach at universities.

See also **corporate personnel practices**.

Address

National Personnel Authority
1-2, Kasumigaseki 2-chome, Chiyoda-ku, Tokyo 100
Tel: (03) 3381-5311

References

Aoki, Masahiko. 1988. *Information, Incentives, and Bargaining in the Japanese Economy.* Cambridge: Cambridge University Press. Ch. 7.

Blumenthal, Tuvia. 1985. The practice of *amakudari* within the Japanese employment system. *Asian Survey* 25: 310–21.

Bureaucrats "descend" into industry boardrooms. *Japan Economic Journal*, Apr. 14, 1990: 22.

Caldor, Kent. 1989. Elites in an equalizing role: Ex-bureaucrats as coordinators and intermediaries in the Japanese government-business relationship. *Comparative Politics*, 21: 379–403.

Fewer senior bureaucrats "retire" to industrial posts. *Japan Economic Journal*, Apr. 15, 1989: 12.

Okimoto, Daniel I. 1990. *Between MITI and the Market.* Stanford: Stanford University Press. Pp. 161–165.

Antimonopoly Law   The law was introduced in 1947 as part of the Allied Occupation's policy to decentralize the postwar economy and to promote competition. The Japanese economy during the war was highly concentrated under the leadership of the **zaibatsu**, the huge conglomerates, which were believed to have contributed to the war effort. Modeled on U.S. antitrust laws, the Antimonopoly Law bans trusts, **cartels**, as well as holding companies, which were an important part of the *zaibatsu* organization. It prohibits "private monopolization, unreasonable restraints of trade and unfair methods of competion" (Article 1). It restricts mergers and prohibits financial institutions from owning more than 5% of any single company's shares to prevent excessive concentration of business ownership. The law was subsequently revised several times.

The Fair Trade Commission was created under the prime minister's office to implement the law. However, it has remained a minor government agency and observers generally regard it as weak and understaffed, a "toothless watchdog" vis-à-vis big business and the Japanese bureaucracy, and too willing to make exceptions. These weaknesses reflect the low priority given by the Japanese government to the implementation of the Antimonopoly Law as compared with other policy areas, particularly the **industrial policy**. The law was sometimes contravened by the industrial policy of the **Ministry of International Trade and Industry** (MITI). In the 1950s the promotion of domestic industries was paramount for the government and the implementation of the Antimonopoly Law was ineffective. Consequently the law was revised in 1953 to ease the restrictions on cartels, trusts, mergers, and other competion-curbing measures. Recession cartels and rationalization cartels were permitted. The revision also exempted import-export businesses from the law. The ceiling on bank holding of company stock was raised to 10%.

In the 1960s, with trade liberalization, industries lobbied for further revision of the law to restrict competition, but their efforts were unsuccessful, in part because of the public's growing support for the law. In the early 1970s, after the oil crisis, there were a number of illegal cartels and other corporate activities that restricted market competition. In response the Diet passed bills in 1975 and 1977 to strengthen the law. Punitive measures such as surcharges and sale of part of operations were provided for the first time to curb violations of the law. As a sign of the growing importance of antimonopoly policy versus the industrial policy, oil company cartels formed in accordance with MITI's **administrative guidance** were found in 1980 to be in violation of the Antimonopoly Law. That was the only antimonopoly dispute ever to go to court in Japan.

Foreign analysts have often criticized the implementation of the law as weak and ineffective and have argued that this has aided Japanese firms' competitiveness in world trade. During the **Structural Impediments Initiative** talks between Washington and Tokyo in 1989–90, U.S. negotiators identified various business practices such as **cross shareholding** in *keiretsu* groups, price cartels, and bid-rigging as violations of the Antimonopoly Law that restrict competition and exclude foreign firms from the Japanese market. Washington requested that Tokyo strengthen its antitrust enforcement in general and that tougher measures be taken against exclusionary business practices.

There are signs that in response to Washington's pressure, Japan is going to implement the Antimonopoly Law more seriously. In December 1990 the Fair Trade Commission announced that it planned to impose surcharges of up to 6% on a company's sales, for a period of up to three years, on companies that formed a cartel to boost prices. Previously the commission imposed an average of 1.5% surcharge on companies on sales in the period the companies were found to have joined an illegal cartel. (In the United States, companies caught in violation of antitrust laws are fined 50% of affected sales.) In FY 1991 the budget and staff of FTC were raised. The commission announced in 1991 that it would investigate Nomura

Securities Co. for allegedly controlling more than 5% of a subsidiary's shares through third-party manipulation. It would also investigate cross-sharedolding in automobiles, auto parts, paper products, and glass industries, which Washington has accused of having exclusionary practices. Also, in late 1991, in its first criminal antitrust complaint in 17 years, FTC accused eight plastic-wrap makers of price fixing.

Some Japanese question whether all Japanese antimonopoly provisions, adopted in 1947 on the basis of the U.S. antitrust laws under pressure from the Occupation, are equally appropriate for Japan in the 1990s. For example, some Japanese argue that holding companies may not be inappropriate in some industries.

See also **cartels, industrial policy, Ministry of International Trade and Industry.**

Address

Fair Trade Commission
2-1, Kasumigaseki 2-chome, Chiyoda-ku, Tokyo 100
Tel: (03) 3581-5471

References

Antimonopoly laws tighten. *Tokyo Business Today*, Apr. 1992: 26–30.

Chipello, Christopher J. 1991. Japanese FTC accuses 8 firms of price fixing. *Asian Wall Street Journal Weekly*, Nov. 11: 12.

Fair Trade Commission. *FTC/Japan Views*. Quarterly.

Nakajima, Ai. 1991. Fair Trade Commission following tougher line. *Nikkei Weekly*, Sept. 28: 3.

Ostrom, Douglas. 1989. Japan's competition politics. *JEI Report*, May 19.

Tsuruta, Toshimas. 1985. Japan's industrial policy. In *The Management Challenge: Japanese Views*, ed. by Lester C. Thurow. Cambridge: MIT Press.

Uekusa, Masu. 1987. Industrial organization: The 1970s to the present. In *The Political Economy of Japan*, vol. 1: The *Domestic Transformation*, ed. by Kozo Yamamura and Yasukichi Yasuba. Stanford: Stanford University Press.

Uekusa, Masu. 1990. Government regulations in Japan: Toward their international harmonization and integration. In *Japan's Economic Structure: Should It Change?* ed. by Kozo Yamamura. Seattle: Society for Japanese Studies.

atogime Deferred price setting, a practice in paper and petrochemical industries of allowing sellers to renegotiate prices after delivery.
See **pricing practices.**

automobile exports and imports
See **automobile industry**.

automobile industry   The automobile industry became one of Japan's most important industries in the postwar period. Automobile production began in Japan in the 1920s when Henry Ford built a factory in Yokohama. In 1933 the Nissan Motor Co. was established to produce small vehicles. In 1937 the Toyota Motor Co. was established. In 1980, less than 50 years after Nissan's founding, Japan became the world's largest producing country of automobiles. It has remained the leader ever since, and Toyota and Nissan have become two of the world's largest automobile manufacturers.

In their early years before World War II, both Nissan and Toyota produced mostly trucks for the military because of the lack of domestic demand for cars. The Ministry of Commerce and Industry, the predecessor of the **Ministry of International Trade and Industry** (MITI), protected the fledgling industry at the urging of the military by restricting imports and subsidizing domestic producers.

In the postwar period vehicle output increased rapidly, particularly between 1960 and 1970 (about elevenfold; see table A.1). Truck output continued to exceed that of cars throughout the 1950s and most of 1960s. By the early 1960s Japan became the world's second largest producer of trucks

Table A.1
Automobile production, exports, and imports (in 1,000 vehicles)

Year	Production	Exports	Imports
1960	482	39	4.3
1965	1,876	194	13.4
1970	5,289	1,087	19.6
1975	6,942	2,678	46.1
1980	11,043	5,967	47.9
1985	12,271	6,730	53.2
1986	12,260	6,605	74.3
1987	12,249	6,305	110.8
1988	12,700	6,104	154.0
1989	13,026	5,884	196.7
1990	13,487	5,832	252.8
1991	13,245	5,753	197.4
1992	12,499	5,668	187.2

Source: Japan Automobile Manufacturers Association.
Note: Figures include cars, trucks, and buses.

after the United States. In 1968, car output began to exceed that of trucks due to expanding domestic market.

In the 1950s and 1960s, MITI provided various assistance to the industry—low interest loans, tax privileges, tariff exemption for imported machinery and tools, and import protection—over the objections of officials at the **Bank of Japan** and the Ministry of Transport, who would liberalize car imports and use Japan's limited resources to develop other industries. MITI argued that by promoting automobile industry, many other industries such as machinery and steel manufacturing would be promoted as well. However, MITI's 1955 plan to promote a mini "people's car" by 1958 failed because no company responded to it due to market considerations. In the mid-1960s MITI recommended mergers or tie-ups between automakers in order to prevent excess competition and promote economies of scale because there were too many auto companies (Nissan, Toyota, Isuzu, Hino, Mitsubishi, Prince, Toyo Kogyo, Daihatsu, Fuji Heavy Industries, Suzuki, and Honda). Only one merger took place between Nissan and Prince in 1966. Tie-ups made Toyota the largest shareholder in Hino and Daihatsu, and Nissan a major shareholder in Fuji Heavy Industries, but they did not reduce domestic competititon or increase production scales because these companies specialized in product lines that Toyota and Nissan did not produce.

Nissan and Toyota have remained the two largest producers in the postwar period. Nissan had 54% of Japan's car output in 1950, with Toyota producing 29%. In 1953 Nissan's share dropped to 34.7%, whereas Toyota's share increased to 40.6% in the same year to become the largest producer. Since then Toyota has remained the leader. In 1992 Toyota produced 3.93 million vehicles (including cars, trucks, and buses) or 31.5% of Japan's total ouput; Nissan produced 2.12 million or 16.9% of the total (see table A.2), giving a combined share of 48.4%. Their share of total exports in 1992 was 30% and 16.6%, respectively. The other producers, in descending order as of 1992, are Mitsubishi, Mazuda, Honda, Suzuki, Daihatsu, Isuzu, Fuji Heavy Industries, Hino, and Nissan Diesel. In the production of passenger cars, the combined share of Toyota and Nissan was at its postwar peak at 88% in 1951. It dropped to about 60% in the 1960s, and fluctuated between 70% and 60% in the 1970s and 1980s. In 1992 it was 52.5%.

Toyota's rise to preeminence in Japan's automobile industry has been aided by its innovations in production management. The most important and widely emulated production management method is the **just-in-time system**, which utilizes the ***kanban*** **system** to keep parts inventory at a

Table A.2
Vehicle production and exports by manufacturer (in 1,000 vehicles)

	Production		Exports	
Make	1985	1992	1985	1992
Toyota	3,666	3,931	1,980	1,698
Nissan	2,500	2,118	1,435	942
Mitsubishi	1,153	1,396	635	653
Mazda	1,194	1,281	844	801
Honda	1,120	1,200	668	589
Suzuki	782	844	303	278
Daihatsu	579	610	130	173
Isuzu	589	473	408	305
Fuji	584	514	284	178
Hino	69	79	28	31
Nissan Diesel	36	52	15	20
Total	12,271	12,499	6,730	5,668

Source: Japan Automobile Manufacturers Association.
Note: Figures include minivehicles. Hino and Nissan Diesel make trucks and buses only.

minimum. In connection with the operation of the just-in-time system, the company has developed an extensive **subcontracting system** to supply parts just before they are needed. In recent years an innovation has been made to link factory production directly to sales.

As Japan's automobile output increased and exceeded domestic requirements, manufacturers began to export. Exports started in the late 1950s at a low level but increased rapidly in the late 1960s, reaching 1.09 million units in 1970 (see table A.1). The greatest increase came after the 1973 oil crisis when the demand for small cars increased, particularly in the United States, Japan's major automobile export market. Between 1973 and 1980 automobile exports increased by 288% to reach 5.97 million units, surpassing domestic sales of 5.02 million units. In 1985 a record 6.73 million units were exported, accounting for a record 54.8% of total production. Since then the number of units exported has declined. The export ratio has also declined steadily to 43.4% in 1991 and 45.3% in 1992.

Alarmed at the rapid increase of auto import from Japan and its impact on the domestic auto industry, Washington requested Japan to institute the "voluntary export restraint" (VER) in order to slow down the increase without having to resort to more restrictive or protectionist measures. The Ministry of International Trade and Industry (MITI) has complied with the request in order to minimize trade frictions between the two countries, and the VER on Japan's passenger car exports to the United States was set at 1.68 million units in fiscal 1981. It was raised to 1.85 million units in fiscal 1984 and 2.3 million units in fiscal 1985. Nevertheless, exports of Japanese automobiles, especially passenger cars, remain heavily dependent on the U.S. market, although the share of total exports to the U.S. has been declining in the late 1980s. In 1991, of the 4.45 million passenger cars exported, 1.76 million or 39.6% went to the United States, down from 45.5% in 1989. Ironically that was below the VER limit of 2.3 million units that MITI allocated to Japanese automakers. Total vehicle exports (including trucks and buses) were 5.67 million units in 1992, of which 1.77 million units or 31.3% went to the United States, down from the peak of 49% in 1987. Furthermore a small number of cars made in the United States by Japanese manufacturers have been imported into Japan.

To soften the impact of the VER and to reduce trade frictions, Japanese automakers have increasinly produced and exported higher priced luxury models to the United States. In addition they have set up factories in North America and Europe for local production. Honda pioneered in U.S. production in 1982, followed by Nissan (1983), Toyota (1984), Mazda (1987), and Mitsubuishi (1988). As a result, although the market share of Japanese exports in the U.S. auto market declined from 20.8% in 1983 to 18.4% in 1991, the market share of combined Japanese exports and domestic makes built by Japanese affiliates increased from 21.3% in 1983 to 35.1% in 1991. Japanese automakers' direct overseas investment has attracted Japanese auto part producers to follow them in order to supply them overseas, touching off foreign criticisms of Japanese companies as extending their exclusionary group business relationships abroad.

In Europe, Toyota and Mitsubishi made capital investment in Portugal as early as 1968 and 1972, respectively. Nissan first produced passenger cars in Britain in 1986. Enticed by the prospect of a united Europe in 1992, Honda and Toyota have also set up plants in Britain to produce cars. In 1991 MITI also agreed with the European Community to limit Japanese auto exports to it to 1.23 million units a year until the end of 1999, but Japanese brand automobiles produced in the EC will not be included in the restrictions. In return the European Community will fully liberalize its auto market by the year 2000.

The automobile industry is the second largest industrial sector of the Japanese economy, after electrical machinery and equipment. Auto and auto parts constituted about 21% of Japan's total exports in 1991. The industry as a whole, including manufacturing, sales and repair services, and gasoline stations, employed over 5.6 million people, more than 10% of the total work force. Many industries, including auto parts, electrical machinery, general machinery, foodstuffs, chemical, iron, and steel, contribute to the production of automobiles.

Japanese automobiles are sold domestically through the manufacturers' sales networks that mostly sell the makers' particular models. According to its American critics, this has inhibited the sales of foreign cars; hence Japan's imports of foreign autos has remained limited—only 187,230 vehicles in 1992, of which 44,386 came from the U.S. and 140,759 from Western Europe. Japanese automakers, on the other hand, attribute the small imports of American cars to U.S. automakers' insufficient effort to produce quality products and to adapt to local conditions (e.g., changing the driver's seat to the right). In January 1992, with continuing imbalance in Japan–U.S. trade and recession in the United States, President George Bush visited Japan in an effort to increase American access to the Japanese market. In response Japanese officials, as well auto executives, promised to step up their imports of American autos and auto parts. Auto dealers reportedly will be allowed to sell foreign cars.

See also **just-in-time system**, **trade pattern**, **trade policy**.

Addresses

Honda Motor Co.
1-1, Minami Aoyama 2-chome, Minato-ku, Tokyo 107
Tel: (03) 3423-1111   Fax: (03) 3423-0511

Japan Automobile Manufacturers Association
6-1, Otemachi 1-chome, Chiyoda-ku, Tokyo 100
Tel: (03) 3216-5771   Fax: (03) 3287-2072

Japan Automobile Manufacturers Association, Washington Office
1050 17th Street, NW, Washington, DC 20036
Tel: (202) 296-8537

Mazda Motor Corp.
1-7, Uchisaiwai-cho 1-chome, Chiyoda-ku, Tokyo 100
Tel: (03) 3508-5055   Fax: (03) 3508-5094

Mitsubishi Motor Co.
33-8, Shiba 5-chome, Minato-ku, Tokyo 108
Tel: (03) 3456-1111   Fax: (03) 3456-2649

Nissan Motor Co.
17-1, Ginza 6-chome, Chuo-ku, Tokyo 014
Tel: (03) 3543-5523   Fax: (03) 3543-5941

Toyota Motor Corp.
4-18, Koraku 1-chome, Bunkyo-ku, Tokyo 112
Tel: (03) 3817-7111   Fax: (03) 3817-9034

References

Clark, Kim B., and Takahiro Fujimoto. 1991. *Product Development Performance: Strategy, Organization, and Management in the World Auto Industry*. Boston: Harvard Business School Press.

Cusumano, Michael A. 1988. Manufacturing innovation: Lessons from the Japanese auto industry. *Sloan Management Review*, 30: 29-39.

Cusumano, Michael A. 1989. *The Japanese Automobile Industry: Technology and Management at Nissan and Toyota*. Cambridge, MA: Council on East Asian Studies, Harvard University.

Garrahan, Philip, and Paul Stewart. 1992. *The Nissan Enigma: Flexibility at Work in a Local Economy*. London: Mansell.

Japan Automobile Manufacturers Association. 1993. *Motor Vehicle Statistics of Japan*.

Japan Automobile Manufacturers Association. 1993. *The Motor Industry of Japan*.

Mutoh, Hiromichi. 1988. The automotive industry. In *Industrial Policy of Japan*, ed. by R. Komiya, M. Okuno, and K. Suzumura. Tokyo: Academic Press Japan.

Toyota: A History of the First 50 Years. Toyota City: Toyota Motor Corp., 1988.

B

Bank of Japan   The Bank of Japan was founded in 1882 as the nation's central bank. It was reorganized in 1942 under the Bank of Japan Law, which is still in effect. In 1949 the Policy Board was established as the highest decision-making body of the Bank. Its members are the governor of the Bank and representatives from **city banks**, regional banks, commerce and industry, agriculture, the **Ministry of Finance**, and the **Economic Planning Agency**.

As with any other central bank, the Bank of Japan's objectives are to regulate money and the **money markets**, and to ensure the stable development of the economy. Its functions include the following:

1. As the only bank of issue, it issues banknotes. The maximum issue limits for banknotes is determined by the minister of finance after consultation with the Cabinet Council, but excess issues may be made for a short period of time if the Bank deems it necessary. Issues of banknotes must be backed by assets (gold and silver bullion, government bonds, commercial bills, loans, etc.) of equivalent value.

2. The Bank of Japan is a bank for financial institutions. As such, it accepts deposits from them, discounts commercial bills, makes loans on bills, buys and sells securities and bills, serves as the settlement institution for transactions among banks, and so on.

3. The Bank intermediates between the government and the private sector. All government receipts and payments are made through balances of government deposits at the Bank. The Bank can extend short-term (less than one year) loans to the government and underwrites or subscribes to government bills. The Bank is prohibited by the Finance Law of 1947 to extend long-term loans to the government or to underwrite government bonds with maturity of greater than one year. The Bank also acts as the government's agent in various types of businesses such as the issue, redemption,

interest payments of government bonds, and intervention in the foreign exchange market as agent for the Ministry of Finance.

The Policy Board is the highest decision-making body of the Bank. It is composed of seven members: the governor of the Bank of Japan, four appointed representatives from the private sector (one each from city banks, regional banks, commerce and industry, and agriculture) and two nonvoting representatives of the government (one each from the Ministry of Finance and the Economic Planning Agency). The former are appointed by the Cabinet with the consent of both houses of the Diet. The Board has broad jurisdiction over the official discount rate, open-market operations, reserve requirements, and regulation of main market interest rates. However, changes in reserve requirements require the approval of the minister of finance, and changes in the maximum limits for market interest rate are to be initiated by the minister of finance.

The main objective of the Bank in monetary policy is price stability, which is regarded as the prerequisite for the objectives of stable employment and growth. In addition equilibrium in the balance of payments is considered important. The policy instruments used by the Bank to pursue its objectives are similar to those of other central banks as outlined below:

1. *The official discount rate.* This is the interest rate on the Bank's discount and loans to client financial institutions. Changes in the discount rate influence the other interest rates in the short-term money market, thereby affecting the cost of raising funds by financial institutions through the lending by the Bank of Japan and in the money market. Changes in the discount rate also serve to signal the Bank's view of the economy and the changes deemed necessary, and are taken seriously by the business community.

2. *Open market operations.* The Bank buys and sells securities and bills in the finanical markets directly, thereby affecting liguidity in the financial system. Open market operations are also conducted with a view to influencing market interest rates.

3. *Reserve deposit requirement.* Financial institutions have to deposit, with no interest, a certain percentage of their liabilities with the Bank of Japan. Changes in the required reserve ratio thus affect their ability to extend loans. The reserve ratio varies with the type of financial institution and the type of deposit.

4. *Window guidance (madoguchi shido).* Started in 1954 and abolished in July 1991, this is the guidance or "moral suasion" issued quarterly by the Bank

to its client financial institutions, particularly city banks, to keep their lending within certain limits. The guidance varied with financial conditions but was usually more important when the Bank pursued a tight money policy. It is considered to have been effective before the late 1970s in supplementing the other monetary instruments. However, its role had since declined because the 1980 revision of the Foreign Exchange Control Law and the financial liberalization of the 1980s have given corporations alternative sources of funds. Hence the Bank of Japan decided to discontinue its use of window guidance. However, some analysts expect it to be used again when the Bank pursues a tight monetary policy. In 1982 the Bank announced it was abolishing window guidance, only to reinstitute it when credit was tightened.

Because the Ministry of Finance shares responsibility with BOJ for monetary policy and has broader power in regulating the financial system, it sometimes differs from the Bank about the latter's actions such as on the discount rate. The Bank of Japan tends to be more concerned with price stability, whereas the Ministry of Finance has to reconcile the competing interests of different financial institutions. Because the Ministry of Finance is arguably Japan's most powerful ministry and the minister is a powerful figure of the ruling Liberal Democratic Party, which has dominated Japanese politics since 1955, the Bank's policy actions cannot be immune from pressures from the Ministry of Finance and from the larger Japanese party politics. For example, Cargill and Hutchinson (1991) have found that Bank of Japan tends to lower interbank interest rate before the Lower House elections.

See also **interest rate structure, Ministry of Finance, money supply**.

Address

Bank of Japan
2-1, Nihonbashi Hongokucho 2-chome, Chuo-ku, Tokyo 103
Tel: (03) 3279-1111

References

Cargill, Thomas F., and Michael M. Hutchinson. 1991. The Bank of Japan's response to elections. *Journal of the Japanese and International Economies* 5: 120–39.

Federation of Bankers Associations of Japan. 1989. *The Banking System in Japan*. Tokyo: Zenginkyo. Ch. 1.

Nakao, Masa'oki, and Akinari Horii. 1991. The process of decision-making and implementation of monetary policy in Japan. *Bank of Japan Special Paper*, no. 198.

Suzuki, Yoshio, ed. 1987. *The Japanese Financial System*. Oxford: Oxford University Press. Ch. 6.

Tatewaki, Kazuo. 1991. *Banking and Finance in Japan*. London: Routledge. Ch. 12.

Bank of Tokyo   A city bank that specializes in foreign exchanges.
See **city banks**.

bankers' acceptance (BA) market   The market in which yen-denominated bills of exchange, guaranteed by banks, are traded.
See **money markets**.

Banking Act, 1982   The first comprehensive revision of banking legislation since 1927, this act permits banks to sell and deal in **government bonds**. Another major provision concerns disclosure requirements for banks.

The provision for banks to deal in government bonds was a logical step and an important milestone in the evolution of Japan's postwar financial system. Since 1965 when the government was permitted by a special one-year law to engage in deficit financing, government deficits have increased steadily in Japan. Initially, when the amount of deficit was small, the **Ministry of Finance** raised the funds by issuing primarily long-term bonds at low interest rate. The bonds were held by banks for one year, after which the **Bank of Japan** was willing to buy back 90% of the bonds from the banks. Only security firms were authorized to deal in government bonds. Banks were not interested in them because they felt that customers would merely shift funds from deposits into government bonds.

In the early 1970s government deficits and bonds increased rapidly due to the oil crisis. By the late 1970s the Bank of Japan was reluctant to buy back from banks large quantities of bonds for fear of inflationary increases in money supply. The banks, on the other hand, were not willing to hold large volumes of government bonds at low interest rates without being able to trade them. Consequently years of debate culminated in the new banking act, which has permitted banks to sell government bonds over the counter since April 1983 and to deal in government bonds in the securities market since June 1984.

See also **government bonds**.

Reference

Rosenblush, Frances M. 1989. *Financial Politics in Contemporary Japan.* Ithaca: Cornell University Press. Ch. 4.

banking regulation and deregulation   Japan's **banking system** in the postwar period has been closely regulated by the **Ministry of Finance** and the **Bank of Japan**, particularly before the mid-1970s, in various areas such as interest rates, types of services permitted, the types of financial instruments permitted, limit on loans to a single party, and capital adequacy requirement. The regulations were mainly enacted to attain stability in the system and to channel low-cost funds to different sectors of the economy.

Stability in the system is considered so important that no Japanese banks have been allowed to fail in the postwar era; the typical solution for ailing banks is merger. As a result commercial banking in Japan before the mid-1970s lacked price competition, and banks competed only in nonprice areas such as the quality of services and even the offering of gifts. Analysts have described commercial banking as a protective "convoy escort system" in which all banks move in tandem at the speed of the slowest members. It has also been characterized as "relationship banking" in which considerations of the long-term business relationship between a bank and its clients, rather than competitive efficiency and innovation, play the most important role.

Another result of regulation is that the banking system is highly segmented; different type of banking institutions are permitted to serve different sectors and different needs of the economy. Thus **city banks** specialize in short-term loans, **long-term credit banks** specialize in long-term development loans, and **trust banks** specialize in trust business, and so on (see **banking system**).

An important aspect of banking regulation is the capital adequacy requirement. Because interest rates were regulated until recent years, banks had to depend on expansion in asset quantity to increase their earnings, and hence they competed with each other in asset expansion. In addition, since bank bankruptcy is nonexistant, they had little incentives to expand their equity capital. Between April 1, 1982, and May 23, 1986, although the Ministry of Finance required Japanese banks to maintain a capital ratio of 10% (the ratio being defined as that between capital and the balance of deposits plus CDs), the actual ratio maintained was much lower than that. On May 23, 1986, the required capital ratio was lowered to 4% (the ratio being defined as that between capital and total assets). For banks with overseas branches, 70% of their "latent" or "hidden" capital (i.e., the difference between market and book value of securities holdings) was added to their capital in the calculation, and the required capital ratio was 6% (Sasaki 1992: 185).

The situation changed after the Basel Agreement of 1988 (Basel Committee on Banking Regulations and Supervisory Practices) in which the rules of the Bank of International Settlement (BIS) required banks engaged in international finance to attain a capital/asset ratio of 8% by March 31, 1993. (However, BIS rules permit Japanese banks to include 45% of their latent capital in the capital). It was after the agreement that Japanese banks had to strive to raise their capital ratio. At first they relied on equity financing. After early 1990, falling share prices made equity financing virtually impossible; the latent capital of the banks was also greatly reduced. Many banks had to curtail risky loans and raise funds through subordinated loans, primarily from life insurance companies.

In the wake of the bursting of the "bubble economy" in which bank loans fueled the land-property speculation in the late 1980s, a new regulation was introduced in 1990 to restrict banks' property-related lending. As a result outstanding bank loans extended to the real estate industry declined from 15.3% of total loans outstanding at the end of March 1990 to 0.3% at the end of March 1991. At the end of March 1987, it was 32.7% according to Bank of Japan statistics.

Regulation of the banking system is only one aspect of the broader regulation of the entire financial system by the Ministry of Finance. On the basis of the Securities and Exchange Act, the Ministry separates banking and securities services by prohibiting banks from offering securities services and securities firms from offering banking services. This began to change in the early 1990s as part of the broader **financial liberalization**.

After the first oil crisis in 1973, fundamental changes in the economy eroded the bases of the traditional regulation and made the deregulation of the banking system inevitable: (1) The slowdown in the economy's growth reduced corporate demand for loans and hence made city banks less dependent on the Bank of Japan for funds and less willing to accept its regulation and guidance. To diversify their business, banks increasingly called for reforms to let them enter the securities business. (2) The increase in public debt to boost aggregate demand led to the establishment in 1977 of a market for **government bonds**, which made it more difficult for the authorities to regulate the interest rate. The **Banking Act of 1982** permits banks to sell and deal in government bonds. (3) The segmentation of the banking system served a useful purpose up to the early 1970s as Japan's capital and **money markets** were underdeveloped and the demand for funds exceeded supply at the low regulated interest rates. With the development of these markets, segmentation became increasingly unnecessary and served mainly to restrict competition in the financial market. (4) The growing internationalization of the Japanese economy gave Japanese companies and financial institutions access to more liberal financial markets and more innovative financial instruments abroad. This in turn led to a growing demand for financial liberalization in Japan in order to enable the Japanese firms and banks to be competitive internationally.

The above factors have led to various reforms in the financial system, referred to as **financial liberalization**. Throughout the 1980s interest rates have been deregulated on many types of deposits, and the minimum amount of deposits required for market rates had been lowered successively. In June 1993 interest rates on bank time deposits were completely deregulated. Complete deregulation of interest rates on nontime deposits is scheduled for spring 1994. Since 1991 the Ministry of Finance has been considering measures to reduce the barriers between short-term and long-term banking by allowing commercial banks to raise long-term funds by accepting three-year large-lot time deposits, and long-term credit banks to offer one-year debentures to raise funds. Also, after years of debate, the Ministry has decided to reduce the separation between banking and securities businesses; banks and securities firms may establish subsidiaries for securities and banking business, respectively (see **financial liberalization**).

Foreign banks are traditionally subject to more stringent regulations in Japan. As part of the financial liberalization, more foreign banks and other financial institutions have been admitted into Japan as Japanese banks expanded their presence abroad. However, a report issued by the U.S. Department of the Treasury in 1990 charged that foreign banks were still blocked from competing on equal terms because of various legal and informal barriers. It complained that no Japanese banks had been acquired by a foreign bank, and foreign banks must pay much higher rates to borrow yen and acquire funds to operate in Japan.

See also **banking system, financial liberalization**.

Addresses

Bank of Japan
2-1, Nihonbashi Hongokucho 2-chome, Chuo-ku, Tokyo 103
Tel: (03) 3279-1111

Banking Bureau, Ministry of Finance
1-1, Kasumigaseki 3-chome, Chiyoda-ku, Tokyo 100
Tel: (03) 3581-4111

References

Crum, Colyer, and David Meerschwam. 1986. From relationship to price banking: The loss of regulatory control. In *America versus Japan*, ed. by Thomas McCraw. Boston: Harvard Business School Press.

Federation of Bankers Associations of Japan. 1989. *The Banking System in Japan*. Tokyo: Zenginkyo. Ch. 2.

Federation of Bankers Associations of Japan. Annual. *Japanese Banks*. Tokyo: Zenginkyo.

Sasaki, Toyonari. 1992. Bank Regulation. In *Capital Markets and Financial Serives in Japan*. Tokyo: Japan Securities Research Institute. Pp. 184–93.

banking system   Japan's modern banking system, established after the Meiji Restoration of 1868, is complex in its organizational structure. It is often described as segmented because it consists of many different categories of banks, each specializing by law in a different type of lending business. The system has been closely regulated by the **Ministry of Finance** and the **Bank of Japan**, especially before the mid-1970s when **financial liberalization** began to take place.

Excluding the Bank of Japan, which is the central bank, banks are classified into two major categories: ordinary banks and specialized banks. Ordinary banks are the regular commercial banks, which accept deposits, provide funds' transfer and short-term loans. They are further classified into three subcategories:

1. *City banks.* There are 11 city banks (13 before April 1990 and 12 before April 1991), which are the largest of Japanese commercial banks, and six of them are among the largest in the world in terms of assets. They have headquarters in the major cities, with over 3,200 branches all over the country. They receive about 20% of all deposits, and have traditionally provided loans to corporations, although consumer loans have increased in recent years. At the end of 1992 city banks had outstanding loans of ¥213.0 trillion and deposits of ¥184.1 trillion. The largest city banks are Dai-ich Kangyo Bank, Sakura Bank, Sumitomo Bank, Fuji Bank, Mitsubishi Bank, and Sanwa Bank.

2. *Regional banks.* There are 64 regional banks and 65 second-tier regional banks (i.e., former *sogo* banks that became members fo the Second Association of Regional Banks in 1989). They are usually based in the principal city of a prefecture and conduct their operations mainly within that prefecture. Their clients tend to be local small- and medium-sized enterprises. As of December 1992 the 64 regional banks had a total of ¥155.1 trillion in

deposits and ¥116.9 trillion in outstanding loans; the members of the Second Association of Regional Banks had a total of ¥58.3 trillion in deposits and ¥47.8 trillion in outstanding loans.

3. *Foreign banks.* These are foreign bank branches in Japan with a license from the Ministry of Finance. At the end of 1992 there were 89 foreign banks with 143 offices in Japan; they had a total of ¥1.6 trillion in deposits, down from a peak of ¥2.2 trillion in 1989, and ¥9.3 trillion in outstanding loans, down from ¥11.2 trillion in 1990. All are heavily involved in foreign currency transactions.

Specialized banks or financial institutions include the following:

1. **Long-term credit banks.** There are three banks in this category: the Industrial Bank of Japan, Long-Term Credit Bank of Japan, and Nippon Credit Bank. These banks specialize in long-term lending to promote industrial development. They served a useful purpose in the postwar era when Japan's capital market was underdeveloped. At the end of 1992, their deposits totaled ¥5.3 trillion, and outstanding loans were ¥47.0 trillion.

2. **Trust banks.** There are seven Japanese trust banks. They are engaged in pension and other trust fund management and administration, as well as in general banking activities. They provide loans to major corporations for long-term capital investment. The largest trust banks are Mitsubishi Trust & Banking, Mitsui Trust & Banking, Sumitomo Trust & Banking, and Yasuda Trust & Banking. At the end of 1992 their total deposits were ¥8.8 trillion, and total loans ¥24.0 trillion.

3. *Financial institutions for small and medium business.* These include *sogo* **banks** (mutual banks) until 1988, *shinkin* **banks** (credit associations), Zenshinren Bank (the national federation of *shinkin* banks), credit cooperatives, and labor credit associations. Credit cooperatives are financial institutions organized in the form of cooperatives to serve their members, who are owners and workers of small- and medium-sized enterprises. Their business consists primarily of taking deposits and installment savings from members and lending to members. At the end of 1992 Japan's 398 credit cooperatives had a total of ¥22.9 trillion in savings and deposits and ¥18.3 trillion in loans and discounts. Labor credit associations accept deposits and make loans to promote the welfare activities of labor unions and consumer cooperatives. At the end of 1992 the nation's 217 labor credit associations had ¥8.2 trillion in savings and deposits and ¥4.3 trillion in loans and discounts.

4. *Financial institutions for agriculture, forestry, and fisheries.* Three levels of financial institutions exist to serve agriculture, forestry, and fisheries. At the level of villages, towns, and cities, there are **agricultural cooperatives**. They accept deposits from members and extend loans to members as well as nonmembers in the rural communities. They also market farm products and purchase farm equipment for their members. They belong to prefectural-level associations called *credit federations*. At the national level there is the Norinchukin Bank (*Norin chuo kinko*), the Central Cooperative Bank for Agriculture and Forestry. Its capital comes from subscription from private agricultural, forestry, and fishery organizations. Its funds are lent to subscribers and individuals engaged in agriculture, forestry, and fisheries and to corporations supplying equipment and facilities to agriculture and forestry. It also invests its surplus funds in securities and in the interbank **money market** such as the **call money market**. As of end of 1992 Japan's 3,223 agricultural cooperatives had ¥63.9 trillion in deposits and ¥17.1 trillion in outstanding loans and discounts; the Norinchukin Bank had ¥27.6 trillion in deposits and ¥14.8 trillion in outstanding loans.

5. **Government financial institutions.** These include two government banks—the Export-Import Bank and the **Japan Development Bank**—which by law are engaged in export-importing finance and regional development, respectively. There are also nine public finance corporations that are established for specific purposes such as housing and small business finance.

The Federation of Bankers Associations of Japan (Zenginkyo) is the umbrella organization of 72 regionally based bankers' associations. It represents the banking community vis-à-vis the government and the public; it operates interbank systems such as check clearing and domestic funds transfer, provides credit information at its Credit Information Center, and is engaged in research and publications.

See also **agricultural cooperatives, Bank of Japan, Banking Act of 1982, banking regulation and deregulation, city banks, financial liberalization, government financial institutions, long-term credit banks, Ministry of Finance, postal savings,** *shinkin* **banks,** *sogo* **banks, trust banks.**

Addresses

Federation of Bankers Associations of Japan
3-1, Marunouchi 1-chome, Chiyoda-ku, Tokyo 100
Tel: (03) 5252-3752   Fax: (03) 5252-3755

Regional Banks Association of Japan
1-2, Uchikanda 3-chome, Chiyoda-ku, Tokyo 100
Tel: (03) 3241-5171

The Second Association of Regional Banks
5, Sanbancho, Chiyoda-ku, Tokyo 101
Tel: (03) 3252-5171

References

Bank of Japan. 1993. *Economic Statistics Annual, 1992.*

Federation of Bankers Associations of Japan. 1989. *The Banking System in Japan.* Tokyo: Zenginkyo.

Federation of Bankers Association of Japan. 1993. *Japanese Banks, '93.* Tokyo: Zenginkyo.

Federation of Bankers Association of Japan. *Zenginkyo Financial Review.* Various issues.

Suzuki, Yoshio, ed. 1987. *Japanese Financial System.* Oxford: Oxford University Press. Ch. 5.

Tatewaki, Kazuo. 1991. *Banking and Finance in Japan.* London: Routledge. Ch. 7.

bankruptcies   Business bankruptcies during the 1980s reached a peak of more than 20,000 in 1984 but declined afterward (see table B.1). In 1991– 92 the figures started to rise over the 1990 figures because of increased

Table B.1
Business bankruptcies

Year	Cases	Total liabilities (in ¥ billions)	Average liabilities (in ¥ millions)
1980	17,884	2,707	151.4
1981	17,610	2,692	152.9
1982	17,122	2,355	137.5
1983	19,155	2,564	133.9
1984	20,841	3,626	174.0
1985	18,812	4,186	222.5
1986	17,476	3,752	214.7
1987	12,655	2,055	162.4
1988	10,123	2,059	203.4
1989	7,234	1,195	165.2
1990	6,468	1,944	300.6
1991	11,767	7,770	660.3
1992	14,069	7,602	540.3

Sources: Teikoku Databank, Ltd. and Nikkei Economic Electronic Databank System.
Note: Figures include bankruptcies of corporations and unincorporated enterprises.

failures in the construction and the real estate industries. Analysts have attributed these failures to softening land prices and higher interest rates.

Ostrom (1991) posits that bankruptcy data are not good indicators of the state of the economy in recent years. The reason is that the annual number of bankruptcies has not always been negatively correlated with the economy's growth rate or employment index. However, bankruptcy figures do indicate the extent of economic difficulties or vulnerability that specific sectors or firms are experiencing due to other changes in the economy. Thus construction and real estate firms are particularly vulnerable to tight credit after years of speculative expansion fueled by easy credit. And small labor-intensive businesses are particularly hurt by the tight labor market, which indicates a high level of aggregate demand. In early 1991 bankruptcies due to labor shortages also increased. However, it is reported that many recently bankrupt firms failed because of their speculation in securities and land, not because of failures in their principal businesses. The record level of average liabilities of bankrupt companies in March and April of 1991 was due to the large liabilities of two bankrupt companies. But, even without them, it is clear that the average liabilities of the failed companies have been rising.

Individual bankruptcies reached 21,160 cases in 1984. Bankruptcies declined steadily afterward and went below 10,000 cases in both 1988 and 1989. They rose to 11,480 in 1990 and 23,491 in 1991. Some analysts attribute the recent rise to consumers' indiscriminate use of credit cards.

References

Isono, Naoyuki. 1991. Bankruptacies, liabilities hint at economic woe. *Japan Economic Journal*, Feb. 23: 5.

Ostrom, Douglas. 1991. Bankruptcies continue rising in Japan. *JEI Report*, June 7, pt. B: 5–6.

Small-business bankruptcies mount as economic downturn takes toll. *Nikkei Weekly*, May 10, 1993: 1, 11.

Yokota, Hayato. 1992. Bankruptcy rise provoking lenders. *Nikkei Weekly*, Feb. 8: 15.

Beef-Citrus Quotas Agreement, 1988   Until 1988 Japan's restrictive import quotas on beef and citrus had long been a source of trade dispute between the United States and Japan. In addition to quotas there were also regulations that constituted trade barriers. For example, only citrus products from California, but not from Florida, were permitted, and imported orange juice had to be blended with domestic tangerine juice. In April 1988, when a previous bilateral agreement on beef-citrus quotas expired and initial negotiations between Washington and Tokyo failed to reach an agreement, Washington filed charges with GATT that Japan violated GATT rules that prohibited agricultural quotas except under extraordinary circumstances such as the need to redress balance-of-payments deficits. At the same time Washington also urged Tokyo to negotiate further for an agreement that would dismantle the quotas, thereby obviating a lengthy GATT investigation.

The Japanese government, for domestic political reasons, initially preferred the dispute to be settled by GATT in order to avoid the appearance of giving in to the United States demand. However, an adverse GATT ruling could force Japan to compensate the United States for trade losses. Subsequently the Japanese government changed its position and resumed trade negotiations with the United States.

In June 1988 an agreement was reached between the two countries. It would permit U.S. beef producers to increase their exports to Japan annually by 60,000 metric tons over the next three years from the 1987 quotas of 214,000 metric tons and to replace the quotas in 1991 with tariffs. The tariff will start at 70% and gradually decline to 50% by 1993. The agreement would permit United States exports of citrus products to increase by 22,000 metric tons annually for three years; then the quotas would be abolished in 1991. During the three-year period exports from Florida would be allowed. The requirement that imported orange juice be blended with domestic tangerine juice would also be eliminated.

Preliminary evidence as of mid-1993 suggests that the lower-priced U.S. beef and citrus products have not inundated the Japanese market and hurt domestic producers in Japan.

Reference

MacKnight, Susan. 1988. Liberalization of Japan's beef and orange markets: Winners and losers. *JEI Report*, no. 42A, Nov. 4.

bill market   An interbank money market where bills are sold at a discount to obtain funds.
See **money markets.**

bond market   Japan's bond market developed only after the mid-1970s because of the rapid increase in government bond issues. It was then and still is dominated by government bonds. However, other types of bonds were issued and actively traded in the 1980s.

Bonds can be classified in different ways—in terms of the issuing body, collateral, linkage with equity, methods of redemption, maturity, methods of interest payment, and so forth. The following system is commonly used to classify the major types of bonds:

1. *Public bonds.* These include **government bonds** issed by the national government, local government bonds, and public corporation bonds. Local government bonds are issued by the prefectural or municipal governments. Public corporation bonds are issued for specific purposes; the bulk are government guaranteed and called *government-guaranteed bonds.* The issuance of government bonds (excluding a small amount of foreign currency bonds) increased rapidly after 1975 following the first oil crisis. The outstanding balance was ¥173.7 trillion at the end of FY 1991. Outstanding local government bonds totaled ¥19.6 trillion at the end of FY 1991 and public corporation bonds stood at ¥54.1 trillion as of November 1991 (see table B.2).

2. *Bank or financial debentures.* These are bonds issued by long-term credit banks (the Industrial Bank of Japan, the Long-Term Credit Bank of Japan, and the Nippon Credit Bank), the Bank of Tokyo, the Norinchukin Bank, the Shoko Chukin Bank, and the Zenshinren Bank. These financial institutions are authorized to issue bank debentures by specific laws because of the long-term nature of their lending or the specialized nature of their operations. There are two types of bank debentures, interest-bearing bank debentures and discount bank debentures. Their outstanding balance was ¥53.46 trillion and ¥20.9 trillion, respectively, at the end of FY 1991.

Table B.2
Outstanding amounts of public and corporate bonds (end of FY; in ¥ trillions)

	1985	1990	1991
Government bonds[a]	136.61	168.55	173.66
Local government bonds	20.76	19.23	19.56
Government guaranteed bonds	16.44	19.59	19.73
Bank debentures	43.52	67.66	74.36
Corporate straights bonds	9.46	11.94	14.90
Convertible bonds[b]	4.55	16.09	16.97
Foreign bonds in yen	5.42	5.98	6.33

Source: Bank of Japan.
a. Domestic bonds only.
b. Including the amount converted to stocks.

3. *Corporate straight bonds.* Corporate bonds are issued by private companies other than financial institutions. They are divided into corporate straight bonds, convertible bonds and warrant bonds. Straight bonds are ordinary corporate debt instruments that do not have special provisions for bondholders to become shareholders, as convertible and warrant bonds do (see below). At the end of FY 1991, there was ¥14.9 trillion outstanding.

4. *Convertible bonds.* These bonds can be converted into stocks under certain conditions. Because of this advantage to investors, the bonds can be issued with lower coupon rates or at lower initial costs than straight corporate bonds. They are less risky to investors than stocks. At the end of FY 1991 there was ¥17.0 trillion outstanding.

5. *Warrant bonds.* These corporate bonds give bondholders the right to subscribe to new shares of the company at a predetermined price during a specified period. They differ from convertible bonds in that the warrant can be detached from the underlying bond and traded separately. Domestic issues of warrant bonds have not been significant. However, warrant bonds issued by Japanese corporations on the Euromarket have been bought by Japanese investors and traded in the **over-the-counter markets** in Japan.

6. *Yen-denominated foreign bonds.* Popularly called **samurai bonds**, these are issued by nonresident institutions in Japan such as international agencies, foreign governments, and foreign private corporations. First introduced in 1970 when the Asian Development Bank issued such bonds in Japan, the outstanding balance was ¥6.33 trillion at the end of FY 1991. *Samurai* bonds should be distinguished from *shogun* bonds which are foreign-currency-denominated bonds isssued by nonresident institutions such as the European Investment Bank and the World Bank. Their outstanding balance at the end of 1990 was only ¥98 billion.

When a bond—public or corporate—is offered publicly for subscription by a large number of unspecified investors, underwriters normally organize a syndicate, consisting of various banks and **securities companies**, for the purpose of underwriting and publicly offering such issue on the open market. However, short-term treasury bills and medium-term notes that are distributed by means of competitive bids do not require underwriting. Financial debentures are issued through public sales and do not require an underwriting syndicate for their distribution. Corporate bonds that are privately placed are sold exclusively to specific institutions such as banks and life insurance companies and do not require underwriting.

Trading on the bond market was active throughout the 1980s, with government bonds dominating the trading volume. Bonds are traded on the securities exchanges and over-the-counter markets. The latter accounted for the bulk (99% in 1992) of the trading volume (see table B.3). Securities companies are the principal participants in the OTC markets as dealers, holding large inventories of bonds. Other major traders in the bond market are **trust banks, insurance companies, investment trusts,** and commercial banks. More than one-third of the OTC trade is in the form of *gensaki* transactions (i.e., transactions with repurchase agreement between a company seeking to invest its surplus funds in short-term investment and another in need of short-term funds).

In 1989 the over-the-counter markets started to offer cash-settlement bond options. The bond market was expanded further in May 1990 with the introduction at **Tokyo Stock Exchange** of bond futures options. Analysts expect this to upgrade Tokyo's bond market with its diversity of bond instruments, including cash bonds, futures, cash-settlement options, and futures options.

Japan has three bond-rating organizations that carry out rankings (AAA, AA, etc.) of bonds and provide the information to investors. They are Japan Bond Research Institute (JBRI), Japan Credit Rating Agency Ltd., and Nippon Investors' Service. They were all established in 1985. JBRI is the largest. In addition to rating domestic bonds and yen-denominated external bonds, these organizations conduct research on both foreign and domestic finanical, economic, and corporate information.

See also **government bonds, over-the-counter market, securities companies, Tokyo Stock Exchange, warrant bonds.**

Table B.3
Total trading volume of bonds in Tokyo

	1987	1990	1992
Tokyo Stock Exchange (in ¥ billions)			
Government bonds	56,918	37,921	6,066
Convertible bonds	50,453	19,842	9,481
Warrant bonds	416	1	0
Foreign bonds in yen	88	12	19
Others	24	13	6
Total	107,899	57,787	15,573
OTC Markets (in ¥ trillions)			
Gensaki trade[a]	1,217	1,106	1,392
Total	5,544	3,360	2,995

Sources: Tokyo Stock Exchange; Securities Dealers Associations of Japan.
a. Transactions with repurchase agreements or "REPOS."

Addresses

Bond Underwriters Association of Japan
5-8, Nihonbashi Kayabacko 1-chome, Chuo-ku, Tokyo 103
Tel: (03) 3667-2431

Japan Bond Research Institute
6-1, Nohonbashi Kayabacho 2-chome, Chuo-ku, Tokyo 103
Tel: (03) 3639-2840   Fax: (03) 3639-2848

Japan Securities Dealers Association
5-8, Nihonbashi Kayabacho 1-chome, Chuo-ku, Tokyo 103
Tel: (03) 3667-8451

References

Bank of Japan. 1993. *Economic Statistics Annual, 1992.*

Choy, Jon. 1988. Japanese debt markets: An overview. *JEI Report,* June 10.

Japan Securities Research Institute. 1992. *Securities Market in Japan, 1992.* Ch. 4.

Elton, Edwin, and Martin J. Gruber, ed. 1990. *Japanese Capital Markets.* New York: Harper and Row.

Fabozzi, Frank J. ed. 1990. *The Japanese Bond Markets: An Overview and Analysis.* Chicago: Probus.

Tokyo Stock Exchange. 1993. *Tokyo Stock Exchange Fact Book, 1993.*

Yamashita, Takeji. 1989. *Japan's Securities Markets: A Practioners' Guide.* Singapore: Butterworths. Chs. 6–7.

Ziemba, William T., and Sandra L. Schwartz. 1992. *Invest Japan.* Chicago: Probus. Ch. 1.

bond-futures options
See **bond market.**

bond-rating organizations
See **bond market**.

bonuses
See **wage structure.**

Bridgestone Corp.   Japan's largest producer of rubber products and the core company of the Bridgestone Group, which comprises some 647 ompanies.

See also *keiretsu* **and business groups**.

bubble economy   A term frequently used in the early 1990s to refer to the asset inflation, or the speculative and inflated wealth in securities and land in 1986–89. The bubble is said to have burst in 1990 when the stock and property markets fell.

See **land use and policies, stock market, Tokyo Stock Exchange**.

burakumin   Literally "hamlet people," these are Japan's untouchable caste who are discriminated against economically and socially because they are the descendents of *eta* (literally the dirty), people who worked as tanners or butchers, jobs considered "unclean" by traditional Japanese standards.

See **employment discrimination**.

business cycles   The Economic Planning Agency of the Japanese government has officially identified 11 business cyles in Japan in the postwar period (see table B.4). The identification is based on macroeconomic indicators in nine broad categories. Thus the identification of peaks and troughs of business cycles can be controversial and is not as clearcut as the U.S. approach, in which a decline in real GNP for two consecutive quarters constitutes a recession.

As in other industrialized market economies, Japan's business cycles vary greatly in duration. In addition specific cyclical changes (inventory cycles, equipment cycles, construction cycles) have combined with autonomous

Table B.4
Reference dates of business cycles (year-month)

Number	Trough	Peak	Trough	Expansion	Contraction
1		1951-6	1951-10		4 months
2	1951-10	1954-1	1954-11	27 months	10
3	1954-11	1957-6	1958-6	31	12
4	1958-6	1961-11	1962-10	42	11
5	1962-10	1964-10	1965-10	24	12
6	1965-10	1970-7	1971-12	57	17
7	1971-12	1973-11	1975-3	23	16
8	1975-3	1977-1	1977-10	22	9
9	1977-10	1980-2	1983-2	28	36
10	1983-2	1985-6	1986-11	28	17
11	1986-11	1991-4		53	

Source: Economic Planning Agency.

changes and external shocks (technological progress, oil crisis, dollar depreciation, Japan–U.S. trade frictions, etc.) to make all cycles multifaceted.

The salient characteristics of some of the cycles are as follows: (1) The expansion of November 1954–June 1957, named the *Jinmu* Boom, is attributed mainly to technological progress and world prosperity. The tight monetary policy adopted to deal with the resultant balance-of-payments deficit is considered to have triggered the subsequent recession. (2) The June 1958–December 1961 expansion, named the *Iwato Boom*, saw increases in equipment investment and personal consumption. Tight monetary policy to control the balance-of-payments deficit also caused the downturn. (3) The short-lived October 1962–October 1964 expansion, also called the *Olympics Boom*, is attributed to the easing of monetary policy and the construction boom for the 1964 Tokyo Olympics. (4) The October 1965–July 1970 expansion, named the *Izanagi Boom*, was the longest (57 months) in the postwar period. During the boom Japan became one of the world's leading exporters, and its balance of payments improved. Worldwide inflation and tight monetary policy brought an end to the boom. (5) The short expansion of December 1971–November 1973 was ended by the first oil crisis of fall 1973, which ushered in a long recession. (6) The economy recovered from the oil crisis during the March 1975–January 1977 expansion in response to appropriate fiscal and monetary adjustments. The rapid appreciation of the yen, however, brought about the downturn. (7) During the October 1977–Feburary 1980 expansion, also called the *First Endaka* (high yen) *Boom*, the economy adjusted well to the higher yen and took advantage of the lower import cost of raw materials (in yen) and stable wages. However, the oil price increase and tighter monetary operation led to the longest postwar recession (36 months). (8) The expansion of Feburary 1982–June 1985 benefited from the expansion of the U.S. economy, the increase in exports to the United States, low oil prices, and increases in domestic consumption and investment. (9) The expansion since November 1986, also called the *Heisei Boom*, or the *Second Endaka* Boom, is one of the longest in the postwar period. It is based on a strong domestic demand due to incresing consumption, residential construction, and equipment investment and on the development of high value-added technologies and products. The boom occurred despite the yen appreciation since the Plaza Accord of September 1985 and despite trade frictions with the United States.

With the exception of the Feburary 1980–Feburary 1983 recession, all postwar recessions are much shorter than the expansionary phases of the business cycles. Thus, disregarding periodic fluctuations, the postwar Japanese economy is basically a dynamic and growth-oriented one.

To help forecast business cycles, the Economic Planning Agency has developed a series of business indicators for short-term forecasting and long-term analysis. The **Bank of Japan** also conducts business surveys and publishes indicators on business conditions.

See also **business-cycle indicators and forecasting**.

References

Boltho, Andrea. 1991. A century of Japanese business cycles: Did policy stabilize activity? *Journal of the Japanese and International Economies* 5, 3: 282–97.

Chandler, Clay. 1991. Economy ties record length of expansion. *Asian Wall Street Journal Weekly*, Sept.: 7.

Ito, T. 1990. The timing of elections and political business cycles in Japan. *Journal of Asian Economics* 1: 135–56.

Ito, Takatoshi. 1992. *The Japanese Economy.* Cambridge: MIT Press. Ch. 4.

Mizuno, Yuko. 1991. Executives less confident in economy. *Japan Economic Journal*, Mar. 16: 1.

West, Kenneth D. 1992. Sources of cycles in Japan, 1975–1987. *Journal of the Japanese and International Economies* 6, 1: 71–98.

Yoshikawa, H., and F. Ohtake. 1987. Postwar business cycles in Japan: a quest for the right explanation. *Journal of the Japanese and International Economies* 1: 373–407.

business-cycle indicators and forecasting   There is a number of official business indicators that are developed to indicate business trends and help forecast business cyles. They include the following:

1. *Leading, coincident and lagging indicators.* The Economic Planning Agency (EPA) has selected 37 series of indicators that are sensitive to changes in business conditions and classified them into three categories—leading indicators (15), coincident indicators (14), and lagging indicators (8)—in terms of the timing of changes in relation to overall changes in business cycles. The leading indicators tend to change before the overall changes in the economy; hence they can help indicate economic conditions 6 to 9 months in advance. Coincident indicators tend to change as the overall economy changes and thus reflect the current state of the economy. Lagging indicators tend to lag behind in changes and thus reflect or confirm economic conditions 6 to 12 months earlier. It should be pointed out, however, that the indicators are not foolproof for forecasting purposes. Some economists therefore do not have much confidence in them.

2. *Diffusion index*. This is an EPA index to indicate the overall direction of changes in the economy. To derive it, the current values of leading, coincident, and lagging indicators are compared with those three months earlier. The number of indicators that have increased is calculated as a percentage of the total number of indicators. That percentage number is the diffusion index. Thus when the diffusion index is over 50%, the economy is considered to be in an expansion. When it is less than 50%, the economy is considered to be in a contraction.

The **Bank of Japan** also has a diffusion index or business-condition index to show the condition of the economy as seen by business managers. From its quarterly survey of a large number of enterprises (more than 8,000 in mid-1991) in various sectors, the responses are sorted out into three groups: those who regard business conditions in their fields as "good," those who say "not so good" and those who say "bad." Discarding the second group, the business-condition index is obtained by substracting the percentage of the "bad" replies from the percentage of the "good" replies. Thus, if the index is high and rising over time, a business expansion is indicated. If it declines, a contraction is indicated.

3. *Composite index*. This is an EPA index designed to measure the relative magnitude of cyclical changes. Using the average rate of change of the coincident indicators in the previous five years as the standard, the rates of change of the leading, coincident, and lagging indicators in each year are compared with that standard, and the differences are averaged and converted into index numbers.

The EPA, however, does not use any one single index to determine the duration of a business cycle, its trough and peak. A special committee is convened to examine a large number of indicators to determine such matters (author's interview, EPA, July 20, 1992). It also utilizes macro and econometric models for forecasting purposes.

In the private sector there are various business and research institutes or "think tanks" such as Japan Economic Research Center and Nomura Research Institute that conduct their own analyses and make predictions about business trends in the economy. Nihon Keizai Shimpun, Inc., publisher of the leading business paper in Japan, publishes the results of its own survey as well as the forecasts made by some research institutes.

See also **business cycles; economic/business research and publications**.

Address

Economic Planning Agency
1-1, Kasumigaseki 3-chome, Chiyoda-ku, Tokyo 100
Tel: (03) 3581-0261

References

Bank of Japan. Quarterly. *Short-Term Economic Outlook (Tankan)*.

Economic Planning Agency. 1991. *Business Cycle Indicators*.

Economic Planning Agency. Quarterly. *Japanese Economic Indicators Quarterly*.

business ethics   Since the late 1980s and early 1990s, Japanese business ethics have come under attack, both at home and abroad. The criticisms stemmed from a number of sensational business scandals uncovered during the period. First, it was revealed in 1988–89 that the Recruit Company had bribed many Liberal Democratic Party officials for favors. In 1991 it was revealed that some large companies, banks, and securities houses had involvement with crime syndicates and that securities companies illegally compensated their big clients for investment losses. These scandals caused an outrage in Japan and raised questions about Japanese business ethics. This was not the first time, however, that such questions were raised. Long before these incidents, business frictions between the Japanese and foreigners had led to recriminatory charges of "unethical" Japanese (and American) business behavior.

Objective observers would agree that no nation has a monopoly on ethics and high morality, and that scandals and unethical behavior are by no means unique to any society. Furthermore, because the ethical norms of a society are invariably rooted in its history and cultural background, what is ethical in one society may be unethical in another. Thus it is hazardous and often invalid to judge the ethical standards of a society with those of another. Nevertheless, scholars can legitimately compare the values and standards of different societies and attempt to understand the differences in terms of their different historical and cultural backgrounds. In addition they can legitimately assess the pros and cons of specific values in a given society, explore their appropriateness to changing circumstances and societal needs, and predict or suggest the direction of future changes.

Analysts who have studied frictions between Japanese and American companies in their business contacts have attempted to explain their behavioral differences in terms of several dichotomies or contrasts in social and business ethics. The first and most commonly mentioned dichotomy is between the Japanese "group orientation" and the American "self-orientation" or between groupism and individualism. The Japanese are said to place group interests above their self-interests, at least as an ideal. Consequently loyalty to the group (or its various forms such as the family, the company, the corporate group, the bureaucratic elite, the nation, etc.) and reciprocal obligations and relationship between group members are considered paramount values. In business practices group loyalty and intragroup reciprocity are manifested in **permanent employment**, corporate paternalism toward employees, a dedicated work force, union-management cooperation (see **labor-management relations**), **cross shareholding** and reciprocal business ties, and a host of other arrangements to ensure that group members receive their "fair share" of benefits.

Unfortunately, group orientation also implies some extent of exclusivity, depending on the importance and cohesiveness of the particular group. Such exclusivity is manifested in subtle exclusion of, or blatant discrimination against, "outsiders," be they foreigners (*gaijin*, literally outside people), domestic rival groups, Korean residents who were born and raised in Japan, the handicapped Japanese, the Japanese outcast (***burakumin***), or Japanese women (in the context of corporate elite). This is the so-called *uchi*-versus-*soto* (inside-versus-outside) consciousness in which being an insider is crucial to almost any type of success. Seen in this light, it is not surprising that a corporate board of directors is typically made up of people who have worked their way up inside the company, not people appointed for their achievements in the outside world, as is the case in the United States. Nor is it paradoxical that Japanese businesses can be paternalistic toward their employees (or regular male Japanese employees) and at the same time be indifferent toward philanthropy for society at large and rarely participate in local volunteer activities.

Schlosstein (1991) has criticized the "hierachical culture" of Japan with its emphasis on control and duty in contrast with the Western values of freedom, liberty, and justice. In theory the concept of hierarchical culture overlaps with the group orientation; in practice it can be misleading to regard it as the cultural foundation of modern business ethics in Japan. It implies a vertical top-down control relationship, whereas Japanese groups usually embody important horizontal as well as vertical dimensions. In addition, although modern corporations in Japan as elsewhere are necessarily hierarchical in their organizational structures, the Japanese corporations tend to be more decentralized than their Western counterparts in **decision making** ("bottom-up" decision making) and in their power structures.

The group orientation of the Japanese is deeply rooted in Japan's historical experiences such as its long history of insular feudalism (late twelfth
century to the 1860s), the rise of militarism in the 1930s, and the hardships
of the early postwar period. It is reinforced by its large homogeneous
population and perhaps also by its compact area geographically separated
from other countries. Furthermore it is consciously and continuously cultivated by companies through such activities/practices as entrance cere-
monies, company songs and uniforms, company guest houses, and group
recreation. Consequently the orientation has proved to be durable and may
not change appreciably for a long time to come. On the other hand, some
authors have suggested that it is already weakening among the young
generation who have grown up in affluence and have not experienced the
early postwar hardships. Miyanaga (1991) suggests that individualism is
emerging in Japan, even among some entrepreneurs.

In any case some business practices that are group oriented have
changed because of changing circumstances. For example, because of labor
shortage midcareer job changes are no longer considered as evidence of
disloyalty to the company. Exclusionary or collusive practices such as bid-
rigging and price-fixing are increasingly regarded as unethical. These atti-
tudinal changes are taking place in the early 1990s because the Japanese
society and economy have become more fluid and pluralistic, Japanese
businesses have become global in scope, and foreign criticisms of exclusionary business practices have intensified. This does not mean, however,
that the Japanese want to replace their traditional values wholesale with
the Western values. The Japanese perceive America's social problems
to be worsening and the Western culture itself as lacking in self-discipline
(including work ethics and frugality) and in the sense of personal commitment. It is therefore not necessarily the model for the Japanese to
emulate.

At the level of managerial rules for business operations and decision
making, observers have pointed out that the Japanese tend to favor pragmatic "case-by-case" decision making on the basis of relationships and to
follow bureaucratic **administrative guidance**, whereas the Americans tend
to follow specific principles and laws and to resort to the legal framework.
The Japanese rule gives decision makers flexibility but can degenerate into
"situational ethics" that bend with the changing wind of financial interests
and foreign pressures. Similarly, because administrative guidance is not
based on specific laws or legal interpretations, it gives Japanese bureaucrats
much discretion in steering the business community. However, it can be
vague and arbitrary and is open to favoritism and other abuses. This does

not mean that administrative guidance is necessarily rigid and control oriented. Some authors have pointed out that administrative guidance is rarely given in a uni-directional relationship based on bureaucratic power and control; suggestions from the business community are usually taken into account in the development and implementation of administrative guidance. Since Japanese bureaucrats themselves are not monolithic, they do not always agree on what guidance to give (see **administrative guidance**). Nevertheless, in the early 1990s a growing number of Japanese have come to agree with foreign critics that operational rules for Japanese businesses, including administrative guidance, should be made more "transparent." To what extent they should be reformed is not yet clear. The "principled" and legalistic approach of American corporate behavior has problems of its own and is not necessarily a model for the Japanese.

The best vehicle of change in business ethics in any society is invariably a well-informed general public. In the past some foreign critics have charged that the Japanese public is unduly influenced by the authorities to support government policies and big corporate interests. Whatever the validity of this charge, this does not seem to be the case in the early 1990s. After the exposure of various cases of big business and government corruption, the Japanese public has become highly suspicious of any possible wrongdoing in high places, although arguably there is also a sense of resignation. The Federation of Economic Organizations (Keidanren), Japan's most important business organization, is aware of the public's changing mood and has initiated measures to restore the tarnished corporate image. For example, it drafted a "Keidanren Charter for Good Corporate Behavior" for corporate executives in 1991 to prevent the recurrence of financial scandals and corporate involvement with the underworld. Although the wording of the charter tends to be vague and compliance is voluntary, analysts expect the new code of conduct to make a positive impact on corporate behavior.

In short, Japanese business ethics in terms of both operational rules and actual practices are not as diametricaly opposed to their Western counterparts as they are often portrayed. Japanese business ethics are changing, just as some American business practices have been changing in response to changing circumstances. For these reasons Gundling (1991: 35) contends that Japanese and American business ethics should not be viewed as neat dichotomies; they are more accurately envisioned as "sets of contrasting cultural ideals embedded within a vast, interlocking web. We are different; we are the same; we overlap; they are our distant reflection." This author agrees with Gundling in this view.

See also **administrative guidance, employment discrimination, labor-management relations, management practices, Structural Impediments Initiative, underworld "businesses."**

References

Gundling, Ernest. 1991. Ethics and working with the Japanese: The entrepreneur and the "elite course." *California Management Review* 33, 3: 25–39.

London, Nancy R. 1990. *Japanese Corporate Philanthropy.* Oxford: Oxford University Press.

Miyanaga, Kuniko. 1991. *The Creative Edge: Emerging Individualism in Japan.* New Brunswick: Transaction Publishers. Chs. 1–2.

Ozaki, Robert. 1991. *Human Capitalism.* New York: Penguin. Ch. 5.

Prestowitz, Clyde V., Jr. 1988. *Trading Places.* New York: Basic Books. Ch. 3.

Sakai, Kuniyasu. 1990. The feudal world of Japanese manufacturing. *Harvard Business Review* 68, 6 (Nov.–Dec.): 38–49.

Schlosstein, Steven. Cracks in the Japanese monolith: A U.S. observer lists 12 political and social seaknesses. *Japan Times* (weekly international ed.), May 6–12, 1991: 8–9.

Seward, Jack, and Howard Van Zandt. 1985. *Japan: The Hungary Guest—Japanese Business Ethics vs. Those of the U.S.* Tokyo: Lotus Press.

Shimada, Haruo. 1991. The desperate need for new values in Japanese corporate behavior. *Journal of Japanese Studies* 17, 1, Spring: 107–25.

Sullivan, Jeremiah J. 1992. Japanese management philosophies: From the vacuous to the brilliant. *California Management Review* 34, 2, Winter: 66–87.

business groups
See *keiretsu* **and business groups**.

business organizations   Japan has four major business organizations, collectively known as *zaikai*. They represent the nation's businesses and top executives; they interact with politicians, bureaucrats, and labor groups and make policy recommendations on economic issues. They were particularly powerful between the 1950s and the mid-1970s when industrial development was the foremost goal of the nation. These four organizations are as follows.

1. *Federation of Economic Organization (Keidanren).* Founded in 1946, this is the largest and most influential business organization. Its members consist of 122 industrial associations and 939 companies as of the end of 1991. Its chairman is known unofficially as the "*zaikai* prime minister." It has 12 vice-chairmen and some 60 committees to focus on different aspects of the

economy. Keidanren leaders are involved in economic policy discussions and make recommendations to the government and the ruling Liberal Democratic Party. Keidanren also coordinates financial contributions to the Liberal Democratic Party made by corporations. In 1992, because of mounting foreign criticisms of Japanese business practices, Keidanren leaders advocated the concept of *kyosei* (symbiosis) for Japanese businessmen to follow both at home and abroad.

2. *Japan Federation of Employers' Association (Nikkenren).* This is the second most important organization. Founded in 1948 by corporate leaders to deal with early postwar labor unrest, it has remained the organization that shapes Japan's corporate policy on organized labor and wage negotiations. It has some 30,000 enterprises as members; it advises them on labor-related issues.

3. *Japan Association of Corporate Executives (Keizai Doyukai).* Founded in 1946, this is a forum for individual executives to express their personal views. Its membership consits of more than 1,500 executives.

4. *Japan Chamber of Commerce and Industry (Nissho).* This organization represents small- and medium-sized enterprises. Founded in 1922, it comprises 501 local chamers of commerce and industry with a total of about 1.4 million members.

Although *zaikai* remains important in Japan, its influence is said to have declined since the mid-1970s partly because of the maturing and diversification of the economy. In recent years its image has also suffered because several of its leaders were tainted by financial scandals and had to resign from their corporate posts. Finally, critics have charged that *zaikai* elders, particularly Keidanren leaders, have failed to adapt to changing economic and social conditions of Japan.

In addition to the four major organizations mentioned above, Japan also has the following business organizations: Japan Junior Chamber, Inc.; Japan Overseas Enterprises Association; Japan Productivity Center; Small Business Corporation; Kansai Committee for Economic Development; Kansai Economic Federation (Kankeiren), and Japan External Trade Organization (JETRO). Kankeiren is western Japan's most powerful business organization. JETRO has more than ten overseas offices to promote trade with foreign countries. Initially set up in 1951 by business leaders in Osaka city, it was taken over in 1954 by the **Ministry of International Trade and Industry** (MITI). In 1958 it was transformed into a public corporation with funding from the central government. Initially it was to deal solely with promoting exports, but its role has expanded to include the furtherance of mutual understanding with trading partners, import promotion, and liason between small businesses in Japan and their overseas counterparts. Finally, all major industries have organized their industry associations, and more than a dozen foreign countries have established their chambers of commerce in Japan.

Addresses

Federation of Economic Organizations
9-4, Otemachi 1-chome, Chiyoda-ku, Tokyo 100
Tel: (03) 3279-1411   Fax: 3279-1501

Japan Association of Corporate Executives
4-6, Marunouchi 1-chome, Chiyoda-ku, Tokyo 100
Tel: (03) 3211-1271   Fax: 3213-2946

Japan Chamber of Commerce and Industry
2-2, Marunouchi 3-chome, Chiyoda-ku, Japan 100
Tel: (03) 3283-7866   Fax: 3211-4859

Japan External Trade Organization
2-5, Toranomon 2-chome, Minato-ku, Tokyo 105
Tel: (03) 3582-5511

Japan Federation of Employers' Association
8-1, Yuraku-cho 1-chome, Chiyoda-ku, Tokyo 100
Tel: (03) 3213-4463   Fax: 3213-4466

Kansai Economic Federation
2-27 Nakanoshima 6-chome, Kita-ku, Osaka 530
Tel: (06) 441-0101

References

Fukuda, Takehiro. Weak leadership, scandal sap power of business old guard. *Nikkei Weekly*, Nov. 2, 1991: 1.

Keidanren—steadily eroding power. *Tokyo Business Today*, Jan. 1986: 38–42.

Ohtuka, Shoji. 1991. *Zaikai*. In *Japan Economic Almanac, 1991*. Tokyo: Nihon Keizai Shimbun.

C

call loans Short-term loans made between financial institutions in the call money market.

See **call money market**.

call money market The call money market is at the center of Japan's interbank money market, which is a short-term financial market for lending and borrowing between financial institutions. Japan's three call markets are located in Tokyo, Osaka, and Nagoya.

City banks are the major borrowers of funds in the call market, accounting for 50% or more of total funds borrowed. Other major borrowers are regional banks and foreign banks. The major lenders are **trust banks**, which provided ¥18.7 trillion or about 48% of the average balance of ¥38.9 trillion of call loans in 1992. In 1990 they provided more than 70%. Other lenders are city banks, regional banks, the Norinchukin Bank, the Zenshinren Bank, and *shinkin* **banks.**

Call market transactions are intermediated by the **money market dealers**, the six *tanshi* companies. There have been a variety of call loans since 1955, classified on the basis of the loan period. Since 1985 non-collaterized loans have been added to the traditional collateralized loans. Currently there are overnight call loans (both collaterized and uncollaterized) and collaterized fixed-date loans with maturity of 2–7 days and 2–3 weeks.

Call rates, or the interest rates on call loans, have been free from government control since 1979. They reflect the supply and demand conditions of the short-term financial market. Call rates vary with type of call money as well as by season of the year as business activities, and hence the demand for money, vary seasonally. For example, the annual rate on overnight call loans without collateral ranged from 6.13% to 9.06% in 1985, 6.47% to 8.34% in 1990, and 3.89% to 5.68% in 1992. The rates on collaterized call money are slightly lower. The rate tends to be highest in December when year-end gift purchases and bonus payments are made. In December 1990 the annual rate on uncollaterized overnight call loans averaged 8.23%. In the recession of 1991–92, however, the opposite was true. The annual rate on uncollaterized overnight loans averaged only 6.31% in December 1991 and 3.91% in December 1992, lower than during the rest of the year.

See also **interest rate structure, money markets**.

References

Bank of Japan. 1993. *Economic Statistics Annual, 1992.*

Suzuki, Yoshio, ed. 1987. *The Japanese Financial System.* Oxford: Oxford University Press. Pp. 112–17.

Tatewaki, Kazuo. 1991. *Banking and Finance in Japan.* London: Routledge. Ch. 4.

capital redevelopment plan   A government plan adopted in 1985 to encourage the relocation of businesses and government agencies from Tokyo to core business cities elsewhere.

See **land uses and policies, Tokyo, Yokohama.**

cartels   A cartel is a formal arrangement or agreement among firms in an oligopolistic market to cooperate on price fixing, maintaining market share, restricting output or imports, and so forth. The purpose is to restrict competition and maintain profitability and market share. In postwar Japan there have been price cartels, import cartels, recession (or antirecession) cartels, rationalization cartels, and so forth. A recession cartel is organized by firms of an industry facing reduced demand in a recession to reduce all firms' output by an agreed-upon percentage. The purpose is to avoid the bankruptcy of the weaker firms and the general debilitating effect on the industry if the firms had to compete for market share to survive. A rationalization cartel emphasizes the restructuring of a declining industry through industry capacity reduction, modernization, and/or reorganization.

Although cartels are banned by Japan's **Antimonopoly Law** because they restrict competition, there are various exceptions provided for by numerous statutes. Cartels were first authorized by the 1953 Export and Import Trading Act, which allowed price cartels and import cartels. The initiative in setting up a cartel is normally taken by the firms, but the consent of the Fair Trade Commission, which is responsible for implementing the Antimonopoly Law, is required. In implementing its industrial policy, the **Ministry of International Trade and Industry** (MITI) in the

1960s and 1970s sometimes permitted or even suggested the formation of cartels in order to restructure an industry or to reduce its capacity. In 1980, however, the oil company cartels established with its permission were found to be in violation of the Antimonopoly Law.

Recession cartels were first authorized in 1953 in an amendment to the Trade Association Act which prohibited groups of firms from operating restrictive practices. The initiative in setting up such cartels is normally taken by the firms, but the consent of the Fair Trade Commission is required. Recession cartels were once relatively common, but since the 1980s the Fair Trade Commission allows them only under strict conditions and within a specific time limit. For example, Japan's Shipbuilders' Association formed a recession cartel in 1987 because of industry recession due to competition from other Asian countries and the yen's sharp appreciation, which reduced Japanese shipbuilders' price competitiveness. By September 1989, however, export contracts were rising because of economic expansion in the other industrial countries. The Association decided to end the cartel itself just when the Fair Trade Commission was considering the ending of its permission for the cartel because of the industry's improved condition.

Because all cartels invariably reduce competition and restrict potential imports, they were criticized by Washington in its **Structural Impediments Initiative** talks with Tokyo in 1989–90. Washington wanted Japan's Fair Trade Commission to strengthen its implementation of the Antimonopoly Law and eliminate cartel practices. As a result, beginning in 1990 the commission has stepped up its investigation of illegal price fixings and other possible violation of the law, and has raised steeply the fines imposed on those found guilty of forming illegal cartels.

At the end of 1965, 1,079 cartels were exempted from the Antimonopoly Law. As of June 1991 the number was reduced to 247 (author's interview, Fair Trade Commission, July 28, 1992).

See also **Antimonopoly Law**, **industrial policy**.

References

Anderson, Douglas D. 1986. Managing retreat: Disinvestment policy. In *American versus Japan*, ed. by Thomas K. McCraw. Boston: Harvard Business School Press.

Cutts, Robert L. 1992. Capitalism in Japan: Cartels and *keiretsu*. *Harvard Business Review*, July–Aug.: 48–55.

Japan Shipbuilders to end an anti-recession cartel. *Wall Street Journal*, Sept. 22, 1989: A10.

Nakajima, Ai. 1991. Fair Trade Commission following tougher line. *Nikkei Weekly*, Sept. 28: 3.

Nester, William R. 1990. *The Foundation of Japanese Power: Continuities, Changes, Challenges.* London: Macmillan. Ch. 11.

Toga, Mitsuo. 1991. Cement makers chip away at illegal cartel. *Nikkei Weekly*, Dec. 28: 11.

Central Union of Agricultural Cooperatives
See **agricultural cooperatives.**

certificate of deposit (CD) market   A money market where negotiable certificate of bank deposits are traded.
   See **money markets.**

Chubu   Central Japan.
   See **Nagoya and Central Japan**.

chugen   Midyear gift-giving season; the fifteenth day of the seventh month of the year according to the lunar calendar.
   See **gift market**.

chu-sho kigyo   Small and medium enterprises.
   See **small and medium enterprises**.

cities   Japan has 656 cities, of which the ten largest in terms of population as of October 1992 are Tokyo (23 wards, 8.13 million), Yokohama (3.27 million), Osaka (2.6 million), Nagoya (2.16 million), Sapporo (1.72 million), Kobe (1.5 million), Kyoto (1.46 million), Fukuoka (1.26 million), Kawasaki (1.2 million), and Kitakyoshu (1.02 million). The largest four cities are also the centers of Japan's three major industrial areas.
   See also **Kansai and Osaka**, **Nagoya and Central Japan**, **Tokyo**, **Yokohama**.

city banks   City banks (*toshi ginko*) are the largest commercial banks in Japan. As of 1993 there are 11 of them. They hold about 20% of all deposits of Japan's financial institutions and supply about 20% of the loans given to private corporations. As of end of May 1993, there are 3,309 branches all over the country and 211 branches abroad. At the end of 1992, city banks had a total of ¥213.0 trillion in outstanding loans and ¥184.1 trillion in deposits, down from a peak of ¥210.5 trillion in 1990.

City banks are the major financial institutions that have lent heavily to industries at low cost to finance their reconstruction and growth in the postwar era. In particular, during the period of rapid growth and capital shortage before the first oil crisis in the early 1970s, large Japanese corporations had high demand for city bank loans, since Japan's capital market was underdeveloped. As a result the banks were often in a situation of "overloan" in which their loans exceeded their deposits, and the deficiency was covered by borrowing from the **Bank of Japan**, the central bank of Japan. Consequently the capital/asset ratio was traditionally very low. By providing funds to large corporations, city banks have contributed greatly to Japan's postwar economic development.

Each of the large city banks serves as the "main bank" to many Japanese corporations. In particular, the six largest of the city banks—Dai-Ichi Kangyo, Sakura (formerly Mitsui and Taiyo Kobe), Sumitomo, Fuji, Mitsubishi, and Sanwa—are the main banks of Japan's six financial *keiretsu*, the giant corporate groups that are organized around the six city banks. The main bank relationship ensures that companies will have access to funds for investment even when company profits are too low for interest payments (*Japan Economic Journal*, Jan. 19, 1991: A1). The Bank of Tokyo is the only city bank that specializes in foreign exchanges.

As part of their regular operation, but particularly in the **crossshareholding** relationship in a *keiretsu*, city banks also hold shares of major client companies as their "stable shareholders" without the intention of selling them for profits. The value of these shares is understated at cost in their balance sheets and thus they are said to have large "latent capital" or *fukumi* (unrealized profits of stock portfolio).

The decline in Japan's stock prices since early 1990 has strained this stable shareholder relationship. A ruling by the International Bank of Settlement that requires the banks to maintain a capital/asset ratio of 8% or more by April 1993 has further eroded the banks' ability to supply cheap credit. Although the rule allows the banks to count 45% of the unrealized profits of stock portfolio as capital, with the falling stock prices, some city banks have difficulties in attaining the 8% capital/asset ratio.

The assets and deposits of the city banks are given in table C.1. It can be seen that the assets of all city banks declined between March 1990 and March 1992 due to the decline of the stock and bond market. The levels of deposits also declined steadily since 1991.

Two of the largest city banks attained their large size through mergers. The first-ranked Dai-Ichi Kangyo Bank came from the merger in 1971 of two well-established city banks, Dai-Ichi Bank and Nippon Kangyo Bank.

Table C.1
Assets and deposits of city banks (in ¥ trillions)

| Bank | Assets | | Deposits[c] |
	March 1990	March 1992	September 1992
Dai-Ichi Kangyo	66.59	61.29	41.22
Sumitomo	62.77	60.21	38.94
Sakura	63.35[a]	59.60	39.76
Fuji	61.90	58.21	36.22
Mitsubishi	60.67	56.57	37.53
Sanwa	58.98	56.22	37.50
Tokai	38.48	35.05	24.13
Tokyo	31.82	28.36	16.50[d]
Daiwa	18.77	18.38	21.95[e]
Asahi	33.21[b]	29.97	22.00
Hokkaido Takushoku	11.75	11.12	7.90

Sources: *The Nikkei Weekly*, June 6, 1992, for assets; Federation of Bankers Association of Japan for deposits.
a. Sum of Mitsui Bank and Taiyo Kobe Bank, which merged on April 1, 1990.
b. Sum of Kyowa Bank and Saitama Bank, which merged on April 1, 1991.
c. Including CDs.
d. Bank debentures and deposits.
e. Including various trust accounts.

Sakura Bank, previously named Mitsui Taiyo Kobe Bank between April 1, 1990, and April 1, 1992, is the result of a merger on April 1, 1990, of Mitsui Bank and Taiyo Kobe Bank. On April 1, 1991, Kyowa Bank and Saitama Bank, two of the smaller city banks, merged into Kyowa Saitama Bank, which was later renamed Asahi Bank. The expected benefits of a merger are economies of scale in bank operations.

See also **banking system.**

Addresses

Dai-Ichi Kangyo Bank
1-5, Uchisaiwai-cho 1-chome, Chiyoda-ku, Tokyo 100
Tel: (03) 3596-1111

Federation of Bankers Association of Japan
3-1, Marunouchi 1-chome, Chiyoda-ku, Tokyo 100
Tel: (03) 5252-3752   Fax: (03) 5252-3755

Fuji Bank
5-5, Otemachi 1-chome, Chiyoda-ku, Tokyo 100
Tel: (03) 3216-2211   Fax: (03) 3201-0527

Mitsubishi Bank
7-1, Marunouchi 2-chome, Chiyoda-ku, Tokyo 100
Tel: (03) 3240-1111   Fax: (03) 3240-3350

Sakura Bank
3-1, Kudan Minami 1-chome, Chiyoda-ku, Tokyo 102
Tel: (03) 3230-3111

Sanwa Bank
5-6, Fushimi-cho 3-chome, Chuo-ku, Osaka 541
Tel: (06) 206-8111

Sumitomo Bank
4-6-5, Kitahama, Chuo-ku, Osaka 541
Tel: (06) 227-2111

References

Bank of Japan. 1993. *Economic Statistics Annual, 1992*. Pp. 47–52.

Federation of Bankers Association of Japan. 1989. *The Banking System in Japan*. Tokyo: Zenginkyo. Ch. 1.

Federation of Bankers Association of Japan. Annual. *Japanese Banks*. Tokyo: Zenginkyo.

Hoiuchi, Akiyoshi, Frank Packer, and Shin'ichi Fukuda. 1988. What role has the "main bank" played in Japan. *Journal of the Japanese and International Economies* 2: 159–80.

Mitsui-Taiyo Kobe merger creates a megabank. *Tokyo Business Today*, October 1989: 16–21.

Outlook bleak for commercial banks. *Nikkei Weekly*, June 6, 1992: 1, 21.,

Suzuki, Yoshio, ed. 1987. *The Japanese Financial System*. Oxford: Oxford University Press. Ch. 5.

Tatewaki, Kazuo. 1991. *Banking and Finance in Japan*. London: Routledge. Ch. 7.

commercial paper market   A commercial paper (CP) is an unsecured promisary note issued by corporations with high credit standing to raise short-term funds. Japan's CP market was first established in November 1987. At the end of 1988 the balance of CPs outstanding on the market was only ¥1.26 trillion. It increased to ¥15.76 trillion in 1990 but declined to ¥12.2 trillion in 1992 because of the recession.

Commercial paper is issued with a face value of ¥100 million or more and with a maturity of between two weeks and nine months. It is a way to raise low-cost funds—the interest rate is calculated from the the discount at which it is sold—and some companies use the funds thus raised to invest in high-yield certificates of deposits. Only corporations with the highest (A-1) or the second highest (A-2) credit rating are eligible for issuing CPs. Prior to April 1, 1992, companies also had to have over ￥33 billion in net assets to be eligible. **Securities companies** were not permitted to issue CPs until February 1990. Since June 1993 **nonbank financial institutions** (nonbanks) with ratings of A-2 or better from at least two credit-rating agencies are permitted to issue CPs.

Commercial papers can be issued and sold only through dealers, which include banks and security houses. Buyers are limited to institutinal investors, usually large companies, especially the large **trading companies**.

See also **corporate finance, money market**.

References

Federation of Bankers Associations of Japan. 1992. *Japanese Banks, '92*. Tokyo: Zenginkyo.

Non-banks step up effort to end CP ban. *Japan Economic Journal*, Nov. 25, 1989: 34.

Securities Market in Japan, 1992. Tokyo: Japan Securities Research Intitute. Ch. 4.

Tatewaki, Kazuo. 1991. *Banking and Finance in Japan*. London: Routledge. Ch. 4.

commodity markets   Japan's commodity markets are relatively small compared with the Chicago Mercantile Exchange, the Chicago Board of Trade, New York's Commodity Exchange, and the gold markets of London and Zurich. However, Japan had the world's first futures market for trading rice in Osaka in the early 1600s. Currently it has the largest trading volumes in platinum in the world. Platinum is the most sought-after precious metal for jewelry in Japan, and Japan's platinum jewelry market amounted to 90% of the world's market in 1988.

There are 16 commodity exchanges in Japan. The **Ministry of International Trade and Industry** (MITI) oversees the trading of metals and other industrial products while the Ministry of Agriculture, Forestry, and Fisheries controls that of agricultural products. The three largest exchanges are Tokyo Commodity Exchange for Industry (TOCOM), Tokyo Grain Exchange, and Tokyo Sugar Exchange, which account for two-thirds of commodity trading in Japan. The other 13 exchanges in the country— including the Osaka Textile Exchange, Osaka Sugar Exchange, and Kobe Grain Exchange—are small.

TOCOM is the world's leading platimum exchange mainly because of demand from local jewelers. Besides precious metals, it also trades rubber, cotton, and wool. The Tokyo Grain Exchange has the bulk of its business in trading soybeans imported from the United States and China. It also trades *azuki* beans. The Ministry of International Trade and Industry is considering the establishment of the Japan Metal Exchange, where aluminum and other nonferrous metals futures can be traded.

TOCOM has some 60 full members, all of which are Japanese firms. According to the Commodity Exchange Act, foreign firms are not permitted to become full members of Japanese exchanges. In April 1989, 30 foreign banks, commodity houses, and metal traders were accepted as associate members of TOCOM. However, they can only trade for their own accounts by placing orders through the Japanese members and pay the relatively high exchange commission fees.

The Nikkei Commodity Futures Index reflects the overall price level of all commodity futures traded. With the 1985 average as 100, the Nikkei Index was between 89 and 90 in early April 1989 and slightly under 63 in late September 1992.

Total turnover on the nation's 16 commodity exchanges for FY 1990 was 43.61 million contracts, an increase of 12.1% from 1989. There were 23.69 million contracts in FY 1986. The increase was most pronounced in three precious metals (gold, silver, and platinum), followed by agricultural products. Trading volume in raw sugar ad textiles remained sluggish.

To facilitate wider investment in commodity futures, a commodity fund market was opened in 1992 to subsidiaries of banks and brokerage houses. These companies could set up commodity futures funds, sell their shares to investors, and manage the funds in the commodity futures market.

See also **Tokyo Stock Exchange**.

Addresses

All Japan Grain Exchange Association
12-5, Nihonbashi Kakigaracho 1-chome, Chuo-ku, Tokyo 103
Tel: (03) 3666-6572

Japan Federation of Commodity Exchanges, Inc.
1-10, Nihonbashi Ningyocho 1-chome, Chuo-ku, Tokyo 103
Tel: (03) 3667-4381

Tokyo Commodity Exchange for Industry
10-8, Nihonbashi Horidomecho 1-chome, Chuo-ku, Tokyo 103
Tel: (03) 3661-9191

References

Inose, Hijiri. 1991. End users hinder commodities futures expansion. *Japan Economic Journal*, May 25: 48.

Inose, Hijiri. 1993. Commodity futures. In *Japan Economic Almanac, 1993*. Tokyo: Nihon Keizai Shimbun.

Shida, Tomio. 1989. Japanese see bright future in futures. *Japan Economic Journal*, May 6: 1, 7.

Taking a shine to Japan's commodities markets. *The Economist*, Aug. 5, 1989: 63–64.

Yamazaki, Akio. 1990. Commodity futures market. In *Japan Economic Almanac, 1990*. Tokyo: Nihon Keizai Shimbum.

commodity tax   A major indirect tax levied by the national government before 1989. Effective April 1, 1989, it was replaced by the new consumption tax.

See **consumption tax, taxation system.**

computer industry
See **electronics industry.**

computer-integrated manufacturing (CIM) system   A production control system that links and coordinates the design, development, planning, production, and marketing activities of a company through sophisticated computers and information networks. With the CIM system changes in one area such as design or sales can be simultaneously conveyed to other areas in order to bring about needed adjustments immediately at a miminum cost.

For the production of a highly complex product that requires the coordination of many production processes and suppliers, as well as branch offices and sales outlets, the CIM system offers the most cost-effective means of wedding computers to manufacturing. It has been increasingly adopted, since the late 1980s, by large manufacturing companies in Japan such as Toyota Motor Corp., Mitsubishi Heavy Industries, and Nippondenso (Japan's largest producer of electrical autoparts). An automobile, for example, has some 20,000 possible specifications. Changes in any of these, coming either from the designing engineer or a customer, can be integrated into the production system immediately. When a customer in Japan orders a Toyota car at a dealer with custom specifications, the order is sent on-line to Toyota plants and parts suppliers under the headquarters' management; many of the parts suppliers are integrated into the system. Within 11 or 12 days the custom-made car is delivered. The CIM system complements and improves on the **just-in-time system.**

A major limitation of the existing CIM systems is that they are limited to individual companies and their affiliates, and lack international compatibility. A problem of noncompatability, for example, is that a computer-aided design system cannot send its design data electronically into an industrial robot, or a new machine developed by a new supplier cannot be connected to an existing system without developing a new interface. To promote widespread use of CIM techniques, the **Ministry of International Trade and Industry** launched in 1990 a ¥50 billion ten-year program to internationalize or standardize CIM techniques around the world so that different manufacturing robots and computer information systems can be integrated or connected. Still in its initial phase, the program has encountered reluctance of Japanese firms in technology transfer and lukewarm response from the United States and Europe.

See also **just-in-time system**.

References

Beatty, Carol A., and John R. Gordon. 1988. Barriers to the implementation of CAD/CAM systems. *Sloan Management Review* 29, 4: 25–33.

Mitsusada, Hisayuki. 1989. Japan seeks U.S., Europe cooperation in plan to create computer-linked factories. *Japan Economic Journal*, July 15: 1.

Mitsusada, Hisayuki. 1989. Toyota computer network speeds car orders. *Japan Economic Journal*, July 15: 4.

Oishi, Nobuyuki. 1989. Computer proves worth as production tool. *Japan Economic Journal*, July 15: 5.

Oishi, Nobuyuki. 1990. Suspicions slow implementation of IMS standard. *Japan Economic Journal*, July 21: 1.

construction industry   Japan's construction industry constitutes a large sector of the economy. It employs nearly 10% of total employees in the economy and construction investment amounted to about 19% of Japan's GNP in 1991.

The industry has some 520,000 companies. Most of them are unincorporated or small-to-medium sized, capitalized at less than ¥100 million. The industry is dominated by five general construction companies—Shimizu, Kajima, Taisei, Takenaka, Obayashi Corp.—each with sales over ¥1 trillion. Shimizu Corp. is the largest one, with sales of ¥2.17 trillion for FY 1992 (see table C.2). Below the top five, there is a second tier of large companies, each with its own specialization such as civil engineering and development. For example, Kumagai Gumi Co., the sixth largest company, is Japan's largest contractor overseas. The small companies work for the large companies as subcontractors under some industry clubs affiliated with the big companies.

Japan's construction investments have grown very rapidly since the late 1980s—from less than ¥50 trillion (15.4% of GNP) in FY 1985 to ¥82.8

Table C.2
Leading construction companies (in ¥ billions)

	FY 1991		FY 1992	
Company	Sales	Profits[a]	Sales	Profits[a]
Shimizu Corp.	2,130	124	2,168	132
Taisei Corp.	1,717	96	1,980	101
Kajima Corp.	1,951	124	1,954	87
Obayashi Corp.	1,509	53	1,519	49
Kumagai Gumi Co.	1,145	38	1,078	29
Fujita Corp.	820	44	849	33
Toda Corp.	780	48	753	41
Hazama Corp.	697	33	663	18
Tokyu Construction Co.	591	22	618	13
Sato Kogyo Co.	543	18	615	13
Nishimatsu Construction Co.	622	27	602	26

Sources: *Japan Company Handbook* for FY 1991; *The Nikkei Weekly*, July 5, 1993 for FY 1992.
Notes: One of the big five, Takenaka, is unlisted.
a. Pretax profits.

trillion in FY 1990 and ¥86.6 trillion (18.8% of GNP) in FY 1991; in dollar amount, they have become the world's largest. About 25% of total construction orders in 1990–91 were government orders as compared with about 50% in the late 1970s. Many large public works projects such as the New Kansai International Airport have attracted the attention of some American construction companies. However, the latter have found the Japanese construction market extremely difficult to enter because of structural barriers such as the government's "designated competitive bidding system" and the industry's *dango* system.

In the designated competitive bidding system, only specific government-appointed contractors are permitted to bid for public works projects. Government offices rank the construction companies on the basis of their scale, performance, technology, and so forth. Depending on the size of a particular project, about ten appropriate companies are selected for bidding. *Dango* literally means consultation, and the *dango* system is the prebidding collusion among the companies to determine the winning contractor and its bidding price for the project. It has been defended by industry people as work sharing, which ensures that smaller firms will have their share of profitable contracts. Government guidelines previously permitted such "information exchange" among contractors, thereby providing a loophole for the **Antimonopoly Law**. Critics have charged that the practice was permitted because local politicians depend heavily on the money and votes of local construction companies and that many government officials retire into the executive ranks of these companies. It has also been suggested that *dango* gives contractors incentives not to refuse unprofitable projects for fear of losing subsequent designations.

Dango incidents have been well documented by the Japanese press. In several instances between 1983 and 1991, projects at U.S. military bases were involved. After the uncovering of such bid-rigging, the U.S. government demanded compensation and eventually did receive some. In 1988, for example, 99 Japanese companies paid ¥4.7 billion to the U.S. government for *dango* at Yokosuka U.S. military base.

Washington's efforts to open up Japanese construction market started in 1986 when it requested international bidding for jobs at the new Kansai International Airport. In the U.S.–Japan construction agreement of May 1988, Tokyo agreed to adopt preferential measures to help U.S. companies participate in 17 public works projects to acquaint them with Japan's bidding system. During the U.S.–Japan **Structural Impediments Initiative** talks, Tokyo agreed in general to implement the Antimonopoly Law vigorously. Subsequently the Fair Trade Commission attempted to deter *dango* practice by raising the penalty for it from 1.5% of sales to 6%. However, industry analysts believe that it is impossible to abolish *dango* altogether and that it will be continued in new guises. In June 1991 another agreement was reached between Washington and Tokyo that will add 17 new public works projects for preferential foreign participation.

The construction industry employed 4.8 million workers in 1991, about 9.6% of total employees. The aging of the work force in construction is said to be faster than in other industries because it is becoming relatively difficult to recruit young construction workers. Many smaller companies have hired workers from other Asian countries on a part-time basis.

See also **Structural Impediments Initiative**.

Addresses

Japan Federation of Construction Contractors, Inc.
5-1, Hatchobori 2 chome, Chuo-ku, Tokyo 104
Tel: (03) 3553-0701

Kumagi Gumi Co.
6-8, Chuo 2-chome, Fukui City 910
Tel: (0776) 21–2700   Fax: (03) 3235-5389

Ministry of Construction
1-3, Kasumigaseki 2-chome, Chiyoda-ku, Tokyo 100
Tel: (03) 3580-4311

Shimizu Corp.
2-3, Shibaura 1-chome, Minato-ku, Tokyo
Tel: (03) 5441-1111   Fax: (03) 5441-0349

Taisei Corp.
25-1, Nishi-Shinjuku 1-chome, Shinjuku-ku, Tokyo 163
Tel: (03) 3348-1111   Fax: (03) 3345-1386

References

Cash flow fosters web of corruption among politicians, contractors. *Nikkei Weekly*, Aug. 23, 1993: 1–2.

The crackdown on construction industry bid rigging. *Tokyo Business Today*, Oct. 1991: 28–30.

Krauss, Ellis S. and Isobel Coles. 1990. Built-in impediments: The political economy of the U.S.-Japan construction dispute. In *Japan's Economic Structure: Should It Change?* ed. by Kozo Yamanura. Seattle: Society for Japanese Studies.

Nishimura, Hiroyuki. 1993. Construction. In *Japan Economic Almanac, 1993*. Tokyo: Nihon Keizai Shimbun, Inc.

Saito, Hitoshi. 1992. Construction. In *Japan Economic Almanac, 1992*. Tokyo: Nihon Keizai Shimbun.

U.S.–Japan construction talks reveal contraditions in American strategy. *Tokyo Business Today*, May 1991: 32–34.

consumer behavior
See **consumer groups, customer sovereignty**.

consumer cooperatives
See **consumer groups**.

consumer credit   Prior to the early 1980s financial institutions provided relatively little credit to consumers. This is considered to be one of the reasons for the high level of household savings. However, the situation started to change in the 1980s. The total amount of consumer credit balance grew from ¥7.1 trillion in 1975 to ¥15.2 trillion in 1980, ¥27.41 trillion in 1985, and ¥53 trillion in 1989. These amounted to 6.5% of household disposable income in 1975, 12.4% in 1985 and 20.1% in 1989 (Economic Planning Agency 1991: 37).

Consumer credit (excluding mortgage loans) consists of two categories: *sales credit* for the payment of goods and services purchased, and *consumer finance*, which is granted directly to the consumer. Until the mid-1980s sales credit was the larger of the two. In the late 1980s consumer finance expanded rapidly due in part to the strong yen and low interest rate. In 1988 consumer finance accounted for about 60% of the outstanding consumer credit balance in 1988.

There are three major sources of consumer credit: banks and other financial institutions, installment credit companies or credit sales companies, and the consumer finance companies. The interest rate charged in the 1980s varied from 12% to 15% for banks, 15% to 30% for installment credit companies, and 35% to 70% for consumer finance companies. The banks have stricter requirements for obtaining consumer loans.

Until the late 1970s Japanese corporations depended heavily on bank loans for investment. Consequently financial authorities have traditionally discouraged banks from extending credit to consumers through ceilings on consumer loan rates and by **administrative guidance**. Since 1986, however, Japan's **city banks** have become increasingly involved in consumer finance, including the fast-growing credit card business (JCB Cards, VISA, MasterCard, etc.). At the end of 1991 city banks' outstanding consumer loans balance was ¥8.9 trillion, more than 12 times that of 1986. For all banks the outstanding consumer credit balance was ¥19.6 trillion at the end of 1992, compared with ¥1.5 trillion at the end of 1986.

The installment credit companies or credit sales companies (*shinpan* companies) are registered with the **Ministry of International Trade and Industries** as firms that intermediate in installment purhases in accordance with the Installment Sale Law of July 1961. They intermediate either in general installment purchases (credit card companies) or in installment purchases of specific goods (installment claims purchasing companies). They have become the major issuers of credit cards in Japan. In 1990, of the 163.23 million credit cards issued in Japan, about 55.7 million or 34% of them were issued by these companies as compared with 48.7 million or 30% issued by bank-affiliated credit card companies. In 1991, a total of 203 million credit cards were in use. Japan's largest credit sales company is Nippon Shinpan.

Consumer finance companies (*sarakin*, from the word "salaryman" and the Japanese word *kinyu*, "finance") used to be an important source of consumer finance. At their peak in the early 1980s, they numbered 220,000 and provided about 13% of consumer credit in 1982. These companies obtain funds from banks and life insurance companies and make small loans directly to individuals at high interest rates, which often exceeded 100% before 1983. In addition they often resorted to threats and harassment in the collection of loans. In 1983 a law was passed to limit their interest rate to 73% per year in 1983, 54.75% in 1986, and 40% in 1991. Because of new competition from other lending institutions in the consumer credit market and tighter regulation by the **Ministry of Finance** of their lending limit and collection practices, these companies have declined since the early 1980s in number (37,000 in early 1990s) and in importance.

For the purchase of houses, the principal source of mortage loans is the public housing corporations (see **government financial institutions**). Interest rates in such loans are generally fixed. For depositors of the **postal savings** service, small loans are available with their deposits as collateral.

Analysts generally expect the consumer credit market, including the credit card market, to continue to grow in the 1990s. One of the reasons is that the **savings** rate of Japanese households is expected to decline and the Japanese society to become more consumer oriented.

See also **credit card industry, savings.**

Addresses

Japan Consumer Credit Industry Association
7, Yotsuyo 4-chome, Shinjuku-ku, Tokyo 160
Tel: (03) 3359-0411

Nippon Shinpan
33-5, Hongo 3-chome, Bunkyo-ku, Tokyo
Tel: (03) 3811-3111   Fax: (03) 3815-6650

References

Alexander, Authur. 1993. Thrifty Japan discovers consumer credit. *JEI Report*, no. 26A, July 16.

Economic Planning Agency. 1991. *Economic Survey of Japan, 1990–1991*.

Feldman, Robert A. 1986. *Japanese Financial Markets*. Cambridge: MIT Press.

Financial markets. *Japan Economic Journal*, Winter suppl., 1990.

Hamada, Koichi and Akiyoshi Horiuchi. 1987. The political economy of the financial market. In *The Political Economy of Japan*. Vol. 1: *The Domestic Transformation*, ed. by Kozo Yamamura and Yasukichi Yasuba. Stanford: Stanford University Press.

Suzuki, Yoshio, ed. 1987. *The Japanese Financial System*. New York: Oxford University Press.

consumer electronics industry
See **electronics industry**.

consumer finance companies
See **consumer credit**.

consumer groups   There are many consumer groups—4,639 at the end of 1988—engaged in consumer-related activities. They can be classified into the following five categories:

1. *Consumer cooperatives (seikyo)*. These groups are set up with funds from members. In 1988 there were 1,271 such cooperatives with 33.7 million members. In FY 1991 the largest consumer cooperatives in terms of sales were Consumers Co-op Kobe (¥92.4 billion), Consumers Co-op Tokyo (¥56 billion), F Consumers Co-op (¥52.1 billion), Osaka Izumi Citizen Co-op (¥49.5 billion), and Chiba Consumers Co-op (¥49.4 billion; *Japan Economic Almanac* 1993: 245). Cooperatives purchase in bulk daily necessities, perishables, and processed foods directly from producers or wholesalers and sell them to members at relatively low prices. The cooperatives may also provide medical treatment, welfare, and housing and run mutual-aid insurance services. There are two types of consumer cooperatives: regional cooperatives, centered mainly on housewives, and employee cooperatives at workplaces and universities. Almost all consumer cooperatives belong to the Japanese Consumers' Cooperative Union.

2. *Housewives organizations*. These groups are involved in various activities such as jointly purchasing products from farmers, price surveys, recycling, testing products, and attending cooking classes. They include the Japan Housewives Association (*shufuren*) and the National Federation of Regional Women's Organizations (*chifuren*). The former was established in 1948 and is the oldest of consumer gropus.

3. *Advocacy groups*. These groups focus on problems of food safety, environmental protection, medical issues, and so on. The largest of these is the Consumer Union of Japan. It publicizes defective products, anticonsumer corporate behavior, and lobbys for consumer interest legislations.

4. *Experts groups*. These groups are made up of lawyers, consultants, and other experts. They attempt to broaden liability for product defects, to ban fraudulent contracts, and so forth.

Because there is no nationwide organization to integrate the consumer groups, the effectiveness of any one group or movement is inevitably limited. However, some analysts contend that the "effectiveness" of Japan's consumer groups, or more broadly the "rationality" of Japanese consumers, should not be viewed from the perspective of Western economic theories of consumer behavior. For example, high retail prices in Japan are accepted by consumers in part because of the Japanese emphasis on high product quality and after-sale service. In this regard Dore (1990: 371) views Japanese consumer behavior from the perspective of the "customer market" as opposed to the theoretical, minimum-price seeking "auction market" and argues that Japanese consumer behavior is rational in the context of a society that values relationships. Similarly the "inefficient" **distribution system** is accepted because consumers like its "personal touch" services; in addition many consumers work in that system. In short, Japanese consumer groups do not necessarily share foreigners' criticisms of the structure of the Japanese economy.

See also **customer sovereignty**.

Addresses

Japan Consumers' Association
5-9, Hacchobori 4-chome, Chuo-ku, Tokyo 104
Tel: (03) 3553-8601

Japan Housewives Association
15, Rokuban-cho, Chiyoda-ku, Tokyo 102
Tel: (03) 3553-8601

References

Dore, Ronald. 1990. An outsider's view. In *Japan's Economic Structure: Should It Change?* ed. by Kozo Yamamura. Seattle: Society for Japanese Studies.

Ishizuka, Masahiko. 1989. Japanese consumers lack group identity, power. *Japan Economic Journal*, Apr. 15: 11.

Nishikawa, Kazuko. 1990. Why Japanese consumer groups oppose market opening measures. *Tokyo Business Today*, Mar.: 40–43.

Wada, Shigeru. 1990. Buyer interest push meets public apathy. *Japan Economic Journal*, May 19: 3.

consumer price index
See **price indexes and price levels**.

consumer sovereignty
See **customer sovereignty**.

Consumer Union of Japan
See **consumer groups**.

consumption   Aggregate consumption (including general government consumption and private consumption) as a share of gross domestic product (GDP) is relatively low in Japan as compared with that of other industrial nations. During the 1970s and 1980s it ranged between 60% and 70%; it was 60% in 1970, 69% in 1980 and 1985, and 66% in 1989 and 1990. The share of government consumption is about 9–10% of GDP. Also government consumption has grown more slowly than that of private consumption.

According to surveys conducted by the Management and Coordination Agency, average household consumption as a ratio of household disposable income was 79.7% in 1970, 77.9% in 1980, 77.5% in 1985, and 74.5% in 1991. Dividing the sample households into five quintile groups by annual income, the average propensity to consume in 1991 ranged from 84.2% for the poorest group to 70.0% for the top income group, all remarkably low by international standards.

Table C.3 compares the composition of household consumption expenditures in 1970 and 1991. The largest single consumption item as of 1991 is food, but its share of the household budget has declined substantially from 34% in 1970 to 25.1% in 1990. On the other hand, expenditures on services (housing, transportation and communication, education, recreation, etc.) have increased by various extents. These changes are consistent with the experiences of other industrial countries. The final category, "other living expenditures," is a broad category of miscellaneous expenditures, of which "social expenses" are the largest item. Social expenses comprise mostly gifts and amount to nearly 10% of household expenditures, making the **gift market** an important segment of Japan's retail market. Between households in large cities and in rural areas, the former spend relatively more on food, **housing**, clothes, and education, whereas the latter spend

Table C.3
Composition of household consumption (in %)

	1970	1990
Food	34.1	25.1
Housing and utilities	9.3	10.6
Furniture and utensils	5.0	4.1
Clothes and footwear	9.4	7.3
Medical care	2.6	2.8
Transportation and communication	5.2	9.3
Education	2.8	4.3
Recreation	9.1	9.6
Other living expenditures	22.6	26.9
(Social expenses)	7.8	9.9

Source: Management and Coordination Agency.

relatively more on utilities, transportation and communication, and "other living expenditures."

Nonfood consumer goods can be divided into consumer semidurables and consumer durables. The former, consisting of items such as clothes and footwear, has declined steadily from more than 15.5% of household budget in 1973 to less than 12% in 1990. Consumers' income elasticity of demand for semidurable goods is relatively low. On the other hand, spending on consumer durables has remained relatively stable; it amounted to 6–6.5% of household spending between 1970 and 1986, and then rose to about 7% in 1987–90 (Economic Planning Agency 1992: 146).

However, consumer spending on specific durable goods such as automobiles, color televisions, washing machines, and air conditioners fluctuates seasonally and over the **business cycles**. The Economic Planning Agency (1992: 136–47) has found that consumer spending on consumer durables is much more sensitive than spending on semidurables to changes in the following variables: (1) household disposable income, (2) interest rate on bank loans, and (3) financial asset balance. Spending on nondurables is also sensitive to changes in household disposable income. In addition households' consumption habits are important with nondurables. Spending on services is heavily influenced by consumption habits and prices.

While the composition of Japanese household consumption changes as household disposable income increases, the average propensity to consume has remained relatively low and stable. This reflects Japanese households' desire to save a sizable portion of their disposable income for various personal reasons (see **savings**). The resultant high saving ratio of the economy has financed the economy's high rate of **investment**. While industries grew rapidly as a result, many consumer goods industries had to rely on the export market to sell their expanded output, thereby contributing to Japan's large and chronic trade surplus. The alternative to this export-driven growth is to rely more heavily on the domestic market for growth, as many countries have urged Japan to do. This would require an increased propensity to consume on the part of the Japanese households. This will not be easy to accomplish in a short period of time because the institutional and psychological factors that have underlied the high saving rate cannot be readily changed. In the longer run, however, many analysts expect Japan's saving ratio to go down as the population becomes older and as more people, not having lived through the hardships of the early postwar period, take an affluent way of life for granted.

See also **savings**.

References

Economic Planning Agency. 1992. *Economic White Paper* (in Japanese). Tokyo.

Ito, Takatoshi. 1992. *The Japanese Economy*. Cambridge: MIT Press. Ch. 9.

Management and Coordination Agency. 1992. *Japan Statistical Yearbook, 1992*.

Takenaka, Heizo. 1991. *Contemporary Japanese Economy and Economic Policy*. Ann Arbor: University of Michigan Press. Chs. 3–4.

Tsukada, Norifumi. 1993. Have consumers given up on the economy? *Tokyo Business Today*, Mar.: 36–40.

consumption tax   Japan's general consumption tax became effective on April 1, 1989. It was part of the **tax reform** package passed by the Diet or parliament under the leadership of then Prime Minister Noboru Takeshita. In the same tax reform, individual income tax, corporation tax, and inheritance tax were simplified and reduced, and a variety of excise taxes eliminated.

The main original provisions of the consumption tax are as follows:

1. A tax of 3% (6% for automobiles) is applied to all sales and service transactions (see exemptions below). Taxes are due twice a year.

2. The tax paid by a company to suppliers is credited against the tax on its sales in order to avoid tax cascading.

3. Small- and medium-sized businesses with sales up to ¥30 million per year are exempt. Companies with sales up to ¥500 million per year may use a fixed value-added rate of 10% for wholesalers and 20% for all others.

4. The following sales are exempt: export, land sales, securities transactions, foreign exchange deals, loan interest, parimutuel betting, postage stamps, medical expenses, education costs, and certain government administrative fees and social welfare payments.

The consumption tax broadens Japan's tax base because its tax system was previously based on wage-withholding income tax, which contained many exemptions for interest groups. The tax is welcomed by foreign exporters because it reduced the tax rate on luxury imports such as luxury cars and fine liquor, which were previously taxed at a higher rate. However, domestic consumers are unhappy about it. Opposition to it by housewives contributed to the strong election victory of Japan's Socialist Party (renamed Social Democratic Party in January 1991) and the first loss of majority control by the Liberal Democratic Party in the Upper House of the Diet in 1989.

Because the Social Democratic Party did poorly in the April 1991 election with its blanket opposition to the tax, it subsequently relaxed its opposition to the tax and cooperated with the ruling Liberal Democratic Party in the revision of the consumption tax in May 1991, to be effective October 1991, to close some loopholes. Originally small- and medium-sized firms with annual sales up to ¥500 million could claim 80% of the sales value (90% for wholesalers) as stocking costs. In the revised tax, the ceiling is lowered to ¥400 million. Manufacturers and service firms with low stocking costs can claim only 60% or 70% of sales as costs. The ceiling for special deductions is lowered from ¥60 million to ¥50 million annual sales.

The revised tax exempts residential rent, childbirth, funeral expenses, and school entry fees. Large firms are to report taxes quarterly instead of semiannually. The opposition parties would also like to exempt food from farm to retail outlets.

See also **tax reform**.

References

Choy, Jon. Tax reform passes lower house. *JEI Report*, Dec. 2, 1988, pt B: 1–8.

Gomi, Yuji. 1992. *Guide to Japanese Taxes*. Tokyo: Zaikeishoho sha.

Isono, Naoyuki. 1991. Some holes in consumption tax expected to be plugged. *Japan Economic Journal*, May 4: 5.

Ministry of Finance. 1991. *An Outline of Japanese Taxes*.

Odden, Lee. 1989. Tax reform 1989. *Tokyo Business Today*, Mar.: 24–27.

convertible bonds
See **bond market**, **corporate finance**.

corporate finance　The nature of a Japanese company's finances varies with its size, its field of business, its business connections, the financial and industrial policies of the government of the particular time period, and so forth. For example, large companies have better access to both debt and equity markets than smaller ones. And at one time or another, companies in certain strategic industries were in a better position to receive long-term bank loans from private banks and **government financial institutions** than companies in other fields. Thus the following generalizations apply mostly to large corporations, but there are always exceptions.

During Japan's high-growth period from the 1950s to the early 1970s, Japanese companies relied mostly on bank loans for financing their invest-

ment, resulting in high debt–equity ratios (Toyota Motor and Matsushita Electric are said to be the major exceptions, relying mostly on internal funds; Abegglen and Stalk, 1985: 151). The main reason for this was the availability of low-cost bank loans as the government encouraged high **savings** and kept interest rates low to promote rapid industrial development. Because of the importance of bank loans, a main-bank system developed in which a company's largest bank-lender would maintain a close relationship with the company to ensure the latter's financial soundness and thus to minimize the risks for all its lenders. The main bank owns a certain percentage (currently up to 5%) of the company's shares, has access to its confidential information, and may advise it on its operations.

Minor sources of debt finance include borrowing from government financial institutions and the issuing of straight corporate bonds. Corporate bond issues have been relatively small in Japan because of the dominance of **government bonds** and the government's policy to keep bond interest rates low. There are also stringent regulations on the amount of bonds that companies can issue.

After the oil crisis of 1973, tighter monetary policy to control inflation led to a cash squeeze and higher interest costs of loans. Banks loans to companies began to decline in importance because equity financing became relatively cheaper. In addition **financial liberalization** since the late 1970s by the **Ministry of Finance** made it easier for companies to issue securities other than straight bonds and equities. Most important among these were equity-linked convertible bonds and **warrant bonds**.

Convertible bonds can be converted into shares under certain conditions. Warrant bonds are similar because the warrants attached permit holders to convert to shares at fixed prices; however, the warrants can be detached and traded separately. Most convertible bonds are issued in Japan, whereas most warrant bonds are issued in the Euromarkets but are purchased by Japanese investors and traded in the **over-the-counter markets.** Because of the advantages of flexibility and reduced risk to investors, these two types of equity-linked bonds became popular in the 1980s. At the same time share prices also rose rapidly in the 1980s, particularly in the late 1980s, making it ever more profitable for big corporations to increase their equity financing. The companies listed on the **Tokyo Stock Exchange** raised through the stock market ¥4 trillion in 1960–69, ¥11.6 trillion in the 1970s, and ¥70 trillion in the 1980s (Zielinski and Holloway, 1991: 161).

Japanese companies typically pay their dividend at ¥5 per share, or 10% of the par value (¥50) of a share. As share prices rose in the late 1980s (see

stock market), the dividend paid out as a percentage of net profits declined—it was 44% in 1977, 37.7% in 1982, and 27.6% in 1990 for all listed companies. In early 1992 the payout ratio remained below 30%, which is lower than that of U.S. and European companies. In order to stimulate the stock market in the midst of a recession, the Japan Securities Dealers Association revised, in March 1992, its guidelines for equity finance, requesting companies that issue new stocks, convertible and warrant bonds to pledge a payout ratio of more than 30%.

Investors traditionally bought shares, not for the dividends, but for their growth potential. The number of shares available in the stock market, however, is limited by the system of **cross shareholding** in which companies that have mutual business ties or are members of the same *keiretsu* group hold each other's shares. These companies are the so-called stable shareholders because they hold other companies' shares for long-term business purposes and are not likely to sell them for short-term gains. Hence the shares they hold are not available for trading in the stock market. When share prices rise, the unrealized capital gains are considered to be the "latent capital" of Japanese companies, which is considered to enhance their financial strength.

The rapid growth in equity financing in the 1980s has provided many companies with excess funds, which were utilized in various ways—for example, deposited in large-denomination deposits or invested in *tokkin* **funds**—to increase corporate profits. *Tokkin* funds are a type of investment trust fund with a tax advantage and high returns. In the 1980, many Japanese companies became heavily involved in *zaitech* (literally financial engineering) or the investment of surplus funds in the stock market for profits. Such profits sometimes exceeded the profits from the main lines of business for many companies. In the stock market boom of the late 1980s, even successful manufacturing firms such as Toyota Motor, Nissan Motor, and Matsushita Electric made 40–65% of their pre-tax profits through *zaitech* (*Economist*, June 25, 1988: 75). Ironically American companies' pursuit of such financial gains outside the firms' main manufacturing activies used to be criticized by the Japanese as a weakness of the American style of management.

After the collapse of share prices in 1990 and the revelation of scandals such as loss compensation made by **securities companies** to their large clients, Japan's stock market has been in the doldrums since the early 1990s. The new issue market for stocks has been inactive, and convertible bond and warrant bond offerings have greatly declined. Thus equity financing is not an easy option for companies. Nor are bank loans easily available at low cost because many banks have to restrict lending to meet the new capital—asset ratio of 8% by the end of March 1993 imposed by the Bank for International Settlements, and because interest rates have gone up due to financial deregulation. To compound the problems, large amounts of convertible and warrant bonds issued during the 1980s will fall due in the early 1990s. Since it is unlikely that share prices in Japan will rebound quickly to induce investors back to the stock market and to encourage conversion of equity-linked bonds to shares, Japanese companies will need large funds for the redemption of maturing bonds. Straight bond issuances may grow in importance, if only for lack of better alternatives; corporate **bankruptcies** may rise, as they did in 1991—92. Also corporations may have to raise their payout ratios to attract investors back to the stock market. Some companies are reportedly preparing to sell some shares of other companies that they have held as stable shareholders. In any case, the early 1990s promise to be a period of financial stringency for Japanese companies.

See also **banking system, bond market, bankruptcies, government bonds, shareownership, stock market, Tokyo Stock Exchange**.

References

Abegglen, James C., and George Stalk, Jr. 1985. *Kaisha: The Japanese Corporation*. New York: Basic Books. Ch. 7.

Ando, Albert, and Alan J. Auerbach. 1990. The cost of capital in Japan: Recent evidence and further results. *Journal of the Japanese and International Economies* 4: 323–50.

Aoki, Masahiko. 1988. *Information, Incentives, and Bargaining in the Japanese Economy*. Cambridge: Cambridge University Press. Ch. 4.

Ballon, Robert J., and Iwao Tomita. 1988. *The Financial Behavior of Japanese Corporations*. Tokyo: Kodansha International.

Hodder, James E., and Adrian E. Tschoegl. 1990. Some aspects of Japanese corporate finance. In *Japanese Capital Markets*, ed. by Edwin J. Elton and Martin J. Gruber. New York: Harper and Row.

Kester, W. Carl, and Timothy A. Luehrman. 1992. The myth of Japan's low-cost capital. *Harvard Business Review* 70, 3: 130–38.

Meerschwam, David M. 1991. The Japanese financial system and the cost of capital. In *Trade with Japan*, ed. by Paul Krugman. Chicago: University of Chicago Press.

Zielinski, Robert, and Nigel Holloway. 1991. *Unequal Equities: Power and Risk in Japan's Stock Market*. Tokyo: Kodansha International. Ch. 6.

corporate groups
See *keiretsu* **and business groups**.

corporate management
See **management practices**.

corporate personnel practices   Japanese corporate personnel practices constitute an important part of **management practices** or the Japanese-style management (*nihonteki keiei*). Although there are exceptions and ongoing changes, the following practices are considered to be dominant.

1. **Lifetime employment** or commitment prevails in large companies. Regular employees are recruited right after college graduation and are expected to stay with the same employer for the rest of their careers. For their part, employers do not lay off or fire their employees, even during recessions, except under extraordinary circumstances. As part of the system, before the 1980s midcareer changes in jobs were discouraged.

2. Temporary workers are hired by large companies for tasks that are not expected to last long. These workers do not enjoy job security and receive less pay and benefits than permanent workers, and are therefore much less costly to hire. For this reason temporary workers may not, in fact, be temporary; they may be rehired year after year as a way of saving labor cost. For the same reason part-time workers are also increasingly employed. Part-time workers are nonagricultural workers who work less than 35 hours per week. In February 1990, of the total number of 46.9 million employees, 5.06 million or 10.8% of them were part-timers. Most of them (4.8 million) were female.

3. Midcareer changes in jobs are becoming increasingly frequent and socially acceptable. As some companies are thinning their ranks of middle management who were recruited before the 1973 oil crisis, this also make midcareer changes inevitable. Labor shortage in the 1980s also contributed to this change.

4. A seniority-based wage system (*nenko*) reinforces the lifetime employment system and minimizes rivalry among colleagues. Promotion is virtually automatic on the basis of seniority in the early years of employment but is increasingly based on individual merit afterward. This system has led to middle-management bulge in the 1980s. As many employees hired before 1973 reached that level, large corporations such as Toyota Motor have acted to eliminate some middle-management positions.

5. Companies routinely rotate and train their new employees in different divisions of the company. They rely on in-house training rather than recruitment of outside experts for specialized skills. Middle-level managers may be sent out to subsidiaries or affiliates for training or for providing technical assistance to a subsidiary. The posting may be for a period of a few months or years. This practice of transferring employees to other related companies is called *shukko*.

6. Early retirement (traditionally at age 55, but increasingly near age 60) is mandatory except for the few who become senior executives or board members. However, employees upon or near retirement may be transfered to an affiliate or subsidiary to set up a new operation and/or to help strengthen the subsidiary and its ties with the parent company. This also helps to make room for their replacement or to trim off redundant personnel. This practice of long-term personnel transfer is called *tenzoku*, meaning literally changing one's affiliation.

7. The majority of executives rise from the ranks on the basis of seniority and proven leadership ability rather than come from outside the company. Even board members will come from company senior executives, and the chairman is typically a former president. This reflects the importance of being an insider in the Japanese corporate culture and society (see **business ethics**). However, some large companies do employ retired high government officials as senior executives. The practice of retired officials seeking employment in private corporations is referred to as *amakudari*, literally "descent from heaven." Presumably companies hire them to benefit from their experiences in government and ties with government bureaucrats, but the practice is being increasingly criticized in recent years for possible abuses.

8. Small businesses do not offer lifetime employment. In addition they often hire part-time workers at low pay and with few benefits.

9. **Employment discrimination** exists in hiring and promotion. Female employees are paid less and have limited prospects for advancement. Minorities such as the outcast **burakumin**, who are ethnic Japanese whose ancesters worked in "unclean" vocations, as well as Japan-born descendents of Korean immigrants tend to be shunned by employers except for lower-paying jobs. Other ethnic minorities also tend to be discriminated against in employment.

10. Foreigners are rarely hired as lifetime employees. They tend to be hired as short-term contract workers (*shokutaku*) on a full-time or part-time basis.

The practices of lifetime employment, seniority-based wages, routine job-rotation, and employee training by companies are the pillars of Japan's corporate personnel system. They are said to have created an internal or internalized labor market within a company. Workers are said to have much work incentives as well mobility in this internal labor market, but have little mobility in the external labor market between firms. Ozaki (1991: 26–30) contends that this type of system is superior to the Western capitalist system in which firms rely on the external labor market for different categories of specialized labor. He argues that the Japanese system is more conducive to higher labor productivity because the company is willing to invest in the continual training of workers without fear of losing them to competitors. On their part, the workers are said to have the incentives to cooperative with and teach other workers, knowing that they have job security and will benefit from the increased productivity of all workers and the higher profits of the firm.

However, Nakatani (1993) argues that this Japanese system is outdated in the 1990s. It was appropriate in the early postwar period when job security was most important to workers. However, the system has produced workers who are inept outside their company of origin. It inhibits external labor market mobility, which is increasingly important because of the need to exchange information with outsiders for a competitive edge.

Whatever the theoretical merits of the two sides of the debate, it is clear that some Japanese companies are already modifying their personnel practices to meet their changing needs.

See also **business ethics, employment discrimination, employment pattern, labor force, women in the labor force**.

References

Ariga, Kenn, G. Brunello, Y. Okhkusa, and Y. Nishiyama. 1992. Corporate hierarchy, promotion, and firm growth: Japanese internal labor market in transition. *Journal of the Japanese and International Economics* 6: 440–71.

Clark, Rodney. 1979. *The Japanese Company*. New Haven: Yale University Press. Chs. 5–6.

Dore, Ronald, Jean Bounine-Cabale, and Kari Tapiola. 1989. *Japan at Work: Markets, Management and Flexibility*. Paris: OECD.

Hamada, Tomoko. 1991. *American Enterprise in Japan*. Albany: State University of New York Press. Ch. 4.

Hasegawa, Keitaro. 1990. The upheaval in personnel management. *Japan Echo* 17, special issue: 21–25.

Nakatani, Iwao. 1993. Corporate paternalism losing symbiotic value. *Nikkei Weekly*, Feb. 22: 6.

Ozaki, Robert. 1991. *Human Capitalism*. New York: Penguin.

Yoshino, M. Y., and T. B. Lifson. 1986. *The Invisible Link*. Cambridge: MIT Press. Ch. 9.

corporate taxes Corporations in Japan pay the national corporate income tax (called "corporation tax" in Japan) levied by the national government, the local corporate "inhabitant tax" levied by the prefectural or the municipal governments, and the prefectural enterprise or business tax.

In the late 1950s and early 1960s, the corporation tax was the most important tax in Japan in terms of tax revenue. Since 1965 it has slipped behind the individual income tax as the second largest tax. In FY 1991 it yielded ¥19.27 trillion, or 29.5% of the total tax revenue collected by the national government.

In FY 1989, as part of the 1988 tax reform to introduce the new **consumption tax**, the national corporate income tax rate on retained income was reduced by steps from 42% to 37.5%, but the rate on income earmarked for dividends was raised from 32% to 37.5%. For **small and medium enterprises** with less than ¥100 million paid-in capital, the tax rate on the first ¥8 million of annual taxable income was reduced from 30% to 28% on retained income, but the rate on income distributed as dividends was raised from 24% to 28% (see table C.4). The reform thus equalized the tax rates on both retained income and distributed dividends after April 1990.

Table C.4
Corporate income tax rate (in %)

	FY 1988	1989	1990
General tax rate			
Retained income	42	40	37.5
Dividend	32	35	37.5
Reduced tax rate[a]			
Retained income	30	29	28
Dividend	24	26	28
Cooperatives			
Retained income	27	27	27
Dividend	22	25	27
Public corporations	27	27	27

Source: Ministry of Finance.
a. Applies to the first ¥8 million annual taxable income of corporations with less than ¥100 million paid-in capital.

The reform did not change the rates of local corporate taxes. The ceiling rates for prefectural and municipal corporate inhabitant tax remain 6% and 14.7%, respectively, of the amount of national corporate tax paid. The top prefectural enterprise tax remains 13.2%.

Other changes related to corporate taxes include the following:

1. Formerly dividend income received from other corporations due to stock ownership was excluded from corporate income tax. Since FY 1990 only 80% of it is exempt. The 100% exclusion still applies to dividends received by companies owning at least 25% of the payer.

2. Formerly the foreign tax credit system was abused by large **trading companies** and other companies to reduce their tax liabilities. All foreign sources were included in the calculation of the foreign tax credit limitation. The reform excludes 50% of any foreign income not subject to foreign tax from the calculation of this limitation. The carry-over period for losses or gains was reduced from five years to three years.

See also **tax reform, tax system**.

References

Ishi, Hiromitsu. 1989. *The Japanese Tax System*. Oxford: Oxford University Press.

Odden, Lee. Tax reform 1989. *Tokyo Business Today*, Mar. 1989: 24–27.

Ministry of Finance. 1991. *An Outline of Japanese Taxes*. Ch. 3.

credit associations   A special type of cooperative financial institutions or *shinkin* banks to serve small and medium enterprises. At the end of 1992 there were 435 of them.

See **banking system, *shinkin* banks**.

credit card industry   As part of the **consumer credit** market, the credit card industry was relatively insignificant until the mid-1980s. This is because Japanese financial institutions have traditionally concentrated on loans to corporations and have neglected consumer credit.

As Japan's financial markets began to mature and alternative sources of funds for businesses developed in the late 1970s, banks began to increase their consumer loans, particularly since 1986. The stronger yen and the low interest rate in the 1980s, as well as the increased affluence of the consumers, have also stimulated the demand for consumer credit and credit cards. As a result credit card–related credit increased 3.5 times from 1978 to 1988. The total number of credit cards issued increased rapidly from about 25 million in March 1979 to 203 million in 1991. This amounts to 1.6 cards per person in Japan.

There are two major types of credit cards, bank-affiliated cards and retailer-affiliated cards. The former have been more popular and growing more rapidly than the latter. Between 1978 and 1988, the outstanding sales balance of the former increased 5.3 times, whereas that of the latter increased 2.4 times.

Major bank-affiliated cards are JCB cards, VISA, and MasterCard, of which JCB cards are the most popular. They are issued by the subsidiaries and affiliates of banks (JCB Co.—Japan's largest credit card company— Sumitomo Credit Service Co., Union Credit Co., etc.), but not by the banks themselves because of a **Ministry of Finance** regulation. They are also characterized as noninstallment (one-time-payment) credit cards because the **Ministry of International Trade and Industry** does not allow bank-affiliated card companies to introduce repayment by installments. As a result these cards are used for travel and entertainment ("T&E cards," similar to American Express and Diners Club cards) and not as everyday "shopping cards" as is the case in the United States. The JCB Co. is Japan's largest credit card company, holding nearly 40% of the Japanese credit card market with 24.6 million cards issued as of 1992. It has established ties with banks abroad in an effort to make its cards international.

Retailer-affiliated cards, such as the "Saison Card" and the "OMC (Orange Members Club) Card," are either issued by retailer-affiliated credit companies or by the retailers themselves. The major ones include the Credit Saison Co. and Daiei Finance Inc., which have recent tie-ups with VISA International and MasterCard International, and Marui Co. and Isetan Co., which offer their in-house department store cards.

With the exception of the Nippon Shinpan Co., consumer credit companies have not done well in the credit card business, even though they had issued 55.7 million credit cards, or 34.1% of the industry total of 163.2 million, as of December 1990. Bank-affiliated card companies had issued 48.7 million, or 29.8% of the total. Distributors (**department stores**, supermarkets, etc.) had issued 30.3% of the cards, and producers (electrical manufacturers and oil companies) 5.5%. In March 1988 the International Credit Card Business Association was established by department stores, supermarkets, manufacturers, and Nippon Shinpan Co. It had issued more than 20 million credit cards for participating companies by November 1989. Thus the industry has become highly competitive.

Compared with its U.S. counterpart, Japan's credit card industry is not yet as well developed. It is still plagued with problems such as inadequate credit management know-how and consumer credit information. On the other hand, the credit card default rate is lower than in the United States, although it has been rising in recent years. Analysts expect the industry to continue to grow and to dominate the consumer credit market.

Credit cards should be distinguished from prepaid cards, in which no credit is involved and a certain amount of cash is already paid by the cardholders. Prepaid cares are a convenient way of obtaining some goods and services such as train tickets and telephone calls without using cash. Prepaid telephone cards, in particular, are widely used.

See also **consumer credit**.

Addresses

JCB Co.
6, Kanda Surugadai 1-chome, Chiyoda ku, Tokyo 101
Tel: (03) 3294-8111

Nippon Shinpan Co.
33-5, Hongo 3-chome, Bunkyo-ku, Tokyo 113
Tel: (03) 3811-3111   Fax: (03) 3815-6650

References

Hardy, Quentin. 1991. Credit-card users facing an unaccustomed crunch. *Asian Wall Street Journal Weekly*, Sept. 16: 3.

Iwasaki, Kazuo. 1990. Burgeoning credit card industry maturing in wake of decade-long consumer binge. *Japan Economic Journal*, Winter suppl.: 12.

Shingai, Koichi. 1991. Credit cards. In *Japan Economic Almanac, 1991*. Tokyo: Nihon Kwizai Shimbun.

Suzui, Yoshio, ed. 1987. *The Japanese Financial System*. New York: Oxford University Press. Pp. 251–54.

Takagi, Hisao. 1990. JCB card aiming to go local abroad. *Japan Economic Journal*, Dec. 8: 6.

Takezawa, Masakide. 1990. Credit cards. In *Japan Economic Almanac, 1990*. Tokyo: Nihon Keizai Shimbun.

credit cooperatives   Financial institutions in the form of cooperatives to serve **small and medium enterprises**. At the end of 1991, there were 398 of them.

See **banking system**.

cross shareholding   The practice of many Japanese companies, banks, insurance companies, and so forth, to hold each other's shares, without the intention of selling them for gains, in order to provide mutual support and maintain friendly business relationships. It is an important part of the larger "stable shareholders" network cultivated by Japanese companies to provide a stable and supportive business environment.

Cross shareholding was an important aspect of the organization of pre-war *zaibatsu* in which members of a *zaibatsu* group held each other's shares. In the postwar period, two types of cross shareholding can be distinguished.

1. Although the *zaibatsu* were dissolved after the war, new postwar **keiretsu**, or business groups of various types, have been established around a city bank, a general trading company, or a large industrial corporation. These *keiretsu* practice cross shareholding as a means to cement group ties; the core company of a group may also use it to exert influence over, and/or to provide support to, its affiliates. In 1988 the average percentage of a member firm's stock held by other group members ranged from 12.2% to 26.9% for the largest *keiretsu*. In FY 1989 the average percentage of cross shareholding in the six bank-centered *keiretsu* was 21.64%. In industrial *keiretsu* such as the Hitachi Group and the Toyota Group which are organized around a large industrial corporation, cross shareholding is mainly one-sided. The Hitachi Corporation, for example, is said to have a policy of holding 50% or more of the shares of every member of the Hitachi Group, which has 688 members (as of March 1989) including Hitachi Cable Ltd, Hitachi Metals Ltd, Hitachi Chemical Co., and Hitachi Construction Machinery Co.

2. Cross shareholding is widely practiced among companies that regularly do business with each other—such as suppliers, distributors, banks, and insurers—even without specific group ties. It is practiced in these cases primarily as a token of goodwill and mutual support, of their intention to continue and foster the business relationship. These friendly shareholders also help to forestall hostile takeovers. For example, after the Japanese **stock market** crash of 1965, many companies were fearful of foreign takeovers because of their depressed share prices and increasingly liberal foreign investment regulations. Consequently they increased their mutual shareholding with friendly firms. In the case of large banks and insurance companies that hold their customers' shares, cross shareholding is one-sided with the banks and insurers providing some needed capital to client companies to maintain or expand business.

All cross shareholders are valued as stable shareholders. Other stable shareholders are institutional investors such as trust funds, pension funds, and **insurance companies** that hold stock portfolios for long-term gains. A 1989 survey by the *Nihon Keizai Shimbun*, a leading business newspaper, shows that more than 60% of publicly traded Japanese companies regard it desirable to have 60% to 70% of outstanding shares held by stable shareholders. The reason is that it gives executives more time to concentrate on business goals and not to worry about possible takeovers. Some scholars agree. Nakatani (1984) describes cross shareholding as a shock-absorbing, "mutual insurance" arrangement that benefits both the company and employees in the long run. Similarly McDonald (1989) considers cross shareholding as part of Japan's reciprocal corporate relationship that contributes to "collective risk reduction." In other words, cross shareholding is an institutional device to combine the best of the two worlds—to have the benefits of the impersonal equity market without its impersonal nature, namely the instability and risks it entails. These are the *mochiai* effect of "joint stockholding" (*kabushiki mochiai*). *Mochiai* literally means to hold mutually; it also implies "shared interdependence" and "helping one another" (Gerlach 1987: 132).

These benefits are not without their social costs. The stable shareholders reduce the competitiveness of the capital market at the expense of outsiders, particularly the small individual investors. From the point of view of the stable shareholders, cross shareholding helps cement business ties at low cost as long as share prices are rising. In fact their unrealized capital gains from such shareholding is recognized in Japan as "latent capital" that can be used as collateral for loans and is calulated as part of banks' own capital. Cross shareholding becomes a burden, however, when share prices decline. For example, share prices declined greatly in 1990 and corporate shareholders saw the value of their stocks decline by about 40%. Reportedly some banks are becoming reluctant to hold more shares at the request of clients because of low returns at a time when financial liberalization makes it necessary to stress competitive efficiency and returns.

Additionally in recent years cross shareholding has generated friction with Washington. American critics of Japan's business practices charge that cross shareholding keeps share prices high and promotes exclusive business ties, thereby making it virtually impossible for foreign companies to purchase complete control of a Japanese company. Consequently, in the U.S.– Japan **Structural Impediments Initiative** talks in 1989–90, Washington pressed Tokyo for changes in disclosure and other rules concerning cross shareholding. The issue has become important to Washington as Japanese companies have bought up American companies and real estate with relative ease while foreign investors face investment barriers in Japan.

In response to Washington's request for more openness, a number of changes have been made. In late 1990 the **Ministry of Finance** enacted a rule requiring members of giant corporate groups, *keiretsu*, to disclose more about transactions within the group. Another new rule requires investors to report holdings of 5% or more in a company.

It should be pointed out that cross shareholding is not unique to Japanese firms. It also exists in Europe, particularly Germany where hostile corporate takeovers are rare. Dore (1989) argues that Japan's market "liberalization" is not necessarily "Americanization" and that there are competing models of capitalism other than that of the Anglo-Saxon countries. He implies that in the evolution of Japanese capitalism, the pros and cons of specific business practices should be assessed from a broader perspective other than that of Japan–U.S. trade relations.

See also *keiretsu* **and business groups**.

References

Choy, Jon. 1991. Patterns and implications of Japanese stockholdings. *JEI Report*, Jan. 25.

Dore, Ronald P. 1989. "Liberalization" not necesarily "Americanization." *Japan Economic Journal*, Nov. 4: 9.

Gerlach, Michael. 1987. Business alliances and the strategy of the Japanese firm. *California Management Review* 30, 1: 126–42.

Japan's stocks caught in vicious circle due to reliance on cross-shareholding. *Asian Wall Street Journal*, Oct. 15, 1990: 32.

Kester, W. Carl. 1991. *Japanese Takeovers: The Global Contest for Corporate Control*. Boston: Harvard Business School Press. Chs. 3, 8.

McDonald, Jack. 1989. The *mochiai* effect: Japanese corporate cross-holding. *Journal of Portfolio Management* 16, 1: 90–95.

Mizuno, Yuko. 1989. Popularity of equity financing threatening *keiretsu* system. *Japan Economic Journal*, Dec. 30: 35–36.

Nakatani, Iwao. 1984. The economic role of financial corporate grouping. In *The Economic Analysis of the Japanese Firm*, ed. by Masahiko Aoki. Amsterdam: North-Holland.

customer sovereignty   It is sometimes said that postwar Japan has been producer oriented rather than consumer oriented, and that the Japanese government has promoted producers' interests at the expense of consumers' interests for the sake of pursuing rapid economic growth. As evidence for this proposition, proponents have pointed to the importance that the government has given to its **industrial policy**, the weak implementation of the **Antimonopoly Law**, the relative weakness of the **consumer groups**, the lack of a product liability system, the high prices of consumer goods and food in Japan, and so forth. The implication is that "consumer sovereignty"—a basic tenet of Western economics—does not exist in Japan.

It should be noted that the pursuit of rapid economic growth is not necessarily contrary to consumers' long-term interests. Consumers' income is increased as more jobs are created and labor productivity is raised. Product quality and variety are improved, and prices are likely to come down as industries grow and companies compete in the market, even to the extent of "excessive competition." New products are created as firms invest in R&D.

Nevertheless, in the context of postwar Japan, the concept of consumer sovereignty, whether it exists or not, is not adequate to capture the all-important relationship between buyers and sellers in the market and their respective power. It is more meaningful to talk about "customers sovereignty" at both the company and industry level to characterize the most important players of the Japanese market place. The term "consumers" as used in Western economics refers to a large, amorphous group of people who are theoretically merely interested in consuming as much final goods and services as possible at the lowest possible prices. It is further postulated in Western neoclassical economics that consumers can best attain their goal in an impersonal, "perfectly competitive" market without any personal ties. In contrast, the term "customers" (or the "honorable customers" in Japanese) is a relation-laden concept, reflecting not only the relationship between buyers and sellers but also the desire to maintain and cultivate that valued relationship, which is essential for long-term business growth. Furthermore "customers" include both individual customers who are consumers and corporate customers who are themselves producers. Viewed in this light, most seasoned observers of Japan would agree with the late Knosuke Matsushita, founder of Matsushita Electric Industrial, that "the customer is God" in Japan. Matsushita might have merely had the individual customers of his world-famous consumer electronic products in mind, and he gave it as an advice to business managers. But it can be taken as an accurate description of the important role and status of the "honorable customers"—both individual and corporate customers—in Japan.

At the retail level, individual customers exert great influence over the retailers. Japanese shoppers are said to be very "fussy" about quality, price, delivery, and services. On the other hand, retailers are said to spare no efforts to please and to retain their customers (Kang 1990). The merchants are very attentive to their customers' needs and whims, not only because it makes good business sense but also because culturally it is deeply ingrained since Japan's feudal period that it is the merchants' obligation to give their best to their customers, who were traditionally considered to be their social superiors (Kang 1990: 4). It is true that retail prices of many products are higher in Japan than elsewhere. However, retail costs are also higher in Japan because land and store space are more expensive. In addition retailing is more labor intensive in Japan because it usually includes personal attention, delivery and postsale services; careful and attractive wrapping is also customary for many consumer goods even if they are not intended as gifts.

Similarly corporate customers are assiduously catered to by their suppliers. Here the unequal bargaining power between the buyers and the sellers further enhances the customer sovereignty. The buyers are often large corporations and members of *keiretsu* or business groups. In some industries such as the automobile and electronics industries, the giant manufacturers have literally hundreds of small subcontractors to supply parts, who in turn may have numerous subcontractors of their own. In this hierachy of large buyers and layers of small suppliers, it is the buyers who dictate, within the bounds of reason, the terms of the transactions. Sakai (1990) likens the power relationship of this hierachical order of Japanese manufacturing to the feudal order of lords—samurai—common people of Japan before the late ninetieth century. Although the analogy exaggerates the permanence and lopsidedness of the business relationship and ignores the fact that such a relationship is voluntary and has to be mutually beneficial to be viable, it does highlight the sovereignty of the corporate customers.

For similar reasons Dore (1990: 371) characterizes Japanese firms' transactions as those of "customers' market" rather than of "auction markets" assumed in Western neoclassical economics. Furthermore he regards their behavior as justified in efficiency terms because such business relationship ensures quality, promp delivery, collaboration in technical improvements, new product design, and so forth.

See also **consumer groups,** *keiretsu* **and business groups, pricing practices, subcontracting system.**

References

Dore, Ronald. 1990. An outsider's view. In *Japan's Economic Structure: Should It Change?* ed. by Kozo Yamamura. Seattle: Society for Japanese Studies.

Kang, T. W. 1990. *Gaishi: The Foreign Company in Japan.* Basic Books. Chs. 1–2.

March, Robert M. 1990. *The Honourable Customer: Marketing and Selling to the Japanese in the 1990s.* Melbourne: Longman Professional.

Saki, Kuniyasu. 1990. The feudal world of Japanese manufacturing. *Harvard Business Review* 68, 6 (Nov.–Dec.): 38–47.

D

Dai-Ichi Kangyo Bank Japan's largest city bank and the world's largest commercial bank in terms of assets and deposits.
See **city banks**.

Dai-Ichi Mutual Life Insurance Co. Japan's second largest life insurance company in terms of assets.
See **insurance companies**.

***daimyo* bonds** Yen-denominated bonds issued in Japan by nonresidents but sold to investors on the Euromarket.
See ***samurai* bonds**.

dango Bid-rigging or the practice of prebidding collusion in the construction industry, resulting in overpricing and the exclusion of foreign firms from Japan's construction market.
See **construction industry, pricing practices**.

decision making Japanese companies and other organizations typically seek a broad-based consensus in their decision making. Consequently decision making often involves a lengthy process of discussions and the formation of consensus.

Two phases of the traditional decison-making process can be distinguished. The first one, sometimes referred to as *nemawashi*, is the informal, pre-decision process of discussions and accommodations of views to prepare the ground for the formation of consensus. In its original usage as a nursery term, *nemawashi* refers to the practice of digging the ground around a large tree and cutting the roots, except for the tap root and large side roots, a year or two before it is to be transplanted, to allow feathery rootlets to grow in order to make it easier to transplant. This is also performed so that trees will bear large fruits. Thus figuratively, it means laying the groundwork to achieve the organization's objective. In consensus-based decision making, such careful preparations are needed.

The second phase involves the formal drafting of a proposal for circulation among units of an organization for consultation, comments and approval. The procedure is referred to as the *ringi* system, where *rin* means submitting a proposal to one's superior for approval and *gi* means deliberations and decisions. In the procedure, a low-echelon management staff member first drafts a formal document (*ringisho*), outlining a problem and his recommendation. The document is then reviewed and approved by the related units of the organization and finally evaluated and approved by the top-level management. After the approval, the document is returned to the original drafter for implementation.

The consensus-based *ringi* system has been described by Western scholars as the "bottom-up" decision making. One implication of the system is that top executives lack the power of their Western counterparts to make quick "top-down" decisions. Even if the idea originally comes from a top executive, he would still entrust a lower staff member who would be involved in its implementation to draft the *ringi* document. In this way the final decision would have the cooperation of more people after the proposal has gone through the "due process."

The system provides a mechanism for consultation with various departments, helps to coordinate their activities, and ensures the smooth implementation of the proposal once it is adopted. However, it is a time-consuming process. In addition consensus-based decision making reduces accountability and shields individuals from direct responsibility if the proposal proves to be ill-advised. Increasingly therefore, in situations in which a quick decision is desirable, Western-style decison-making involving only top-level management has been adopted. This can take the form of issuing and circulating the *ringisho* at the upper management level, thereby shortening the decision-making process (author's interview with NEC management, June 16, 1993). It is also noteworthy that the Japanese decision-making system has not always worked well in Japanese subsidiaries in the United States for precisely the reasons mentioned above.

At the operational or shop-floor level of an enterprise, decision making tends to be decentralized and organized on the basis of small groups. The famous **quality control** circle is an example. Ozaki (1991: 30–34) argues that this type of decision making is superior to the more centralized type of the American firms because it promotes the sharing of technical know-how among workers and cultivates "a habit of thinking holistically" on the part of workers, thereby avoiding the demoralization and alienation of workers found in an American firm.

Finally, the **subcontracting system**, which is prevalent in Japanese manufacturing industries, is tantamount to delegating decision making on the production of parts to the subcontractors (Ozaki 1991: 52–53). Compared with the alternative system of relying on in-house production of parts, the subcontracting system effectively decentralizes decision making at some stages of the manufacturing process, thereby giving both large manufacturing firms and their numerous subcontractors the benefits of specialization and flexibility in the organization of production.

References

Lincoln, James R. 1989. Employee work attitudes and management practice in the U.S. and Japan: Evidence from a large comparative survey. *California Management Review* 32, 1: 89–106.

Lincoln, James, and Arne L. Kalleberg. 1989. *Culture, Control, and Commitment: A Study of Work Organizations and Work Attitudes in the U.S. and Japan*. Cambridge: Cambridge University Press.

Ozaki, Robert. 1991. *Human Capitalism*. New York: Penguin.

Takeuchi, Hiroshi. 1985. Motivation and productivity. In *The Management Challenge: Japanese Views*, ed. by Lester C. Thurow. Cambridge: MIT Press.

Yoshino, M. Y. 1968. *Japan's Managerial System: Tradition and Innovation*. Cambridge: MIT Press. Ch. 9.

declining industries   Any growing economy has its declining industries, and Japan is no exception. In Japan, public policy has played an active role along with voluntary industry efforts in promoting the necessary structural adjustments in declining industries in response to shifting market demand.

Prior to 1978 only ad hoc government measures were taken to facilitate adjustments in declining industries such as textiles and shipbuilding. However, the first oil crisis (1973–75) adversely affected so many industries that a comprehensive legislation for assistance became necessary. Consequently the 1978 Law of Temporary Measures for Stablization of Specific Depressed Industries was enacted. It provided for low-interest loans to "structurally depressed industries" for shifting production to a new line of business and for retiring redundant personnel. It also provided for guarantees for new private bank loans to pay off existing loans on plants and equipment.

The criteria for structurally depressed industries are (1) more than 50% of the industry's firms experiencing financial difficulties due to changes in domestic or international economic conditions, (2) severe overcapacity of the industry with poor prospects for improvement, (3) firms representing two-thirds of the industry's capacity seeking designation as structurally depressed, and (4) a consensus that some scrapping of facilities has become necessary. Fourteen industries met these criteria, including electric and open-hearth steel, aluminum smelting, nylon staple, polyester staple, polyesterfilament, ployacrylnitrate filament, ammonium, urea, phosphoric acid (by wet process), cotton and wool spinning, wool yarn, ferrosilicon, corrugated cupboard, and shipbuilding.

The law authorizes the **Ministry of International Trade and Industry** (MITI) or some other designated agency to formulate, after consultation with advisory committees, a "Basic Stabilization Plan" for the specific industries. The plan would establish the extent of overcapacity on the basis of supply and demand forecasts and determine the proper method of reducing excess capacity. The plan has to be approved by the Fair Trade Commission, after which it would be implemented by industrial **cartels**, formed under MITI's guidance and exempted from the **Antimonopoly Law**.

The following measures were taken to help implement the capacity-reduction plan: (1) A total of $148 million loans and loan guarantees was given between 1978 and 1983. (2) In the textile industry, a special "scrapping fund" was created to guarantee repayment of loans collateralized by equipment that was to be scrapped. (2) **Administrative guidance** was used by the Ministry of Transport to curtail output in the **shipbuilding industry**. (4) Administrative guidance was used to encourage or assist industries to shift to other product lines.

The implementation of the stabilization plan has had different successes in different industries. It was very successful in alumimum smelting—an industry that is extremely energy intensive—where actual reduction in capacity has exceeded the plan target by 70%. It was also successful in shipbuilding in which about 100% of the target was achieved. It was moderately successful in all other structurally depressed industries except cotton spinning where actual reduction in capacity fell short of targeted reduction by 22%. Analysts attribute the failure to reduce capacity in the textile industry to its fragmented structure, because of ease of entry, and to its political clout.

As the 1978 Law expired in 1983, the 1983 Law of Temporary Measures for the Structural Adjustment of Specific Industries was enacted. It has the same criteria and procedure as the 1978 Law for the designation of structurally depressed industries. As a result 11 of the previous 14 industries remain covered by the 1983 Law (excluding shipbuilding, cotton, and wool). In addition 11 new industries are covered, including fertilizer, eth-yline, polyolefine, polyvinyl chloride, ethylene oxide, unpasticized poly-vinyle chloride pipes, paper, viscose rayon staple, sugar refining, and cement.

The 1983 Law provides for a wider range of monetary and fiscal support measures, including low-interest loans, government subsidies for invest-ment in energy-conserving equipment, and a special depreciation system for modernization and capacity-reduction investment. In addition it pro-vides for various types of business tie-ups to cut cost—production tie-ups allow an underutilized company to produce for a competitor, transporta-tion tie-ups allow a company nearest the customer to make delivery for sales made by other companies in order to reduce cross-hauling, and sales tie-ups utilize a common selling agent for several companies. All these tie-ups require prior approval by the Fair Trade Commission.

See also **industrial policy**.

References

Anderson, Douglas D. 1986. Managing retreat: Disinvestment policy. In *American versus Japan*, ed. by Thomas K. McCraw. Boston: Harvard Business School Press.

Lesbirel, S. Hayden. 1991. Structural adjustment in Japan: Terminating "old King Coal." *Asian Survey* 31: 1079–1094.

Peck, Merton J., Richard C. Levin, and Akira Goto. 1987. Picking losers: Public policy toward declining industries in Japan. *Journal of Japanese Studies* 13: 79–123.

Sekiguchi, Sueo, and Toshihiro Horiuchi. 1988. Trade and adjustment assistance. In *Industrial Policy of Japan*, ed. by Ryutaro Komiya, Masahiro Okuno, and Lotaro Suzumura. Tokyo: Academic Press Japan.

Sheard, Paul. 1991. The role of firm organization in the adjustment of a declining industry in Japan: The case of aluminum. *Journal of the Japanese and International Economics* 5: 14–40.

Uekusa, Masu. 1987. Industrial organization. In *The Political Economy of Japan*. Vol. 1: *The Domestic Transformation*, ed. by Kozo Yamamura and Yasukichi Yasuba. Stanford: Stanford University Press.

defense expenditures   Japan's peace constitution, adopted under U.S. pressure, renounces "war as a sovereign right of the nation and the threat or use of force as a means of settling international disputes" (Article 9). Only a small Ground Self-defense Force is maintained, authorized in 1976 at 180,000 personnel. However, the Treaty of Mutual Cooperation and Security of 1960, through which the United States created a special re-lationship with Japan as part of its postwar strategy, has provided Japan with U.S. military protection, including the stationing of some 50,000 U.S. troops in Japan.

Consequently throughout most of the postwar period Japan's defense expenditures as a percentage of GNP was often below 1% (see table D.1), although the percentage would be higher if officers' pension costs were included. By contrast, the United States spends a much higher percentage of its GDP (5.8% in 1990) on defense. However, Japan's average annual rate of increase in defense spending during 1980–90 was 6.4%, which was consistent with the 6%-plus spending increases that Pentagon officials had urged Tokyo to maintain. Also, in absolute dollar figures, Japan is now the second largest military spender in the world behind the United States.

Japan's relatively light defense burden during the postwar period is considered by many analysts to have contributed to its fast economic growth. As U.S.–Japan trade frictions mounted in the 1970s and 1980s, it has also prompted foreign criticism of Japan for enjoying a "free ride" on security from the United States and has led the U.S. Congress to demand greater Japanese defense burden sharing.

Partly as a response, since the early 1980s Japanese leaders have broadened their concept of defense to include foreign aid as part of Japan's "comprehensive security." They are willing to step up their aid to developing countries as Japan's contribution to world security. Japan was the largest aid donor in the world in 1989 and 1991–92.

Table D.1
Defense budget

Fiscal year	Initial budget (in ¥ billions)	Ratio to GNP
1955	134.9	1.78
1965	301.4	1.07
1975	1,327.3	0.84
1980	2,230.2	0.90
1985	3,137.2	0.99
1986	3,343.6	0.99
1987	3,517.4	1.00
1988	3,700.3	1.01
1989	3,919.8	1.01
1990	4,159.0	0.95
1991	4,386.0	0.94
1992	4,552.0	0.94

Source: Japan Defense Agency.

Because of the ending of the cold war, Tokyo plans to have slower increases in defense spending in the foreseeable future. The Medium-Term Defense Plan for fiscal years 1991–95 adopted by the National Security Council in 1990 envisions total expenditures of about ¥23 trillion for the five years, starting April 1, 1991. It would limit annual increase in spending to about 3%. In late 1992, because of the collapse of the Soviet Union, the government decided to cut ¥580 billion from that plan and to limit the growth in defense budget for FY 1993 to 1.95%. This is the lowest annual rate of growth in defense spending since 1960.

See also **foreign aid**.

References

Auer, James E. 1991. Defense Burdensharing and the U.S.–Japan Alliance. In *Japan and the United States: Troubled Partners in a Changing World*. Cambridge, MA: Institute for Foreign Policy Analysis.

Balassa, Belas, and Marcus Noland. 1988. *Japan in the World Economy*. Washington: Institute for International Economics. Pp. 158–66.

Japan Defense Agency. Annual. *Defense of Japan*.

Sharing the defense burden with Japan: How much is enough? *JEI Report* 19A, May 13, 1988.

defense industry   Japan's defense industry is dominated by a small group of firms. Mitsubishi Heavy Industries is by far the largest defense contractor, followed by Kawasaki Heavy Industries, Mitsubishi Electric, Ishikawajima-Harima Heavy Industries, and Toshiba (see table D.2). However, these companies are generally diversified companies and are not engaged solely or mainly in defense production. For example, in FY 1991

Table D.2
Leading defense contractors (FY 1991; in ¥ billions)

	Defense sales	Market share
Mitsubishi Heavy Industries	440.8	28.0%
Kawasaki Heavy Industries	146.5	9.3
Mitsubishi Electric	100.3	6.4
Ishikawajima-Harima Heavy Industries	78.6	5.0
Toshiba	59.9	3.8
NEC	54.5	3.5

Source: Japan Defense Agency.

Mitsubishi Heavy Industries and Kawasaki Heavy Industries derived only 17.7% and 15.7%, respectively, of their revenues from defense contracts. The figures for the other defense contractors are even lower. By contrast, the figures for McDonnel Douglas and General Dynamics, the two top U.S. defense contractors, were 53.1% and 68.3%, respectively, in 1988.

The industry is constrained first and foremost by the relatively low level of **defense expenditures**—generally around 1% of GNP in the 1980s. Of those expenditures, only about 28% was spent in FY 1988 and 1989 on equipment purchases. As a result defense production as a share of industrial production was only 0.36% in 1980, 0.51% in 1985, and 0.58% in 1987. The contractors are paid on a cost-plus basis, with profit margins consistently at 6–7%.

The industry is also constrained by Japan's ban on the export of military hardware, although the line between military and nonmilitary equipment is often blurred because of the proliferation of dual-use technologies. Analysts believe that Tokyo is not likely to lift the ban in the foreseeable future, since the world's arms market is already oversupplied and any such exports from Japan will only aggravate the strained economic relations between Japan and the United States.

Most of Japan's advanced weapon systems are produced under license from U.S. manufacturers. For example, Mitsubishi Heavy Industries makes F-15 fighter and the surface-to-air Patriot missile, and Mitsubishi Electric Corp. makes the second-generation Hawk surface-to-air missile, all built with technology licensed from the United States.

However, Japanese companies have developed some weapons on their own, including anti-tank missiles, air-to-air missiles, and Mitsubishi Heavy Industries' ground-based anti-ship missiles (SSMI). According to some Western analysts, Japan's strength lies in dual-use technologies, which were originally developed for civilian uses but subsequently have military applications. For example, Toray Industries produces carbon-fiber composites, a tough, light material for tennis rachets and golf clubs. The product is also sold to the United States for use in jet-fighter airframes. NEC's telecommunication technologies and semiconductors are used in military telecommunication systems. Toshiba's electrooptics used in home-video cameras can be used in missile-guidance systems.

Given the relatively small size of Japan's defense industry, it makes economic sense for Japan to import advanced defense technology from the United States rather than developing it on its own, as some American officials and Japan's own critics of "buy Japanese" policy have argued. In some cases the cost differentials between Japanese-designed or produced weapons and foreign equivalents are said to be substantial (*Nikkei Weekly*, June 22, 1991: 3). However, until 1991 Tokyo was interested in promoting self-sufficiency in arms production, even at the cost of economic efficiency. This is shown in its initial decision in the late 1980s to develop a new fighter plane for the 1990s by Mitsubishi Heavy Industries. After much urging from Washington, the two governments agreed in 1988 to jointly develop an advanced version of F-16, code-named FSX, by Mitsubishi Heavy Industries and General Dynamic. However, because of the intractable U.S. trade deficits with Japan, some members of the U.S. Congress subsequently objected to the joint project, fearful that it would give Japan undue technological and commercial advantages. Consequently the United States has refused to hand over software for the flight-control system, forcing the Japanese to develop it themselves. As of 1991 that project is nearly four years behind the original 1994 production target.

There were indications in 1991 that because of increased pressure from Washington, Tokyo would relax its policy of nurturing Japan's armaments industry and increase imports of U.S.-made weapons. The Gulf War played a major role in this policy change because of the growing consensus to support U.S. military power.

See also **defense expenditures**.

References

Auer, James E. 1991. Defense Burdensharing and the U.S.–Japan Alliance. In *Japan and the United States: Troubled Partners in a Changing World*. Cambridge, MA: Institute for Foreign Policy Analysis.

"Buy Japanese" called inefficient, expensive in weaponry. *Nikkei Weekly*, June 22, 1991: 3.

Defense industry. *Japan Economic Almanac*, various years. Tokyo: Nihon Keizai Shinbum.

Drifte, Reinhard. 1986. *Arms Production in Japan: The Military Applications of Civilian Technology*. Boulder, CO: Westview.

Japan Defense Agency. Annual. *Defense of Japan*.

Japan's weapons makers: Ready and able. *The Economist*, Feburary 2, 1991: 67.

Samuels, Richard J., and Benjamin C. Whipple. 1989. The FSX and Japan's strategy for aerospace. *Technology Review*, Oct.: 43–51.

Wanner, Barbara. 1993. Japanese defense industry grapples with post–cold war conversion. *JEI Report*, no. 12A, Apr. 12.

deferred pricing   The practice of finalizing prices after sales in some industires.

See **pricing practices**.

demography
See **population**.

department stores   Sales of all department stores (total of 2,004), large
and medium sized, amounted to ¥19.6 trillion in 1991, or about 14% of
total retail sales in Japan. Of these department stores in 1991, 416 were
large-scale department stores, defined as employing 50 or more employees
and having 3,000 square meters or more of store space in the ten largest
cities and 1,500 square meters or more in the rest of the country. These
large department stores accounted for about 8.6% (¥12.1 trillion) of all
retail sales in 1991.

The market shares of Japan's department stores in the retail business
are low compared with the situation in other industrial countries. The
growth of the number of "large-scale" department stores in the postwar
period has also been slower than the growth of total retail sales. The
number was 325 in 1975, 360 in 1985, and 416 in 1991. The reason for this
is that until 1990, the government had protected small retailers by restricting the establishment of large department stores and supermarkets
through the Department Store Law of 1956 and the **Large Retail Store
Law** of 1974 which superseded the 1956 law. It was not until Washington
complained about the restriction and its impact on imports during the
Structural Impediments Initiative talks between Washington and Tokyo
in 1989–90 that changes were made. In May 1990 the government relaxed
the implementation of the Large Retail Store Law. In 1991 revisions were
made in the law to shorten the period before large department stores can
be opened. Thus analysts expect large department stores to grow in the
future in terms of store numbers and retail market share. During the late
1980s the stock market boom and economic growth in Japan led to high
levels of consumer spending. Department stores experienced rising sales
and profits. Thus as soon as the implementation of the Large Retail Store
Law was relaxed, large department stores were engaged in a competition
to build new and ever-larger stores in the major cities during 1990–92.
However, just as the large investment and expansion scheme was taking
place, the economy was hit with a recession that depressed sales and profits
(see table D.3).

Of Japan's top department stores, Mitsukoshi is particularly prestigeous.
Originally founded as a dry goods store in 1673 by the merchant Mitsui
family (founder of the Mitsui *zaibatsu*), it became Japan's first modern
department store in 1904. In the postwar era it is a core member of the
Mitsui Group, reputed for its wide variety of deluxe merchandise, both

Table D.3
Leading department stores (in ¥ billions)

	FY 1991[a]		FY 1992[a]	
	Sales	Profits[b]	Sales	Profits[b]
Mitsukoshi	876.6	11.0	842.4	−2.1
Seibu Department Stores	916.9	—	808.1	—
Takashimaya	843.0	13.4	788.6	4.9
Daimaru	608.3	6.1	569.8	4.7
Marui	569.1	57.3	539.1	35.0
Matsuzakaya	502.0	10.0	491.4	3.8
Isetan	468.2	14.1	442.9	5.0
Tokyu Department Stores	410.6	9.2	378.8	6.7
Hankyu Department Stores	355.2	15.1	344.7	6.6
Sogo	310.6	7.3	280.0	3.8

Source: *Japan Economic Almanac*, 1993: 239; *The Nikkei Weekly*, Apr. 26, July 5, 1993.
a. Business FY 1991 ended in 1992 at the end of January for Marui and Tokyu, end of March for Isetan and Hankyu, and end of February for the rest.
b. Pretax profits.

Japanese and foreign. It has 14 stores, including operations in Europe and the United States. Seibu Department Stores Ltd. is the core company of the Saison Group.

In addition to merchandise, Japanese department stores ordinarily offer various types of services, entertainment, and regular cultural exhibitions. The more prestigeous department stores carry a wide variety of high-priced brand-name products, including imports. Because many Japanese consumers are brand-name conscious and are willing to pay substantially higher prices for the presumed quality and prestige, especially when shopping for the obligatory biannual gift giving, large department stores have long occupied a special niche in the Japanese retail market, particularly in the **gift market**.

See also **distribution system, gift market, Large Retail Store Law**.

Addresses

Japan Department Stores Association
2-1-10 Nihonbashi, Chuo-ku, Tokyo 103
Tel: (03) 3272-1666

Mitsukoshi
1-4-1 Nihonbashi-Muromachi, Chuo-ku, Tokyo 103
Tel: (03) 3241-3311

Seibu Department Stores
28-1, Minami Ikebukuro 1-chome, Toshima-ku, Tokyo 171
Tel: (03) 3462-0111

Takashimaya Department Store
4-1, Nihonbashi 2-chome, Chuo-ku, Tokyo 103
Tel: (03) 3211-4111

References

Japan Company Handbook. Quarterly. Tokyo: Toyo Keizai.

Japan Economic Almanac. Annual. Tokyo: Nihon Keizai Shimbun.

Japan Statistical Yearbook. Annual. Tokyo: Management and Coordination Agency.

deposit insurance system   Jointly established by the government and
private financial institutions, the system protects depositors and covers
their demand deposits, time deposits, money trusts, and loan trusts with
principal compensation contracts. It will reimburse depositors up to ¥10
million per depositor in case of bank failure, although this has not been
necessary to date. All banks and credit cooperatives are required by law to
join the sytem. Annual insurance fee amounts to 0.012% of the insured
deposit.

The Deposit Insurance Corporation was established in 1971 to adminis-
ter the system. Its initial capital of ¥455 million was jointly contributed by
the government, the **Bank of Japan**, and private financial institutions. Its
director is the deputy governor of the Bank of Japan as stipulated by law.
As of end of March 1991, the system had a fund balance of ¥513.6 billion.
In 1973 a separate Savings Insurance Corporation was established to cover
agricultural cooperatives and fishery cooperatives.

When a financial institution becomes, or is in danger of becoming insol-
vent, rescue attempts are encouraged. Since 1986 the insurance system has
the authority to provide low-interest loans to help another insitution take
it over in a merger or other form of rescue. Each category of financial
insitutions also has mutual aid schemes for such emergencies, with the help
of the deposit insurance system if necessary.

References

Federation of Bankers Associations of Japan. 1989. *The Banking System in Japan.* Pp. 32–34.

Suzuki, Yoshio, ed. 1987. *Japanese Financial System.* Oxford: Oxford University Press. Ch. 5.

Yokota, Hayato. 1991. Deposit insurance behind bank merger. *Nikkei Weekly,* Aug. 3: 5.

deposits system   Deposits are a major source of funds for many financial institutions and an important type of financial assets to households and business firms, which use them as a means of payment and a means of savings. Deposits are offered by all commercial banks, *shinkin* **banks**, credit cooperatives, labor credit associations, **agricultural cooperatives**, and fishery cooperatives. The **postal savings system** also offers deposits, although it is not a financial institution.

Deposits are classified according to whether or not interest rates are regulated and whether or not their term is fixed. The major categories of deposits are as follows:

I. Deposits with regulated interest rates

1. *Demand deposits*

• Current deposits (current accounts). These are non-interest-bearing deposits used mainly by business firms for the payment of bills by checks drawn on the account. Other payments can also be made automatically through current deposits.

• Ordinary deposits. Held by individuals and business enterprises, these are payable on demand and have no restrictions on deposit or withdrawal amounts. They differ from current deposits in that withdrawals are made by presentation of a passbook and not by writing checks. Deposits and withdrawals may also be made at automatic teller machines (ATMs) or cash dispensers (CDs) through the use of cash cards. They can be used to accept salary, pension, and fund transfer payments, and for automatic payments of public utility charges, taxes, insurance premiums, credit card payments, and so forth. Interest is paid semiannually.

• Notice deposits. These cannot be withdrawn until seven days after the day of deposits and require two days' notice. They are used mainly by companies for investing temporary surplus funds. The minimum deposit is ￥50,000, and the unit for calculating interest is ￥10,000. The interest is slightly higher than that paid on ordinary deposits.

2. *Fixed-term deposits*

• Time deposits. The term of the deposits is fixed (three months, six months, one year, and two years), and the deposit cannot be withdrawn during the period. Before 1988, as part of Japan's *maruyu* system (tax exemption for small savers), interest on time deposits up to certain limits could be tax exempt. In June 1993 the interest rate on bank time deposits was deregulated.

• Installment savings. A fixed amount of money is deposited regularly (usually monthly) during a certain period, and a specified amount is given back to the depositor on the date of maturity. Bank employees usually come to the depositor to collect the deposits. Individuals usually use this type of savings for a specific purpose such as for education or a wedding. Installment savings tend to be concentrated in *shinkin* **banks**, credit cooperatives, and agricultural cooperatives.

II. Deposits with free interest rates

1. *Negotiable certificates of deposits (CDs)*. First issued in 1979, CDs may be sold to third parties. The buyers are mostly corporations and local government bodies because of the high minimum unit of issue (reduced from ¥100 million to ¥50 million since April 1988). The maturities are between one month and one year. The interest rate is freely determined in the money market.

2. *Money market certificates (MMCs)*. These are large denomination time deposits, introduced in 1985 and abolished in 1989. The minimum deposit was reduced successively from ¥50 million in 1985 to ¥10 million in October 1987. The term of deposit was between one month and two year. MMC interest rates were set freely by each bank, but the maximum rate was computed at 0.75% below the average CD issue rate.

3. *Large time deposits*. There are two types of large time deposits. The first type was introduced in 1988. The minimum deposit was initially ¥50 million but was reduced to ¥10 million in 1989 after successive reductions. The term is between one month and two years. The second type was introduced in 1991 with a minimum deposit of ¥3 million and a term of between three months and three years. The interest rates on both types of large time deposits are determined by each bank.

4. *Small money market certificates*. Introduced in 1989, these have a term of between three months and three years. The minimum deposit was reduced from ¥3 million to ¥0.5 million in April 1991, and to zero in June 1992. The ceiling of interest rates on small MMCs was linked to the large time deposit interest rates. In June 1993 this type of deposits was abolished.

Deposits are insured by the **deposit insurance system**. The **postal savings** service is discussed separately because it is not part of the private financial system.

See also **interest rate structure, money market, postal savings**.

References

Federation of Bankers Associations of Japan. 1989. *The Banking System in Japan*. Tokyo: Zenginkyo.

Federation of Bankers Associations of Japan. 1992. *Japanese Banks, '92*. Tokyo: Zenginkyo.

Suzuki, Yoshio, ed. 1987. *The Japanese Financial System*. Oxford: Oxford University press. Ch. 5.

Tatewaki, Kazuo. 1991. *Banking and Finance in Japan*. London: Routledge.

Depressed Industries Law, 1978   A law enacted to reduce capacity and balance supply and demand in structurally depressed industries.

See **business-cycle indicators and forecasting, declining industries, industrial policy, steel industry.**

diffusion index of business condition
See **business-cycle indicators and forecasting.**

direct overseas investment   Japan's direct overseas investment (DOI) has increased rapidly since the early 1980s. From a modest $4.7 billion in FY 1980, it rose to $22.3 billion in 1986, and to a peak of $67.5 billion in 1989; it declined in 1991–92 because of declined corporate profits due to the recession (see table D.4). The accumulated total as of March 31, 1992, was $352.4 billion, which makes Japan the third largest foreign investor in the world behind the United States and Britain. It dwarfs the amount of total accumulated **foreign direct investment** in Japan, which was only $22.8 billion as of March 31, 1992.

The rapid increase of Japan's DOI is the result of various factors. Before the 1980s Japan's DOI was primarily for the purposes of securing the supply of raw materials and fuels and for taking advantage of cheaper

Table D.4
Direct overseas investment (in $ billions)

Fiscal year	Amount	Fiscal year	Amount
1951–1975	$15.9	1984	10.2
1976	3.5	1985	12.2
1977	2.8	1986	22.3
1978	4.6	1987	33.4
1979	5.0	1988	47.0
1980	4.7	1989	67.5
1981	8.9	1990	56.9
1982	7.7	1991	41.6
1983	8.1	1992	34.1

Source: Ministry of Finance.
Note: The figures are the accumulated value of approvals and notification.

skilled labor in developing Asian and South American countries. Thus countries such as Hong Kong, South Korea, Indonesia, Brazil, and Australia have been important recipients of Japanese DOI. In the 1980s, as Japan's trade surplus and excess domestic savings accumulated and its industrialized trading partners became more protectionist, it became desirable for Japanese companies to make defensive investment in the United States and Western Europe to protect their market share (see table D.5). For example, Japanese automakers and consumer electronics firms have set up plants in the United States and Western Europe. Defensive investment in Western Europe has been accelerated by the European integration in 1992, with a large share going to Britain.

This trend to invest in the industrialized countries in the 1980s is reinforced by other economic factors. As Japanese industries became more knowledge intensive after the oil crises, raw materials have become relatively less important. The appreciation of the yen since the mid-1980s has made it cheaper to acquire assets and to produce in the industrial countries. Finally, through acquisitions, Japanese banks and investment firms have also utilized their excess funds to expand their presence abroad, especially in the United States and Western Europe, as these service-oriented industries have to be located near the market. Direct overseas investment has thus become an attractive outlet for Japan's large trade surplus and excess savings.

These factors discussed above can be seen in the distribution of Japanese DOI by industry. Of the $352.4 billion total DOI as of March 31, 1992,

Table D.5
Direct overseas investment by area (in $ billions and %)

	FY 1990	FY 1991	Total[a]	Share of total
North America	27.2	18.8	155.0	44.0%
United States	26.2	18.0	148.6	42.2
Europe	14.3	9.4	68.6	19.5
Asia	7.1	5.9	53.5	15.2
Oceania	4.2	3.3	21.4	6.1
Middle East	0.3	0.1	3.5	1.0
South America	3.6	3.3	43.8	12.4
Africa	0.6	0.7	6.6	1.9
Total	56.9	41.6	352.4	100.0

Source: Ministry of Finance.
a. Accumulated total as of March 31, 1992.

$93.9 billion (26.6%) was in manufacturing, $70.3 billion (20%) in finance and insurance, $36.6 billion (10.4%) in commerce, and only $17.5 billion (5.0%) in mining.

In the future, analysts expect the share of Japan's DOI in the United States to decline and that in East and Southeast Asia to increase more rapidly. The reasons are the following: (1) DOI in the United States has yielded lower rates of return than elsewhere. (2) Much DOI in manufacturing such as steel, electronics, and auto in the United States is already in place (author's interview with James Abeggalen, Chairman, Gemini Consulting, July 7, 1992). (3) East and Southeast Asian economies have grown rapidly and have become technologically more sophisticated. Wage rates in these economies are lower than in the United States, while their growth prospects are better.

As Japanese corporations invested abroad, they have also brought with them Japanese business practices, which have been met with mixed responses. First, Japanese business managers are said to favor Japanese suppliers, especially those from the same *keiretsu*, in their business dealings to the chagrin of local companies and officials. Second, Japanese group-oriented management practices have been introduced with mixed success, but the job security of Japanese personnel practice has been welcomed by local workers.

See also **mergers and acquisitions, trade pattern.**

References

Balassa, Bela, and Marcus Noland. 1988. *Japan in the World Economy*. Washington: Institute for International Economics. Ch. 5.

Drake, Tracey A., and Richard E. Caves. 1992. Changing determinants of Japanese foreign investment in the United States. *Journal of the Japanese and International Economies* 6, 3: 228–46.

Encarnation, Dennis J. 1986. Cross-investment: A second front of economic rivalry. In *America versus Japan*, ed. by Thomas K. McCraw. Boston: Harvard Business School Press.

Kester, W. Carl. 1991. *Japanese Takeovers: The Global Contest for Corporate Control*. Boston: Harvard Business School Press.

Tejima, Shigeki. 1992. Japanese foreign direct investment in the 1980s and its prospects for the 1990s. *EXIM Review* 11, 2: 25–51.

Tokunaga, Shojiro, ed. 1992. *Japan's Foreign Investment and Asian Economic Interdependence*. Tokyo: Tokyo University Press.

Yamamura, Kozo, ed. 1989. *Japanese Investment in the United States: Should We Be Concerned?* Seattle: Society for Japanese Studies.

Yoshida, Mamoru. 1987. *Japanese Direct Manufacturing Investment In the United States*. New York: Praeger.

Yoshihara, Hideki. 1991. Overseas transfer of the Japanese-style production system. *Japanese Economic Studies* 19, 3: 19–42.

distribution *keiretsu*
See **distribution system**, *keiretsu* **and business groups**

distribution system   Japan's system for distributing products, including imports, to the consumers and industrial users is characterized by the predominance of numerous small retailers, the existence of multi-layers of small- and medium-sized wholesalers, and the prevalence of the sole import agents. It is considered by foreign critics, and some Japanese as well, as inefficient and exclusionary but is defended by many Japanese as open and functionally efficient in the Japanese context.

At the retail level there were 1.62 million retail stores in 1988, or 132 retail stores per 10,000 poeple; in 1991 there were 1.59 million retail stores. In comparison, there were 2.4 million retail stores in the United States in 1987 or 66 retails stores per 10,000 people. Small food retail stores in particular proliferate in Japan. In 1989 there were 45 small food stores per 10,000 people in Japan compared with 10 in the United States and 20 in Britain.

There are three categories of retail establishments in Japan:

1. *Small- and medium-sized retail stores that employ 1–49 persons.* As of 1991 there were 1.59 million such retail stores. They accounted for 99.5% of all retail establishments and 84% of total retail sales in 1990. About 80% of them are small "Mom-and-Pop" stores, employing only 1–4 persons. Since most Japanese housewives buy their groceries daily, the convenience and customer services provided by these small stores are extremely important to them. This type of store also provides employment to a large number of elderly people with inadequate pensions. However, their number and market share have been declining. On the other hand, medium-sized discount store chains and self-service stores have grown, particularly in the 1970s. They are usually located in populated suburban residential areas and carry foods, clothing, and many other consumer goods.

2. *Large **department stores** and self-service stores or supermarkets that employ more than 50 persons.* In 1991 they had total sales of ¥22.16 trillion, which accounted for only 15.7% of total retail sales, far below that of other industrialized countries. The government has restricted their growth and

protected the small retailers through the Department Store Law of 1956, the **Large Retail Store Law** of 1974, and other restrictive regulations. The number of department stores has grown slowly, from 325 at the end of 1975 to 360 in 1985 and 416 at the end of 1991. The number of large self-service stores has also grown slowly, from 1,613 at the end of 1980 to 2,013 at the end of 1991.

3. *Nonstore retailers, which include businesses that sell through catalogs, telephones, and door-to-door sales.* Their sales are relatively small but have expanded rapidly in recent years, reaching ¥4.25 trillion in 1990. Some department stores also have mail-order business.

At the wholesale level there were about 476,000 wholesale establishments in 1991, or about 38 per 10,000 people, compared with 466,680 in the Unites States in 1987, or 19 per 10,000 people. Most Japanese wholesalers are relatively small. In 1988 about 75% of them employed 1–9 employees. Most goods go through two or more layers of wholesalers. As a result the ratio between the total value of wholesales and that of retails (*W/R*) is much higher in Japan (about 4 in 1991) than in other industrialized market economies (about 1.6 in the United States).

Wholesalers are very important in the distribution system because they provide a number of important functions to the retailers: (1) Because most retailers are small and have minimal floor space and stocking capacity, wholesalers usually make daily deliveries of small quantities. (2) Wholesalers provide financing to retailers by accepting long-term payments. (3) Because retailers usually buy on commission, wholesalers accept the return of unsold merchandise, thus bearing the burden of inventory risk.

In the consumer electronics industry, some large manufacturers circumvent the traditional wholesalers by establishing their own distribution networks, referred to as distribution **keiretsu**. Matushita Electric, for example, has a network of 60 wholesalers and 25,000 "National Shops." They are either wholly owned by, or affiliated with, the company. Toshiba Corp. has 12,500 *keiretsu* shops, Hitachi Ltd, 10,000, and Sanyo Electric Co., 6,000. In the automobile industry, automobiles are domestically sold through the manufacturers' sales networks that sell only their automaker's models.

In international trade, the traditional "general import agents" system gives exclusive contracts to some wholesalers, particularly the large **trading companies**, to import brand-name products. This has given them the monopoly power to control the marketing channels and the prices of imported goods, even though the Japanese government authorized the "parallel import" system as early as 1972. Under this system any company can import any foreign product in parallel with the general import agents. One problem with the system is post-sale services because general import agents have refused to service products imported under parallel import.

Japan's foreign competitors have long complained that Japan's complex distribution system has effectively kept them out of the Japanese market and is responsible for the high prices in Japan. Consequently, in the **Structural Impediments Initiative** talks between Washington and Tokyo in 1989–90, Washington made reforms in the distribution system one of its key demands. In particular, it wanted to see the removal of restrictions on the establishment of large retail stores, which are said to be more likely to carry imports. In early 1990 Tokyo decided to revise the Large Retail Store Law. Starting in May 1990, the implementation of the law was relaxed. Effective January 31, 1992, revisions were made to shorten government approval for a large store to a maximum of one year.

Defenders of the Japanese distribution system, including many ordinary citizens and authors, contend that the Japanese system is open to foreign companies and products, and oppose imposing changes on it on cultural and functional grounds. Culturally it is contended that the system was formed over a long period of time, integrating aspects of the culture, economy, and society. Hence the government should let it evolve on its own, and should not force it to change under U.S. pressure (Shioya 1989). Functionally it is argued that the existence of numerous neighborhood retail stores generates employment for a large number of people, provides quality services, and makes daily household shopping more convenient for urban households without the need to drive to suburban areas where larger supermarkets tend to be located. Daily grocery shopping is necessary in Japan to economize household storage space in small living quarters. For the small retailers to function efficiently with their limited resources and space, a large number of wholesalers are needed to provide the essential services to the retailers, as mentioned above. Thus Japan's distribution system has a logic of its own, given Japan's socioeconomic conditions, and the supposedly more efficient American system is not appropriate for Japan. Finally, Itoh (1991) argues that Japan's decentralized distribution system faciliates information sharing and coordination between manufacturers and wholesalers, and between wholesalers and retailers, which promotes product improvement/development and superior services far beyond what a simple market mechanism can ever provide.

Whatever the merit and demerit of the Japanese distribution system, there is evidence that it is changing with the times. From a peak of 1.72 million in 1982, the number of retail establishments has declined slowly to

1.59 million in 1991. The number of large- and medium-sized retail outlets and wholesalers has also grown. Furthermore the Japanese government is promoting the "parallel import system" in order to increase competition and reduce import prices. Reimports of Japan-made products intended for foreign markets are also finding their way back to Japan to be sold at discount prices.

In regard to market access for foreigners, there is growing evidence that foreign companies can successfully join or circumvent the Japanese distribution network. For example, in the 1980s the American Amway Corp. successfully organized a direct-distribution system in Japan, which comprises of some 700,000 Japanese distributors who are also its customers, to sell its products, thus bypassing the complex Japanese distribution system. An alternative strategy is to utilize Japan's own distributional network. In October 1989 the Swedish appliance giant AB Electrolux formed an alliance with Japan's Sharp Corp. to market household appliances in Japan; its products will be marketed through Sharp's retail stores. Finally, in late 1991 the American firm Toys R Us established its new branch store in Japan, directly retailing toys from the manufacturers at discounts. Preliminary evidence suggests that it is doing well.

See also **department stores, Large Retail Store Law, pricing practices, trading companies**.

Addresses

Japan Chain Stores Association
13-1, Toranomon 5-chome, Minato-ku, Tokyo 105
Tel: (03) 3433-1290

Japan Department Store Association
1-10, Nihonbashi 2-chome, Chuo-ku, Tokyo 103
Tel: (03) 3272-1666 Fax: (03) 3281-0381

References

Cyinkota, Michael R. and Jon Woronoff. 1991. *Unlocking Japan's Markets*. Chicago: Probus.

Fields, George. 1989. The Japanese distribution system: Myths and realities. *Tokyo Business Today*, July: 57–59.

Itoh, Motoshige. 1991. The Japanese distribution system and access to the Japanese market. In *Trade with Japan*, ed. by Paul Krugman. Chicago: Chicago University Press.

Itoh, Motoshige, Seung-Jaei Lee, and Takatoshi Yajima. 1990. Creating a competitive commercial sector. *Japan Echo* 17, 3: 17–22.

Ito, Takatoshi. 1992. *The Japanese Economy*. Cambridge: MIT Press. Ch. 3.

Laumer, Helmut. 1986. The Distribution system: Its social function and import-impeding effects. In *Japan's Response to Crisis and Change in the World Economy*, ed. by Michele Schiegelow. New York: Sharpe.

Sakaiya, Taichi. 1990. Retailing on the eve of a revolution. *Japan Echo* 17, 3: 12–16.

Shioya, Takafusa. 1989. Japan's distribution system is a result of economy, society and culture—MITI. *Business Japan*, no. 8, Aug.: 57–63.

Takahashi, Hideo. 1989. Structural changes in Japan's distribution system, *JEI Report*, no. 43A, Nov. 10.

Weigand, Robert E. 1989. The gray market comes to Japan. *Columbia Journal of World Business* 24, 3: 18–23.

dollar-call market   An interbank money market in which financial institutions trade foreign currency funds among themselves for short periods. See **money markets**.

E

Economic Council   A top advisory council to the prime minister on economic policies and economic planning. It is assisted by the Economic Planning Agency in the latter task.

See **economic planning, housing**.

economic planning   Although Japan's postwar economy has never been a centrally planned economy, the Economic Planning Agency has made economic plans to provide economic projections and growth targets to the private sector and to help coordinate government economic policies and activities. Economic planning started in 1948 with the Five-Year Economic Recovery Plan for 1948–52. Since then, 12 other plans have been made—most of them for a five-year period and a few for six to ten years. These include the Five-Year Plan for Economic Self-support (1956–60), the New Long-Range Economic Plan (1958–62), the National Income Doubling Plan (1961–70), various socioeconomic development plans throughout the 1970s and early 1980s, and the current Five-Year Plan (1992–96). There are no formal annual plans derived out of the five-year plans. Instead the Economic Planning Agency publishes an annual "Economic Outlook" early in the year that outlines its projections for the year and the government's basic policy position on the economy.

The Economic Recovery Plan of 1948 mainly provided background information for the government in requesting U.S. aid. The National Income Doubling Plan for 1961–70 was well known because of its broad scope and long-term nature, and because Japan was then entering the period of high growth (more than 10% annually). It had a target GNP growth rate of 7.8% annually to double the national income within a decade. It attempted to develop social overhead capital, human resources, and science and technology, to accelerate industrialization and eliminate the dual industrial structure, and to promote export. Between the early 1970s and the early 1980s, changes in the domestic and world economy—higher Japanese standard of living, the oil crises and the stagflation it brought about in various industrial countries, the floating exchange rate system, and Japan's increased role in world trade and its surpluses in the balance of payments, and so on— have prompted planners to pay more attention to the improvement in the quality of life and to restoring equilibrium in the international balance of payments. Since the late 1980s, because of continuing changes in Japan and the world economy, planners are increasingly focusing on the development of new technology, market liberalization, overseas investment, and the aging of the population. The current Five-Year Plan (1992–96) emphasizes improvements in the quality of life—a 40-hour workweek, affordable housing, and improved social infrastructure—and Japan's contribution to global issues such as enviromental issues and assistance to formerly communist countries.

In terms of planning organization, the Economic Stabilization Board was established in 1946 on the recommendation of the Allied Occupation Forces to stabilize and reconstruct the economy. It was reorganized as the Economic Deliberation Board in 1952. In 1954 the present Economic Planning Agency was established as Japan's economic recovery was completed and government priority was shifted to economic growth.

Currently the Economic Planning Agency serves as the secretariat of the Economic Council, a top advisory committee to the prime minister appointed to deliberate on important economic policies and to formulate long-term economic planning. The Economic Planning Agency, comprising mainly of economists, assists the Council in the technical tasks of econometric estimates and projections. The planning procedure is as follows: First the prime minister conveys to the Economic Council the major goals of the plan. The Council deliberates on various policy aspects of the goals. The Economic Planning Agency works on various policy implications in consultation with other ministries and uses macroeconometric models to develop detailed estimates and projections. When the plan is completed, it is submitted by the Economic Council to the Cabinet for approval. When approved, it becomes the official National Economic Plan.

Japan's national economic plan is broadly based in its making, and in turn it helps to form consensus in the government and to coordinate the policies of various ministres. Since any minister in the cabinet can veto it, the Economic Planning Agency has to consult with various ministries, particularly the **Ministry of Finance** and the **Ministry of International Trade and Industry** during the drafting of the plan to incorporate their views. In addition it has to communicate with other ministries to utilize their special expertise and to obtain statistics in their respective specialized fields. The Economic Council is composed of prominent and experienced persons from diverse backgrounds, including the academe, business, labor, the press, and retired officials. Its members therefore reflect the diverse interests and experiences of mainstream Japan. Once the plan is adopted by the Cabinet, various specialized plans and programs of the government such as the National Land Use Plan, plans for regional development, or public investment plans, as well as the policies of each ministry, are expected to be consistent with it. In addition, because all government ministries and agencies and public enterprises have to submit budget requests for deliberation and approval by the Ministry of Finance, the latter makes sure that the approved budget is consistent with the economic plan. In this manner the plan is integrated into the government budgeting process for implementation (author's interview, Economic Planning Agency, July 20, 1992).

One weakness of the plan is that local governments do not participate in the planning process. Yet their collaboration is important to the success of the plan becuase more than half of government expenditures in a plan are those of local governments. There are two ways through which the central government can influence local governments. First, the central governments allocate subsidies to local governments, although this does not guarantee plan implementation at the local level. Second, and more important, the National Land Agency makes the National Development Plan for regional development, which is formulated to be consistent with the economic plan, and each local government is required to draw up a long-term plan that is consistent with the Land Agency's plan.

However, Japan's economic plan is indicative in nature as in many Western European countries, unlike the central planning of the former Soviet Union. It provides desired targets and projections for various areas of the economy that are consistent with government policy priorities and the underlying capabilities of the economy, but it does not provide mandatory directives to the private sector to follow in order to reach the targets. Hence its ability to affect the overall allocation of resources in the economy is limited. Major plan targets such as GNP growth rate, inflation rate, and balance of payments are often very different from the initial plan figures. Before the oil crises of the early 1970s, the planned annual real GNP growth rates were invariably below the actual rates by 2.5–3.5%, whereas after the early 1970s the planned growth rates tended to be above the actual rates. In the three plan periods between 1967 and 1977, projected annual inflation rates (3–4.4%) were much lower than the actual rates

(5.7–12.8%). Projected balance-of-payments surpluses throughout 1961 to 1980 were far below the actual figures. When such discrepancy develops between the initial plan and the actual economic conditions, the Economic Planning Agency will revise its plan figures accordingly.

See also **business-cycle indicator and forecasting, economic/business research and publications**.

Address

Economic Planning Agency
1-1, Kasumigaseki 3-chome, Chiyoda-ku, Tokyo 100
Tel: (03) 3581-0261

References

Economic Planning Agency. 1990. *Economic Planning in Japan.*

Economic Planning Agency. 1991. *Economic Survey of Japan, 1990–1991.*

Economic Planning Agency. 1992. *The Five-Year Economic Plan—Sharing a Better Quality of Life around the Globe.*

Komiya, Ryutaro. 1990. *The Japanese Economy: Trade, Industry, and Government.* Tokyo: University of Tokyo Press. Ch. 7.

Okita, Saburo. 1985. Economic planning in Japan. In *The Management Challenge*, ed. by Lester Thurow. Cambridge: MIT Press.

Economic Planning Agency   A government agency under the prime minister's office responsible for drafting the national economic plan and for monitoring, analyzing, and forecasting economic trends.

See **business cycles, economic planning, economic/business research and publications, price indexes and price levels**.

economic/business research and publications   Economic/business research and publishing are essential to an economy in the information age. In Japan such research is conducted at a variety of institutions—universities, government ministries and agencies, government-affiliated research institutes, private research institutes, and private business publishers.

1. *Universities.* Scholars at major universities conduct research on various economic issues. These universities include Tokyo University, Kyoto University, Hitotsubashi University, Keio University, Waseda University, Sophia (Jochi) University, Aoyama University, and Osaka University, among others. Distinguished economists from top universities often serve

on government commissions or research panels or work with private research institutes. The University of Tokyo Press is a major publisher of
scholarly books. However, compared with the government's program in
economic research and publishing, that of Japanese universities is very
limited. Also, compared with major research universities in the United
States, Japanese universities are not considered to be active in their research
and publishing.

2. *Government research departments and institutes.* Japanese government research and publishing on the economy is well organized and very comprehensive. All government ministries and agencies have their research/
statistics departments to serve the needs of their respective policymakers
and to author official publications of the organizations, including annual
reports (usually in the form of White Papers) and statistical yearbooks.
In addition several ministries have separate in-house research institutes for
research and publications on broader or longer-term policy issues in which
academicians from Japanese universities may participate. Most notable in
these endeavors are the following:

• The Research and Statistics Department of the **Bank of Japan** publishes
the *Economic Statistics Annual* and *Economic Statistics Monthly* (in both Japanese and English) and other research reports, including a closely watched
quarterly industry survey, *Tankan* (Short-Term Economic Outlook). The
Institute for Monetary and Economic Studies of the Bank publishes the
Bank of Japan Monetary and Economic Studies.

• The Economic Planning Agency under the prime minister's office publishes the annual *Keizai Hakusho* (Economic White Paper; English version
published as *The Economic Survey of Japan*), which surveys trends in the
economy and gives in-depth analyses of selective aspects of the economy
such as **income distribution**, household saving rates, energy supply and
demand, and regional development. It also publishes annual reports on
business cycle indicators, for example. The Economic Research Institute
of the Agency compiles the national income accounts of Japan and publishes such statistics in great detail in its *Annual Report on National Accounts*
(in Japanese).

• The Statistics Bureau of the Management and Coordination Agency
under the prime minister's office conducts regularly 15 different surveys
(including the quinquennial population census, monthly labor force survey,
monthly retail price survey, and annual family savings survey) and publishes the survey results; it also publishes the voluminous *Japan Statistical
Yearbook* (in both Japanese and English).

• The **Ministry of Finance** publishes various financial reports. Its Institute of Fiscal and Monetary Policy publishes the *Monthly Finance Review*.

• The **Ministry of International Trade and Industry** publishes the important *White Paper on International Trade*, which details Japan's trade performance and policy. The Ministry's Research Institute of International Trade and Industry publishes special monographs on various aspects of the economy and the Ministry's policies.

The research institutes at both the Ministry of International Trade and Industry and the Bank of Japan have special research programs that accept eminent scholars from abroad to conduct research at the institutes. Most government publications can be purchased at the Government Publications Service Center in Tokyo, which also has branches in all major cities.

3. *Government-affiliated research institutes*. These are semigovernmental, nonprofit research institutes, established in accordance with a legislation and subsidized by the government. They are affiliated with a ministry and/or other government agencies and sponsor research conducted by either in-house researchers or outside scholars. For example, the Japan Institute of Labor was founded in accordance with a 1958 law passed by the Diet and is affiliated with the Ministry of Labor. It published a series of monographs on aspects of the labor force authored by experts. The Japan Real Estate Institute is affiliated with the Ministry of Finance, the Land Planning Agency, the Ministry of Construction, and the Ministry of Home Affairs. The Institute of Developing Economies, founded in 1958, is affiliated with the Ministry of International Trade and Industry and conducts research on developing countries. It publishes *The Developing Economies* (quarterly, in English), *Ajia Keizai* (Asian Economies, monthly in Japanese) and several other periodicals in Japanese on Asia, Middle East, Latin America, and Africa.

4. *Private research institutes*. All large banks, securities companies, industrial corporations, and trading companies have their in-house research departments and experts. In addition a number of them have set up separate but affiliated research institutes or *shinku tanku* (think tanks) for research in their specific areas of interests. There are also a few nonprofit economic research institutes that are not affiliated with any financial institution or corporation and conduct research projects for clients. All of these institutes are members of the Japan Association of Independent Research Institutes ("Japan Association of Think Tanks"). Leading private research institutes include the following:

• Daiwa Institute of Research. Concerned with macro- and microeconomic trends, general financial and management studies. Affiliated with Daiwa Securities Co.

• Japan Center for Economic Research. A member-supported nonprofit research organization established in 1963. Engaged in short-term and longer-term economic projection of the economy. Also trains forecasting specialists for corporate clients and conducts contract research (author's interview, Aug. 7, 1992). Publishes series of special reports on domestic and international economic issues, including *JCER Report* and *Quarterly Forecast of Japan's Economy*.

• Japan Research Institute. Established in 1962 and serves as a research forum for big business in general. Sponsors general economic and industry studies. Publishes topical reports in its *Business Japan* series in English and various reports in Japanese.

• Mitsubishi Research Institute. Founded in 1932. Engaged in macro-economic forecasting, industry studies, corporate management, urban and regional economic studies, data processing and database services. Also strong in public policy studies, with more than 50% of its annual research revenues coming from government projects. Publishes the *MERI's Monthly Circular* in English and various other publications in Japanese. Affiliated with the **Mitsubishi Group**.

• Nikko Research Center. Specializes in macro- and microeconomic fore-casting, international and domestic money markets, and capital asset man-agement. Affiliated with Nikko Securities Co.

• Nomura Research Institute. The largest of the private research institutes. Conducts macro- and microeconomic surveys and projections, investment research, public policy analyses, and provides consulting services among other services. Affiliated with Nomura Securities Co. Publishes the *Quar-terly Economic Review* and *NRI Quarterly* in English and a large number of reports in Japanese.

These private research institutes are regarded by some observers as more closely resembling American-style management consulting firms rather than genuine "think tanks" such as the Brookings Institution or the Rand Corporation in the United States. However, their access to informa-tion is considered excellent. In addition Nomura Research Institute has established collaboration with the Brookings Institution and a number of other well-known foreign research institutes in an effort to expand the scope of its research (author's interview, Nomura Research Institute, August 20, 1992).

It should also be added that the Japan Research Institute, based in Washington, is a U.S. research organization funded in part by Japan's Ministry of Foreign Affairs. It publishes a weekly two-part *JEI Report*, which contains timely background information on current development in Japan and in Japan–U.S. relations. It is authored by the Institute's in-house experts on Japan. It also publishes *Japan–U.S. Business Report* (monthly) and *Japan Economic Survey* (monthly).

5. *Private business publishers.* Japan's major business publishers not only report significant findings of government and private economic studies, they also conduct periodic industry surveys and opinion polls and undertake industry and market analyses of their own. The two largest business publishers are

• Nihon Keizai Shimbun, Inc. (Nikkei). This is the oldest (1876) and by far the largest business publisher in Japan. It publishes Japan's largest business daily, *Nihon Keizai Shimbun* (Japan Economic Daily, circulation about 3 million in 1991) and its weekly English version, *Nikkei Weekly* (formerly *Japan Economic Journal* before June 1, 1991). It also publishes three other Nikkei newspapers in Japanese—*Nikkei Kinyu Shimbun* (Nikkei Financial Daily), *Nikkei Sangyo Shimbun* (Nikkei Industrial Daily), and *Nikkei Ryutsu Shimbun* (Nikkei Marketing Journal)—and many other Japanese publications on business and corporations. On the basis of its database on the stock market, it calculates and publishes the Nikkei Stock Average (Nikkei 225) Index and other market indexes. Finally, it publishes the *Japan Economic Almanac* (in English), an annual survey of various sectors of the Japanese economy.

• Toyo Keizai, Inc. It publishes more than 20 periodicals, including the *Shukan Toyo Keizai* (Weekly Toyo Keizai, in Japanese) and the *Tokyo Business Today* (monthly, in English; formerly the *Oriental Economist* during 1934–85). On the basis of its database on Japanese companies, it publishes a quarterly report on Japanese companies—*Kaisha Shikiho* in Japanese and *Japan Company Handbook* (two volumes) in English. The quarterly report gives comprehensive information on all Japanese companies (1,638 as of August 1992) listed on the first and second sections of the **Tokyo Stock Exchange**. A new 1991 English publication, the *Japan Company Datafile*, is an encyclopedia of Japanese companies. It covers all corporations listed on the first sections of the Tokyo, Osaka, and Nagoya Stock Exchanges.

See also **business-cycle indicators and forecasting, education system**.

Addresses

Government Publications Service Center
2-1, Kasumigaseki 1-chome, Chiyoda-ku, Tokyo 100
Tel: (03) 3504-3885

Institute of Developing Economies
42, Ichigaya Onmuracho, Shinjuku-ku, Tokyo 162
Tel: (03) 3353-4231

Japan Center for Economic Research
6-1, Nohonbashi Kayabacho, 2-chome, Chuo-ku, Tokyo 103
Tel: (03) 3639-2801   Fax: (03) 3639-2839

Mitsubishi Economic Research Institute
3-1 Marunouchi, 3-chome, Chiyoda-ku, Tokyo 100
Tel: (03) 3214-4416   Fax: (03) 3214-4415

Nihon Keizai Shimbun, Inc.
1-9-5 Otemachi, Chiyoda-ku, Tokyo 100
Tel: (03) 3270-0251

Nomura Research Institute
27-1, Shinkawa 2-chome, Chuo-ku, Tokyo 104
Tel: (03) 3297-8100   Fax: (03) 3297-8364

Toyo Keizai, Inc.
1-2- Nihonbashi Hongokucho, Chuo-ku, Tokyo 103
Tel: (03) 3246-5655   Fax: (03) 3241-5543

References

Tomkin, Robert. 1990. Japanese "think tanks": An imperfect hybrid. *Japan Economic Journal*, Feb. 24: 26.

Institutes consulting more than "thinking." *Japan Economic Journal*, Feb. 24, 1990: 27.

Zielinski, Robert, and Nigel Holloway. 1991. *Unequal Equities*. Tokyo: Kodansha International. Pp. 83–95.

eigyo tokkin   Corporate investment accounts directly managed by brokerage houses on a discretionary basis.
   See **securities companies, *tokkin* funds**.

education system   Japan's formal education system consists of kindergartens, elementary schools, lower secondary schools, high schools, technical colleges, junior colleges, universities, special training schools, and miscellaneous schools (see table E.1). There are also special education schools for the blind, the deaf, and other handicapped people. Informal education consists of educational programs of the national public television,

Table E.1
Number of schools and students (May 1, 1991)

	Schools[a]	Students (1,000)	Student–teacher ratio[b]
Kindergartens	15,041	1,978	19.5
Elementary schools	24,798	9,157	20.6
Lower secondary schools	11,290	5,188	18.1
High schools	5,503	5,455	19.1
Technical colleges	63	54	13.2
Junior colleges	592	504	24.1
Universities	514	2,206	17.4
Special training schools	3,370	835	24.9
Miscellaneous schools	3,309	407	21.7

Source: Ministry of Education.
a. Include branches
b. Include full-time teachers only.

cram schools that prepare students for examinations, and various types of company in-house training for employees.

Japan's compulsory education includes six years of elementary school and three years of lower secondary school (*chugakko*). Students enter elementary school at age six and graduate from lower secondary school at 15. Virtually all elementary schools and about 94% of lower secondary schools are public schools, established and supervised by prefectural or municipal authorities. There is a very small number of national schools and private schools at the elementary and lower secondary levels.

Nearly all lower secondary schools graduates (95% in 1991) enter high schools or upper secondary schools (*koto gakko*) and technical colleges. The dropout rate for high school students was only 2.2% in 1990, compared with 28.4% in the United States. Japanese secondary education is widely regarded as highly efficient in teaching fundamental skills, factual knowledge, and cooperative group behavior, which are the foundation of Japan's well-trained cooperative labor force. International comparative studies invariably rank Japanese secondary students among the top in math skills and scientific knowledge. However, because the main focus of Japanese high schools is to prepare students for passing rigorous university entrance examinations ("examination hell"), skills such as verbal expressions, critical and creative thinking, and cultural values that are not tested in written examinations tend to be neglected. Furthermore most high school students attend private cram schools (*juku*) that drill them for university entrance examinations. Many lower secondary school students also attend cram schools to prepare for high school entrance examinations; it is important to enter high schools with a good track record of sending students to the elite universities. About a quarter of the nation's high schools are private ones.

Technical colleges (*koto senmon gakko*) are five-year technical schools for lower secondary school graduates. Most of them are run by the national government, and 89% of their students in 1991 were male. Special training schools (*senshu gakko*) and miscellaneous schools (*kakushu gakko*) are private schools that offer vocational and practical training to graduates of lower secondary schools for 1–5 years. The special training school system was first established in 1976. The majority of students are enrolled in curriculums in medical science, technology, and home economics. Miscellaneous schools are those that cannot meet the requirements for special training schools. The most popular types in terms of enrollment are preparatory schools (*yobi-ko*), automobile driving schools, and schools for foreigners.

In 1991, 31.6% of Japan's high school graduates entered junior colleges (*tanki daigaku*, literally short-term universities) and universities. Junior colleges offer two-year education to predominantly female high school graduates (91.6% in 1991). Regular four-year universities are male dominated both in terms of students (72% in 1991) and faculty (more than 90%). Of the 514 universities as of May 1, 1991, 97 are national universities run by the Ministry of Education, 39 are public universities founded and run by prefectural or municipal authorities, and 378 are private ones. Several of the nation's top universities, including Tokyo University, Kyoto University, and Hitotsubashi University, are national universities. Tokyo University, in particular, is the most prestigious university in the nation. Initially established in 1877 to train top government officials, its graduates still far outnumber those of other elite universities among top government officials and corporate executives. Top private universities such as Keio University and Waseda University are also prestigious, and their alumni are influential in business and political circles.

Because the status of the universities is very important to their graduates' career, studying to enter an elite university by passing entrance examinations has been the abiding obsession of Japan's high school students. Once they enter universities, however, the intensity of their education is said to slacken off considerably. According to Rohlen (1992: 338), "undergraduate instruction is notoriously lax and uninspired. Elite universities are aspired to more for their status than their quality of instruction."

Japanese education at the graduate level is said to be weak by international standards and "very few Japanese universities today can be said to be oriented toward either world-class research or training" (Rohlen 1992: 337). In 1990 there were only 90 graduate schools in the nation (41 in 1970), and in 1991 only 7.0% of the nation's university graduates entered graduate schools (4.5% in 1970). This ratio is much lower than that in the United States, England, and France. In addition the areas of graduate training are very uneven; about half of the graduate students are enrolled in engineering. Not surprisingly, MBA programs are virtually nonexistent; those offered at Keio University, Waseda University, and Nihon University are the few exceptions, and even these cater heavily to foreign students.

The above discussion does not mean that practical postgraduate training and research are lacking in Japan. In Japan's corporate system, companies themselves provide their employees with continuous in-house business and technical training, much more than their Western counterparts. Large companies also train their own R&D personnel. The skills thus learned are much more company-specific and immediately applicable. These training activities are an integral part of the Japanese corporate culture that emphasizes long-term employment, continual skill improvement, and intrafirm labor mobility.

See also **corporate management practices**.

Addresses

Hitotsubashi University
1, Naka 2-chome, Kunitachi, Tokyo 186
Tel: (0425) 72-1101

Keio University
15-45, Mita 2-chome, Minato-ku, Tokyo 108
Tel: (03) 3453-4511

Kyoto University
Yoshida Hon-machi, Sakyo-ku, Kyoto 606
Tel: (075) 753-7531

Ministry of Education
2-2, Kasumigaseki 3-chome, Chiyoda-ku, Tokyo 100
Tel: (03) 3581-4211

Tokyo University
3-1, Hongo 7-chome, Bunkyo-ku, Tokyo 113
Tel: (03) 3812-2111

Waseda University
6-1, Nishi Waseda 1-chome, Shinjuku-ku, Tokyo 113
Tel: (03) 3203-4141

References

Duke, Benfamin. 1987. *The Japanese School: Lessons for Industrial America*. New York: Praeger.

Ishikawa, Toshio. 1991. *Vocational training*. Tokyo: Japan Institute of Labor.

Leestma, Robert, and Herbert Walberg, eds. 1992. *Japanese Educational Productivity*. Ann Arbor: Center for Japanese Studies.

Ministry of Education. 1992. *Basic Statistical Survey on Schools, 1991*.

Rohlen, Thomas P. 1983. *Japan's High Schools*. Berkeley: University of California Press.

Rohlen, Thomas P. 1992. Learning: The mobilization of knowledge in the Japanese political economy. In *The Political Economy of Japan*. Vol. 3: *Cultural and Social Dynamics*, ed. by Shumpei Kumon and Henry Rosovsky. Stanford: Stanford University Press.

White, Merry I. 1989. *Japan's Educational Challenge: A Commitment to Education*. New York: Free Press.

electronics industry   The premier industry of the 1980s, the electronics industry occupies a special place in Japan's manufacturing industries. It exemplifies excellence in manufacturing, quality product, and continual product development through R&D.

The industry produces a wide range of products. They can be classified into three categories: (1) consumer electronics (audiovisual equipment, etc.), (2) industrial electronics (communication gear, computers, measuring devices and office automation equipment, etc.), and (3) electronic parts (semiconductor parts, liquid crystal display devices, etc.). In terms of production value, in 1990 industrial electronics led with ¥11.3 trillion, followed by consumer electronics (¥4.3 trillion) and electronic parts (¥1.2 trillion). Industrial electronics (especially computers) and electronic parts (especially memory chips) are known to go through generational changes in technology and cyclical changes in demand ("silicon cycle"), affecting production and the market in a cyclical manner. The industry as a whole experienced rapid, double-digit annual growth rates during the 1980s through 1988. Growth slackened to 6.7% in 1989 and to slightly less than 6% in both 1990 and 1991. The year 1990 is considered to be a year of cyclical slowdown for industrial electronics and electronic parts, but industry sales remained weak in 1991–92 partly because of the economy's recession.

The industry has a sizable number of famous companies whose products are world reknown. Most of the companies make a large variety of products, but they have different strengths in different products, as seen in their market shares (in %) of major products in 1991 (*Japan Economic Almanac 1993*: 214–17, 232):

1. Color TVs (domestic shipments): Matsushita, 22.5%; Toshiba, 14.5%; Sharp, 14.5%; Hitachi, 10.5%; Sony, 10.5%.

2. Home VCRs (domestic shipments): Matsushita, 25.0%; JVC, 13.0%; Toshiba, 13.0%; Mitsubishi Electric, 12.5%; Sharp, 12.0%.

3. Camcorders (domestic shipments): Sony, 43.0%; Matsushita, 32.0%; JVC, 10.0%; Hitachi, 3.0%.

4. Compact disks (domestic production): Sony Music Entertainment, 18.4%; Toshiba EMI, 12.9%; Pony Canyon, 9.0%; Victor Musical, 7.7%; BMG Victor, 5.9%.

5. Video disk players (domestic shipments): Pioneer, 50.0%; Sony, 17.0%; Nippon Columbia, 14.0%; Matsushita, 4.0%.

6. Mainframe computers (domestic installation): Fujitsu, 25.0%; IBM, 23.8%; Hitachi, 18.0%; NEC, 17.3%; Nihon Unisys, 10.1%.

7. Personal computers (domestic shipments): NEC, 53.1%; Fujitsu, 12.7%; Toshiba, 10.8%; Seiko Epson, 8.2%; IBM, 7.0%.

8. Integrated circuits (domestic production): NEC, 21.0%; Toshiba, 17.1%; Hitachi, 13.4%; Fujitsu, 12.5%; Mitsubishi Electric, 9.9%.

The industry owes much of its initial success to the "founder type of personality." Kinosuke Matsushita (1894–1991), founder of Matsushita Electric Industrial, did not finish grade school, and had a humble beginning as a mechanic in a bicycle-repair shop. Through personal ingenuity, perseverance, and emphasis on technology, he led the company he founded in 1935 through difficult periods of Japan to become the world's largest electronics firm. He created harmonious labor relations in his company and his management philosophy is much revered in Japan. Another prominent personality of the industry is Akio Morita, cofounder and chairman of Sony Corporation. Unlike Matsushita, Morita is a graduate of science and engineering at Osaka University, a globe-trotter, and very internationally oriented. His emphasis on research, product development, and product quality guided the company from its small postwar beginning into one of the world's leading electronic firms, and its products have become a symbol of quality in consumer electronics.

Althouth emphasis on R&D characterizes all firms in the electronics industry, computer-related companies have also benefited from active government promotion of high technology, including computer technology. Government support took various forms, including subsidies in R&D, infant industry protection, and technical assistance as part of the **industrial policy** of the **Ministry of International Trade and Industry** (MITI).

Japan is not unique in this respect; it is well known that many American high-technology companies have benefited, perhaps to a greater extent, from government-supported research and from defense contracts. The extent of Japanese government subsidies to computer companies was modest and limited to the phase of technology research rather than the commercialization of the product development.

An example of government-assisted R&D project is the VLSI (very large-scale intergrated circuit) Research Cooperative, set up by MITI to develop the technology required for the fourth generation computers. MITI took the initiative to set up and coordinate the joint R&D venture of five computer companies (Fujitsu, Hitachi, Mitsubishi Electric, NEC, and Toshiba) in 1976. The purpose of the cooperative was to integrate the research capacities of the five companies, to capture the large externalities associated with R&D. The cooperative was disbanded in April 1980 after it had accomplished its objective. The legal life of the cooperative was limited in order to prevent it from extending monopolistically into the joint production and marketing of the product that results from the new technology. MITI paid ¥29.1 billion, or 39.5%, of the project's costs. Its role of initiation and coordination, however, was more important. It consulted with potential corporate participants who helped select promising technologies to research and develop.

In consumer electronics, although the Japanese makers are well known for their excellent manufacturing, some analysts have criticized them as relatively lacking in innovative product development. They are said to have a "pack mentality," with many companies producing the same line of goods but reluctant to try something new unless it has been tried somewhere else first (Schlesinger 1992: 4). Sony is considered to be the outstanding exception, with its innovative products such as the Walkman, the Handycam, and the recordable compact disk player.

See also **industrial policy, Semiconductor Agreement**.

Addresses

Electronic Industries Association of Japan
7-2, Otemachi 1-chome, Chiyoda-ku, Tokyo 100
Tel: (03) 3231-3156

Fujitsu Ltd.
6-1, Marunouchi 1-chome, Chiyoda-ku, Tokyo 100
Tel: (03) 3216-3211   Fax: (03) 3216-9365

Hitachi, Ltd.
4-6, Kanda-Surugadai, Chiyoda-ku, Tokyo 101
Tel: (03) 3258-1111   Fax: (03) 3258-5480

Matsushita Electric Industrial Co.
1006, Kadoma, Kadoma City, Osaka Prefecture 571
Tel: (06) 908-1121   Fax: (06) 908-2351

NEC Corp.
7-1, Shiba 5-chome, Minato-ku, Tokyo 108
Tel: (03) 3454-1111   Fax: (03) 3457-7249

Sony Corp.
6-7-35 Kitashinagawa, Shinagawa-ku, Tokyo 141
Tel: (03) 3448-2111   Fax: (03) 3448-2183

Toshiba Corp.
1-1, Shibaura, 1-chome, Minato-ku, Tokyo 105-01
Tel: (03) 3457-4511   Fax: (03) 3456-4776

References

Anchordouguy, Marie. 1990. A challenge to free trade? Japanese industrial targeting in the computer and semiconductor industries. In *Japan's Economic Structure: Should It Change?* ed. by Kozo Yamamura. Seattle: Society for Japanese Studies.

Electronics. In *Japan Economic Almanac*, various years. Tokyo: Nihon Keizai Shimbun.

Fransmain, Martin. 1990. *The Market and Beyond: Cooperation and Competition in Information Technology in the Japanese System*. Cambridge: Cambridge University Press. Ch. 3.

Imai, Ken'ichi. 1988. Industrial policy and technological innovation. In *Industrial Policy of Japan*, ed. by Ryutaro Komiya, Masahiro Okuno, and Kotaro Suzumura. Tokyo: Academic Press Japan.

Morita, Akio. 1986. *Made in Japan*. New York: Dutton.

Ouchi, William, and Michele Kremen Bolton. 1988. The logic of joint research and development. *California Management Review* 30, 3: 9–33.

Prestowitz, Clyde V., Jr. 1988. *Trading Places*. New York: Basic Books Ch. 2.

Schlesinger, Jacob M. 1992. Japan's vaunted electronics industry hits rut as lack of innovation hinders growth. *Asian Wall Street Journal Weekly*, May 4: 4, 6.

Shinjo, Koji. 1988. The computer industry. In *Industrial Policy of Japan*, ed. by Ryutaro Komiya, Masahiro Okuno, and Kotaro Suzumura. Tokyo: Academic Press Japan.

Yamashita, Toshihiko. 1987. *The Panasonic Way*. Tokyo: Kodansha International.

employment discrimination   As in many other countries, discrimination in employment exists in Japan, reflecting the prejudices of society. Victims of discrimination include women, social outcasts, foreign residents, and the handicapped.

1. *Women.* Japanese female workers generally do not receive the same treatment as male workers at major Japanese companies. Their earnings

are lower, and they are not usually eligible for promotion to executive positions. The disparity is considered by many to be the worst among the industrialized nations. Although the **Equal Employment Opportunity Law** of 1986 was enacted to rectify this, progress has been slow. Various manifestations of the disparity are discussed in **labor force** and **women in the labor force**.

2. *Social outcasts*. More than one million Japanese are social outcasts called *burakumin* (literally the hamlet people) because their ancestors during the feudal period were *eta* (literally the dirty), people who worked as butchers and tanners; these occupations were and still are considered unclean by traditional Japanese standards. Although *burakumin* are ethnic Japanese, they face severe discrimination in employment, housing, and marriage. They are physically indistinguishable from the ordinary Japanese, but potential employers or marriage partners can find out their outcast background by checking their household registry record. As a result they tend to earn their living by engaging in their ancestors' occupation of leather working and other low-status jobs while living in traditional *burakumin* ghettos.

3. *Foreign residents, particularly Koreans*. There are 1.22 million foreigners living in Japan as of December 31, 1991, of which some 693,100 are Koreans and 171,100 Chinese. Although all foreign residents, particularly Asian and black residents, face various degrees of employment discrimination, Koreans are said to have fared worst. Reportedly, many Japanese are prejudiced against the Koreans. The bulk of the Koreans in Japan are descendents of the two million forced laborers conscripted from the former Japanese colony of the Korean peninsula before and during World War II to work in munition plants, coal mines, and construction projects. Korean residents are discriminated against in employment, **housing**, and education. Because naturalization is extremely difficult in Japan for foreign residents— even if they are born in Japan and are the second-and third-generation holders of permanent residence—their "alien" legal status also disqualifies Korean residents for government employment and the legal profession. As a result Korean residents in Japan are forced to perform low-paying, unskilled labor or to operate their own businesses in areas in which barriers to entry are low such as construction, drinking establishments, *pachinko* (pinball) parlors, and services.

4. *The handicapped*. Japanese companies are said to be reluctant to hire handicapped workers, reportedly for the same reason that *burakumin* and Koreans are discriminated against: strong Japanese cultural bias against

those who are different. As a result of Japan's 1.3 million disabled citizens of working age, only 20% have jobs. The government has adopted measures to help employing the handicapped. A 1960 law, amended in 1976, requires that in private companies with more than 63 employees, 1.6% of employees be workers with physical or mental disability. For public organizations and special corporations, the quota is 1.9%. Subsidies are given to companies that achieve the quota, while public disclosure and a fine (¥40,000 per month for every quota person not hired) are the penalty for noncompliance. Unfortunately, the implementation of the law has not been effective. As of June 1991 the government had not disclosed the name of any company that had not complied with the law. Two-thirds of the companies covered by the law routinely pay the small fine rather than hire more disabled workers. A survey taken by the Ministry of Labor in June 1990 shows that 47.8% of the 48,149 companies surveyed failed to achieve the legal quota. The number of handicapped employees working in all these companies was 203,634, or 1.32% of their employees. Large companies with over 1,000 employees had attained only 1.16%. On the other hand, small companies achieved 2.04%.

In addition to employers' reluctance to hire them, the wheelchair-bound encounter extreme difficulties commuting in crowded trains and suffer from lack of special access facilities in train stations with steep stairs and in office buildings. As a result many handicapped persons are discouraged from seeking employment. In 1991 there were about 55,000 handicapped people registered at the unemployment office, but the actual number of unemployed is believed to be much higher. Ironically Japanese companies have long complained about a labor shortage, and many jobs, both unskilled and skilled, have gone unfilled.

See also **labor force, women in labor force.**

Address

Physically Handicapped Persons' Employment Council, Ministry of Labor
2-2, Kasumigaseki 1-chome, Chiyoda-ku, Tokyo 100
Tel: (03) 3593-1211

References

Fabre, Olivier. 1991. Physical, mental barriers hinder the disabled. *Japan Economic Journal,* Feb. 16: 6.

Itoh, Yoshiaki. 1991. Ministry gives firms 5 months to increase hiring of disabled. *Nikkei Weekly,* June 22: 4.

Ministry of Labor. 1992. *Labor Administration: Seeking a More Comfortable Life for Workers.*

Murdo, Pat. 1992. Roles of government, industry in the life of disabled Japanese. *JEI Report,* no. 41A, Oct. 30.

Park, Yonug Myung. 1990. Japan's Koreans live with prejudice, fear. *Tokyo Business Today,* Feb.: 40–44.

Suh, Yong Dal. 1991. Many doors in Japan remain closed to minorities. *Asian Wall Street Journal Weekly,* July 29: 12.

employment insurance   Japan's employment insurance is broader than Western unemployment insurance; it includes unemployment benefits and employment promotion. It is based on the Employment Insurance Law enacted in 1974 and is administered by the Employment Security Bureau of the Ministry of Labor. It covers employees in the private sector and daily laborers. Seamen are covered by a separate Seamen's Insurance scheme.

For unemployment benefits, both employees and employers contribute 0.55% of wages. However, older workers who are seeking employment after having retired from a company are exempt from paying the premiums. For services in employment promotion, work force development and training, employees contribute 0.35% of their wages.

The amount and duration of unemployment benefits are determined as follows:

1. *Amount of benefits.* The daily amount of basic allowance depends on the level of wages and the nature of employment. For regular workers the benefits range from ¥2,390 to ¥9,040 in 1991, depending on their wage levels. For daily wages between ¥2,970 and ¥3,960, the allowance is 80% of the wages. The percentage declines to 60% when daily wages are between ¥9,560 and ¥15,070.

2. *Duration of benefits.* This is determined by the period of employment ensured, the age of the worker and the nature of employment. Table E.2 shows the duration of benefits for regular workers in 1991. For example, for regular workers younger than 30, they are eligible for 90 days of benefits if they are insured for 5–9 years, and for 180 days if insured for 10 years or more. For disabled persons who have difficulty in obtaining employment, the duration is increased selectively. The duration of benefits for part-time workers (who work 22–33 hours a week) is reduced somewhat, with the same minimum of 90 days but maximum of 210 days (with ten years or more of insured employment). For anyone ensured for less than one year, the duration of benefits is 90 days. Unemployed seasonal

Table E.2
Duration of unemployment benefits, for regular insured workers, 1991 (unit: days)

Age	Period of employment insured		
	1–4 years	5–9 years	10 and more years
Below 30	90	90	180
30–44	90	180	210
45–54	180	210	240
55–64	210	240	300
Disabled			
Below 55	240	240	240
55–64	300	300	300

Source: Ministry of Labor.
Note: For employment of less than one year, the duration of benefits is 90 days for regular workers, disabled workers, and part-time workers.

workers are entitled to a lump-sum equivalent to only 50 days of benefits.

A system of employment adjustment subsidies was established in 1975 as part of the employment insurance scheme to improve employment. Under the system employers who need to reduce employment because of recessions can receive subsidies from the government up to one-half (for large firms) or two-thirds (for small- and medium-sized firms) of their payments to their temporarily laid-off workers for a maximum of 75 days. These temporarily laid-off workers are not counted as unemployed in the Japanese labor statistics.

Address

Employment Security Bureau, Ministry of Labor
2-2, Kasumigaseki 1-chome, Chiyoda-ku, Tokyo 100
Tel: (03) 3593-1211

References

Employment and Employment Policy. 1988. Tokyo: Japan Institute of Labor.

Hiraishi, Nagahisa. 1987. *Social Security.* Tokyo: Japan Institute of Labor.

Ministry of Labor. 1992. *Labour Administration: Seeking a More Comfortable Life for Workers.*

employment pattern   Of Japan's total employed labor force of 63.7 million in 1991, about 13.5% were self-employed/employers, 7.7% were fam-

Table E.3
Employment by sector (in million people and %)

	1980		1990	
Total	55.4	100%	63.7	100%
Agriculture and forestry	5.3	9.6	3.9	6.1
Fisheries	0.5	0.8	0.4	0.6
Mining	0.1	0.2	0.1	0.1
Construction	5.5	9.9	6.0	9.5
Manufacturing	13.7	24.7	15.5	24.3
Transportation, communications, and utilities	3.8	6.9	4.1	6.5
Wholesale/retail and food	12.5	22.5	14.3	22.5
Finance, insurance, and real estate	1.9	3.5	2.6	4.1
Services	10.0	18.1	14.5	22.7
Government	2.0	3.6	2.0	3.1

Source: Management and Coordination Agency.

ily workers, and 78.5% were employees. By sector, only 6.1% of them were engaged in agriculture. Manufacturing is the largest sector—employing about a quarter of the labor force—followed by wholesale/retail trade (22.5%) and services (22.7%), as shown in table E.3. Between 1975 and 1991, agriculture's share of employment has declined, while that of services has grown. The other industries' shares have remained relatively stable. Of these industries, mining, construction, transportation and communications, and government employ much more male than female employees. In wholesale/retail trade, finance, and services, the numbers of male and female employees are close.

Of all employees, about three-quarters are regular employees and the rest nonregular employees. The latter consist of different groups of workers with various status such as temporary employees (1–4 month employment term), day laborers, part-timers (less than 35 hours a week), and *arubaito* workers (side-job holders, usually students). Table E.4 shows the number of regular and nonregular employees by sex.

As Table E.4 shows, while about a quarter of all employees are nonregular employees, the percentage is much higher for women (about 41% in 1992). In particular, part-time workers are predominantly (93%) female, constituting 27% of all female employees.

See also **labor force, women in the labor force.**

Table E.4
Regular and nonregular employees (as of February 1992)

	Regular employees	Nonregular employees		
		Total	Part-timers	*Arubaito*, etc.
Number (in million)				
Total	50.3	37.1	13.3	5.6	2.3
Male	31.1	25.7	5.4	0.3	1.1
Female	19.2	11.4	7.9	5.2	1.2
Percentage				
Total	100.0	73.7	26.3	11.0	4.5
Male	100.0	82.6	17.4	1.0	3.6
Female	100.0	59.2	40.8	27.3	5.9

Source: Management and Coordination Agency.

References

Japan Institute of Labour. 1992. *Japanese Working Life Profile, 1991–92.*

Management and Coordination Agency. Annual. *Labor Force Survey.*

Management and Coordination Agency. 1992. *Japan Statistical Yearbook, 1992.*

endaka   High yen or yen appreciation; often specifically used to refer to the yen's appreciation after the September 1985 Plaza Accord.
　　See **yen–dollar exchange rates**.

enterprise tax (or business tax)   A prefectural tax levied on the net incomes of corporations and unincorporated businesses located in the prefectures. Also called the *business tax.*
　　See **tax system**.

enterprise unions
See **labor unions**.

Equal Opportunity Employment Law, 1986   Legislated in 1985 after heated debate in Japan, the law became effective in April 1986. It was inspired by and conformed with the United Nations Convention on the Elimination of All Forms of Discrimination against Women, which Japan signed in 1980.

The law forbids employers to discriminate on the grounds of sex in regard to employee training, retirement, and benefits and requires employers to "endeavor" to provide women the same opportunities as men in recruiting, hiring, job assignment, and promotion. It forbids employers to require female employees alone to be unmarried or below a certain age, or to require female employees to do work that would be detrimental to pregnancy, childbirth, and breastfeeding. It extends maternity leave from 12 weeks as provided for in the Labor Standards Law of 1947 to 14 weeks.

Thus the law combines protective provisions for women with promotion of equality between the sexes. Protective legislation for women in postwar Japan started as early as 1947 with the Labor Standards Law which restricted overtime and night work for women. However, such protection has been criticized as counterproductive because it raised the price of female labor and thereby gave employers an excuse for their reluctance to hire and promote women. Although the overtime and night work restrictions were relaxed in 1986, Saso (1990: 106) questions whether equal opportunity can be implemented while a certain measure of protective legislation remains in force.

The law has no sanctions for violations and complaints are to be mediated or submitted to arbitration committees. Although it is too early to assess the law's long-term impact, some changes have already been brought about. Some companies have begun to ask female employees when they are hired whether they prefer a career on the general management (sogo shoku) track with all its commitments or just a job on the clerical (ippan shoku) track. The former provides extensive training and advancement opportunities but may entail long hours and transfers; the latter offers lower salaries, little promotion opportunity, and shorter working hours. Previously companies would automatically place women on the clerical track and men on the general managment track. Thus opportunites for women have increased, although the number of women actually selected for management track remains small (Mordo 1991: 16). Also, in many professions formerly open only to men, the law has made it possible for some women to enter.

The Japanese national government has been at the forefront of promoting female employment, but overall it remains male dominated. As of 1991, only 17.5% of the national government's work force is female.

See also **employment discrimination, women in labor force**.

References

Hasegawa, Michiko. 1984. Equal opportunity legislation is unnecessary. *Japan Echo* 11, 4: 55–58.

Murdo, Pat. 1991. Women in Japan's work world see slow change from labor shortage, Equal Employment Law. *JEI Report*, 33A, Aug. 30.

Omori, Hiroko. 1990. Equality proves elusive for women in job market. *Japan Economic Journal*, Dec. 15: 4.

Saso, Mary. 1990. *Women in the Japanese Workplace*. London: Hilary Shipman.

equity-warrant bonds
See **warrant bonds**.

Eurodollar warrants   Warrant bonds denominated in dollar, issued by Japanese corporations, and traded on the Euromarket and in Japan.
  See **warrant bonds**.

Euroyen bonds   These are yen-denominated bonds issued on the Euro-market. Before June 1986 the Euroyen bond market was generally confined to Japanese and foriegn corporations, sovereign countries, and suprana-tional organizations such as the World Bank; foreign banks were restricted to issuing Euroyen certificates of deposits. Beginning in June 1986, U.S. and other non-Japanese banks are allowed by Japan's **Ministry of Finance** to raise cash in yen as part of the liberalization of the Japanese financial markets, thus giving non-Japanese banks access to low-cost funds and a new investor base.

  The volume of new Euroyen bonds issued was ¥2,938 billion in 1987 and ¥3,060 billion in 1991. It was larger than that of its major competing debt instrument, the *samurai bonds*, which are yen-denominated bonds issued in Japan by nonresidents.
  See also *samurai* **bonds**.

References

Senner, Madis. 1989. *Japanese Euroderivaties*. London: Euromoney Pulications.

Viner, Aron. 1987. *Inside Japan's Financial Markets*. London: The Economist Publications. Ch. 6.

Euroyen futures   Contracts to trade three-month deposits at a given interest rate on a specific future date on the Euromarket.
See **financial futures market**.

Export-Import Bank of Japan   A government bank specialized in extending loans to export and import businesses.
See **government financial institutions.**

export pricing
See **pricing practices**.

exports
See **trade pattern**.

F

Fair Trade Commission   A government commission under the prime minister's office established to implement the Antimonopoly Law of 1947.
See **Antimonopoly Law, cartels**.

farm lobby
See **agricultural cooperatives, Zenchu**.

Federation of Economic Organizations (Keidandren)   Japan's most important business organization.
See **business organizations**.

female labor force
See **women in labor force**.

financial debentures   Bonds issued by long-term credit banks, the Bank of Tokyo, the Norinchukin Bank, and the Shoko Chukin Bank.
See **bond market**.

financial futures market   Formally called the *Tokyo International Financial Futures Exchange* (TIFFE), this market was established in June 1989 by the Federation of Bankers' Associations of Japan. Membership includes banks, **securities companies**, and other financial companies, Japanese and foreign. Three financial instruments are traded: yen-dollar currency futures, three-month Euroyen, and Eurodollar interest-rate futures. Euroyen futures are the world's first and account for 99% of its total transactions.

Yen futures consist of contracts to buy or sell yen at a given exchange rate on a specific future date. Euroyen and Eurodollar interest-rate futures are contracts to buy or sell three-month deposits at a given interest rate on a specific future date on the Euromarket. These financial instruments are designed to protect investors, banks, and companies against unpredictable future fluctuations in exchange rate and interest rates.

TIFFE has become one of the world's top three futures exchanges in terms of trading volumes. About 90% of total trading volumes consist of deals involving banks' own accounts for their own hedging purposes. Corporations and nonbank financial institutions account for the rest. Euroyen contract proves to be highly popular and dominates the trading because it is the only instrument available to hedge and speculate in short-term yen interest rates. The volume of Euroyen futures transactions increased rapidly from 9 million contracts in 1989 to 28.8 million contracts in 1990 but leveled off at 29.3 million and 29.9 million contracts in 1991 and 1992, respectively. Yen-dollar futures and Eurodollar futures have not done well, and trading in them constitutes less than 1% of the total volume.

Analysts expect trading in yen-based financial futures to remain TIFFE's strength and foresee listing of new yen-based products and diversified contract terms as its next step of development.

References

Bank of Japan. 1993. *Economic Statistics Annual, 1992.*

Shindo, Masashi. 1991. TIFFE to list Europen futures options. *Japan Economic Journal,* March 23: 30.

Weinberg, Neil. 1990. Tokyo financial futures' first year marked by mixed success, growing pains. *Japan Economic Journal Special Report: Financial Markets,* summer suppl.: 3.

financial institutions
See **Bank of Japan, banking system, city banks, government financial institutions, insurance companies, postal savings, securities companies**.

financial *keiretsu*
See ***keiretsu* and business groups**.

financial liberalization   The gradual decontrol by the government, and hence the growing market orientation, of the Japanese financial system since the late 1970s. It consists of many changes in different areas of the financial system, including the introduction of new financial instruments and markets, the decontrol of foreign exchange, the gradual deregulation of deposit interest rates and of banking businesses.

From the immediate postwar period to the early 1970s, Japan's financial system was highly regulated by the authorities for the purpose of providing abundant and cheap funds for rapid industrialization in a stable environment. Bank deposit rates were regulated at low levels, bank activities were regulated by the **Ministry of Finance** and the **Bank of Japan**, banks were obliged to purchase and hold **government bonds** at low yields, opportunities for financial investment were very limited, and foreign exchange was controlled.

The oil crisis of the early 1970s led to stagnation and inflation. This made the low deposit rates untenable as the public could not hedge against inflation. The rapid increase in the issue of government bonds after 1975—more than what the banks were willing to hold at low yields—caused the Bank of Japan to rely increasingly on the purchase of bonds rather than lending as the main monetary instrument for controlling **money supply**; hence its open market operations became increasingly important.

In the late 1970s various short-term **money markets** and instruments—including the *gensaki* market, the negotiable certificate of deposit (CD) with a free market interest rate—as well as a secondary bond market developed. These developments made the financial system increasingly market oriented. The Foreign Exchange Law of 1980 eased foreign exchange controls and made it possible for both residents and nonresidents to invest in domestic and overseas markets. In April 1984 the acquisition of commercial papers (CPs) and CDs issued overseas was permitted for investors. In December 1984 the issuance of the Euroyen CD was allowed for overseas branches of Japanese banks. In July 1985 foreign currency–denominated convertible bonds were issued by banks in overseas market. At the same time access to free overseas financial markets prompted Japanese investors and financial institutions to demand further domestic financial liberalization.

Throughout the 1980 new financial instruments and markets were introduced and the banking businesses were increasingly deregulated. For example, dealing in public bonds by banks was started in June 1984, yen-denominated bankers' acceptance market was opened in June 1985, short-term (six-month) treasury bills were first issued in February 1986, public issue of 20-year governments bonds began in October 1986, and the auction method for underwriting them was implemented in September 1987. **Stock-index futures trading** was started in September 1988. In June 1989 the stock index option was started, and the Tokyo **financial futures market** was established. The Japanese government bond futures option was started in May 1990.

The deregulation of deposit interest rates proceeded at a slow pace. It consists of the gradual lowering of the minimum amount required for four types of large deposits that have unregulated or deregulated interest rates so that the market-determined rate of return becomes increasingly within the reach of the average depositor. These types of deposits are (1) negotiable certificate of deposit (the minimum amount was ¥500 million in May 1979; it was lowered to ¥50 million in April 1988), (2) large time deposits (the minimum was ¥1 billion in October 1985; it was lowered in several steps to ¥100 million in April 1988 and to ¥10 million in October 1989), (3) money market certificate (MMC) (the minimum was initially ¥50 million in April 1985; it was lowered to ¥10 million in October 1987, and in October 1989, MMC was abolished), and (4) small MMC (the minimum was ¥3 million in June 1989; it was lowered to ¥1 million in April 1990 and ¥500,000 in April 1991. In June 1992 it was reduced to zero, and in June 1993 small MMC was abolished).

Effective June 22, 1992, interest rates on all bank deposits and **postal savings**, excluding three-year bank time deposits and ten-year term postal savings (*teigaku*), are liberalized. Interest rates on bank time deposits were deregulated in June 1993. The barriers between banking and securities businesses was reduced in April 1993 when the Financial System Reform Act went into effect. It permits banks to set up subsidiaries to enter some securities business and securities houses to set up subsidiaries to enter some trust-banking businesses.

Analysts have criticized Japan's financial liberalization as too slow and incremental. It has taken more than ten years since it first started, and it still has years to go before it is completed.

See also **banking regulation and deregulation, bond market, deposit system, *gensaki* market, interest rate structure, money markets**.

References

Federation of Bankers Association of Japan. Annual. *Japanese Banks*. Tokyo: Zenginkyo.

Royama, Shoichi. 1985. The Japanese financial system: Past, present, and future. In *The Management Challenge: Japanese Views*, ed. by Lester C. Thurow. Cambridge: MIT Press.

Royama, Shoichi. 1990. Aspects of financial restructuring in contemporary Japan. *Japan Review of International Affairs* 4: 42–65.

Shigehara, Kumiharu. 1991. Japan's experience with use of monetary policy and the process of liberalization. *Bank of Japan Monetary and Economic Studies* 9, 1: 1–21.

financial markets
See **bond market, money markets, over-the-counter market, postal savings, stock index futures trading, stock index options trading, stock market, Tokyo Stock Exchange.**

Fiscal Investment and Loan Program (FILP)   An important government credit program that uses funds from **postal savings**, public pension funds, insurance funds, and so forth, to make loans to, and to invest in, various public corporations, local government bodies, for example, in order to promote social and economic development or specific policy objectives. In addition it makes loans to selected categories of private business that are regarded as particularly important for the development of the economy or for social policy objectives. It may also fund projects that cannot find adequate financing in the private sector. Most government loans to private enterprises are administered through special banks or finance corporations.

Introduced in 1953, FILP has grown rapidly in size over the years. Because of its importance every year the proposed FILP has to be approved by the Diet along with the regular government budget. Throughout the 1970s, 1980s, and the early 1990s, the annual FILP amounted to about one-half the size of the general account of the central government. In FY 1991, for example, the general account of the central government was ¥70.35 trillion, whereas the FILP was ¥36.81 trillion. The ordinary account of local governments totaled ¥70.88 trillion.

The major sources of funds for FILP are postal savings, public pensions (e.g., National Pension, Employees' Pension), and postal life insurance. Money from these sources is deposited in the following four funds:

1. Funds of the Trust Fund Bureau of the **Ministry of Finance** (77.9% in FY 1991). Postal savings, employees' pensions, and national pensions are deposited in this fund.

2. Postal Life Insurance Fund (16.9% in FY 1991).

3. Government-guaranteed bonds and borrowings (5.1% in FY 1991). When government institutions, public corporations, or public bodies issue bonds or borrow funds from private financial institutions, the government may guarantee the payment of interest and principal.

4. Industrial Investment Special Account (0.2% in FY 1991). The investments of the FILP are made through this special account. It provides funds as capitalizations, which are free of debt-servicing requirements, to government banks, public finance corporations, public bodies, and so forth.

The funds from these sources are dispensed, primarily in the form of loans, by the FILP to the following organizations and special accounts for use:

1. Special accounts such as National Forest Service Special Account, National Schools Special Account, Postal Savings Special Account.

2. **Government financial institutions** such as Housing Loan Corporation, People's Finance Corporation, Small Business Finance Corporation, Japan Finance Corporation for Municipal Enterprises, **Japan Development Bank**, and Export-Import Bank of Japan.

3. Public Corporations such as Pension Welfare Service Corporation, Japan Highway Corporation, Japan National Railways Settlement Corporation, and Overseas Economic Cooperation Fund.

4. Local governments.

5. Others such as the Shoko Chukin Bank, Kansai International Airport Co., the East Japan Railway Co., Electric Power Resources Development Co.

The Housing Loan Corporation and the Pension Welfare Service Corporation have been the two top recipients of funds from the FILP. In FY 1991 they received ¥6.4 trillion and ¥4.18 trillion, respectively. In terms of final uses, the bulk of the funds in the past has gone to the following areas: **housing** (32.6% in FY1991), small- and medium-sized enterprises (15.4%), living environment improvement (14.8%), and roads (10.2%).

References

Bank of Japan. 1993. *Economics Statistics Annual, 1992.*

Ministry of Finance. 1991. *Financial Statistics of Japan, 1991.*

Ishi, Hiromitsu. 1986. The government credit program and public enterprises. In *Public Finance in Japan*, ed. by Tokue Shibata. Tokyo: University of Tokyo Press.

Ogura, Seiritsu, and Naoyuki Yoshino. 1988. The tax system and the fiscal investment and loan program. In *Industrial Policy of Japan*, ed. by Ryutaro Komiya, Masahiro Okuno, and Kotaro Suzumura. Tokyo: Academic Press Japan.

Suzuki, Yoshio, ed. 1987. The *Japanese Financial System*. Oxford: Oxford University Press. Pp. 273–87.

fiscal policy
See **Fiscal Investment and Loan Program, government bonds, tax reform, tax system.**

flexible manufacturing system (FMS)   Order-based small-batch production with computer-aided design and manufacturing to increase product variety and to cut labor and inventory costs. A growing number of companies are introducting FMS because of the rising demand for product varieties in Japan as well the need to cut cost to be competitive. In the semiconductor industry, for example, the demand for mass-produced general-use chips has declined and that for application-specific integrated circuits (ICs) increased. In the auto market the demand for customized features has also increased.

FMS takes different forms in different industries and companies. At Yokogawa Electric Corp., Japan's largest maker of industrial measuring instruments, various machines and tools are used to change assembly line configurations quickly to enable workers to assemble different products. At Mitsubishi Electric Corporations's Kochi prefecture plant, computer-controlled assembly lines can process up to 2,000 different types of application-specific ICs. In the auto industry, it takes the form of engineering workstations and robots, which allow the same assembly line to produce different models. It is estimated that robot sales for the automakers in 1990 was about ¥120 billion, up from less than ¥40 billion in 1984. In all these cases FMS results in "soft automation."

Thus the FMS enables factories to easily switch from mass production of a small number of products or models to small-batch production of a broad range of products or models. In addition it reduces the need for new equipment investment, although R&D spending may increase. When factories change to the production of new items, it is not necessary to retool, as is necessary with traditional mass production. Technicians simply reprogram machines to handle different products.

While FMS yields these benefits, its successful implementation demands high exacting skills as well. Technologist Kodama (1991) estimates that the standards of a FMS require efficiency increases by a factor of one or two over traditional mass production in every aspect of processing precision, **quality control**, reliability, maintenance, and worker skills.

See also **computer-integrated manufacturing system**.

References

Kagawa, Masato. 1990. Flexible plants allows customized production. *Japan Economic Journal*, Feb. 24: 24.

Kodama, Fumio. 1991. Flexible manufacturing frees industry to concentrate on visions of the future. *Japan Economic Journal*, May 25: 8.

Kumar, K. R., A. Kusiak, and A. Vannelli. 1986. Grouping of parts and components in flexible manufacturing system. *European Journal of Operation Research* 24: 387–97.

Kusiak, A. 1985. The part families problem in flexible manufacturing systems. *Annals of Operations Research* 3: 279–300.

Oishi, Nobuyuki. 1990. Automakers boosting factory use of robots. *Japan Economic Journal*, May 5: 15.

Owa, Masataka. 1990. Flexible assembly eases inventory needs. *Japan Economic Journal*, Mar. 3: 21.

foreign aid   Japan's foreign aid or official development assistance (ODA) program originated in its payments of war reparations to Asian nations from the mid-1950s through 1965. Since then the amount of aid has increased steadily, and since 1986 it has been the second largest donor in the world except in 1989 when it was the largest donor in the world. In 1991 and 1992 Japan was again the world's largest donor.

Before the first oil crisis of 1973, Japanese aid was extended primarily to Asian nations and was tied to the purchase of Japanese products. After the oil crises of the 1970s, Tokyo felt the need to strengthen its ties with other regions, particularly the Middle East. From 1980 to 1990, the share of Asia declined from 71% to 59% (see table F.1). Of all recipients of Japan's aid, Indonesia and China were the two top recipients in 1987–90, followed by the Philippines and Thailand. In the early 1990s Eastern Europe began to receive aid from Japan.

To counter the criticism that its aid program was export oriented, Tokyo increasingly shifted the focus of its aid during the 1980s from large-scale infrastructural projects to projects to meet "basic human needs" such as rural and agricultural development, human resource development, and small- and medium-sized businesses. In response to the criticism that its aid projects were destructive of the local environment, in 1990 Japanese aid

Table F.1
Japan's aid to developing countries (in $ millions; multilateral aid excluded)

Region	1980	1988	1990
Asia	1,383 (70.5%)	4,039 (62.8%)	4,117 (59.3%)
Middle East	204 (10.4%)	583 (9.1%)	705 (10.2%)
Africa	223 (11.4%)	884 (13.8%)	792 (11.4%)
Latin America	118 (6.0%)	399 (6.2%)	561 (8.1%)
Oceania	12 (0.6%)	93 (1.4%)	114 (1.6%)
Eastern Europe			153 (2.2%)

Source: Ministry of Foreign Affairs.

officials first took into account the environmental impact of projects in screening aid projects. In 1991 the government attempted to use foreign aid for strategic purposes. It indicated that it would take into account, when offering aid, the potential recipients' military spending, weapon production and trade, and promotion of democracy, market orientation, and human rights. These new aid principles have been criticized as impractical, and for making Japan's aid program susceptible to political pressures.

In 1986 Japan surpassed France to become the second largest aid donor in the world—$5.6 billion as compared with $9.6 billion given by the United States. The figure increased to $7.5 billion in 1987, $9.1 billion in 1988, and $9 billion in 1989, which made Japan the largest aid donor in the world compared with $7.7 billion given by the United States in 1989. In 1990, however, Japan slipped back to the second place with $9.1 billion as the United States regained its top rank with $11.4 billion in aid. This U.S. figure includes $1.2 billion of military debt forgiveness for Egypt in return for its support in the Persian Gulf War, which in Tokyo's view should not be counted as foreign aid. In 1991 and 1992 Japan was the largest donor, with $11.03 billion and $11.15 billion given.

Part of the increase in Japan's dollar-denominated aid reflects the yen appreciation since 1985. As a percentage of GNP, Japan gave annually about 0.31% of its GNP in 1987–90 and 0.32% in 1991, the twelfth among the 18 industrialized aid donors. The U.S. gave 0.20% of its GNP in 1987, 0.21% in 1990 and 0.17% in 1991, which was the second lowest among aid donors.

Japan's aid consisted primarily of loans, which are not as desirable as grants; the latter constituted only 14–15% of the total aid given in 1990–91. Other forms of aid are technical assistance, cultural activities, and contributions to international agencies (multilateral aid; see table F.2).

Table F.2
Composition of Japan's foreign aid (in $ millions; disbursement basis)

Type of aid	1970	1980	1985	1989	1990	1991
Bilateral aid	372	1,961	2,557	6,779	6,940	8,870
Loans	250	1,308	1,372	3,741	3,920	5,475
Grants	100	375	636	1,556	1,374	1,525
Technical assistance	22	278	549	1,481	1,645	1,870
Multilateral aid	87	1,343	1,240	2,186	2,282	2,163
Total aid	458	3,304	3,797	8,965	9,222	11,034

Source: Ministry of Foreign Affairs.

The Foreign Ministry has the greatest influence over aid policy. However, the **Ministry of Finance**, the **Ministry of International Trade and Industry**, and the Economic Planning Agency also share the responsibility. The Japan International Cooperation Agency coordinates grant giving and technical cooperation, and the Overseas Economic Cooperation Fund administers concessional loans. Thus there is no unified leadership in the administration of Japan's aid program. Efforts have been made to name a foreign aid minister, but so far they have been unsuccessful.

It can be expected that in the future Japan's foreign aid will continue to increase. Many Japanese officials willing to increase foreign aid see it as Japan's only way to increase political influence in the world, given Japan's limited military role prescribed by its constitution. In addition increased aid will help to deflect foreign criticism that Japan is getting a "free ride" in the Western alliance. Since the early 1980s Japanese leaders have included aid as part of their concept of "comprehensive security."

See also **defense expenditures**.

Addresses

Japan International Cooperation Agency
1-1, Nishishinjuku 2-chome, Shinjuku-ku, Tokyo 163
Tel: (03) 3346-5311

Ministry of Foreign Affairs
2-1, Kasumigaseki 2-chome, Chiyoda-ku, Tokyo 100
Tel: (03) 3580-3311

Overseas Economic Cooperation Fund
4-1, Otemachi 1-chome, Chiyoda-ku, Tokyo 100
Tel: (03) 3215-1311

References

Grimm, Margo. 1992. Japan's foreign aid program: Setting priorities, policies in 1992. *JEI Report*, no. 46A, Dec. 11.

Iida, Tsuneo. 1991. In defense of Japan's aid program. *Japan Echo* 18, 3: 41–44.

Islam, Shafiqul, ed. 1991. *Yen for Development: Japanese Foregin Aid and the Politics of Burden Sharing*. New York: Council on Foreign Relations Press.

Japan's ODA: The blessing and the bane. *Tokyo Business Today*. Sept. 1991: 10–17.

Klamann, Edmund. 1990. Aid machine struggles with ecology issue. *Japan Economic Journal*, June 30: 1, 5.

Kusano, Atsushi. 1991. Rebutting the aid critics: A report from India, *Japan Echo* 18, 3: 45–53.

Ministry of Foreign Affairs. Annual. *Japan's Official Development Assistance: Annual Report.* Tokyo.

Orr, Robert M., Jr. 1990. *The Emergence of Japan's Foreign Aid Power.* New York: Columbia University Press.

Yasutomo, Dennis T. 1986. *The Manner of Giving: Strategic Aid and Japanese Foreign Policy.* Lexington, MA: D.C. Heath.

foreign direct investment (FDI)   Compared with Japan's **direct overseas investment**, FDI in Japan is not large relative to the large size of the Japanese economy. The reasons are the perceived difficulties for foreign companies to do business in Japan. Aside from the differences in business practices, government regulation of foreign investment was relatively restrictive until 1980.

As shown in table F.3, FDI in Japan grew steadily in the 1980s, particularly since 1987. Japan's economic boom of the late 1980s and its increasingly liberalized policy toward FDI are the main reasons for the increase. Until the early 1970s the government restricted FDI on the ground that domestic industry was weak and needed protection. Liberalization reforms made during 1967–73 permitted foreign ownership with prior government approval in all but 17 industries. Further reform in 1980 reduced the restricted industries to four—petroleum, leather, mining and agriculture, and forestry and fishery. Instead of prior government approval, only prior notification to the **Ministry of Finance** was required. In 1991, with Wash-

Table F.3
Foreign direct investment in Japan (in $ millions)

Fiscal year	Number of cases	Amount
1951–80	8,826	$2,979
1981	919	432
1982	1,052	749
1983	2,363	813
1984	3,685	493
1985	3,370	930
1986	3,079	940
1987	3,946	2,214
1988	4,268	3,243
1989	5,688	2,860
1990	5,939	2,778
Total	43,135	18,432

Source: Ministry of Finance.

ington's prodding for further liberalization, the requirement of prior notification was changed to ex post facto reports except for the four restricted industries.

As shown in table F.4, the United States is by far the largest foreign investing country in Japan in terms of the cumulative total. The Netherlands and Switzerland are, respectively, the second and third largest. The amount of FDI in Japan is dwarfed, however, by Japan's direct overseas investment, which amounted to $67.5 billion in FY 1989 and $41.6 billion in FY 1991. The cumulative total of Japan's direct overseas investment during FY 1951–91 is $352.4 billion, more than 15 times that of FDI in Japan during FY 1950–91.

Of the $18.4 billion total FDI in Japan in FY 1950–90, $11.8 billion or 63.9% was invested in manufacturing, particularly machinery ($6.2 billion) and chemicals ($3.2 billion). Nonmanufacturing accounted for $6.7 billion, or 36.1%, of which commerce ($2.9 billion) and services ($1.1 billion) are the most important.

In a 1991 survey of more than 1,200 American companies, the respondents cited the following as the major problems in investing in Japan: high rents and land prices, difficulties in hiring and keeping personnel, complicated business practices and **distribution system**, exclusionary *keiretsu* practices, and vague government regulations (Saito 1991: 7). Related to these is the fact that corporate **mergers and acquisitions** are relatively rare in Japan and particularly difficult for foreign companies. Most of these

Table F.4
Foreign direct investment in Japan by country (as of March 31, 1992; in $ million)

Country	FY 1991	FY 1950–91	Share (in %)
United States	1,344	9,907	43.5
Netherlands	323	1,787	7.8
Switzerland	176	1,334	5.9
Germany, F.R.	172	1,122	4.9
Canada	764	1,093	4.8
Britain	431	1,083	4.8
Hong Kong	60	575	2.5
France	51	352	1.5
Japanese firms[a]	639	2,721	11.9
Other	388	2,797	12.3
Total	4,339	22,771	100.0

Source: Ministry of Finance.
a. Investments by Japanese firms with significant foreign participation.

difficulties were raised by Washington in the **Structural Impediments Initiative** talks with Tokyo in 1990 and will presumably ease in the future.

In addition to these "host country" factors, Mason (1992) points out that there are important "home country" factors. First, American companies have slipped in their competitiveness in some industries behind their Japanese counterparts. Second, as many observers have noted, American firms have not tried hard enough to invest in Japan. They are critized for making three strategic errors—lack of patience, lack of knowledge, and lack of effort.

See also **direct overseas investment, mergers and acquisitions.**

References

Brauchli, Marcus W. 1989. U.S. to prod Tokyo on easing investment. *Wall Street Journal,* Nov. 2: A14.

Feldberg, Gregory H. 1990. Joint ventures in Japan suffering wedding bell blues. *Japan Economic Journal,* Aug. 25: 1, 7.

Kester, W. Carl. 1991. *Japanese Takeovers.* Boston: Harvard Business School Press.

Lacktorin, Michael J. 1989. *Foreign Direct Investment in Japan: The Long-Term Strategy for the Japanese Market.* Tokyo: Sophia University.

Mason, Mark. 1992. United States direct investment in Japan: Trends and prospects. *California Management Review* 35, 1: 98–115.

Saito, Tadashi. 1991. Foreign direct investment in Japan. *JEI Report,* no. 35A, Sept. 20.

foreign exchange rates
See **yen-dollar exchange rates**.

foreign securities companies in Japan
See **securities companies, Tokyo Stock Exchange**.

foreign workers in Japan   There are two categories of foreign workers in Japan, legal and illegal. Under the Immigration Control Law the admission of foreigners for legal employment in Japan is restricted to business managers, university-level instructors, entertainers, providers of advanced or specialized know-how, and others with special skills not possessed by the Japanese (cooks in Chinese or French restaurants, Western-style confectioners, language teachers, etc.). Illegal foreign workers tend to be tourists, trainees, and students from Southeast Asia and other East Asian countries who overstay or who are in Japan legally but work illegally. The presence of growing illegal foreign workers has touched off heated debates in Japan in recent years concerning the appropriate policy toward them in view of the labor shortage in the economy.

The total number of foreigners admitted for legal employment is relatively small, but it has grown rapidly throughout the 1970s and 1980s (22,173 in 1976, 43,994 in 1985, 81,407 in 1988, and 94,000 in 1990). The vast majority of them were in entertainment (87% in 1988), followed by business (8%), language teachers (2.5%), and company employees (1.6%). They tend to work as short-term contract workers (*shokutaku*) on a full-time or part-time basis or as "international trainees." Because the inflow of legal workers has been small, the total number of legally employed foreign residents is also small—68,000 at the end of 1990, or only 0.6% of the Japanese population.

There are no accurate statistics on the number of illegal foreign workers in Japan. According to the Immigration Bureau of the Ministry of Justice, as of November, 1992, there were 292,791 illegal foreigners in Japan. They came mainly from Thailand, Iran, Malaysia, South Korea, and the Philippines in descending order. That total number, however, does not include many foreigners who are in Japan legally as tourists or students but are illegally employed. The number of students taking part-time jobs illegally is estimated at 50,000. Illegal workers tend to work as construction workers, factory workers, restaurant workers, bar hostesses, and so on. In other words, they tend to fill the undesirable 3-K jobs (*kitanai, kiken, kitsui*, or dirty, dangerous, and demanding).

In the 1960s and 1970s Japanese employers and **labor unions** resisted foreign workers. Although a shortage of unskilled workers developed after years of economic growth, Japanese industries decided to automate to relieve the shortage rather than to hire foreign workers. As the labor shortage spread to many sectors of the economy in the 1980s, many small businesses began to hire illegal foreign workers willing to take low-paid undesirable jobs shunned by the Japanese. Thus illegal foreign workers have contributed to Japan's economic growth by performing useful functions at relatively low-wage costs.

Yet the presence of a growing number of foreign workers in a hitherto homogeneous society has created various problems and concerns for the Japanese. Foreign workers tend to concentrate in ghettos with poor living conditions. Their different cultural backgrounds have caused social frictions with the Japanese. They are said to have a higher crime rate and to ignore Japanese social customs. Critics also believe that if their numbers continue to increase, they will take jobs away from unskilled Japanese workers and will slow the modernization of labor-intensive industries. As a result growing incidents of Japanese discrimination against foreign workers have been reported. Reportedly foreign workers have encountered discrimination in housing and are not given as much job safety protection and benefits as the Japanese workers.

There is no consensus among Japanese employers on the issue of foreign workers. Owners of small businesses in the service sector, particular construction where the shortage of labor is most acute, tend to welcome foreign workers, whereas executives and union leaders at large corporations tend to have the opposite view. The latter favor hiring more women and retirees. To alleviate the problems of labor shortage and illegal foreign workers, the Japanese government decided in 1991 to set up a foreign trainee program. The Japan International Training Cooperation Organization (JITCO) was established under the government's auspiece to train 100,000 foreigners a year for member companies, who pay membership fees to support such training and can request trainees through the organization. Trainees receive living expenses but not salaries, are allowed to stay as interns but must return home after completion of training (maximum of two years). In this way technology transfer to developing countries is also effected. However, early evidence indicates that few companies are hiring foreign interns.

There is a group of foreign workers who have been given special treatment. They are the *nikkeijin*, foreigners of Japanese descent, usually from Brazil, Peru, and other South American countries. Revisions of Japan's immigration law in June 1990 gave *nikkeijin* the status of long-term residents that allows them to work legally in the country. Some companies are actively recruiting them because of the labor shortage and the fact that it is easier for *nikkeijin* to adjust to the Japanese society. As a result their number in Japan soared from 8,500 at the end of 1988 to 148,000 at the end of June 1991.

See also **labor force**.

Addresses

Immigration Bureau, Ministry of Justice
1-1, Kasumigaseki 1-chome, Chiyoda-ku, Tokyo 100
Tel: (03) 3580-4111

Ministry of Labor
2-2, Kasumigaseki 1-chome, Chiyoda-ku, Tokyo 100
Tel: (03) 3593-1211

References

Foreign workers in Japan: Needed but not wanted. *The Economist*, Aug. 12, 1989: 58–59.

Ihoh, Yoshiaki. 1991. Japan to help industry train 100,000 foreigners. *Nikkei Weekly*, Oct. 19: 1.

Labor ministry plans to ease restrictions on foreign workers. *Nikkei Weekly*, May 30, 1992: 11.

Low-cost, illegal workers boon for business, worry for society. *Nikkei weekly*, Aug. 1, 1992: 11.

Nishio, Kanji. 1990. The danger of an open-door policy. *Japan Echo* 17, 1: 51–56.

Shimada, Haruo. 1990a. A possible solution to the problem of foreign labor. *Japan Review of International Affairs* 4, 1: 66–90.

Shimada, Haruo. 1990b. The labor shortage and workers from abroad. *Japan Echo* 17, 1: 57–62.

Takahashi, Hideo. 1990. Illegal foreign workers in Japan. *JEI Report*, June 15, 1990.

Watanabe, Toshio. 1990. A flawed approach to foreign labor. *Japan Echo* 17, 1: 45–50.

Fuji Bank　One of Japan's six largest city banks and a core member of the Fuyo Group.
　See **city banks**, **keiretsu** **and business groups**.

Fujitsu Ltd.　Japan's largest domestic computer maker.
　See **electronics industry**.

fukumi　"Latent capital" or the unrealized value of assets when market prices exceed their book value.
　See **banking system, city banks**.

futures markets
See **bond market, commodity market, financial futures market**.

G

general import agents   Exclusive importers of brand-name products.
See **distribution system**.

general trading companies
see **trading companies**.

gensaki **market**   The market for the trading of bonds with a repurchase
agreement.
See **bond market, money markets**.

gift market   For centuries gift giving has been a very important part of
the social and business life in Japan, so much so that in premodern times
there were formal guidelines prescribing various aspects of the practice,
from the appropriate gift for various occasions to the wrapping materials.
Although such formalities are no longer important, gift giving remains
very important in social and business relations as an approprite expression
of appreciation and goodwill and an indispensable means to cement the
existing relationship. Consequently the gift market constitutes an important segment of the consumer market.

The gift market is highly seasonal. Although gifts are given throughout
the year, there are two major gift-giving seasons, midyear (*chugen*) in July
and end of year (*seibo*) in December. The latter is the bigger of the two,
in part because of the rising popularity of Christmas gifts. During these
two seasons, gifts are given to those to whom the giver is indebted.
Thus companies give presents to important clients; families give to friends,
superiors, teachers, doctors, and so forth. Leaders of the major factions of
the Liberal Democratic Party give year-end gifts to members of their groups.

Throughout the year, gifts are given for various reasons. Cash gifts
are popular for weddings, funerals, births, and illnesses. Members of the

Parliament give gifts throughout the year for weddings and funerals of their constituents. It is also customary to give parting gifts to someone leaving on a long trip, which obligates the receiver to bring back gifts for the givers. One gift-giving custom imported or adapted from the West is the so-called *giri* or obligatory chocolates given on St. Valentine's day by women to male associates at work, which is said to express a sense of group belonging. On "White Day" some weeks later, gifts go the other way from men to women.

For **department stores**, gift purchases account for as much as one-fifth of annual sales. It is estimated that, in December 1990 alone, as much as ¥3 trillion was spent on gifts. Popular gifts are the higher-priced varieties of alcohol, seasoning, canned goods, soap, towels, and confectionery. Department store gift certificates are becoming increasingly popular; customers are encouraged to buy them to avoid the delays in gift deliveries due to the labor shortage and traffic jams during gift-giving seasons. As a result there is even an active secondary market for gift certificates. In Tokyo alone there are reportedly more than 50 shops buying and selling gift certificates at discount prices. They usually buy them at 6−8% below the par price and sell them at 2−4% below par.

Japanese companies pay out their semiannual bonuses at midyear and year-end, coinciding with the gift-giving seasons. Thus the size of the bonuses, which varies with the comapany's profits and may amount to several months' salary, influences the amount of gift spending.

References

Craft, Lucille. 1986. Presents at *o-seibo* time. *Tokyo Business Today*, Nov.: 60−63.

Gift certificates overcome tacky image. *Nikkei Weekly*, Feb. 1, 1992: 18.

Gift rapt. *The Economist*, Dec. 13, 1986: 78.

Oshima, Izumi. 1989. Summer gift certificate sales soar. *Japan Economic Journal*, July 29: 6.

Takeuchi, Hiroshi. 1989. Gift-giving transends traditional role as urbanites seek sense of belonging. *Japan Economic Journal*, Aug. 12: 10.

Weisman, Steven R. 1990. The days of wine and $115 mellons: It's gift time. *New York Times*, Dec. 21: A4.

GNP, GNP per capita, and GDP   From the devastation of World War II, Japan has succeeded in building one of the most dynamic economies of the world, which is also the second largest in the world after the United

States (see table G.1). This dynamism is reflected in various ways—the rapid development of Japan's industries, the rapid growth of its exports, and the rapid growth of its gross national product (GNP), which is the sum of all final goods and services produced by residents in a year, including the income residents receive from abroad for their factor services (capital and labor).

Annual growth rate of real GNP (in constant prices) has been on average the highest over the past four decades among the major industrial countries, although it has fluctuated cyclically as in other countries. In the 1950s and 1960s the annual growth rate exceeded 11% in most years. It slowed down to 4–8% in 1971–73, and then to record low of 0.8% in 1974 and 2.9% in 1975 in the aftermath of the first oil crisis in 1973. After the recovery to about 5% and more in 1977–79, it slowed down to a level slightly above 3% in 1980–83, but began to grow after 1984 at 4.3% or higher (except in 1986 due to the **yen shock**).

Because Japan's GNP has been growing much faster than its population, its GNP per capita has been growing at a higher rate than other major

Table G.1
GNP and growth rates (in ¥ trillions and %)

	Nominal GNP	Real GNP	Annual growth rate
1955	8.40	42.94	—
1960	16.00	65.15	13.1
1965	32.77	100.82	5.8
1970	73.19	171.29	10.2
1975	148.17	212.88	2.9
1980	240.10	266.63	3.5
1985	321.56	321.53	5.2
1986	335.84	330.02	2.6
1987	350.48	344.33	4.3
1988	373.73	365.82	6.2
1989	399.05	383.45	4.8
1990	428.67	403.37	5.2
1991	456.12	412.32	4.5

Source: Economic Planning Agency.
Note: Average annual growth rate of real GNP:
1971–75: 4.8%
1976–80: 4.6%
1981–85: 3.8%
1986–90: 5.1%
Nominal GNP is calculated in current prices. Real GNP is calculated in 1985 prices. Annual growth rate is that of real GNP.

industrial countries. When converted at the average **yen–dollar exchange rate** for each year, Japan's GNP per capita in current dollars began to exceed that of the United States in 1987 ($19,553 versus $18,570). In 1988, at $23,382, it was the second highest in the world after Switzerland, with a growing lead over that of the United States ($19,813 in 1988). By any standard this is a remarkable accomplishment by the Japanese and understandably a source of pride for them, who had to start from a very low income level after World War II.

However, international comparison of GNP per capita by using simple annual exchange rates can be misleading because exchange rates can fluctuate wildly from year to year and differences in the prices of countries are not fully reflected by the exchange rates. In the case of Japan–U.S. comparison, the use of the yen–dollar exchange rate can be particularly misleading because Japan's chronic trade surplus has led to a strong yen vis-à-vis the dollar since 1985 that does not reflect the real purchasing power of the yen in Japan. In other words, the yen–dollar exchange rate does not correspond to the purchasing-power parity of the two currencies; a dollar can buy more in the United States than its yen equivalent can in Japan at the prevailing exchange rate.

To minimize such problems, the World Bank has used since 1985 modified exchange rates in the so-called "*World Bank Atlas* method" in its international comparison of GNP per capita in dollars. It uses the average of the exchange rate for the particular year and the exchange rates for the two preceding years, after adjusting them for differences in relative inflation between the particular country and the United States. This three-year average smoothes fluctuations in prices and exchange rates for each country. Calculated in this way, Japapn's GNP per capita did not exceed that of the United States until 1988, and did so only by a small margin (see table G.2).

The same rapid economic growth can also be seen in Japan's gross domestic product (GDP), which is the sum of all goods and services produced by residents and nonresidents in the country in a year. Thus it equals GNP minus net factor income from abroad and plus income payments made to nonresidents who contributed to the domestic economy. Japan's GDP differs only slightly from its GNP. Prior to 1982 the two were virtually the same. Since 1983 Japan's GNP began to exceed its GDP slightly because its residents were receiving more factor income from abroad than what nonresidents were receiving from Japan for their factor services. This reflects the growing importance of Japanese investments made overseas. The excess, however, was not large. In 1989 Japan's GNP

Table G.2
GNP per capita, Japan and the United States (in current ¥ and $ prices)

Year	Japan		United States
1955	¥94,000	$261[a]	$2,705
1970	707,000	1,964[a]	4,995
1985	2,662,000	11,322 (11,300)	16,690
1986	2,765,000	13,552 (12,840)	17,480
1987	2,872,000	19,959 (15,760)	18,530
1988	3,049,000	23,382 (21,020)	19,840
1989	3,239,000	23,485 (23,810)	20,910
1990	3,469,868	24,184 (25,430)	21,790
1991	3,664,000	28,937 (26,930)	22,240
Average annual growth rate			
1965–89		4.6	1.6%

Sources: Economic Planning Agency; the World Bank.
Note: Japanese GNP per capita in dollars in parentheses are calculated by the World Bank using modified exchange rates (three-year average, inflation adjusted).
a. Converted at ¥360 = $1.

was greater than its GDP by ¥3.2 trillion, a record that amounted to less than 1% of GNP. The disparity declined to ¥2.4 trillion in 1990.

See also **price indexes and price levels, yen–dollar exchange rates.**

References

Economic Planning Agency. Annual. *Annual Report on National Accounts.*

Saito, Tadashi. 1992. Quality of life in Japan: Is it affluent or not? *JEI Report,* no. 22A, June 12.

Summers, R. and A. Heston. 1984. Improved international comparison of real product and its composition. *Review of Income and Wealth* 2 (June): 207–60.

The World Bank. Annual. *The World Bank Atlas.*

The World Bank. Annual. *World Development Report.*

government bonds   The major type of public bonds issued by the national government (the other public bonds are local government bonds and public corporation bonds). On the basis of their authorized purposes, government bonds are classified into construction bonds, deficit-financing bonds, and refunding bonds. In terms of maturity, they consist of interest-bearing long-term government bonds (10 and 20 years), interest-bearing medium-term government bonds (2 to 4 years), discount government bonds (5 years), and short-term treasury bills (introduced in 1985 and included in bond statistics). Long-term bonds constitute about 90% of the total.

Before the mid-1970s the amounts of government bonds were relatively small (see table G.3), and their yields very low. The sale of long-term bonds was negotiated between the **Bank of Japan** and an underwriting syndicate composed of all types of banks and other financial institutions. The bonds were simply allocated to the syndicate members according to negotiated fixed shares. Syndicate members were willing to hold the mandatory low-yield bonds in exchange for access to the Bank of Japan's discount window. On the other hand, the Bank of Japan used the monthly amount of of bond issue as an important monetary tool to adjust the liquidity of the banks and the economy.

The banks were not allowed to resell them to the public. After 1975 flotations of government bonds increased rapidly because of rising government deficits. It became too costly for banks to continue to hold them. Thus, starting in 1977, banks were allowed to resell the bonds to the public at free prices if they had held them for more than a year. In April 1981 the minimum holding period imposed on banks before resale was reduced to one hundred days. Since April 1983 banks were allowed to make over-the-counter sales of new issues of long-term government bonds.

As of October 1990 there were 839 members in the underwriting syndicate. The number of foreign members has been increased from three in the

Table G.3
Government bonds, outstanding amount (in ¥ trillions)

End of fiscal year	Amount
1965	0.69
1970	3.60
1975	15.78
1980	71.91
1985	136.61
1986	147.33
1987	154.11
1988	159.10
1989	161.10
1990	168.55
1991	173.66

Source: Ministry of Finance.
Note: Domestic bonds only.

1970s to more than 60. However, the share alloted to foreign firms has remained small (under 7%). As yields on government bonds have increased, foreign banks and security firms have requested larger shares in underwriting government bonds. In addition they have requested more openness in the determination of the bond prices. Until April 1989 the coupon rate, as well as the issuing price of the ten-year bonds, the major long-term government bonds, was determined through negotiations between the **Ministry of Finance** and the syndicate.

In response to the foreign underwriters' request, the Ministry of Finance has gradually opened up the government bond market. In April 1989 40% of new issues of ten-year bonds was put to auction instead of syndicate allocation. The ratio was raised to 60% in October 1990 and 100% in April 1991. Bonds of other maturities are offered to the public on the basis of competitive bidding.

Yields on Japanese government bonds have fluctuated from year to year and from month to month in tandem with changes in the economic conditions and Japanese monetary policy (see table G.4). In the late 1980s they were substantially lower than those on U.S. goverment bonds, prompting sizable Japanese investment in U.S. government bonds. For example, in early 1989, 10-year Japanese government bonds carried a yield of about 5% as compared with about 9% for the U.S. equivalent. In early 1990, however, Japanese 10-year bonds yields increased rapidly toward 7% because of the higher Bank of Japan discount rate. This caused concern in

Table G.4
Yields on government bonds (10 years)

Year	Month	Coupon rate	Issue price	Yield
1989	3	4.8	98.75	4.987
	6	4.9	98.75	5.088
	9	4.9	100.04	4.894
	12	5.3	99.96	5.306
1990	3	6.4	99.99	6.401
	6	6.4	100.97	6.242
	9	7.3	98.66	7.534
	12	6.9	100.60	6.799
1991	3	6.4	101.14	6.215
	6	6.5	100.07	6.488
	9	6.3	100.00	6.300
	12	6.0	101.03	5.836

Source: Bank of Japan.

the United States that Japanese funds would be pulled out of U.S. government bonds.

See also **bond market**.

References

Bank of Japan. 1993. *Economic Statistics Annual, 1992.*

Choy, Jon. Japanese debt markets: An overview. *JEI Report*, June 10, 1988.

Japan Securities Research Institute. 1992. *Securities Market in Japan, 1992.* Ch. 4.

Ohkawa, Masazo. 1986. Government bonds. In *Public Finance in Japan*, ed. by Tokue Shibata. Tokyo: University of Tokyo Press.

Pettway, Richard H. 1990. Underwriting Japanese long-term national bonds. In *Japanese Capital Markets*, ed. by Edwin J. Elton and Martin J. Gruber. New York: Harper and Row.

Tatewaki, Kazuo. 1991. *Banking and Finance in Japan.* London: Routledge. Ch. 6.

government financial institutions   Aside from the central bank, the **Bank of Japan**, government financial institutions in Japan include two banks—the Export-Import Bank of Japan and **Japan Development Bank**—and nine finance corporations. As stipulated by law, the two government banks concentrate their loans in export-import and development finance. At the end of 1991 the Export-Import Bank had capital of ¥967 billion, borrowed money of ¥5.43 trillion, and loans and discounts of ¥7.08 trillion. Japan Development Bank's capital was ¥234 billion. Its borrowings from the government were ¥8.43 trillion, while its loans outstanding were ¥10.01 trillion at the end of 1991.

Table G.5
Government finance corporations (end of 1992; in ¥ trillions)

Name	Outstanding loans
Agriculture, Forestry, and Fisheries Finance Corp.	5.36
Environmental Sanitation Business Finance Corp.	0.87
Housing Loan Corp.	47.41
Hokkaido-Tohoku Development Corp.	1.20
Japan Finance Corp. for Municipal Enterprises	13.82
Okinawa Development Finance Corp.	1.20
People's Finance Corp.	8.12
Small Business Credit Insurance Corp.	0.43
Small Business Finance Corp.	8.32

Source: Bank of Japan.

The names and outstanding loans of the nine government finance corporations are given in table G.5. It is clear that the Housing Loan Corporation is by far the most important of the government finance corporations. Its outstanding loans were larger than those of the others put together. All the finance corporations finance their loans with funds borrowed from the government (Trust Fund Bureau and **postal savings**) and with funds raised by issuing debentures. They cannot accept deposits because they are designed to supplement private-sector finances and are prohibited by law from competing with private financial institutions.

In a broader sense, the post offices—with their life insurance and postal annuity accounts—and the Trust Fund Bureau of the **Ministry of Finance** can be regarded as government financial institutions as well. The government also has a small capital share in the Shoko Chukin Bank and the Norinchukin Bank, but these are not considered to be government financial institutions.

See also **Japan Development Bank, postal savings**.

Addresses

Export-Import Bank of Japan
4-1, Otemachi 1-chome, Chiyoda-ku, Tokyo 100
Tel: (03) 3287-1221

Housing Loan Corporation
4-10, Horaku 1-chome, Bunkyo-ku, Tokyo 112
Tel: (03) 3812-1111

Japan Development Bank
9-1, Otemachi 1-chome, Chiyoda-ku, Tokyo 100
Tel: (03) 3270-3211

References

Bank of Japan. 1993. *Economic Statistics Annual, 1992.*

Suzuki, Yoshio, ed. 1987. *The Japanese Financial System.* Oxford: Clarendon. Ch. 5.

Tatewaki, Kazuo. 1991. *Banking and Finance in Japan.* London: Routledge. Ch. 9.

gross domestic product (GDP)
See **GNP, GNP per capita and GDP**.

gyosei shido   Administrative guidance, the guidance or suggestions given by bureaucrats to firms.
See **administrative guidance**.

H

handicapped workers
See **employment discrimination, social security system.**

health insurance   Japan has a number of health insurance plans to cover different groups of people—company employees, day laborers, seamen, government employees, teachers, the self-employed, and so forth. Most of these plans are based on employment or occupation, while one is based on the local community. Thus virtually everyone in the country is covered by one of the following insurance plans:

1. A health insurance (*kenko hoken*) plan for employees of large corporations (with more than 300 employees) managed by the company's health insurance society (or a joint society of several companies). As of March 31, 1990, this plan covered 31.5 million people, about 25% of the population, including the dependents of the insured. The premiums may vary from one society to another. The average was 8.2% of the employee's monthly wages as of March 31, 1989, shared equally between the employee and the employer. The plan offers the following benefits as of March 31, 1990: 90% of medical costs for the insured and 70% of outpatient costs and 80% of hospital costs for the dependents. The insured pay the balance, up to the monthly maximum of ¥57,000 (¥31,800 for low-income earners).

2. A health insurance plan, managed by the government, for employees of small- and medium-sized companies. As of March 31, 1990, this plan covers 33.7 million people or about 29% of the population. The premiums are about 8.3% of the insured worker's monthly pay, shared equally by the insured and the employer. The benefits and monthly maximum are the same as in the plan for employees of large companies.

3. Government-managed health insurance for day laborers, including construction workers and workers hired by the day (about 0.1% to 0.3% of the

population). The employers pay 60% of the premiums and a special stamp fee and the workers pay 40% of the premiums, which are based on the wages.

4. Seamen's insurance, organized by the government (0.4% of the population). The coverage is similar to that of other employer-based plans. Premiums are 8.5% of the insured's monthly pay.

5. Insurance managed by mutual aid associations for government employees and private school teachers and employees (9.7% of the population). Premiums are 8.1% of the insured's monthly pay. The coverage is the same as the other employer-based plans.

6. The community-based national health insurance (*kokumin kenko hoken*) covers the self-employed (farmers, doctors, etc.) and employees of small businesses not otherwise covered. Also, when members of employee-based insurance funds retire, they typically join this plan. The plan is managed by the municipalies (covering 43.8 million people or 35% of the population as of March 31, 1990) and the National Health Insurance Associations (covering 3% of the population). The benefits cover 70–80% of the medical costs for both the insured and dependents. Premiums are fixed locally on the basis of income, property, and the number of people to be covered. Maximum monthly payments by the insured is the same as in other schemes.

7. Health insurance for the aged. This program was established in 1983 because of the aging population. As of March 31, 1990, the elderly (those over age 70 and those between ages 65 and 70 with disability) pay a fixed charge of ¥400 per day (¥300 per day for low-income elderly up to two months) for hospitalization and ¥800 per month for outpatient care. About 70% of the costs are covered by various group insurers (employees' insurance—e.g., government-managed health insurance or mutual aid association—and the national health insurance). The national government and local governments (municipalities and prefectures) contribute 20% and 10%, respectively, in subsidies.

Finally, when the patients are indigent, their costs are paid by the government's livelihood protection subsidies.

The comprehensiveness of Japan's health insurance is said to be an important factor in giving Japan the world's longest life expectancies (76.1 years for men and 82.1 years for women in 1991) and one of the world's lowest infant mortality rates (5.2 deaths per 1,000 births).

See also **social security system.**

Addresses

Health Insurance Bureau, Ministry of Health and Welfare
2-2, Kasumigaseki 1-chome, Chiyoda-ku, Tokyo 100
Tel: (03) 3503-1711

References

Fujii, Mitsiru, and Michael Meich. 1988. Rising medical costs and the reform of reform of Japan's health insurance system. *Health Policy* 9: 9–24.

Inglehart, John K. 1988a. Health policy report: Japan's medical care system. *New England Journal of Medicine* 319, 12 (Sept. 22): 807–12.

Inglehart, John K. 1988b. Health policy report: Japan's medical care system, part two. *New England Journal of Medicine* 319, 17 (Oct. 27): 1166–72.

Ministry of Health and Welfare. 1991. *White Paper on Health and Welfare*.

Murdo, Pat. 1991. Japanese health-care system no panacea for ailing U.S. program. *JEI Report*, July 5.

Norbeck, Edward, and Margaret Lock, eds. 1987. *Health, Illness and Medical Care in Japan: Cultural and Social Dimensions*. Honolulu: University of Hawaii Press.

Powell, Margaret, and Masahira Anesaki. 1990. *Health Care in Japan*. London: Routledge.

Heisei Boom   The economic expansion in Japan from November 1986 to July 1991 (preliminary estimate), one of the longest in the postwar period.
   See **business cycles**.

Hitachi Group   Japan's largest industrial group, consisting of Hitachi, Ltd., and its more than 680 subsidiaries, including Hitachi Cable, Hitachi Metals, Hitachi Chemical, Hitachi Construction Machinery, and Hitachi Credit Corp. Hitachi, Ltd., holds a high percentage of the shares of the other companies.
   See **cross shareholding,** *keiretsu* **and business groups**.

Hitachi, Ltd.   Japan's largest comprehensive electric machinery manufacturer and second largest industrial corporation. It has many subsidiaries in various fields.
   See **cross shareholding, electronics industry,** *keiretsu* **and business groups**.

Honda Motor Co.   Japan's fifth largest automobile manufacturer (as of 1992) and the first to set up a plant in the United States to produce passenger cars.

See **automobile industry**.

housing   Because of the shortage of land and a high population density, houses in Japan are typically smaller and less well equiped than their Western counterparts. The average floor space per new dwelling was only 80.5 square meters (867 square feet) in 1990, down from the postwar peak of 93.9 square meters (1,011 square feet) in 1982. The percentage of houses with flush toilets was 65.8% in 1988. Most houses have no central heating and use kerosene heaters for heating. In 1988, 9% of Japanese houses had no bathtub.

Housing services are not as bad as the figures given above would suggest, however. The Japanese have traditionally adopted various practices to compensate for their limited floor space and facilities. Many rooms can serve multiple purposes; people may sleep on a *tatami* floor (*tatami* is the traditional Japanese floor mat) and room furnishings are minimal to save space, and many people go to a public bath. These practices are still preserved by many people as part of their way of life so that comparative statistics between Japan and other countries on housing have to be interpreted with caution.

The number of new housing starts fluctuated greatly with the conditions of the economy. According to the Ministry of Construction, it was only 843,000 units in 1965, with an average floor area of only 58.9 square meters. It rose rapidly and reached a postwar peak of 1.91 million units in 1973 with an average of 75.4 square meters and then plunged to 1.32 million units in 1974 because of the 1973 oil shock. It rose again around the mid-1970s and then declined again. The bottom was reached in 1983 at 1.14 million units. During the real estate and stock market boom years of 1987–89, housing starts were at a high level of more than 1.66 million units annually. The number reached 1.71 million in 1990, the highest since 1973. It then declined to 1.37 million in 1991.

The high price of housing is a serious problem. The ownership of a small suburban house, particularly in the Tokyo metropolitan area, is virtually beyond the reach of most middle-class families because of its very high price. In 1989 a small condominium with 75 square meters of floor space costed an average of ¥54,975,000, about 8.62 times the average annual wage of salaried workers (*Japan Economic Journal*, January 20, 1990: 11). In 1991, a new condo of the same size would cost an average of ¥65.6

million in Tokyo, ¥54.4 million in Osaka, and ¥36.9 million in Nagoya (*Nikkei Weekly*, May 30, 1992: 4). Although the prices have come down by about 10% by April 1992 following the collapse in 1990–91 of the speculative real estate market, house prices are still about 8 times the average family income or higher. By contrast, the ratio between the average price of new houses and annual family income was 3.4 in the U.S. (1987), 4.4 in Britain (1987), and 4.6 in West Germany (1986; Takagi 1991: 75).

The major cause of high housing price is the high price of land, particularly in the major metropolitan areas, which was fueled by large bank loans for speculative real estate development in the late 1980s. Since the real estate bubble burst in 1990–91, land prices have come down somewhat, but not enough to make the housing prices affordable. The Economic Council, which advises the prime minister, has suggested that house prices should average five times the average family income. For most Japanese that goal is still unattainable. The Economic Council proposed that 2.6 million housing units be built within a 30-kilometer radius of Tokyo by the year 2000 to help achieve that goal.

The high price of housing has prompted large companies to increase company housing construction as well as housing loans to employees. For example, in 1989 Mitsubishi Electric Corp. launched a multibillion-yen company housing project in metropolitan Tokyo and raised its ceiling on housing loans to employees from ¥14 million to ¥23 million. Hitachi Ltd. and Toshiba Corp. have launched similar housing projects.

See also **housing finance**, **investment**.

References

Hayakawa, Kazuo. 1987. Japan. In *Housing Policy and Practice in Asia*, ed. by Seong-kyu Ha. London: Croom Helm.

Ito, Takatoshi. 1993. The land/housing problem in Japan: a macroeconomic approach. *Journal of the Japanese and International Economies* 7, 1: 1–31.

Oshima, Izumi. 1989. Pricey land drives firms to offer lifetime housing. *Japan Economic Journal*, May 20: 5.

Ostrom, Douglas. 1989. Japanese housing: The international dimension. *JEI Report*, no. 30A, Aug. 4.

Sanger, David. 1990. Tatami or colonial, a house is wishful thinking. *New York Times*, Oct. 17: A4.

Takagi, Shintaro. 1991. Are land and house prices too high in Japan? *Japanese Economic Studies* 20, 1: 57–86.

housing finance   Housing in Japan is financed by a number of financial institutions. Table H.1 gives the shares of housing credit provided by various sources.

Some trends can be seen in table H.1: (1) The share of **city banks** in housing credit has increased significantly since 1985. At the end of 1992 their outstanding loans were ¥25.21 trillion. (2) The share of other banks such as regional banks and *shinkin* **banks** has declined steadily since 1975. (3) The shares of financial institutions set up for specific sectors such as labor, agriculture, forestry, and fisheries have declined steadily. (3) The role of specialized financial institutions for housing has increased. At the end of 1992 they provided 46.5% of total housing credit. Housing loan companies are subsidiaries set up by banks after 1971 specifically for housing finance. There are eight such companies. The Housing Loan Corporation is a government financial institution. It is now the largest housing credit institution, extending more than one-third of the total. At the end of 1992 its outstanding loans were ¥41.78 trillion.

The total amount of outstanding housing credit has grown from ¥21.2 trillion at the end of 1985 to ¥115.4 trillion at the end of 1992. The interest rate on housing loans is based on the long-term prime lending rate.

See also **housing**.

Table H.1
Main sources of housing finance (end of month; in % of total loans outstanding)

Institutions	March 1975	December 1985	December 1992
City banks	16.9	13.6	21.8
Regional banks	14.3	10.3	8.6
Regional banks (II)[a]	7.6	5.6	4.7
Trust accounts, all banks	6.8	5.6	2.4
Shinkin banks	11.7	8.1	6.5
Labor credit associations	4.0	2.3	1.7
Financial institutions for agriculture, forestry, and fisheries	7.9	3.4	2.6
Insurance companies	3.8	6.6	5.9
Housing loan companies	3.9	8.3	10.3
Housing Loan Corporation	19.5	35.0	36.2

Source: Bank of Japan.
Note: The figures do not add up to 100% because some minor institutions are not included.
a. Second-tier regional banks, called *sogo* banks before 1989.

Address

Housing Loan Corporation
4-10, Koraku 1-chome, Bunyko-ku, Tokyo 112
Tel: (03) 3812-1111

References

Bank of Japan. 1993. *Economic Statistics Annual, 1992.*

Suzuki, Yoshio. 1987. *The Japanese Financial System.* Oxford: Oxford University Press. Pp. 248–51.

housing loan companies   Subsidiaries of commercial banks that specialize in housing loans. They have provided about 10% of the nation's outstanding housing credit.

See **housing finance.**

Housing Loan Corp.   A government financial institution set up for the purpose of providing housing credit. It receives investments and loans from the government's **Fiscal Investment and Loan Program** and has extended more than one-third of the nation's outstanding housing credit.

See **Fiscal Investment and Loan Program, government financial institutions, housing finance.**

human resource development
See **corporate personnel practices, education system, labor-management relations, lifetime employment, population.**

I

impact loans Bank loans in foreign currency by foreign exchange banks with no restrictions on the use of the funds. Unlike domestic yen loans, they are not subject to the window guidance by the **Bank of Japan** as to their growth rate. Hence banks often extend impact loans to meet fund demands by small- and medium-sized businesses. In fiscal year 1990 a total of ¥21.9 trillion impact loans was made.

Until the early 1990s the amount of total impact loans extended grew very rapidly. It increased by 50% in FY 1989. The growth rate declined to 17% in FY 1990 as banks curtailed their overall loans to meet the new 8% capital adequacy requirement set by the Bank for International Settlements.

See also **city banks.**

References

New BIS rules curtailed impact loan growth. *Japan Economic Journal*, Apr. 27, 1991: 43.

Suzuki, Yoshio, ed. 1987. *The Japanese Financial System*. Oxford: Oxford University Press. Ch. 5.

imports
See **trade pattern**.

income distribution Japan's income distribution is quite equal by international standards. This is reflected in the fact that, in government surveys conducted annually since 1960, more than 85% of the respondents have consistently indicated that they belonged to the middle class except for 1960 with 76.2%. The percentage reached a peak of 90.7% in 1975, declined slightly to 87.6% in 1986, and remained at 87.7% in 1989. It was 89.9% in 1991. This predominance of middle-class consciousness has contributed greatly to the country's social stability and low crime rate.

Because the Japanese perception of middle-class status is cultural as well as economic—middle class is perceived as diligent and frugal, which are widely shared values—the above figures are not the best indicator of income distribution. A better indicator is the Gini coefficient, which is a widely used measure of income inequality (it ranges from zero, perfect equality, to 1, perfect inequality). Table I.1 gives the official estimates of the Gini coefficients of household income and wage earners' disposable income in selected years. These official figures are all below 0.3; they are very low by international standards and thus have to be interpreted with caution. Alternatively, Bronfenbrenner and Yasuda (1987: 110–111) and Choo (1991: 5) have cited higher Gini coefficients of Japan estimated by other scholars. They range from 0.313 for 1955, to 0.319 and 0.407 for the 1960s and 1970s, to 0.334 for 1980 (no figures for other years in the 1980s). Even these higher estimates, however, are slightly lower than the Gini coefficients of the other industrialized countries in the same period. Choo (1991: 5) also cites estimates of Gini coefficients of Japanese farm households, which range from 0.229 to 0.327 for selective years in 1955–89. Thus one can conclude that income distribution in Japan has remained relatively equal throughout the postwar period.

One reason for this relative income equality is that Japan has no "permanent economic underclass" due to large-scale immigration of cheap labor (Brongenbrenner and Yasuda 1987: 110). Another reason is that among company employees, the income differentials between different groups with different education and employment status are relatively small. Table I.2 gives the annual earnings (wages plus bonuses) in 1990 of male employees with different educational background at different ages. Thus at age 22, a university graduate just starting work made less than a lower secondary-school graduate with several years of seniority or an upper

Table I.1
Official Gini coefficients

Year	Family income	Wage earners' disposable income
1970	0.2669	0.1787
1975	0.2742	0.1883
1980	0.2596	0.1832
1985	0.2785	0.1973
1989	0.2894	0.1965
1990	0.2905	

Source: Economic Planning Agency.

secondary-school graduate with four years of seniority. At age 30 the university graduate's earnings slightly exceeded those of these other two groups. At age 55, near retirement, the earning ratio between univeristy graduate and lower secondary-school graduate was 1.69 and between university graduate and upper secondary-school graduate was only 1.25.

Table I.3 gives the annual earnings (wages plus bonuses) of different groups of corporate employees. It is shown that the directors' incomes are less than double that of chief clerks, and no more than 2.5 times that of blue-collar workers. These numbers should not be taken as indicators of the distribution of real income, however. Corporate executives often enjoy huge fringe benefits such as a chauffeur-driven car, dining and drinking and golfing on expense accounts, and various other benefits that are said to be more than what their counterparts in other countries enjoy.

All employees' earnings constitute the labor income component of national income; other components are income from assets and business income. As shown in table I.4, the share of labor income in national income has increased from 54% in 1970 to nearly 71% in 1991. This rising share of labor income has contributed to the overall income equality in Japan, given the fact that the distribution of labor income is relatively equal as discussed above.

See also **wage structure.**

Table I.2
Earnings of male standard employees by education (1991; in ¥1,000 per year)

Age	Lower secondary	Upper secondary	University
22	2,678	2,962	2,300
30	4,036	4,227	4,706
40	4,997	6,174	7,685
50	6,230	8,583	10,931
55	6,822	9,051	11,712

Source: Ministry of Labor.

Table I.3
Employee earnings by positions (in ¥1,000 per year)

Position	1978	1980	1985	1990	1991
Director	6,201	6,966	8,420	9,958	10,384
Section chief	4,926	5,491	6,762	7,999	8,256
Chief clerk	3,979	4,448	5,451	6,393	6,645
Regular worker	2,482	2,795	3,498	4,138	4,327
Top/bottom ratio	2.50	2.49	2.41	2.41	2.40

Source: Ministry of Labor.

Table I.4
Distribution of national income (in %)

Income category	1970	1975	1980	1985	1990	1991
Employees' income	54.0	67.5	66.8	68.8	69.2	70.8
Income from assets	8.3	10.9	10.6	9.7	11.0	12.1
Business income[a]	37.7	21.6	22.6	21.4	19.7	17.1

Source: Economic Planning Agency.
a. Includes incomes of private corporations, public corporations and individual proprietorships, agriculture, forestry, and fishery, imputed service from owner-occupied dwellings, net of dividend receipts and payments.

References

Bronfenbrenner, Martin, and Yasukichi Yasuba. 1987. Economic welfare. In *The Political Economy of Japan*, vol. 1: *The Domestic Transformation*, ed. by Kozo Yamamura and Yasukichi Yasuba. Stanford: Stanford University Press.

Choo, Hakchung. 1991. A comparision of income distribution in Japan, Korea and Taiwan. In *Making Economies More Efficient and More Equitable*, ed. by Toshiyuki Mizoguchi. Tokyo: Kinokuniya.

Economic Planning Agency. Annual. *Economic White Paper*.

Jones, Randall S. 1987. Japanese income distribution. *JEI Report*, Aug. 28.

Ministry of Labor. Annual. *Basic Survey on Wage Structure*.

Ostrom, Douglas. 1991. Economic Equality in Japan. *JEI Report*, Feb. 1.

individual income taxes   For individual or personal income tax, the individual rather than the household is the unit of taxation. Two–wage earner couples are taxed separately. Individuals in Japan pay two types of income tax—national individual income tax (called *income tax* in Japan) levied by the national government and local income tax (called *inhabitant tax*) levied by the 47 prefectures and over 3,000 municipalies.

National income tax is the largest source of tax revenue for the national government. In FY 1992 the national government collected ¥25.35 trillion, or 41.9% of its total tax revenue, from the tax. Prefectural inhabitant tax is the second largest tax for the prefectural governments. In FY 1992 it yielded ¥5.31 trillion, or 32.8% of total prefectural tax revenue. Municipal inhabitant tax has been since 1964 the most important municipal tax. In FY 1992 it yielded ¥10.1 trillion or 53.4% of the total municipal tax revenue.

Effective January 1, 1988, both national and local income taxes were reformed as part of the 1988 tax reform package to introduce the new

consumption tax. The number of income brackets and the tax rates were reduced, and the level of exemptions was increased, as explained below:

1. *National income tax.* The number of income brackets was reduced from 12 to 5. The previous tax rate ranged from 10.5% for annual income below ¥1.5 million to the top rate of 60% for income over ¥50 million. The new tax rates are 10% for income below ¥3 million, 20% on incomes between ¥3 and 6 million, 30% on incomes between ¥6 and 10 million, and the top rate of 50% on incomes above ¥20 million. Before January 1989 personal exemptions included a basic exemption of ¥330,000 for a spouse and dependents, and a special exemption of ¥250,000 for the handicapped, widows, and working students. Starting in 1989 the basic exemption was raised to ¥350,000 for a spouse and dependents, and the special exemption for the handicapped, widows, and working students was raised to ¥270,000.

2. *Local income (inhabitant) tax.* The number of income brackets was reduced from 6 to 3. The range of tax rates was reduced from 3–12% to 3–11%.

One problem with the income tax before reform was that different types of income were treated unequally. Wages and salaries were taxed by withholding at the source. Dividends and capital gains on stocks were almost tax free. Interest incomes from a variety of savings—*maruyu* savings, **postal savings**, national and local bonds, savings for the formation of employee's assets, and postal installment savings for housing—were tax exempt within certain limits. Since April 1988 tax exemption for interests from these privileged savings was eliminated except for the handicapped, people over 65, and working widows. A 20% witholding tax is imposed on nearly all interest incomes from deposit accounts. Since April 1989 capital gains earned by individuals are subject to a flat tax rate of 26% (20% for national and 6% for local income tax).

See also **corporate income tax.**

Addresses

National Tax Administration Agency
1-1, Kasumigaseki 3-chome, Chiyoda-ku, Tokyo 100
Tel: (03) 3581-4161

Local Tax Bureau, Ministry of Home Affairs
1-2, Kasumigaseki 2-chome, Chiyoda-ku, Tokyo 100
Tel: (03) 3581-5311

References

Ishi, Hiromitsu. 1989. *The Japanese Tax System*. Oxford: Oxford University Press.

Ministry of Finance. 1992. *An Outline of Japanese Taxes*, 1991.

Odden, Lee. Tax reform 1989. *Tokyo Business Today*, Mar. 1989: 24–27.

Industrial Bank of Japan   Japan's largest long-term credit bank, considered by many Japanese analysts to be the best managed bank in Japan in recent years.
See **long-term credit banks**.

industrial groups
See *keiretsu* **and business groups**.

Industrial Investment Special Account   A special government account that finances the investment activities of the government's fiscal investment and loan program.
See **Fiscal Investment and Loan Program**.

industrial policy   Once officially defined as the systematic selection of industries to be encouraged or discouraged by government action or deliberate inaction, industiral policy entails the use of various government policy measures to change the allocation of resources among industrial sectors and to influence the organization of specific industries in accordance with the economic objectives of the government and its selection of priority industries for development. The **Ministry of International Trade and Industry** (MITI), formed in 1949, is the principal designer and executor of industrial policy.

Industrial policy in Japan has gone through three major periods. During the first period from 1949 to 1965, the policy was to revive and expand basic manufacturing industries such as coal, steel, electric power, transport industries, automobile, petrochemicals, petroleum refining, and machinery industries. The second period, from 1965 to 1973, was a transitional one. Liberalization of trade policies took place as Japan joined GATT in 1963 and IMF and OECD in 1964. The industries promoted by MITI shifted from basic manufacturing to knowledge-intensive industries. In the third period, from 1973 to the present, trends of the second period continued. In addition, because the first oil crisis (1973–75) adversely affected many industries in Japan, MITI adopted additional policy measures to facilitate structural adjustment and capacity reduction in the **declining industries**.

Industrial policy is implemented mainly through **administrative guidance**, that is, suggestions given by MITI bureaucrats to companies for voluntary compliance. This is reinforced with other measures such as relaxing the **Antimonopoly Law** by permitting the formation of **cartels**, and the provision of financial incentives, trade protection, and so forth, to help promote priority industries or to reduce the capacity of declining industries. For example, in the early 1960s MITI encouraged the mergers of firms in steel and auto industries in order to attain economies of scale to compete with foreign producers; the **steel industry** followed the suggestion but not the **auto industry**. Trade protection in the forms of tariffs, quotas, restrictive standards, and regulations for imports have been used to protect some industries. Special tax exemptions have been granted by MITI to favored industries. Subsidies and technical assistance were given to various priority industries, particularly the **electronics industry**, to foster technical development. However, the amount of funds involved was relatively small. For example, in the VLSI (very large-scale integrated circuit) project of 1976–80 to develop VLSI circuits for the fourth-generation computers, only ¥29.1 billion or 39.5% of total R&D expenditures came from the government. MITI's important role lay in the coordination of the project of five major computer firms. In 1990 MITI launched a ¥50 billion 10-year program to promote the **computer-integrated manufacturing system**.

For declining industries slated for capacity reduction such as textiles and shipbuilding in the 1970s, administrative guidance has been used to encourage shift into new product lines. Cartels have been permitted for industry rationalization. The Depressed Industries Law was passed in 1978 and extended in 1983 to provide financial incentives to declining industries to reduce capacity.

There is no consensus among scholars on the effectiveness and prospects of Japan's industrial policy. Among believers of its efficacy and success, Johnson (1982) attributes the "success" to the capability, dedication, and wide authority of the elite MITI bureaucracy and the "market-comforming" nature of their policy measures. Noboru Makino, former chairman of Mitsubishi Research Institute, attributes the strength of Japanese manufacturing to MITI's policy of weeding out the weak in industry in contrast to the **Ministry of Finance**'s "convoy system" policy of keeping weak financial institutions alive (*Japan Economic Journal*, Apr. 13, 1991: 14).

Critics of industrial policy question the wisdom and visions of MITI officials and the prospects of industrial policy in Japan. For example, Eads and Yamamura (1987) contend that industrial policy has often merely reflected the needs and demands of those being "guided," not the other way around. They predict that the role of industrial policy will decline in the future in Japan because of the reduced policy tools available to policy-makers due to capital market liberalization, trade liberalization, diminished funds for subsidies, and so on. Another criticism of industrial policy is that the use of subsidies by MITI is susceptible to political influence. For example, Okimoto (1989) charges that the coal and textile industries have been given much more subsidies than are justified on economic grounds. A more fundamental criticism is that MITI is not omniscient, as shown in its failed plan in the mid-1960s to create a world-class petrochemical industry despite Japan's total dependency on oil imports, given that industry has encountered serious problems since the first oil crisis. Okimoto (1989) argues that given its fallibility, MITI's involvement in high-tech R&D in the future can send companies into the wrong directions with costly consequences.

One interesting assessment of industrial policy is offered by Prestowitz (1988: 150) from a broad comparative perspective. He feels that industrial policy has served Japan well, given Japan's own policy objective. "Japan's industrial policy response is essentially an expression of its age-old drive to preserve its exclusivity. It does violence to American economic thinking, but it is not necessarily wrong. It is difficult, after all, to criticize Japan's economic performance, and the policy is only wrong if one accepts Western economic theory, which Japan does not."

See also **administrative guidance, declining industries, Ministry of International Trade and Industry**.

References

Dore, Ronald. 1987. *Taking Japan Seriously*. Stanford: Stanford University Press. Ch. 10.

Eads, George C., and Kozo Yamamura. 1987. The future of industria policy. In *The Political Economy of Japan*, vol. 1: *The Domestic Transformation*, ed. by Kozo Yamamura and Yasukichi Yasuba. Stanford: Stanford University Press.

Johnson, Chalmers. 1982. *MITI and the Japanese Miracle: The Growth of Industrial Policy, 1925–1975*. Stanford: Stanford University Press.

Komiya, Ryutaro, Masahiro Okuno, and Kotaro Suzumura, eds. 1988. *Industrial Policy of Japan*. Tokyo: Academic Press Japan.

Komiya, Ryutaro, and Keiichi Yokobori. 1991. *Japan's Industrial Policy in the 1980s*. Tokyo: Research Institute of International Trade and Industry, MITI.

Nester, William R. 1990. *The Foundation of Japanese Power: Continuities, Changes, Challenges*. London: Macmillan. Ch. 11.

Okimoto, Daniel I. 1989. *Between MITI and the Market: Japanese Industrial Policy for High Technology*. Stanford: Stanford University Press.

Okuno-Fujiwara, Masahiro. 1991. Industrial policy in Japan: A political economy view. In *Trade with Japan*, ed. by Paul Krugman. Chicago: University of Chicago Press.

Prestowitz, Clyde Jr. 1988. *Trading Places: How We Allowed Japan to Take the Lead*. New York: Basic Books. Ch. 5.

Woronoff, Jon. 1992. *Japanese Targeting*. New York: St. Martin's Press.

industrial regions　Japan has three major industrial regions. They are, in order of importance, the Tokyo-Yokohama area, Kansai area with Osaka as the center, and Central Japan with Nagoya as the center.

　　See **Nagoya and Central Japan, Kansai and Osaka, Tokyo, Yokohama**.

industrial relations
See **labor-management relations, labor unions**.

inhabitant tax　A type of local income tax levied by prefectural and municipal governments on individuals and corporations.

　　See **corporate taxes, individual income taxes, tax system**.

inheritance tax　A national tax imposed on the statutory heirs of inherited assets.

　　See **tax reform, tax system**.

insurance companies　Japan's insurance industry consists of life insurance companies and nonlife or casualty-liability insurance companies. They are regulated by the banking bureau of the **Ministry of Finance** in terms of entry into the market, product type, industrywide premiums, and dividend rates on policies.

　　Life insurance in Japan is concentrated in relatively few companies. In 1990 there were only 27 life insurance companies in Japan, whereas there were more than 2,000 in the United States. The assets as of March 31, 1992, of the top eight are given in table I.5, along with their premium income. In FY 1991 these eight companies had a combined market share of 70% in life insurance premium income and about 80% in assets.

　　Japanese life insurance companies grew very rapidly in the 1980s. Their total assets grew from ¥22.7 trillion on March 31, 1980, to ¥116.2 trillion at the end of FY 1989 and ¥130.3 trillion at the end of FY 1991 (Ministry of Finance). Several factors may account for their rapid growth: (1) Since the disposable incomes of Japanese households continued to increase in the 1980s, most households (92% in 1989) had some type of life insurance,

Table I.5
Leading life insurance companies (FY 1991; in ¥ trillions)

Company	Premium revenue	Total assets
Nippon Life Insurance	5.32	29.51
Dai-Ichi Mutual Life Insurance	3.84	20.62
Sumitomo Life Insurance	3.40	18.03
Meiji Mutual Life Insurance	2.41	12.42
Asahi Mutual Life Insurance	1.81	9.56
Mitsui Mutual Life Insurance	1.61	7.78
Yasuda Mutual Life Insurance	1.47	6.77
Chiyoda Mutual Life Insurance	0.96	5.62

Source: *The Nikkei Weekly,* June 20, 1992: 18.

with increasingly larger or multiple policies. (2) Since the interest rates were low in the second half of the 1980s, life insurance companies were able to siphon much in deposits from banks with high-yielding policies such as the popular single-premium endowment insurance. (3) Companies made intensive door-to-door sales efforts, employing more than 400,000 saleswomen. Utilizing personal connections and persistent persuasion, these "Life Insurance Ladies" have greatly promoted sales. This type of sales technique also makes it difficult for foreign insurance companies to enter the Japanese insurance market. (4) The elimination in 1988 of tax-exemption for small savers at banks and the post office (*maruyu*) increased the tax advantages of life insurance. Since dividends of interest for policies with terms of more than five years are still treated as temporary untaxable income, these policies give higher yields than other financial instruments.

In order to increase their investment incomes, life insurance companies have diversified their investment. Up to 1984 more than 50% of their funds were used as loans to corporations. Since then, that percentage has declined (36% in 1989); more funds have been invested in securities both in Japan and overseas. The companies have also invested in domestic and foreign real estate and in tie-ups with foreign (mainly European) financial institutions. With the depressed stock and property prices in 1991–92, the financial conditions of the companies have caused concern in Japan.

Casualty-liability insurance covers property insurance, automobile insurance, workers compensation, cargo insurance, and so forth. The industry is highly concentrated. In 1990 Japan had 22 companies compared with more than 3,500 in the United States. Their total assets amounted to ¥20 trillion in 1990. The largest five as of March 31, 1992, are Tokio Fire and Marine Insurance Co., Yasuda Fire and Marine Insurance Co., Mitsui Marine and

Fire Insurance Co., Sumitomo Marine and Fire Insurance Co., and Nippon Fire and Marine Insurance Co. They have a combined market share of 50%.

Most of the individual casualty-liability insurance policies have an attractive feature—premiums are invested and returned to policyholders when their policies mature. They combine, in effect, savings with insurance protection.

With its abundant funds for investment, the insurance industry would like to enter foreign exchange and corporate bond underwriting businesses, which are now the preserve of banks and the securities industry, respectively. This would entail relaxing the operating rules of the Insurance Business Law. Reportedly such changes are being considered by the Ministry of Finance, which is the regulatory authority of the industry.

The Ministry of Finance is also said to be considering a proposal to permit life and nonlife insurers to enter each other's business areas through the establishment of subsidiaries. The objective is to promote greater competition by merging the two sectors.

Foreign companies play a minor role in Japanese insurance industry. In both life and nonlife insurance, their share of the market is about 2–3%.

See also **financial liberalization.**

Addresses

Life Insurance Association of Japan
4-1, Marunouchi 3-chome, Chiyoda-ku, Tokyo 100
Tel: (03) 286-2624

Marine and Fire Insurance Association of Japan
9, Kanda Awajicho 2-chome, Chiyoda-ku, Tokyo 101
Tel: (03) 255-1211

Nippon Life Insurance Co.
1-1, Yuraku-cho 1-chome, Chiyoda-ku, Tokyo 100
Tel: (03) 3503-0311

References

Insurance. In *Japan Economic Almanac.* Various years. Tokyo: Nihon Keizai Shimbun.

Komiya, Ryutaro. 1990. *The Japanese Economy: Trade, Industry, and Government.* Tokyo: University of Tokyo Press. Ch. 6.

Life insurance companies. *Japan Economic Journal Special Survey: Tokyo Financial Markets,* summer 1989: 24–26.

Ministry of Finance. Annual. *The Insurance Yearbook.*

Mizuno, Yuko. 1990. Saleswomen strengthen position of insurers. *Japan Economic Journal*, May 19: 35.

Omori, Hiroko. 1991. Housewives challenged in insurance sales. *Nikkei Weekly*, Dec. 7: 15.

Ostrom, Douglas. 1992. Japan's sleeping insurance giants: Roused and ready? *JEI Report*, no. 17A, May 1.

Tatewaki, Kazuo. 1991. *Banking and Finance in Japan*. London: Routledge. Ch. 8.

intellectual property protection
See **patent system**.

interest rate structure   There are many types of interest rates in Japan. Interest rates used to be strickly regulated, but under the **financial liberalization policy**, some deregulation of interest rates has occurred. The most important types of interest rates are discussed below.

1. *Official discount rate.* This is the basic interest rate that the **Bank of Japan** charges commerical banks for its loans. Determined by the Policy Board of the Bank, it is an important policy instrument, for it affects other interest rates and the conditions of the financial markets. The discount rate has changed over time in terms of categories and percentage levels. Before 1972 there were several discount rates for different types of loans. They were generally in the 4.25–5.75% range; the rates were lowest (4.25% in early 1972) on commercial bills, on loans secured by government securities, and on export bills.

Since 1972 there are two types of discount rates: the discount rate on commercial bills and on loans secured by government bonds or specially designated securities, and the discount rate on loans secured by other assets. The latter is usually higher than the former. The discount rate on commercial bills rose from 4.25% in October 1972 to 9.0% in December 1973, and it declined steadily thereafter, remaining in the 4–6% range throughout the 1970s. With the exception of the relatively high rate in 1980 (8.25–9%) and the low rate in early 1987 (2.5%), it fluctuated in the low-level range of 3–6% throughout most of the 1980s and during 1990–91. Both discount rates are usually lower than those in other industrialized countries.

2. *Deposit rates.* All categories of banks as well as the **postal savings** system accept deposits. With the exception of rates on negotiable certificates of deposits (CDs), large time deposits, and foreign currency deposits, there are ceiling on deposit rates established by the **Ministry of Finance** in accordance with the Temporary Interest Rates Adjustment Law

of 1949. There are also guidelines on different types of deposits provided by the Bank of Japan, which are followed by financial institutions. Postal savings offer higher deposit rates, which are determined by the Ministry of Posts and Telecommunications. Deposit rates vary with the type of deposits and maturity period. A few deposit rates, as of December 1991, are

Commercial banks	Installment deposits	3.1% per annum
	Ordinary deposits & savings	1.5%
	Time deposits	6 months, 4.5%; 1 year 5.25%
Trust banks	Designated money in trust	1 year, 5.25%
		5 year, 5.9%
Postal savings	Fixed-sum deposit certificate (*teigaku chokin*)	Rises from 3.75% for less than 1 year to 4.25% for more than 1 year and 5.25% for more than 3 years
	Ordinary savings	2.88%
	Time savings	6 months, 4.5%
		1 year, 5.25%

3. *Lending rates. Short-term lending rates* on loans of less than one year in maturity are subject to ceilings set by the Ministry of Finance in accordance with the Temporary Interest Rates Adjustment Law of 1947. In addition the *short-term prime rate* (the interest rate that banks charge their most favored corporate clients on loans and discount of bills of high creditworthiness) serves as the lower limit for lending rates. Since 1975 short-term lending rates are determined by negotiations between banks and their customers; the upper limits, however, have varied with the official discount rate at the request of the Bank of Japan. The average short-term lending rate of all banks at year-end was 4.71% in 1978, 5.796% in 1985, and 8.022% in 1990, and 6.859% in 1991. Short-term prime rates were reformed in January 1989 to reflect market interest rate, that is, to be based on short-term money rates in the money market plus other fixed costs. However, changes in short-term prime rates tend to be announced by a price leader among the banks, invariably one of the large banks, and quickly followed by other banks, leading some analysts to suspect that the rates are really decided among bankers at behind-the-scene discussions.

Long-term lending rates are interest rates on loans of more than one year in maturity. They are not subject to ceiling regulations but are said to be tied to *long-term prime rates*, which are the lending rates charged by **long-term credit banks** and **trust banks** on long-term loans to highly credit-worthy corporations such as electric power companies. However, as Suzuki (1987: 147) notes, long-term prime rates have not always been the basic rate for long-term lending; since the mid-1980s both **city banks** and long-term credit banks have used lower rates for long-term lending. The average long-term lending rate of all banks at year-end was 7.589% in 1978, 7.282% in 1985, and 7.558% in 1990, and 6.971% in 1991. The long-term prime rate was between 7.0% and 7.7% in 1985, and between 6.8% and 8.9% in 1990. It declined below 8% in 1991. Since April 1991 some city banks have adopted a new formula for determining the long-term prime rate. It is calculated by adding to the short-term lending rate 0.3% for loans up to three years and 0.5% for loans of more than three years.

4. *Call rates.* These are the interest rates on call loans. The **call money market** is the central part of the short-term interbank **money markets** where banks with deficient funds borrow from banks with temporary surplus. The rate is determined by the market and has not been controlled by the Ministry of Finance or the Bank of Japan since 1979. However, it has had little influence on other interest rates. Since the 1950s different types of call rates have been introduced. The overnight call rate, averaging 8.034% in 1970 and 4.175% in 1979, was abolished in April 1979. The new collateralized overnight call rate averaged 7.457% in 1991. The noncollateralized overnight call rate averaged 3.669% in 1987 but rose to 7.525% in 1991. The seven-day call rate, abolished in November 1988, averaged 11.053% in 1980 and 3.825% in 1988.

For much of the postwar era, Japan's various interest rates are considered by most analysts to have been lower than their counterparts in the United States and Europe. This has led to the widespread belief that Japan has pursued a "low interest rate policy" in the postwar era and that this policy has greatly stimulated Japan's rapid economic growth. However, Horiuchi (1984) has argued that Japan's interest rates are not really low, and that they have been high enough to reflect the scarcity price of capital in Japan. In any case, because the rate of inflation since 1975 has been lower in Japan than in the United States, the Japan–U.S. differentials in real interest rates (net of inflation) are smaller than the differentials in nominal interest rates.

The actions of both the Bank of Japan and the Ministry of Finance affect interest rates—the former through the official discount rate and **money supply** and the latter through the deposit rate and lending rate ceilings. The two monetary authorities often have differing views on how interest rates should be changed.

Interest rates on negotiable certificate of deposits (CDs) and large time deposits are not regulated. However, the minimum amount for these deposits were initially set at very high level, beyond the reach of most individual depositors: ¥500 million for the former and ¥1 billion for the latter. As part of the **financial liberalization**, these minimum requirements have been successively lowered. In April 1988 the minimum amount for CDs was reduced to ¥100 million. The minimum amount for large time deposits was reduced in October 1989 to ¥10 million. In June 1993 the interest rates on bank time deposits were deregulated. The Ministry of Finance has announced that it will deregulate the interest rates on ordinary bank deposits by the spring of 1994. Western critics and many Japanese analysts have argued that this pace of liberalization is too slow.

See also **banking system, call money market, deposits system, financial liberalization, money markets, postal savings**.

References

Bank of Japan. 1993. *Economic Statistics Annual, 1992*.

Federation of Bankers Associations of Japan. 1989. *The Banking System in Japan*. Ch. 7.

Horiuchi, Akiyoshi. 1984. The "low interest rate policy" and economic growth in postwar Japan. *Developing Economies* 22: 349–71.

Isono, Naoyuki. 1991a. Long-term prime rise tempers relief from debt. *Japan Economic Journal*, Apr. 13: 31.

Isono, Naoyuki. 1991b. Yen jitters: World watches BOJ–MOF tussle. *Japan Economic Journal*, Apr. 21: 1.

Kester, W. Carl, and Timothy A. Luehrman. 1992. The myth of Japan's low-cost capital. *Harvard Business Review*, 30, 3: 130–38.

Suzuki, Yoshio, ed. 1987. *The Japanese Financial System*. Oxford: Oxford University Press. Ch. 4.

Tatewaki, Kazuo. 1991. *Banking and Finance in Japan*. London: Routledge. Ch. 3.

investment   Aggregate investment as a ratio of GNP was 32.3% in 1975, 32.1% in 1980, 28.1% in 1985, 32.6% in 1990, and 32.1% (¥146.9 trillion) in 1991. These are higher than those in the other industrial nations. Investment in the economy comprises housing investment, equipment investment, inventory investment, and general government investment. They are affected by different factors, but all fluctuate over time.

1. *Housing investment* in the form of new housing starts has experienced two long-term cycles in the postwar period. From a low level in the 1950s,

it rose steadily in the 1960s, reached a peak of 1,863,000 units in FY 1972, and then declined in the rest of the 1970s and the first half of the 1980s. After it bottomed at 1,135,000 units in 1983, it rose again. It peaked at 1,729,000 units in FY 1987, but remained at a high level of more than 1,660,000 units yearly during 1988–90. It declined to 1,370,000 units in 1991. Its value was ¥24.9 trillion.

There are three categories of new housing construction, namely rental housing, owner-occupied housing, and houses for sale in order of importance. The latest upswing in new housing starts began with a boom in the construction of rental housing in greater **Tokyo** in 1986, which was followed by a boom in Osaka and Nagoya. According to the Economic Planning Agency (1991: 48–49), all types of housing starts are inversely related to the level of interest rate and the price of land. In addition the amount of **savings** is positively correlated with owner-occupied housing starts; the number of marriages affects housing starts for owner-occupied housing and houses for sale, while the number of people in the 15–24 age bracket affects rental housing starts. The demand for building replacements also plays a role. In 1990 the size of housing stock was 43.6 million units and the average replaement period was 34 years, down from more than 40 years in the early 1980s.

2. *Equipment investment* is made for various reasons—for replacement, to save energy, to save labor, for expanded production and increased sales, for R&D, new products, and so on. Because the Japanese economy is becoming more service oriented, the rate of equipment investment is increasing faster in nonmanufacturing industries than in manufacturing industries. The Economic Planning Agency (1991: 66) has found that rate of increase in real equipment investment is closely correlated with the rate of return on assets over and above the rate of interest on loans. The value of equipment investment was ¥94.8 trillion in 1991.

3. *Inventory investment* in manufacturing and mining tends to fluctuate with **business cycles**. First, as the economy recovers from a business cycle, accumulated inventories will be reduced as shipments increase. Then, as production picks up during the economy's expansion, the decline in inventories will be halted, and inventories will be maintained at a suitable level. Finally, as the economy slows down in its expansion and eventually enters a recession, inventories will accumulate again. Overall, however, inventory investment is relatively small (¥3.2 trillion in 1991) and less important than housing investment and equipment investment in influencing the economy.

4. *General government investment* takes the form of infrastructural capital projects such as highways and airport construction. Hence it is determined by government policy objectives. As a percentage of aggregate investment in the economy, it was 16.8% in 1985, 16.6% in 1988, 15.5% in 1990, and 15.8% in 1991. The value was ¥21.5 trillion in 1990 and ¥23.1 trillion in 1991.

In terms of the origin of investment, nonfinancial corporations make the bulk of investment in the economy (68% in FY 1990), followed by the government (18.6%), households [10.3%), and financial institutions (2.5%). See also **savings**.

References

Balassa, Bela, and Marcus Noland. 1988. *Japan in the World Economy*. Washington: Institute for International Economics. Ch. 5.

Bank of Japan. 1993. *Economic Statistics Annual, 1992*.

Economic Planning Agency. 1991. *Economic Survey of Japan, 1990–1991*.

Economic Planning Agency. 1992. *Anual Report on National Accounts* (in Japanese).

Takenaka, Heizo. 1991. *Contemporary Japanese Economy and Economic Policy*. Ann Arbor: University of Michigan Press. Chs. 5–6.

investment advisory companies   Japan has some 138 licensed investment advisory companies or asset management companies and 596 registered investment advisory companies as of March 31, 1990. The licensed companies are licensed to manage clients' financial assets, to provide investment information, and to give investment advice, and so forth, for fees. Also called *securities investment advisers*, they differ from the securities investment trust management companies because they are not involved in **investment trusts** business.

Securities companies (through affiliated companies) and **trust banks** were first engaged in investment advisory business in the early 1960s. Life **insurance companies** followed quickly. Since the 1970s many independent investment advisory companies were founded in response to growing demand. In 1985 **city banks** started establishing affiliated investment advisory companies. In 1986 the Law Concerning Regulation of Investment Advisory Industries Related to Securities was legislated, providing a system of registration and disclosure.

Total contracted assets for the 138 investment advisory companies were nearly ¥30 trillion at the end of 1989. Affiliates of Japan's four leading securities companies dominate the industry, but bank affiliates have grown more rapidly in recent years. The top four companies and the amount of contract assets as of December 1989 are Nomura Investment Management (¥3.24 trillion), Daiwa International Capital Management (¥2.06 trillion), Nikko International Capital Management (¥1.81 trillion), and Yamaichi International Capital Management (¥1.68 trillion).

See also **investment trusts, securities companies**.

References

Big Four keep lead despite faster growth of bank affiliates. *Japan Economic Journal*, Mar. 31, 1990: 35.

Japan Securities Research Institute. 1992. *Securities Market in Japan*, 1992. Ch. 9.

Suzuki, Yoshio, ed. 1987. *The Japanese Financial System*. Oxford: Oxford University Press. Pp. 296–297.

investment trusts   Investment trusts are a special type of investment instrument whereby funds of the general investing public are channeled by investment management companies into trust funds for investment in securities. The system generally works as follows, although the details may vary with the type of trust: First, the "securities investment trust management company," or fund manager, who is the manager as well as owner of the trust, sells beneficiary certificates to the general public (the beneficiaries) who do not have large funds or knowledge to make their own investment. The funds thus collected are then entrusted through a trust contract to a trust bank (the trustee) as trust funds for investment in securities in accordance with the directions of the trust owner. They can be invested in stocks, **government bonds**, corporate bonds, and foreign securities. The trust owner will manage the payment of dividends and redemption of principal to the beneficiaries.

There are 15 securities investment trust management companies in Japan as of 1990—including Nomura Securities Investment Trust Manaagement Co. and Nikko Securities Investment Trust and Management Co.—all of which are affiliates of securities houses. When the system of securities investment trusts was first established under the Securities Investment Trust Law of 1951, the management operations for investment trusts were carried out by **securities companies**. In 1960 the management of trusts was separated from securities companies and assigned to independent securities investment trust management companies. These companies are licensed by the **Ministry of Finance** to meet certain requirements.

Investment trusts have always been viewed as a conservative savings instrument. Investors are said to have valued stability over the rate of return (Tomkin 1990). Although there are several types of investment trusts, the basic distinction is between the open-end trust fund and unit-type or closed-end trust fund. The latter was, until 1990, the more popular type, accounting for about 64% of the total as of December 1990, in which trust share is sold to investors at a fixed amount per share. Once the trust fund is established, no new principal can be added, and the funds can only be partially redeemed during the trust period, which can range from two to seven years. In the open-end trust the principal can be added whenever market conditions justify it, and the funds can be redeemed by investors at any time.

Trust management companies have traditionally preferred the closed-end trust funds because they provide a more stable fund to manage. However, with the **stock market** slump in 1990, investors saw the value of their shares plummet by nearly 30% in the closed-end funds. In 1991 the open-end funds became more popular than the closed-end ones. The Ministry of Finance allowed four foreign asset management firms to set up Japanese investment trust units. The purpose was to make the industry more competitive.

Table I.6
Size of investment trusts (in ¥ trillions)

Year	Stock investment trusts[a]		Bond investment trusts	
	Net increase[b]	Net assets[c]	Net increase[b]	Net assets[c]
1976	0.31	2.49	0.15	1.59
1980	−0.34	4.03	0.17	2.02
1985	2.18	10.38	−0.76	9.59
1986	7.09	19.12	3.27	12.96
1987	12.61	30.61	−0.45	12.30
1988	5.32	39.25	1.28	13.65
1989	2.21	45.55	−0.81	13.10
1990	0.24	35.07	−2.30	10.92
1991	−6.44	28.56	1.72	12.91
1992	−7.40	21.10	9.11	22.20

Source: Tokyo Stock Exchange.
a. Convertible bonds investment trusts are included in stock investment trusts.
b. Net increase is the difference between new issues and redemptions.
c. Net assets are year-end figures.

Table I.6 shows the size of stock investment trusts and bond investment trusts. The former is about three times as large as the latter in the late 1980s. The fall of the stock market in 1990–91 also reduced the total size of the investment trusts.

See also **Tokyo Stock Exchange.**

Addresses

Japan Investment Trusts Association
5-8, Nihonbashi, Kayabacho 1-chome, Chuo-ku, Tokyo 103
Tel: (03) 3667-7471

References

Japan Securities Research Institute. 1992. *Securities Market in Japan, 1992.* Ch. 8.

Koyanagi, Takehiko. 1990. Market forces loom for investment trusts. *Japan Economic Journal,* July 14: 31–32.

Tanabe, Noboru. 1992. Japan's investment trust: The current evolution and issues toward the future. In *Capital Markets and Financial Services in Japan.* Tokyo: Japan Securities Research Institute.

Tomkin, Robert. 1990. Fund managers to assume limelight as investment trusts take center stage. *Japan Economic Journal,* winter suppl.: 22.

Tokyo Stock Exchange. 1993. *Tokyo Stock Exchange Fact Book, 1993.*

Ishikawajima-Harima Heavy Industries   A comprehensive heavy machinery maker and Japan's second largest shipbuilder.

See **defense industry, shipbuilding industry**.

Itochu Corp.   One of Japan's largest general **trading companies** with strength in importing textiles. It is better known in the West by its English name, C. Itoch & Co., which was dropped in October 1992.

See **trading companies**.

Izanagi Boom   The 57-month economic expansion from October 1965 to July 1970 that set a postwar record.

See **business cycles**.

J

Japan Airlines Co. (JAL)   Japan's national flag carrier, privatized in 1987.
  See **airline industry**.

Japan Associated Finance Co.   Japan's largest venture capital company,
set up by Nomura Securities Co. in 1973 to finance start-up companies.
  See **venture capital industry**.

Japan Association of Corporate Executives (Keizai Doyukai)   A leading business organization.
  See **business organizations**.

Japan Chamber of Commerce and Industry (Nissho)   A leading business organization.
  See **business organizations**.

Japan Development Bank   Created in 1951, this is a major government
bank that is essential for the implementation of **industrial policy**. Its initial
capital of ¥10 billion came from the U.S. Aid Counterpart Fund—the yen
proceeds from the sale in Japan of U.S. aid products—provided by the
Supreme Command for the Allied Powers. Its objective is to provide long-
term equipment loans to private enterprises for economic reconstruction
and industrial development for which financing by private financial institutions is difficult.
  The banks's principal sources of funds are the capital subscription by the
Industrial Investment Special Account—a special government account established to succeed the Counterpart Fund for capital subscriptions of and
loans to government institutions—and borrowings from the government,
especially from the Trust Fund Bureau of the **Ministry of Finance**. Total
loans outstanding at year-end increased rapidly from ¥374 billion in 1955

to ¥3,341 billion in 1975, ¥7,609 billion in 1885, ¥10,007 billion in 1991, and ¥11,318 billion in 1992. The loans are extended mostly in the form of joint financing with private financial institutions. The amount of money it borrowed from the government was ¥8,434 billion at the end of 1991.

The bank is under the administrative jurisdiction of the Ministry of Finance. However, it has become a major policy instrument of the **Ministry of International Trade and Industry** (MITI) because of the latter's responsibility in assessing industry capital needs and in screening the bank's loan applications. For example, in the 1950s the bulk of the bank's loans went to MITI's designated strategic industries—electric power, shipping, coal, and steel. In the 1960s the bank also extended large "structural credit" loans to large companies that merged. Mergers were promoted by MITI in the mid-1960s as a way to achieve economies of scale, thereby cutting the prices of Japanese products and promoting export.

See also **government financial institutions, industrial policy**.

Address

Japan Development Bank
9-1, Otemachi 1-chome, Chiyoda-ku, Tokyo 100
Tel: (03) 3270-3211

References

Japan Development Bank. *Annual Report*. Various years.

Johnson, Chalmers. 1982. *MITI and the Japanese Miracle*. Stanford: Stanford University Press. Ch. 6.

Suzuki, Yoshio, ed. 1987. *The Japanese Financial System*. Oxford: Oxford University Press. Ch. 5.

Tatewaki, Kazuo. 1991. *Banking and Finance in Japan*. London: Routledge. Ch. 9.

Japan External Trade Organization (JETRO)   A public organization with branches abroad to promote trade with foreign countries.

See **business organizations**.

Japan National Railways (JNR)   Japan's former government-run railway system until it was privatized and broken up, in 1987, into six regional Japan Railway companies and one national freight company.

See **railway companies**.

Japan offshore market
See **Tokyo offshore market**.

Japan Railway Group (JR Group)   The group of six regional Japan Railway companies and a national freight company created through the privatization and breakup of the Japan National Railways in 1987.
See **railway companies**.

Japan Securities Finance Co.   The largest of three securities financing companies in Japan that specialize in the financing of securities.
See **securities finance compancies**.

JCB card   Japan's most popular credit card, issued by JCB Co, Japan's largest bank-affiliated credit card company.
See **credit card industry**.

Japan–U.S. economic relations
See **automobile industry, Beef-Citrus Quotas Agreement, direct overseas investment, foreign investment in Japan, Semiconductor Agreement, steel industry, Structural Impediments Initiative, trade pattern, trade policy, yen–dollar exchange rates**.

JTUC-Rengo   Japan Trade Union Confederation.
See **labor unions**.

just-in-time system   Also called the *Toyota production system*, or the *kanban* system, this is an inventory-control system developed by Toyota Motor Company in which materials and parts are produced and delivered just before they are needed. The objective is to minimize the level of inventories, especially when different models or parts are to be produced. Toyota Motor Company developed the system to coordinate in-plant activities between different processes of production and also to control the timing of deliveries made by subcontractors. The system is now widely used in Japan.

The system is commonly referred to as the *kanban* system in Japan because it relies on *kanban*, a type of production-ordering cards, in its implementation. Literally a "shop sign," a *kanban* card comes in the form of a small piece of paper in a square vinyl holder. It indicates the type and quantity of parts needed and the production process using them, and is attached to the container holding the parts. When the parts are assembled, the worker at the process returns the *kanban* to the preceding process to pick up a new batch of parts needed. The workers at the preceding process then produce and supply the amount of parts written on the just returned *kanban*. For the production-ordering *kanban* card to a subcontractor, delivery times, the store shelf to deliver, and the gate to receive, for example, are also specified. In this way the parts are produced or delivered "just in time" to eliminate or minimize inventories. The system has been characterized as a "pull" system because parts are pulled from parts fabrication into assembly just when they are needed in accordance with the latter's production schedule. By contrast, in the traditonal "push" system, parts are produced according to a separate schedule and pushed into inventories regardless of subsequent processing needs.

Initially introduced by Toyota in the early 1950s, the system spread throughout Japan in the 1970s. When Toyota set up plants overseas, the system was also introduced. In addition a growing number of Western firms have also adopted it. Newly industrializing countries such as South Korea and Taiwan began adopting the system in the late 1980s.

Starting in 1982, some Japanese companies have tried to extend the *kanban* system to production and marketing. The idea of the so-called New Production System (NPS) is to link production directly to sales at market outlets without the need for inventory. The rationale for this is the belief that, because of volatile consumer demand, companies need to produce more varieties of products in small quantities to meet current market demand, hence the need to base production on current sales data instead of market forecast. For the same reason mass production and distribution are inappropriate in many industries because they result in slow responses to changing market demand and expensive inventories.

To implement the new production system, Toyota Motor has completed an on-line computer system that links its production division to its nationwide dealership communications network in order to meet new orders quickly. Similarly Sekisui Chemical Co. and a growing number of other companies have set up a network to communicate directly with retail outlets in order to respond immediately to market changes.

One problem with the just-in-time system in the Japanese automobile industry in its relationship with subcontractors is that it requires frequent deliveries. This is said to have aggravated the labor shortage of some firms and to have contributed to air pollution and traffic jams. Accordingly the system is being reviewed by the industry.

In the United States where the JIT system has been adopted by many companies, it has not always worked smoothly. Zipkin (1991) states that it has strained some companies' supplier relations and that it has created stress among workers. The basic reason is that "JIT requires patient effort, persistence, and meticulous care on the factory floor," and such qualities are often in short supply.

See also **automobile industry, *kanban* system.**

References

Abegglen, James C., and George Stalk, Jr. 1985. *Kaisha: The Japanese Corporation.* New York: Basic Books. Ch. 5.

Alonso, Ramon L., and Cline W. Frasier. 1991. JIT hit home: A case study in reducing management delays. *Sloan Management Review* 32, 4: 59–67.

Black, J. T., ed. 1987. *JIT Factory Revolution.* Cambridge, MA: Productivity Press.

Cusumano, Michael A. 1985. *The Japanese Automobile Industry.* Cambridge: Harvard University Press. Pp. 275–305.

Karmarkar, Uday. 1989. Getting control of just-in-time. *Harvard Business Review* 67, 5: 122–31.

Monden, Ysuhiro. 1983. *Toyota Production System.* Atlanta: Industrial Engineering and Management Press.

NPS tries to improve on the just-in-time production system. *Tokyo Business Today,* Sept. 1989: 28–30.

Zipkin, Paul H. 1991. Does manufacturing need a JIT revolution? *Harvard Business Review* 69, 1: 40–50.

K

kaisha   The (Japanese) corporation.

See **corporate finance, corporate personnel practices, corporate taxes, decision making, *keiretsu* and business groups, labor-management relations, management practices.**

kanban **system**   One of the core techniques of the **just-in-time system**. The *kanban*, literally a "shop sign," is used here as an production order in the form of a small piece of paper in a square vinyl holder. The *kanban*, indicating the kind and quantity of parts, is attached to the container holding the parts. When the parts are assembled, the worker at the process returns the *kanban* to the preceding process to pick up the necessary amount of parts. The workers at the preceding process then produce and supply the amount of parts written on the just returned *kanban*. The idea of the system is that the parts are produced "just in time" to minimize the inventory level.

Toyota engineers have worked out the following *kanban* formula (Cusumano 1985: 292):

$$y = \frac{D(Tw + Tp)(1 + n)}{a},$$

where

y = the number of *kanban*,

D = demand (units per period),

Tw = waiting time for *kanban*,

Tp = processing time,

a = container capacity (not more than 10% of daily requirement),

n = policy variable (not more than 10% of daily requirement).

The Toyota Motor Company introduced the system in its production in the late 1960s. It has also used the system with its subcontractors or parts suppliers in ordering parts.

See also **just-in-time system.**

Address

Toyota Motor Corporation
1, Toyota-cho, Toyota City, Aichi Prefecture 471
Tel: (0565) 28-2121

References

Cusumano, Michael A. 1985. *The Japanese Automobile Industry.* Cambridge: Harvard University Press. Pp. 275–305.

Japan Management Association, ed. 1989. *Kanban: Just-in-Time at Toyota.* Trans. by David J. Lu. Cambridge, MA: Productivity Press.

Shingo, Shigeo. 1989. *A Study of the Toyota Production System from an Engineering Viewpoint.* Trans. by Andrew P. Dillon. Cambridge, MA: Productivity Press. Ch. 9.

Suzuki, Kioyoshi. 1987. *The New Manufacturing Challenge: Techniques for Continuous Improvement.* New York: Free Press. Pp. 146–168.

Kansai and Osaka   Literally "west of the pass," Kansai refers to the prosperous region in southwestern part of Honshu that encompasses seven prefectures (Hyogo, Kyoto, Mie, Nara, Osaka, Shiga, Wakayama) and that has Osaka as its principal city. The region also includes the port of Kobe and the ancient capital of Kyoto, but it is the city of Osaka that is the hub of the region. Kansai's gross regional product accounted for 19% of Japan's gross national product in FY 1985 and 18.2% in FY 1988.

Osaka is Japan's third largest city in terms of population. As of May 1992, it has 2.6 million people. Its daytime population, however, rises by 41% because many workers communte from the surrounding areas to Osaka to work. Osaka has Japan's second biggest stock market after **Tokyo**, is home to one of Japan's largest city banks (Sakura Bank, previously Mitsui Bank) and some of Japan's largest trading houses (Itochu Corp., Marubeni Corp., Nissho Iwai Corp., Sumitomo Corp.), and manufacturers (Matsushita Electric Industrial, Sanyo, Sharp, etc.). In FY 1975 it accounted for 10% of Japan's GNP, and in FY 1988, 8.5% (Tokyo's share was 17% and 18%, respectively). Among Japan's large cities, Osaka ranked first in 1990 in the production of chemicals and petroleum, a close second behind Tokyo in metals, and a close third behind Tokyo and **Yokohama** in the production of general machinery.

The Kansai region has become increasingly important since the late 1980s for two reasons. (1) Because the Tokyo area is already saturated and overcrowded, Kansai provides the major alternative, particularly to overseas companies, for expansion in Japan. (2) There are currently hundreds of development projects under construction in Kansai, providing much business opportunities.

Two large infrastructural projects are currently under way to help stimulate the economy of Kansai: the ¥2.1 trillion Kansai Internatinal Airport, scheduled to come into operation in 1994, and Kansai Science City, a satellite city to be built between Osaka, Kyoto, and Nara for high-tech research institutes, costing over ¥4 trillion. The latter will not be completed, however, until the beginning of the twenty-first century.

See also **Tokyo**.

Addresses

Kansai Committee for Economic Development
2-27, Nakanoshima 6-chome, Kita-ku, Osaka 530
Tel: (06) 441-1031

Kansai Economic Federation
2-27, Nakanoshima 6-chome, Kita-ku, Osaka 530
Tel: (06) 441-0101

Osaka Chamber of Commerce and Industry
2-8, Hommachibashi, Chuo-ku, Osaka
Tel: (06) 944-6484   Fax: (06) 944-6250

References

Kansai: New focus of international attention. *Tokyo Business Today*, Oct. 1991: 54–57.

Kansai: Second wind or second best? *The Economist*, June 20, 1987: 76–77.

Osaka: Searching for a new role. *Far Eastern Economic Review*, Aug. 18, 1988: 41–62.

Kanto   Japan's most industrialized region that includes Tokyo and six neighboring prefectures.

See **Tokyo, Yokohama**.

karoshi   Death from overwork, said to be more common in Japan than in other countries because of long working hours and stress.

See **working hours and stress**.

Kawasaki Heavy Industries   A large machinery producer and Japan's second largest defense contractor.
See **defense industry**.

Keidanren   Federation of Economic Organizations, Japan's most powerful business organization.
See **business organizations**.

keiretsu **and business groups**   Variously translated as business groups, corporate groups, enterprise groups, industrial groups, and supplier-manufacturer-distributor networks, *keiretsu* are groups of affiliated companies in related or unrelated fields that were formed in Japan in the postwar period. However, there is no consensus on the proper scope or exact meaning of the term. Originally it referred to groups of large firms organized around a bank, the so-called horizontal *keiretsu* or financial *keiretsu* (*kingyu keiretsu*). Subsequently it has been extended to hierachical or vertically related production groups (*sangyo keiretsu*), manufacturers-distributor groups or distribution *keiretsu* (*ryutsu keiretsu*), and even groups of parent company—subsidiaries that have capital ties but not business ties (*shihon keiretsu* or *Konzern*; Gerlach 1992a: 68–69). Thus the term has proliferated in common usage, but some scholars do not approve of such expanded usage because it weakens the meaningfulness of the term and insist that only the horizontal type or the vertical type of grouping is the legitimate or meaningful category of *keiretsu*. There is no consensus among scholars on this issue.

Whatever the proper scope of *keiretsu*, the following categories of business groups can be distinguished in Japan:

1. Six horizontal *keiretsu* or financial *keiretsu*. These are groups of affiliated companies loosely organized around a large city bank. These six can be further classified into two subcategories:

• Three groups—Mitsubishi, Mitsui, and Sumitomo Groups—are based on prewar **zaibatsu** (financial cliques) ties. These ex-*zaibatsu* groups consist of dozens of large corporations, along with a major **city bank** as the main bank and a giant general **trading company**, most of them using the same former *zaibatsu* name. The **Mitsubishi Group**, the largest and most cohesive of the three, contains 29 core companies that are closely associated as members of the Presidents' Club where company presidents meet regularly. The **Mitsui Group** and **Sumitomo Group** have 24 and 20 core companies in their respective Presidents' Club. All three groups have a much larger number of loosely affiliated companies.

• The other three groups are Fuyo, Sanwa, and Dai-Ichi Kangyo Groups. They contain a somewhat smaller number of member companies, but they also include a large city bank (Fuji, Sanwa, and Dai-Ichi Kangyo banks) and a general trading company (Marubeni, Nissho-Iwai, and Itochu). However, members of these groups do not have the prewar *zaibatsu* ties as those of the first type. In addition analysts feel that they are less cohesive and that their group relations are largely limited to bank-client relations with little interactions among nonfinancial members.

In these financial *keiretsu*, members of the groups are linked primarily by finances—by **cross shareholding** and bank loans from the group's main bank. Otherwise they are independent companies operating in diverse areas of business. However, since the financial power of the large corporations grew in the 1980s, the role of the main bank is no longer that important. The extent of cross shareholding has also declined. According to the Fair Trade Commission, the cross-shareholding ratio within a group averaged 21.64% in fiscal 1989, down from 25.5% in 1981 and 22.7% in 1987.

2. Vertical production *keiretsu* such as the Toyota Group and the NEC Group that consist of a core manufacturing company and its numerous subcontractors, subsidiaries, and affiliates, linked by manufacturer-supplier business relations, stockholdings, and personnel ties. For example, the Toyota Motor Co. is engaged primarily in automobile assembly and relies on numerous primary, secondary, and tertiary subcontractors for the supply of parts. Some 175 primary subcontractors are part of the Toyota Group, with substantial cross ownership within the group. Some 4,000 secondary subcontractors have looser affiliation with the group. Often the core companies of these groups are themselves members of other horizontal *keiretsu*. For example, Toyota is a member of the Mitsui Group, NEC is a member of the Sumitomo Group, and Nissan Motor is a member of the Fuyo Group.

3. In the electronics industry, vertical distribution *keiretsu* with a large number of affiliated retail shops ("*keiretsu* stores") formed by giant manufacturers in order to boost sales and maintain high prices. For example, Matsushita Electric has 25,000 *keiretsu* stores; Toshiba Corp. has 12,500, Hitachi has 10,000, and Sanyo Electric Co. has 6,000. However, these manufacturers also sell through other retailers such as consumer electronics stores, department stores, and chain stores. Some *keiretsu* stores have been dissovled because of low profitability.

4. Dozens of other groupings are based on the flow of capital from a parent company and not on manufacturer-supplier or distributor relationships.

Some of these consist of a big industrial corporation (Hitachi, Bridge-stone, Matsushita Electric, Toshiba, etc.) and its numberous subsidiaries. The core company of the group is usually the largest shareholder of the other group members. The Hitachi Group is the largest of such groups, comprising some 680 subsidiaries of Hitachi Ltd., which is Japan's largest comprehensive electric machinery manufacturer and its second largest industrial corporation after Toyota Motor Co. Hitachi Ltd. is reputed to hold more than 50% of the shares of the group's member companies, but otherwise group members are independent and do not have much intragroup business. Other groups do not have an industrial corporation as the core company. For example the Saison Group has the Seibu Department Store at the top, and include a supermarket chain, a consumer credit company, an insurance company, and a hotel chain. The Seibu Railway Group, a brother group to Saison, consists of a railway company at its core and diverse leisure businesses. The Tokyu Group also consists of a railway company and many other businesses (see **railway companies**).

5. Finally, there are diverse small-business groups and strategic alliances. In the former, small firms in local communities form producer and purchaser cooperatives, industrial estates, neighborhood associations, and so on, to collaborate with each other and to better compete with the larger firms. Strategic alliances are ad hoc cooperative groupings formed between large firms and small high-technology firms to utilize new technology for specific purposes such as joint ventures, project consortia, and other forms of cooperation (Gerlach 1992a: 69).

Horizontal *keiretsu* have been of particular interest to scholars because they include many of Japan's largest and most prestigeous corporations. In addition, unlike vertical *keiretsu*, they are not based on, or justified by, direct production or distrubtion relationships. Yet in a broad business context they are said to yield business benefits to group members. These may include information exchange, lower transaction costs, sharing the expertise of other member firms, and lower costs of funds from the group bank. Nakatani (1984) emphasizes the benefit of risk sharing in a group. Imai (1990, 1992) also argues that business groups, seen as "corporate networks," reduce risk and facilitate information exchange for innovation and investment, which the market alone cannot provide. Similarly Kester (1991: 13) contends that Japanese companies in *keiretsu* groups enjoy the "best of both worlds" because they have the incentives of the market and the benefits of selective market intervention by large banks, trading companies, and other stable shareholders.

However, the benefits of being a *keiretsu* member are by no means guaranteed. Caves and Uekusa (1976) suggest that the group bank might have exploited its privileged position as a stockholder. But this is unlikely to be the case any more because the financial power of big corporations has grown since the late 1970s. There is also evidence that *keiretsu* firms are not necessarily more profitable than non-*keiretsu* firms (Nakatani 1984). In recent years *keiretsu* stores in the electronics industry have not been doing very well because discount stores offer lower prices. Some observers suggest that electronics manufacturers have engaged in price fixing with their *keiretsu* stores, which is a violation of Japan's **Antimonopoly Law**.

Washington believes that *keiretsu* are unfairly closed to foreign companies, thereby keeping Japanese industries and market impenetrable by foreign companies. U.S. trade negotiators therefore have made *keiretsu* a central issue in the U.S.–Japan **Structural Impediments Initiative** talks in 1989–90 and in their subsequent follow-up meetings. Washington's demand is that intra-*keiretsu* dealings should be made more "transparent" and less exclusionary. As part of the agreement resulting from the talks, the **Ministry of Finance** issued in late 1990 a ruling requiring *keiretsu* members to disclose more about transactions within the group. Also investors have to report holdings of 5% or more in a company.

Lending support to Washington's position, Lawrence (1991) contends that the level of manufactured imports tends to be lower in sectors of the Japanese economy in which *keiretsu*-related firms are dominant. He also argues that the horizontal keiretsu are more exclusionary; the vertical ones may be exclusionary, but they also enhance efficiency. However, the validity of his methodology is challenged by Saxonhouse (1991). Gerlach (1992b) concludes, after a comprehensive survey of the literature, that the criticism of *keiretsu* as a closed trading system underestimates its significance and viability in the Japanese economy.

Many Japanese scholars and officials, in responding to American criticisms of *keiretsu*, have reiterated the benefits of *keiretsu* in the Japanese economy, as mentioned above. In addition some of them have discussed the issue of the alleged *keiretsu* exclusivity. The discussions include three major points:

1. The horizontal *keiretsu* are only loosely organized and do not make decisions for their members. For this reason Ken-ichi Imai of the Stanford Japan Center has suggested to Japan's business leaders that the Presidents' Clubs of the three *keiretsu* based on ex-*zaibatsu* ties be dissolved to avoid foreign misunderstanding (author's interview, July 8, 1992). Furthermore

the intragroup transactions of the horizontal *keiretsu* are not inordinately high and have been declining. For example, the Fair Trade Commission reported in early 1992 its investigative finding that horizontal *keiretsu* are no more prone to conduct intragroup business than to deal with outsiders. In FY 1990 sales generated by intra-*keiretsu* businesses, excluding financial institutions, constituted only 7.28% of the aggregate sales of member companies, down from 10.8% in 1981. Intragroup procurement as a percentage of the aggregate purchases was 5.1% in FY 1990 as compared with 8.1% in FY 1981 (*Nikkei Weekly*, Mar. 7, 1992: 4).

2. It is recognized that vertical *keiretsu* involving subcontracting tend to be closed to outsiders, although such subcontracting relations are economically efficient. In this trade-off between efficiency and openness, Masu Uekusa of Tokyo University is willing to sacrifice some efficiency in order to have more openness and harmonious relations with foreigners. He has even suggested to the **Ministry of International Trade and Industry** that regional distribution centers be built in Japan for foreign parts-producers so that they can supply Japanese manufacturers expeditiously (author's interview, July 13, 1992).

3. It is admitted that distribution *keiretsu* would have violated the Anti-monopoly Law if the manufacturers set and enforced high retail prices for the *keiretsu* stores. In any case, it is agreed that the distribution *keiretsu* should be made more open.

See also **corporate finance, cross shareholding, Mitsubishi Group, Mitsui Group, Structural Impediments Initiatives, Sumitomo Group, zaibatsu**.

References

Caves, Richard, and Masu Uekusa. 1976. Industrial organization. In *Asia's New Giant*, ed. by Hugh Patrick and Henry Rosovsky. Washington: Brookings Institution.

Gerlach, Michael L. 1992a. *Alliance Capitalism: The Social Organization of Japanese Business*. Berkeley: University of California Press.

Gerlach, Michael L. 1992b. Twilight of the *keiretsu*? A critical assessment. *Journal of Japanese Studies* 18, 1: 78–118.

Hoshi, T., A. Kashyap, and D. Scharfstein. 1991. Corporate structure, liquidity, and investment: Evidence from Japanese industrial groups. *Quarterly Journal of Economics*, 106: 33–60.

Imai, Ken-ich. 1990. Japanese business groups and the Structural Impediments Initiative. In *Japan's Economic Structure: Should It Change?* ed. by Kozo Yamamura. Seattle: Society for Japanese Studies.

Imai, Ken-ich. 1992. Japan's corporate networks. In *The Political Economy of Japan*, vol. 3: *Cultural and Social Dynamics*, ed. by Shumpei Kumon and Henry Rosovsky. Stanford: Stanford University Press.

Keiretsu: What they are doing, where they are heading. *Tokyo Business Today*, Sept. 1990: 26–36.

Kester, W. Carl. 1991. *Japanese Takeovers: The Global Contest for Corporate Control*. Boston: Harvard Business School Press. Chs. 3, 8.

Lawrence, Robert Z. 1991. Efficient or exclusionist: The import behavior of Japanese corporate groups. *Brookings Papers on Economic Activity*, no. 1: 311–30.

Nakatani, Iwao. 1984. The economic role of financial corporate grouping. In *The Economic Analysis of the Japanese Firm*, ed. by Masahiko Aoki. Amsterdam: North-Holland.

Odagiri, Hiroyuki. 1992. *Growth through Competition, Competition through Growth*. Oxford: Clarendon. Ch. 7.

Sakai, Kuniyasu. 1990. The feudal world of Japanese manufacturing. *Harvard Business Review* 68, 6: 38–49.

Saxonhouse, Gary R. 1991. Efficient or exclusionist: The import behavior of Japanese corporate groups. Comments and discussion. *Broomings Papers on Economic Activity*, no. 1: 331–36.

Uekusa, Masu. 1990. Government regulations in Japan: Toward their international harmonization and integration. In *Japan's Economic Structure: Should It Change?* ed. by Kozo Yamamura. Seattle: Society for Japanese Studies.

Keizai Doyukai   Japan Association of Corporate Executives, a leading business organization.
See **business organizations**.

kenko hoken   Health insurance plans for company employees and day laborers.
See **health insurance**.

Kenshinren   The prefectural-level credit federations of agricultural cooperatives.
See **agricultural cooperatives**.

Kinki Nippon Railway Co.   The largest private railway company in Japan and the core company of the Kintetsu Group.
See **railway companies**.

Kintetsu Group   A business group consisting of Kinki Nippon Railway Co. and its more than 160 subsidiaries, including the Kintetsu Department Store.
See **railway companies**.

kinyu keiretsu Financial *keiretsu*, the six bank-centered business groups (Mitsubishi, Mitsui, Sumitomo, Fuyo, Sanwa, and Dai-Ichi Kangyo).
See ***keiretsu* and business groups**.

kokumin kenko hoken National health insurance.
See **health insurance**.

kokumin nenkin National pension that covers the self-employed and other people.
See **pension system**.

Korean residents The largest group of "foreign" residents born and/or raised in Japan, who are said to face employment and social discrimination.
See **employment discrimination**.

kosei nenkin Employees' pension insurance, which covers most salaried workers of private companies.
See **pension system**.

kyosai nenkin Mutual aid associations pensions, which cover employees of the national government, local governments, private schools, and cooperative associations.
See **pension system**.

kyosairen The 47 prefectural insurance cooperatives.
See **agricultural cooperatives**.

L

labor credit associations   Cooperative-type financial institutions to serve labor unions, consumer cooperatives, and so on.
See **banking system**.

labor disputes
See **labor-management relations**.

labor force   Japan's labor force is a well trained and motivated work force and arguably the mainspring of Japan's economic growth. Because of continuous economic and social development, particularly in the 1980s, it has also undergone significant changes.

Of Japan's total **population** of 123.6 million in 1990, 100.9 million were 15 years old and over. Of this number 63.8 million were in the labor force—employed or actively seeking employment—giving Japan a labor force participation rate of 63.3%. Of this labor force 62.5 million were employed and 1.3 million unemployed, giving an unempoyment rate of 2.1% of the labor force, which is among the lowest in the world (see table L.1). Employed workers are further classified into self-employed workers, family workers, and employees. Employees include regular employees and nonregular employees (part-timers and temporary workers).

Labor force participation rate has declined in the postwar period, reflecting mainly the longer schooling years of the young people. It was 69.2% in 1960 and is projected to reach 62.5% in 2,000. Of Japan's labor force women constituted 31.8% in 1965, 34.1% in 1980, and 39.9% in 1990. However, female labor force participation rate has been much lower than that of men. The rate was 54.5% and 84.8% for women and men, respectively, in 1960. It declined to a postwar low in 1975 for both sexes before it gradually increased again for women. It was 50.1% and 77.2% for women and men, respectively, in 1990.

Table L.1
Population, labor force, and employment (in millions)

Year	Total population	Aged 15 and over	Labor force	Employed	Unemployment rate (%)
1965	98.3	72.9	47.9	47.3	1.2
1975	111.9	84.7	53.4	52.4	1.9
1980	117.1	89.6	56.7	55.5	1.7%
1985	121.0	94.7	59.6	58.1	2.6
1986	121.7	95.9	60.2	58.5	2.8
1987	122.3	97.2	60.8	59.1	2.8
1988	122.8	98.5	61.7	60.1	2.5
1989	123.3	99.7	62.7	61.3	2.3
1990	123.6	100.9	63.8	62.5	2.1
1991	124.0	102.0	65.1	63.7	2.1

Source: Ministry of Labor.

Partly because of the increasing number of **women in the labor force**, the number of part-time workers—nonagricultural workers who work less than 35 hours a week—in the labor force has increased, from 0.7 million in 1975 to 2.3 million in 1985 and 5.1 million in 1990. Although this represented less than 8% of the total labor force in 1990, part-time workers constituted a sizable percentage of employees in specific industries, such as wholesale and retail trade (18.1% in 1990) and manufacturing (10.1% in 1990). As of February 1990, 27.2% of women workers were part-timers, whereas the figure was only 9% for male workers. Compared with other industrial nations, however, these figure are still relatively low.

The average educational background of the labor force is high and is becoming higher as more graduates of junior colleges and universities enter the labor market. As shown in table L.2, the number of labor market entrants with only lower secondary-shool education decreased dramatically in the early 1970s, whereas the number of entrants with junior college and university education has increased steadily.

Because of the relatively slow growth of the population and of the labor force in comparison with the rate of economic growth and job expansion, a labor shortage occurred in the 1980s, which was particularly acute in the late 1980s and in 1990. This can be seen in the job openings/applications ratio for various age categories. For example, for employees aged 19 or under, the ratio was 1.6 in 1965, 2.6 in 1980, 3.6 in 1989, and 4.3 in 1990. For those aged 30 to 34, it was 0.6 in 1965, 0.9 in 1980, 2.5 in 1989, and 2.6 in 1990. In other words, for both unskilled and skilled or experienced

Table L.2
Educational level of labor market entrants (in 1,000 persons)

Year	Lower secondary	Upper secondary	Junior college	University
1965	549	690	35	135
1975	63	577	103	233
1980	44	581	129	285
1985	50	547	141	288
1986	48	622	140	292
1987	46	589	133	295
1988	45	578	161	298
1989	43	591	174	300
1990	40	608	181	324
1991	36	607	188	348

Source: Ministry of Education.

labor, a severe labor shortage existed in the late 1980s and 1990. The shortage eased, however, in 1991–92 because of the recession in the economy.

Partly as a result of the labor shortage, the number of **foreign workers** has also grown. The number of legally employed foreigners remains very small—20,500 in 1984, 36,300 in 1987, and 49,400 in 1989—because of a strict immigration policy. These foreign workers constituted merely 0.8% of the labor force in 1989. However, the number of illegally employed foreign workers in Japan is estimated to be 292,791 as of November 1992, although no accurate statistics exist.

The percentage of the labor force that is unionized has declined from a postwar peak of 46.2% in 1950 to 30.8% in 1980 and 24.5% in 1991 (see table L.4, **labor unions**). This is the result of the relative decline of the traditional manufacturing sector and the rise of the nonunionized service and high-technology sectors, the increase of part-time workers in the labor force, and other factors.

See also **employment pattern, foreign workers in Japan, labor unions, unemployment, women in labor force.**

Addresses

Japan Institute of Labor
7-6 Shibakoen 1-chome, Minato-ku, Tokyo 105
Tel: (03) 5470-4065

Ministry of Labor
2-2, Kasumigasek 1-chome, Chiyoda-ku, Tokyo 100
Tel: (03) 3593-1211

References

Hashimoto, Masanori. 1990. *The Japanese Labor Market in a Comparative Perspective with the United States*. Kalamazoo, MI: W.E. Upjohn Institute for Employment Research.

Japan Institute of Labor. 1991. *Japanese Working Life Profile*.

Management and Coordination Agency. Annual. *Labor Force Survey*.

Ministry of Labor. 1992. *Labour Administration*. Tokyo: Japan Institute of Labor.

labor laws A number of labor laws were enacted in 1945–48 by the Supreme Commander of the Allied Powers (SCAP) in an attempt to improve workers' welfare and to democratize the Japanese society. The most important of them were the Trade Union Law (1945), the Labor Relations Adjustment Law (1946), and the Labor Standards Law (1947).

The Trade Union Law was modeled on the American Wagner Act. It gave workers, with the exception of cetain classes of public servants, the right to organize, to bargain collectively, and to strike. It also provided, along with the Labor Relations Adjustment Law, for the establishment of the machinery for bargaining. A National Labor Relations Board and 46 prefectural boards, consisting of equal numbers of workers, employers, and public representatives, were set up with the power to mediate and arbitrate in industrial disputes.

The Labor Standards Law was based essentially on International Labor Organization conventions and was introduced to protect workers. It set up legal minimums for working conditions and terms of work. It laid down maximum hours (8 hours per day and 48 hours per week), minimum holidays, overtime provisions, and so on, and had protective provisions for women and children. It also dealt with such matters as unemployment insurance, workers' compensation, and old age social security programs. To implement these laws, the Ministry of Labor was set up in 1947. As a result of these laws, union membership increased rapidly from zero in 1945 to more than 6 million in 1948.

Employees in public corporations are governed by Public Corporation and National Enterprise Labor Relations Law enacted in 1948. They are allowed to bargain collectively but are prohibited from striking. Civil service trade unions are governed by the National Public Service Law.

In the 1980s, as the Japanese economy prospered and trade surplus developed and persisted, Japanese workers' long working hours and few vacation days were criticized by foreigners as having contributed to Japan's alleged "oversaving" and "underconsumption," including the the underconsumption of imports. Partly as a response to foreign criticism, the Labor Standards Law was revised in 1988 to help introduce a shorter 40-hour work week and to ensure that employees take all the holidays that they are entitled to. Japanese employees customarily take less vacation days than they are entitled to in compliance with the social pressure that equates it with dedication to one's company. The new law also makes the normal working hours more flexible.

See also **Equal Employment Opportunities Law**.

References

Gould, William B. 1984. *Japan's Reshaping of American Labor Law*. Cambridge: MIT Press.

Saso, Mary. 1990. *Women in the Japanese Workplace*. London: Hilary Shipman.

Sugeno, Kazuo. 1992. *Japanese Labor Law*, trans. by Leo Kanowitz. Tokyo: University of Tokyo Press.

Woodiwiss, Anthony. 1992. *Law, Labour, and Society in Japan*. London: Routledge.

labor-management relations   The right to organize, to bargain collectively, and to strike is provided by Japan's **labor laws** for private-sector employees. Labor-mangement relations in Japan, however, is generally characterized by cooperation, not confrontation, since the early 1970s.

Labor-management relations in postwar Japan have gone through two period of changes. In the 1950s–1960s period radical unionism emerged, and there were cases of serious labor disputes. Strikes were staged at a number of large enterprises such as Nissan Motor, Omi Henshi, Amagasaki Seiko-sho, Japan Steel Works, Oji Paper Co., and Mitsui Mining Co., with disruptive consequences. Toward the end of the period, however, both labor and management realized the futility of confrontation and the number of labor disputes gradually decreased. In the second period since the first oil crisis, the number of labor disputes decreased steadily, and labor-management relations have been generally cooperative and harmonious.

This cooperative labor-management relations can be seen in a number of ways. Annual wage increases, for example, are determined in an institutionalized bargaining process called the **spring offensive** (*shunto*) with reasonable outcomes and without serious work stoppage. Table L.3 compares labor disputes in Japan, the United States, Germany, and Britain in terms of workdays lost due to labor disputes. It is clear that Japan and Germany have very low numbers compared with those of the United States and Britain. The United States has a labor force nearly twice as large as that of

Table L.3
Workdays lost due to labor disputes (in 1,000 days)

Year	Japan	United States	Germany, FR	Britain
1978	1,353	23,774	4,281	9,405
1980	1,001	20,844	128	11,964
1982	538	9,061	15	5,313
1984	354	8,499	5,618	27,135
1986	253	11,861	28	1,920
1988	174	4,364	42	3,702
1989	220	16,996	100	4,128
1990	145	5,926	364	1,890
1991	96	4,584	—	—

Source: International Labor Organization.

Japan, but the number of workdays lost in 1989 was more than 77 times as large. Britain has a labor force that is slightly less than half that of Japan, but its workdays lost in 1989 was nearly 19 times that of Japan. In terms of the number of workers involved in labor disputes (not shown in the table), Japan and Germany again have much lower numbers, although the number for Germany fluctuated much more every few years.

The rate of unionization among workers declined in Japan in the 1970s and 1980s due to the decline of traditional industries with heavy unionization and the increased use of nonunionized temporary and part-time workers in the economy. This may have contributed to the low incidences of labor dispute in Japan, but most analysts attribute Japan industrial peace to more fundamental reasons. A widely accepted thesis is that of the "company community"—that the company in Japan is a community with which all employees identify and in which they have important stakes in terms of profit sharing (bonuses), job security, and participation in **decision making** (Abegglen and Stalk 1985; Dore 1987; Ozaki 1991). Or as Shimada (1992) puts it, both Japanese management and unions operate within the same "industrial culture." Workers are not treated as hired labor, bought and sold in the corporate labor market, and the company is not the property of the stockholders to be bought or sold as they wish. Thus the Japanese corporate model differs fundamentally from the Western neoclassical model of the firm (Aoki 1988), which originated in nineteenth-century Britain and is still practiced and taught there as well as in the United States. Interestingly Dore (1989), Thurow (1992: 32–39), and others have also pointed out that the German company approximates the community model but not the Anglo-Saxon neoclassical model, and that it is no coincidence that Japanese and German companies are more successful than American and British ones.

In Japan the sense of corporate community on the part of workers is strengthened by the fact that there are no marked differences between blue-collar and white-collar workers within a company; both belong to the same enterprise union, and income differentials between top executives and the rank and file workers are relatively small (see **income distribution**). Workers are trained by the companies to acquire wide-ranging skills, which further blurs the distinction between blue-collar and white-collar workers. All these constitute what Koike (1988) calls the "white-collarization" of workers. Workers' sense of participation is enhanced by such widespread practices as workers' participation in **quality control** circles for product improvement, joint labor-management consultation system concerning various aspects of work, and complaint settlement system to adjudicate workers' grievances. In all of these practices the Japanese respect for consensus ensures that workers' views are taken seriously.

In the public sector, civil servants at the national and local levels do not have the right to bargain over pay or to strike. The National Personnel Authority and the local personnel commissions make recommendations to the government on pay adjustments for civil servants on the basis of wage conditions in the private sector; the government may revise it, depending on the budget conditions. Employees of public corporations and national enterprises have the right to bargain collectively but not to strike. The right to bargain collectively is considered by Shirai (1987) to be meaningless because public corporations and national enterprises are not in a position to negotiate pay increases with unions since their budgets are controlled by the **Ministry of Finance**. Ultimately therefore it is up to the National Enterprise and Public Labor Relations Commission to mediate between the employees and the management and establish a compulsory arbitration for implementation, subject to legislative approval.

See also **corporate personnel practices, decision making, labor laws, labor unions, quality control, spring offensive**.

References

Abegglen, James C., and George Stalk, Jr. 1985. *Kaisha: The Japanese Corporation*. New York: Basic Books.

Aoki, Masahiko. 1988. *Information, Incentives, and Bargaining in the Japanese Economy*. Cambridge: Cambridge University Press.

Dore, Ronald. 1987. *Taking Japan Seriously*. Stanford: Stanford University Press.

Dore, Ronald. 1989. "Liberalization" not necessarily "Americanization." *Japan Economic Journal*, Nov. 4: 9.

Inagami, Takeshi. 1988. *Japanese Workplace Industrial Relations*. Tokyo: Japan Institute of Labor.

International Labor Organization. Annual. *Yearbook of Labour Statistics*.

Kinzley, W. Dean. 1991. *Industrial Harmony in Modern Japan*. London: Routledge.

Koike, Kazuo. 1988. *Understanding Industrial Relations in Modern Japan*, trans. by Mary Saso. London: Macmillan.

Kuwahara, Yasuo. 1989. *Industrial Relations System in Japan*. Tokyo: Japan Institute of Labor.

Ozaki, Robert. 1991. *Human Capitalism*. New York: Penguin.

Shimada, Haruo. 1992. Japan's industrial culture and labor management relations. In *The Political Economy of Japan*, vol. 3: *Cultural and Social Dynamics*, ed. by Shumpei Kumon and Henry Rosovsky. Stanford: Stanford University Press.

Shirai, Taishiro. 1987. Recent trends in collective bargaining in Japan. In *Collective Bargaining in Industrialized Market Economies: A Reappraisal*. Geneva: International Labor Office.

Sumiya, Mikio. 1990. *The Japanese Industrial Relations Reconsidered*. Tokyo: Japan Institute of Labor.

Thurow, Lester. 1992. *Head to Head*. New York: William Morrow.

labor productivity
See **corporate personnel practices, working hours and stress**.

labor unions   There were 33,271 labor unions (or 72,202 basic union units) in Japan in 1990, of which about 95% were enterprise unions, 2% crafts unions, and 1.6% industrial unions. An enterprise union is organized on the basis of an enterprise or workplace rather than a trade or an industry. It includes all regular employees in the enterprise, both blue- and white-collar workers, as its members. Thus line managers, supervisors, and junior management personnel are included. Gould (1984: 5) contends that this has affected the style and attitude of unions in Japan by "inhibiting militance, providing expertise, and creating more contact and perhaps some egalitarianism between blue-collar and white-collar employees." Temporary workers and subcontract workers, however, are not included.

Japanese unions play an active role in matters of direct concern to workers such as wage increases, employee benefits, and working conditions. In addition enterprise unionism is said to have various advantages over trade unionism, which is typical in the West. One advantage is that there are no jurisdictional disputes concerning union jobs in enterprise unions. This permits flexibility in in-company training and job assignment and is conducive to greater labor productivity. Under enterprise unions, **labor-management relations** have been remarkably cooperative except for the early postwar period. Labor disputes and union strikes have been more serious in the public sector.

Enterprise unions are usually members of a union federation that covers one or more industries. Until late 1987 labor unions were led by four major federations: Sohyo (the General Council of Trade Unions of Japan), the largest, which included government employees; Rengo, the association of private-sector unions; Domei (the Japanese Confederation of Labor), a right-wing splinter of Sohyo, and Churitsu Roren (the Federation of Independent Unions). In November 1987 a new labor federation, the Japan Trade Union Confederation (JTUC-Rengo), or the new Rengo, was founded by the private sector unions. It became the largest federation in Japan with 5.55 million members drawn from a number of other federations, and Domei and Churitsu Roren voluntarily disbanded. In 1989 Sohyo dissolved itself and merged with the new Rengo, boosting membership in the latter to over 8 million workers, or 65% of Japan's organized labor. For the first time in Japan, both public and private sector unions are under the same national leadership.

Neither the union federations before 1987 nor the new Rengo since 1987 took part in collective bargaining with employers. It is the enterprise unions themselves that negotiate with the management of their firms in the annual **spring offensive**. Rengo, however, serves as the voice for unions in general and publicizes unions' general demands concerning wages and other working condtions. It also represents labor's interests vis-à-vis government ministries and business organizations.

Union membership has increased only very slowly since the 1960s, from 10.1 million in 1965 to 12.6 million in 1975. Since then it has declined slightly to 12.4 million in 1991. As a percentage of the labor force, the unionization rate declined from 35.4% in 1970 to slightly less than 30% in 1983 and 24.5% in 1991 (see table L.4).

The major reason for the declining unionization rate is the sectoral shift of employment in the economy—from the more highly unionized manufacturing, transportation, and communication to the lowly unionized wholesale and retail trade and services. In particular, the decline in employment in steel, shipbuilding, and electrical machinery industries has eroded the traditional center of union strength. Retail and service businesses tend to be small establishments that are difficult to organize, and they employ many part-time and temporary workers who do not see benefits in union membership.

Table L.4
Union membership and unionization rate

Year	Membership (in millions)	Unionization rate (in %)
1965	10.1	34.8
1970	11.6	35.4
1975	12.6	33.7
1980	12.4	30.8
1983	12.5	29.7
1985	12.4	28.9
1988	12.2	26.8
1989	12.2	25.9
1990	12.3	25.2
1991	12.4	24.5

Source: Ministry of Labor.

Table L.5
Unionization rate by industry (in %)

Industry	1980	1990
Agriculture, forestry, fishery, and mining	30.3	15.0
Construction	16.5	17.1
Manufacturing	35.3	30.1
Electricity, gas, heat supply, and water	80.1	70.7
Transportation and communication	62.3	48.3
Wholesale and retail trade, eating and drinking places	9.4	9.0
Finance, insurance, real estate	56.1	49.7
Service	21.0	14.8
Public service	74.6	74.9

Source: Japan Institute of Labor.

The erosion of union strength, however, is evident in virtually all sectors of the economy. As shown in table L.5, with the exception of construction and public service, the unionization rate has declined in all other sectors between 1980 and 1990. The decline was particularly large in the service sector, from 21.0% to 14.8%, as employment in the sector expanded rapidly in the 1980s to reach 23.4% of total employment in the economy in 1990. It is interesting to note that public service has become the most highly unionized sector of the economy just as privatization of some public companies took place in the 1980s.

In addition to the sectoral shift in employment, other factors have contributed to the decline of the unions. The slower growth of the economy in the 1970s and early 1980s and the yen appreciation in the 1980s have forced companies to eliminate excess workers, resist large wage increases and unionism, and move labor-intensive production to cheap-labor countries. These changes have reduced the unions' wage bargaining power for the workers and hence the benefits of union membership. The increase in the labor force of part-time workers who are not unionized also contributes to the lower unionization rate. Finally, the JTUC-Rengo leadership itself acknowledges that traditional union activities—which are characterized as "top-down" in organizational method and "fighting spirit" oriented in work style—no longer appeal to today's young workers (author's interview, JTUC-Rengo, July 9, 1991).

In response to these socioeconomic changes, union federations were consolidated into the new Rengo in 1987, as mentioned above. The JYUC-Rengo has announced a goal of restoring the union membership rate to 30% of the labor force. In addition to improving wages and working conditions, it has included improvements in the quality of life—such as working hours, child care, housing conditions, and social security—as its goals.

Although there is a growing number of **foreign workers in Japan**, they are rarely in the unions. Legal foreign workers are mostly specialists who do not see the need for union membership. Illegal foreign workers are not willing to be organized for fear of exposure.

In the literature on the union movement in Japan, enterprise unionism is generally credited with having contributed to postwar corporate growth and the improvement of the working conditions and living standards of company employees. Kawanishi (1992) surveys various Japanese authors' theories of enterprise unions and raises some questions about the validity of the theories by presenting his own case studies.

See also **labor-management relations, labor laws, spring offensive**.

Address

Japan Trade Union Confederation
1-10-3 Mita Minato-ku, Tokyo 108
Tel: (03) 3456-3061

References

Freeman, R. B., and M. E. Rebick. 1989. Crumbling pillar? Declining union density in Japan. *Journal of Japanese and International Economics* 3: 578–605.

Gould, William B. 1984. *Japan's Reshaping of American Labor Law*. Cambridge: MIT Press.

Japan's labor unions work to meet new challenges. *JEI Report*, no. 2A, Jan. 15, 1988.

Japan Trade Union Confederation. 1992. *The Spring Struggle for a Better Living; Rengo White Paper, 1992.* Tokyo: JTUC-Rengo.

Kawanishi, Hirosuke. 1992. *Enterprise Unionism in Japan*, trans. by Ross E. Mouer. London: Kegan Paul International.

Koike, Kazuo. 1987. Human resource development. In *The Political Economy of Japan*, vol. 1: *The Domestic Transformation*, ed. by Kozo Yamamura and Yasukichi Yasuba. Stanford: Stanford University Press.

Koike, Kazuo. 1988. *Understanding Industrial Relations in Modern Japan.* London: Macmillan. Ch. 7.

Ministry of Labor. 1991. *Basic Survey on Labor Unions.*

Shirai, Taishiro. 1984. A theory of enterprise union. In *Industrial Relations in Japan*, ed. by Tashiro Shirai. Madison: University of Wisconsin Press.

Sumiya, Mikio. 1990. *The Japanese Industrial Relations Reconsidered.* Tokyo: Japan Institute of Labor.

land reform
See **land uses and policies**.

land tax
See **land uses and policies**.

land trust
See **land uses and policies, trust banks**.

land uses and policies   Of Japan's total land area (377,700 square kilometers), 66.9% consists of woodlands, 14.2% is used as agricultural land, 4.2% is occupied by dwellings, 3.5% is taken up by rivers and 3% by roads. The amount of land is so small—smaller than California—relative to its **population** that Japan has one of the highest population densities in the world. In 1990 Japan had 327 persons per square kilometer (or 132 persons per 100 acres) compared with 27 persons per square kilometer in the United States and 252 in India. Furthermore the population is heavily concentrated in the major metropolitan areas. Agricultural land is fragmented into small farms.

In Japan as in any other country, land uses are determined by geo-environmental factors, the stage of economic development, and government policies on land use. However, because of the severe shortage of land in Japan, government planning and control are particularly important. The National Land Agency under the prime minister's office heads the nation's land planning and control. It works with prefectural and municipal government agencies to develop guidelines and programs for land use. All major land uses—residential, commercial, industrial, forest, recreational, and agricultural—are subject to national, prefectural, municipal, and neighborhood plans and controls. The instruments used in land policy implementation are land price approval and publication, building codes, zoning ordinances, building permits, designation of urban promotion and urban control areas, expropriation, preemptive rights, and environmental controls. Because of the wide ramifications of land use, policy coordination between the National Land Agency and other ministries and agencies—such as the Ministry of Agriculture, Forestry, and Fisheries, the Ministry of Construction, the Ministry of Transport, and the National Tax Administration Agency—are needed to effectively implement land use policies.

Agricultural land use and urban housing land supply have been two major policy concerns. In the immediate postwar period, a land reform was carried out in 1945–49 (in accordance with Owners-Farmer Establishment Law of 1946) as part of the Occupation's attempt to democratize and decentralize the economy. It limited landlord's holding to one *cho* or 2.45 acres (10 acres in Hokkaido); the excess was sold to the government. Tenant farmers acquired land from the government. As a result the proportion of total agricultural land area worked by tenant farmers was reduced from 46% in November 1946 to 10% in August 1950. In 1952 the Agricultural Land Act was enacted. It severely restricted land transfers, tenure, tenant rents, and so forth, in an attempt to prevent reconcentration of land and to protect the welfare of tenants.

The postwar land reform was successful in promoting widespread ownership of farmland. In addition subsequent inflation reduced the value of land compensation to the landlords and the cost of land to the farmers. On the other hand, farmland became fragmented and many farms are too small to be efficient; the average farm—about 1.65 acres— became smaller than the prewar average. The policy of banning joint-stock companies from owning farmland and allowing agricultural cooperatives to own farmland only if they do actual farming also prevents the consolidation of land into large farms.

Because of the limited supply of urban land and the growing demand for land for housing and commercial uses, land prices in Japan's large cities have become very high by world standards. Several factors on the supply and demand sides are involved. On the supply side, one factor that has contributed to the shortage of land for urban housing and buildings is the government's rice policy. The high prices of rice due to government subsidies and the ban on the import of cheaper foreign rice have given farmers the incentives to remain in farming, with many small plots of farms in metropolitan areas cultivated by part-time or "weekend" farmers, who derive the bulk of their incomes from nonfarm activities. Another supply-side factor is that because of low fixed property taxes, high transactions taxes, and a law that makes it extremely difficult for owners of buildings to evict tenants, landowners have little incentives to sell or redevelop their land. In addition, prior to 1992, farmland was subject to lower rate of taxation than nonfarmland, giving farmers in urban areas no incentive to convert their land to other uses (author's interview, National Land Agency, Aug. 13, 1992).

On the demand side, steady economic growth in Japan and the continuing concentration of business activities in the large cities have led to a growing demand for urban land. There is also the speculative demand for land based on the popular belief that land prices in Japan can only go up, and hence landholding is a good investment. In the late 1980s the booming **stock market** and easy credit from financial institutions to developers and real estate firms helped to fuel a speculative investment boom in urban land and property. As a result residential land prices rose 2.5 times in **Tokyo** and 3 times in Osaka between 1983 and 1991, far greater than the rate of wage increases, making a house beyond the reach of the average salaried employee. This has led to a growing realization that changes in land use policies are needed to relieve the shortage of urban land for housing.

The government has adopted some measures since 1990 to alleviate urban land problems. In April 1990 the **Ministry of Finance** imposed temporary restrictions on real estate lendings by **nonbank financial institutions**. In January 1991 the government urged local governments to use their authority to convert most farmland in city areas to sites for housing and public facilities. The National Tax Administration Agency sharply raised the assessed values of real estate for inheritance and gift taxes to prevent speculation and thus slow the rise in real estate prices. Finally, after much debate a new landholding tax was introduced in January 1992 to make landholding less lucrative. However, because of opposition from businesses, the tax rate is only 0.2% in 1992 and 0.3% from 1993 onward of the official assessed value for calculating inheritance tax, which is only about 50–60% of the actual market value. In addition the basic deduction from the landholding tax is high: ¥1 billion or ¥30,000 times the square meter area of each plot, whichever is higher. Consequently analysts doubt that the new tax itself will be effective in inducing changes in land uses. They suggest that additional measures such as a new land use plan and the revision of the Land Lease and Rental House Law should be adopted to stabilize land prices and ensure the supply of land for housing.

A serious aspect of land use problems in Japan stems from the excess concentration of businesses and government offices in Tokyo. Unless this is changed, the demand for land in Tokyo will remain at a high level. Some steps have been taken to encourage the dispersion of corporate and government offices to other areas. In 1985 the government announced the Capital Redevelopment Plan to develop core business cities and secondary core business cities such as **Yokohama** and Kawasaki for the relocation of some government agencies. In 1988, 79 government agencies were selected for such relocations. As of 1992, 16 government offices and agencies were planning to relocate in Yokohama. The Construction Ministry indicated in October 1991 that, starting in 1992, it would select up to 10 areas of development under a system to relieve concentration in the country's three large metropolitan areas (Tokyo, Osaka, and Nagoya). Under the system, selected areas will receive preferential treatment in the allocation of public works projects and in undertaking land redemarcation.

In the 1980s land trusts were popular with urban landowners as a means of having their land developed and receiving income from it. Under the system a landowner would entrust his land to a **trust bank**, which would raise funds, build a commercial building, manage or sell the building (not including the land), and pay the trust owner earnings from the operation. After the contract expires (usually after 20 years), the owner would get the property back. However, the popularity of land trusts has declined because of the subsequent "bursting" in 1990–91 of the speculative stock market and the real estate market, the twin pillars of the "bubble economy" of the late 1980s. On the other hand, the Japanese government is said to be considering the use of land trusts for the effective management of national land, especially in the major cities. Land trusts are considered a way to circumvent public land sales. The Ministry of Finance is reportedly also considering allowing regional banks to serve as commission-earning agents for land and loan trusts, which are traditionally the preserve of trust banks.

See also **housing, rice production and distribution.**

Address

National Land Agency
2-2, Kasumigaseki 1-chome, Chiyoda-ku, Tokyo 100
Tel: (03) 3593-3311

References

Dore, R. P. 1959. *Land Reform in Japan*. London: Oxford University Press.

Economic Planning Agency. 1991. *Economic White Paper*.

Hanayama, Yuzuru. 1986. *Land Markets and Land Policy in a Metropolitan Area*. Boston: Oelgeschlager, Gunn and Hain.

Hines, M. A. 1987. *Investing in Japanese Real Estate*. New York: Quorum Books.

Ito, Takatoshi. 1993. The land/housing problem in Japan: A macroeconomic approach. *Journal of the Japanese and International Economies* 7, 1: 1–31.

National Land Agency. 1991. *Annual Report* (in Japanese).

National Land Agency. 1992. *White Paper on Land* (in Japanese).

Saito, Tadashi. 1991. Government unveil land reform package. *JEI Report*, Feb. 8, no. 5B, 5–6.

Sunohara, Tsuyoshi. 1990. Public, private sectors call for land use poliy. *Japan Economic Journal*, Nov. 17: 4.

Takagi, Keizo. 1989. The rise of land prices in Japan: The determination mechanism and the effect of taxation system. *Bank of Japan Monetary and Economic Studies* 7, 2: 83–139.

Takagi, Shintaro. 1991. Are land and house prices too high in Japan? *Japanese Economic Studies* 20, 1: 57–86.

landholding tax
See **land uses and policies**.

Large Retail Store Law, 1974   Also translated as Large-Scale Retail Store Law (*Daitenho*), this law superseded the Department Store Law of 1956 to protect the small retailers by regulating the growth of large-scale stores, including department stores and chain supermarkets. It stipulates that the establishment of stores with store area of 3,000 square meters or more in the ten biggest cities and of 1,500 square meters or more in the rest of the country is to be supervized by the **Ministry of International Trade and Industry** (MITI). After consultations with local retailers and city officials, MITI could order the reduction of the planned floor space, postponement of the opening, earlier closing hours, or more days on which the store has to remain closed, if these are thought to be necessary to mitigate the effect of the store on the resident small shops.

As originally intended, any big store could open and any necessary adjustments made within a year or two after the application has been filed.

In practice, however, it has taken seven to as long as ten years from the initial planning for a large store to open.

When **department stores** and supermarket chains began to open stores all over the country with a selling area below 1,500 square meters, local governments demanded regulations on medium-sized stores. Consequently in 1979 MITI extended the law to stores with a shopping area of 500 square meters. In 1982 MITI issued new guidelines governing the size of stores that could be opened in cities of various population and increased the role of localities in the opening of big retail operations. MITI also used **administrative guidance** to slow the spread of supermarket chains. Thus the establishment and expansion of supermarket chains were made more difficult, reflecting the political power of the smaller retailers and the government policy that favors them.

In the late 1980s the law was increasingly under attack. Some domestic business groups argue that it should be abolished. U.S. trade officials regard it as limiting American access to the Japanese **distribution system** and foreign imports into Japan (since large stores are more likely to carry imports) and would like to see it repealed. Japanese defenders of the law admit that small retail stores are inefficient but argue that they promote full employment and that their presence is important for elderly consumers who live in downtown areas and cannot drive to suburban areas where large retailers are usually located.

Members of the ruling Liberal Democratic Party, however, have been reluctant to abolish the law for fear of losing the political support of small retailers. In June 1989 a MITI advisory panel recommended that the law be applied more flexibly to implement its original intent. In 1990, as part of the basic agreement between Japan and the United States on the removal of "structural impediments" to trade, Tokyo agreed to revise the law in stages so that the power of small shopowners to block the construction of large stores in their districts could be curtailed. Starting in May 1990, the implementation of the law was relaxed. On January 31, 1992, revisions went into effect that would shorten the time needed for final government approval for a large store to a maximum of one year. Two years after the revision, the law would be reviewed completely, with the possibility of excluding large metropolitan areas from its application.

A large American toy retailer, Toys "R" Us, succeeded in opening its store in Japan in 1991.

See also **department stores, distribution system**.

References

Ito, Takatoshi. 1992. *The Japanese Economy*. Cambridge: MIT Press. Ch. 13.

Ito, Takatoshi, and Masayoshi Maruyama. 1991. Is the Japanese distribution system really inefficient? In *Trade with Japan*, ed. by Paul Krugman. Chicago: University of Chicago Press.

Sekiguchi, Waichi. 1990. Big-store law revision means small change for imports. *Japan Economic Journal*, Apr. 14: 1, 5.

Smith, Charles. 1991. Reforms in store. *Far Eastern Economic Review*, Jan. 17: 44–48.

Takahashi, Hideo. 1989. Structural changes in Japan's distribution system. *JEI Report*, Nov. 10: 7–10.

latent capital   Unrealized capital gains, namely the difference between book value and market value of a stock portfolio and property.
   See **cross shareholding**.

leading indicators   Some 15 business indicators selected by the Economic Planning Agency that are sensitive to, and tend to lead, changes in overall business conditions.
   See **business-cycle indicators and forecasting**.

Liberal Democratic Party (LDP)   The dominant political party in Japan since its founding in 1955.
   See **political parties**.

lifetime employment   This refers to the commitment by both employers and employees to maintain the employment relationship throughout an employee's career. This practice was developed by large companies during the early postwar period to attract and retain scarce skilled labor, although the practice also existed in the 1910s and 1920s on a smaller scale. Currently it still prevails in most large corporations. Fresh college graduates are hired by large firms with the understanding that they will stay with the same company for the rest of their careers. For their part, the companies train the new employees and reward their loyalty with seniority-based salary increases and advancements. Employees therefore have the incentives to stay with the same company. Midcareer job changes were shunned as signs of disloyalty. However, smaller companies have not adopted the system.
   There are various ways to avoid the high cost of being saddled with incompetent and highly paid senior employees. (1) An early mandatory retirement age of 55 to 60 is adopted, after which the retired employee may

work at a subsidiary of the company at a reduced pay. (2) A large company may hire temporary workers for tasks that are not expected to last long. These workers are paid less than regular workers and do not enjoy job security, although they may be rehired year after year. (3) The company may rely on subcontractors for many tasks. The subcontracted work can be curtailed as needed.

Since the early 1980s the slower growth and restructuring of the economy have put strains on the system. The strong yen has forced companies to cut costs, including hiring part-time workers, resisting large wage increases, and moving labor-intensive production abroad. As a result lifetime employment is no longer as highly valued. In some cases companies are willing to assist employees in job changes, although they are still reluctant to fire them. Midcareer job changes are becoming more common as opportunities for advancement in the same company are becoming scarce or as new job openings at other companies become available. In 1987 about 2.7 million workers, or 4.4% of the work force, changed jobs. That was an 80% increase from five years earlier. In a 1990 survey it was found that one-third of Japanese workers under 30 years old had changed jobs at least once, and there was no difference between male and female workers.

See also **corporate personnel practices**.

References

Hasegawa, Mina. 1992. Slump strains lifetime employment. *Nikkei Weekly*, Oct. 3: 1.

Job-hopping no longer a dirty word. *Japan Economic Journal*, Oct. 6, 1990: 10.

Kimindo, Kusaka. 1988. Dawn of a new employment era. *Japan Echo* 15, 3: 63–67.

Lifetime employment in its death throes? *Japan Economic Journal*, Mar. 24, 1990: 27.

Nishimura, Hiroyuki. 1993. System of lifetime jobs resisting change. *Nikkei Weekly*, Feb. 1: 1.

list price system   The government-guided pricing system in the steel industry during 1958–91. Also called the *"open sales system."*
    See **steel industry**.

livelihood protection   Public assistance given to the indigent for medical care and living expenses.
    See **health insurance, social security system**.

local taxes   Taxes levied by the 47 prefectural governments and more
than 3,000 municipal governments, including inhabitant tax, business tax,
and property tax.
See **tax system**.

long-term credit banks   Japan has three long-term credit banks, which
were founded in accordance with the Long-Term Credit Bank Law of
1952 to specialize in extending long-term loans. They are the Industrial
Bank of Japan, the Long-Term Credit Bank of Japan, and the Nippon Credit
Bank.

Before World War II long-term financing was provided by the semigovernmental "special banks." After the war the Occupation authority
abolished the special banks in favor of the capital market for providing
long-term funds. Because the capital market was too inadequate at that
time, the Long-Term Credit Bank Law was passed in 1952 to establish the
system of long-term credit banks.

These banks have played an important role in Japan's postwar banking
system and industrial growth by supplying long-term credit to industries,
thereby relieving the ordinary banks of the pressure for long-term financing. This was particularly important during Japan's high-growth period
before the early 1970s. As a means of raising funds for long-term lending,
they are authorized to issue five-year interest-bearing debentures as well as
one-year discount debentures up to 30 times their combined total of capital
and reserves. However, they are restricted in deposit taking; they can only
accept deposits from their borrowers. They also have fewer branches than
ordinary banks.

With the slower growth of the economy after the first oil crisis in 1973,
the growing trade surplus since the late 1970s, and the maturing and
liberalization of the capital and money markets in Japan in the 1980s, the
financial needs of the economy have changed as well. The long-term credit
banks have responded to the changes by lending actively to wholesale and
service trades, private housing finance companies, and consumer credit
companies. They have also been active in lending to foreign operations of
Japanese corporations as well as to foreign governments and corporations.

The Industrial Bank of Japan, the largest of the three long-term credit
banks, had total assets of ¥42.87 trillion at the end of March 1992, down
slightly from the the previously year's level because of the recession (see
table L.6). However, these assets were more than two-thirds those of Dai-
Ichi Kangyo Bank, Japan's largest city bank in terms of assets. The Industrial Bank of Japan was originally founded before World War II. According

Table L.6
Long-term credit banks (in ¥ trillions)

Bank	Assets (March 31, 1992)	Deposits (September 31, 1992)
Industrial Bank of Japan	42.87	31.79
Long-Term Credit Bank of Japan	31.58	24.90
Nippon Credit Bank	18.09	14.35

Sources: *The Nikkei Weekly* (June 6, 1992: 21) for assets; Federation of Bankers' Association of Japan for deposits.

to surveys conducted by Nihon Keizai Shimbun, Inc., publisher of Japan's leading business daily, it is by far the most highly regarded bank by Japanese financial experts for four consecutive years (1988 to 1991) because of its managerial efficiency and operational expertise. The Long-Term Credit Bank of Japan and the Nippon Credit Bank were established in 1952 and 1957, respectively.

With the continuous liberalization and development of the capital and **money markets** in Japan, analysts expect the need for traditional long-term credit banks to decline. Reportedly the **Ministry of Finance** plans to help transform these banks into ordinary banks.

See also **banking system, city banks**.

Addresses

Industrial Bank of Japan
3-3, Marunouchi 1-chome, Chiyoda-ku, Tokyo
Tel: (03) 3214-1111   Fax: (03) 3213-6066

Long-Term Credit Bank of Japan
2-4, Otemachi 1-chome, Chiyoda-ku, Tokyo
Tel: (03) 3211-5111   Fax: (03) 5252-8701

Nippon Credit Bank
13-10, Kudan-kita 1-chome, Chiyoda-ku, Tokyo
Tel: (03) 3263-1111   Fax: (03) 3239-8065

References

Federation of Bankers Association of Japan. 1989. *Banking System in Japan*. Tokyo: Zenginkyo. Ch. 1.

Hamada, Koichi and Akiyoshi Horiuchi. 1987. The political economy of the financial market. In *The Political Economy of Japan*, Vol. 1: *The Domestic Transformation*, ed. by Kozo Yamamura and Yasukichi Yasuba. Stanford: Stanford University press.

Suzuki, Yoshio, ed. 1987. *The Japanese Financial System*. Oxford: Oxford University Press. Ch. 5.

Tatewaki, Kazuo. 1991. *Banking and Finance in Japan*. London: Routledge. Ch. 7.

Viner, Aron. 1987. *Inside Japan's Financial Markets*. London: The Economist Publications. Ch. 7.

long-term prime rates   The lending rates charged by long-term credit banks and trust banks on long-term loans to credit-worthy corporations.

See **interest rate structure**.

M

madoguchi shido   Window guidance given by the Bank of Japan to commercial banks concerning the amounts of their loans and the direction of their operations. It was abolished in mid-1991.

See **Bank of Japan**.

main bank system
See **city banks, corporate finance**.

Management and Coordination Agency (Somu-cho)   A large government agency under the prime minister' office in charge of the central management and coordination of the national government. It is responsible for the following areas: (1) personnel management, (2) government administrative management, (3) administrative inspection, (4) traffic safety and youth affairs, (5) pension programs, and (6) government statistics.

See also **economic/business research and publications**.

management practices   The term "Japanese-style management" (*nihon-teki keiei*) is used by many Japanese and Western authors to refer to a host of "traditional" management practices outlined below that have been common until recently in large corporations in postwar Japan. Since the early 1980s the Japanese economy has been in a state of flux, and many changes have been introduced in the midst of tradition. "Continuity and change" best characterize Japanese management practices of the early 1990s.

1. Market share or corporate growth, rather than short-term profits or share prices, are considered to be the dominant corporate goal. This is consistent with the Japanese management emphasis on long-term performance rather than short-term profits. As a result the Japanese company pursues high corporate **investment** rather than high dividend distribution.

This does not mean that profits are not important. However, some analysts argue that profits are important to Japanese firms mainly because they are a means to investment and not because they are the primary corporate goal itself. In the early 1990s, however, an increasing number of Japanese companies and managers are emphasizing the primacy of profits.

2. Corporate management is influenced by both shareholders and employees, and hence Aoki's (1990) characterization of Japanese firms as being subject to dual control in contrast to Western firms which are subject to unilateral control by ownership. More broadly, Kester (1991: 79) characterizes Japanese managers as "agents of the entire coalition of stakeholders rather than of the shareholders or any other single group." Stakeholders include workers, management, and shareholders, which include banks and other companies who are the "stable shareholders" in **cross-shareholding** relationships as well as individual shareholders. The company's main bank, in particular, is much more important than individual shareholders; the latter do not exercise much control and are likened by Abegglen and Stalk (1985) to preferred stockholders in a Western company. Employees participate in company **decision making** and share in profits in the form of semiannual bonuses.

3. **Corporate personnel practices** include **lifetime employment** and a senority-based wage system and promotion, which are considered to be conducive to employee loyalty and work incentives. Companies also regularly undertake extensive employee training without fear of losing trained personnel. These personnel practices suggest to Ozaki (1991) and others that the Japanese management system values corporate human resources more than its Western counterpart.

4. Enterprise-based **labor unions** and extensive consultation between management and employees contribute to cooperative **labor-management relations** and productivity growth in contrast to the adversarial labor-management relations commonly observed in the West.

5. **Decision making** emphasizes group consensus. This faciliates the implementation of the decision.

6. Management respect for workers' views helps to mobilize workers' initiatives, as reflected in their active participation in the **quality control** circles.

7. Innovative and cost-cutting production management methods, particularly the **just-in-time system**—a production system that minimizes the level of inventories—are characteristics of the Japanese style of manage-

ment. Since the late 1980s the **computer-integrated manufacturing system** and **flexible manufacturing system** have been increasingly introduced.

8. Aspects of Japanese **corporate finance**, such as a relatively high debt–equity ratio and a low dividend–payout ratio, are considered by some authors to be an integral part of Japanese approach to management in order to have a high rate of investment and growth.

These management practices are considered by Ozaki (1991) to be superior to American management practices in generating a high level of workers' incentives, productivity, and corporate growth. He characterizes the Japanese enterprise system as "human capitalism" for the high value it places on its human resources over capital resource. In a large comparative survey of workers in the United States and Japan, Lincoln (1989) finds that the Japanese management practices produced higher work motivation, although American workers have a high level of satisfaction.

It should be emphasized that there are always important exceptions to the above generalizations. In addition, since the late 1970s or early 1980s, various changes in management practices have been gradually introduced as economic conditions change. For example, a growing number of companies are stressing merit over seniority in employee promotion, and midcareer job changes are increasingly accepted. In the late 1980s the debt–equity rato of the average company declined because of the increased importance of equity finance.

Recently Akio Morita (1992), chairman of Sony Corp. and long an advocate of the Japanese style of management, questions the appropriateness of some Japanese management practices in the contemporary world in an article published in a Japanese magazine, *Bungei Shunju*. In particular, he criticizes Japanese companies for paying workers too little while demanding long working hours, and for paying small dividends to shareholders while operating on small profit margins to keep investment high and prices low. In addition he is concerned that these practices may have given Japanese manufacturers unfair competitive advantages in pricing in the world market (author's interview with Sony management, July 10, 1992). Although many top Japanese corporate leaders disagree with Morita, the ensuing discussions touched off by his criticisms can be seen as manifestations of a serious and timely self-examination by the Japanese corporate world about its own management practices. As Japanese companies become more globalized and integrated in the world economy, Japanese management practices are likely to undergo more changes in the future.

See also **business ethics, corporate finance, Structural Impediments Initiative**.

References

Abegglen, James C. 1992. Morita's argument misses bigger issues. *Tokyo Business Today*, Apr.: 14–16.

Abegglen, James C., and George Stalk, Jr. 1985. *Kaisha: The Japanese Corporation*. New York: Basic Books. Chs. 7–8.

Aoki, Masahiko. 1988. *Information, Incentives, and Bargaining in the Japanese Economy*. Cambridge: Cambridge University Press. Ch. 3.

Aoki, Masahiko. 1990. Toward an economic model of the Japanese firm. *Journal of Economic Literature* 28: 1–27.

Chandler, Clay. 1992. Japan market slide sparks debate on future of entrenched corporate management practices. *Asian Wall Street Journal Weekly*, May 4: 1, 7, 8.

Hiromoto, Toshiro. 1988. Another hidden edge: Japanese management accounting. *Harvard Business Review* 66, 4: 22–26.

Dore, Ronald. 1987. *Taking Japan Seriously*. Stanford: Stanford University Press. Chs. 6–8.

Kester, W. Carl. 1991. *Japanese Takeovers: The Global Contest for Corporate Control*. Boston: Harvard Business School Press.

Lincoln, James R. 1989. Employee work attitudes and management practice in the U.S. and Japan: Evidence from a large comparative survey. *California Management Review* 32, 1: 89–106.

Morita, Akio. 1992. A critical moment for Japanese management. *Japan Echo* 19, 2: 8–14 (abridged trans. from *Bungei shunju*, Feb. 1992: 94–103).

Morita shock: New paradigm needed for Japanese management. *Tokyo Business Today*, Mar. 1992: 40–42.

Mroczkowski, Tomasz, and Masao Hanaoka. 1989. Continuity and change in Japanese management. *California Management Review* 31, 2: 39–53.

Ozaki, Robert. 1991. *Human Capitalism*. New York: Penguin.

Marubeni Corp.   One of Japan's largest general trading companies. See **trading companies**.

maruyu   A privileged saving system which, until 1988, exempted the interest earnings of small savers from income tax in order to encourage individual savings. As of the end of September 1987, about ¥300 trillion ($2.3 trillion) of Japan's ¥637 trillion of personal savings were in accounts benefiting from the tax exemption. In 1987 these savings constituted nearly all of Japan's **postal savings** and about two-thirds of personal deposits in commercial banks. However, the interest rate paid was controlled by the government at a low level—0.2% on a savings account at a commercial bank, 2.7% on a one-year time deposit, and 3.64% on the popular ten-year savings certificates at the post office.

Although there was a limit of ¥3 million per savings account that was eligible for the tax-exempt privilege, there were various abuses such as illegal multiple accounts, sometimes under assumed names, that circumvented the limit. As a result large savers benefited much more from it than small savers. Ishi (1989: 128) shows that in 1986, 78.9% of families used the *maruyu* system. For families with annual incomes of less than ¥2 million, only 56.4% used the system. The percentage increased as the income level rose. For families with annual incomes over ¥7 million, 93.0% benefited from it.

Starting in April 1988, as part of Japan's tax reform, eligibility for the tax exemption is restricted to disabled, ederly people over 65 and working widows. A 20% withholding tax is imposed on nearly all interest income from deposit accounts.

See also **postal savings, tax reform**.

References

Ishi, Hiromitsu. 1989. *The Japanese Tax System*. Oxford: Oxford University Press.

Loss of small-saver tax breaks slows city bank deposit growth to 7.8%. *Japan Economic Journal*, Apr. 22, 1989: 16.

Viner, Aron. 1987. *Inside Japan's Financial Markets*. London: The Economist Publications. Ch. 7.

When $2.3 trillion looks for a new Japanese home. *The Economist*, Feb. 20, 1988: 83–84.

Matsushita Electric Industrial Co.   The largest electronics company in Japan and in the world and the core company of the Matsushita Group.
    See **electronics industry, *keiretsu* and business groups**.

Matsushita, Kinosuke (1894–1991)   Founder of Matsushita Electric Industrial Co. and a venerated pioneer entrepreneur in Japan.
    See **electronics industry**.

mergers and acquisitions (M&A)   In the West a corporate merger or the acquisition of an existing firm is often a convenient way for a company to grow or to diversify, and for investors, particularly foreign investors, to enter a business; hence it is widely practiced. However, until the late

1980s the number of M&A in Japan is small. Wholesale and retail trade is the industry that has had the highest number of M&A, followed by manufacturing.

Mergers have to be reported to the Fair Trade Commission in accordance with the **Antimonopoly Law**, but not acquisitions. Hence reliable statistics on acquisitions are diffcult to obtain, and different sources give different figures, as can be seen from table M.1. Furthermore these statistics understate the real extent of acquisitions because the acquisitions of small companies are not recorded (author's interview with Kanji Ishizumi, attorney at Chiyoda Kokusai Law Offices, Aug. 11, 1992). In any case analysts agree that M&A transactions are small in Japan and that it is rare for foreign firms to acquire Japanese firms.

Analysts have offered several reasons for the traditional paucity of M&A transactions in Japan. The first is the unfavorable sociocultural attitude. The company is regarded by Japanese managers and workers alike as a family or a community, and the idea of selling a company by its owner or CEO for financial considerations has the connotation of "flesh peddling" (Kester 1991a: 12) or as much a betrayal as "the captain of a ship deserting his crew in a storm" (Ishizumi 1988: 14). Even in a friendly merger between two Japanese companies, the firms reportedly often have difficulty integrating because of employees' continuing loyalties to the former firms (Choy 1990: 10). These are consistent with Ito's (1991) finding that M&A

Table M.1
Number of mergers and acquisitions

	Japanese firms acquired		Foreign firms acquired	
	Japanese firms	Foreign firms	Japanese firms	Mergers
1981	122	48	6	1,044
1984	140	44	6	1,096
1985	163	100	26	1,113
1986	226	204	21	1,147
1987	219	228	22	1,215
1988	223 (227)	315 (307)	17 (9)	1,336
1989	240 (272)	405 (415)	15 (19)	1,450
1990	293 (306)	440 (464)	18 (17)	1,751
1991	386	257	12	
1992		(198)	(36)	

Sources: Yamaichi Securities Co., Ltd. Figures in parentheses are from Daiwa Securities Co. Figures for 1991 are from Nomura Research Institute. Figures on mergers are from the Fair Trade Commission.

activities substantially increase the stock market valuation of target firms in the United States but lower that of both acquiring and target firm in Japan.

Furthermore Kester (1991b) argues that given Japan's economic institutions and business practices, the purposes that are served in the West by means of M&A are more readily served in Japan in the traditional ways that are more socially acceptable. For example, in the West M&A serve to extend corporate control over another company or business area (vertical integration). This is not necessary for Japanese companies that maintain long-term stable relationships with their suppliers, distributors, customers, and subcontractors. Alternatively, M&A might be pursued in the West as a means to correct abuses by stakeholders, including management. Such abuses are said to be fewer in Japan and more easily corrected without gaining majority control. Thus there has been much less incentive for Japanese companies to use M&A to achieve what it is used to achieve in the West.

It is difficult and rare for foreign companies to acquire Japanese companies. The reasons are that in addition to the traditional reluctance to sell, the idea of selling to a foreign firm is particularly alien and unsettling to the Japanese. It is feared that foreign companies will pursue short-term profits and disregard long-term relationships and time-honored practices, including job security for employees. The practice of **cross shareholding** also facilitates the defense against any hostile takeover. Finally, the gove. n-ment did not ease its restrictions on **foreign direct investment** in Japan until 1980.

The situation started to change in the 1980s, particularly after the mid-1980s, as Japanese corporate relationships, economic structure, social attitude, and government policies were changing. Japanese corporations were acquiring a lot of cash, became less dependent on their banks in their business relations, and had more incentives to invest their funds for higher returns. As a result the practice of cross shareholding is not as important as previously. Government **financial liberalization** is easing the restrictions on foreign ownership in Japan as well as increasing competition in the financial market. Socially M&A is said to be increasingly acceptable as making money becomes more important and business managers realize what can be accomplished with M&A in their global business plans (Choy 1990: 13). For these reasons analysts expect Japanese M&A to increase in the future.

Japanese M&A activity abroad increased rapidly between 1986 and 1990, but declined in 1991–92. About half of the transactions took place in the United States (176, 194, and 229 cases in 1988, 1989, and 1990, respectively; about $15 to 18 billion annually during 1988–90). These changes reflect changes in the Japanese domestic economy itself. Between 1986 and 1990 a number of factors enabled Japanese companies to acquire firms in the United States. The yen's appreciation after the Plaza Accord of 1985 has reduced Japanese companies' competitiveness in some export markets and hence increased the need to diversify; it has also reduced the cost of acquiring foreign assets. The Japanese **stock market** boom facilitated the raising of equity capital, and the low interest rates and the rising real estate values enabled companies to borrow more money at low cost, using their inflated properties as collateral. These conditions changed in 1991 as the Japanese stock market and real estate market declined and the economy entered a recession.

The average size of Japanese acquisitions of U.S. companies is relatively modest—$99 million in 1988, $77 million in 1989, and $62 million in 1990 (Sano 1992: 53). However, it was mega-deals such as the following that dominated the headlines and caused some concern in the American public: Sony's acquisition of CBS Records (1988, $2.0 billion), Bridgestone's acquisition of Firestone Tire and Rubber (1988, $2.6 billion), Saison Group's acquisition of Intercontinental Hotel (1988, $2.2 billion), Mitsubishi Estate's acquisition of Rochefeller Group (1989, $0.8 billion), and Sony's acqustion of Columbia Pictures (1989, $3.4 billion).

Analysts expect Japanese M&A acitivity in the domestic market and abroad and American participation in the Japanese market through joint ventures to increase once the two economies emerge from the recession. For foreign firms interested in entering the Japanese market through M&A, Ishizumi (1988) gives practical step-by-step guide from the perspective of an experienced M&A attorney in Japan. Eide (1991) gives advices on legal issues such as taxation, labor, and establishing technicalities.

See also **direct overseas investment**.

References

Choy, Jon. 1990. Japan and Mergers: Oil and Water? *JEI Report*, no. 14A, Apr. 6.

Daiwa Securities Co. 1992. M&A transactions by Japanese Companies. In *Capital Markets and Financial Services in Japan*. Tokyo: Japan Securities Research Institute.

Eide, Tord. 1991. *How to Establish Business in Japan*. Deventer, the Netherlands: Kluwer Law and Taxation Publishers.

Fair Trade Commission. Annual. *Antimopoly White Paper*.

Ishizumi, Kanji. 1988. *Acquiring Japanese Companies*. Tokyo: Japan Times.

Ito, Kunio. 1991. The effect of M&A activity on company value in Japan and the United States: A comparative study. *Hitotsubashi Journal of Commerce and Management* 26, 1: 1–14.

Kester, W. Carl. 1991a. *Japanese Takeovers: The Global Contest for Corporate Control*. Boston: Harvard Business School Press.

Kester, W. Carl. 1991b. Global players, Western tactics, Japanese outcomes: The new Japanese market for corporate control. *California Management Review* 33, 2: 58–70.

Odagiri, Hiroyuki. 1992. *Growth through Competition, Competition through Growth*. Oxford: Oxford University Press. Ch. 5.

Pettway, Richard H., Neil W. Sicherman, and Takeshi Yamada. 1990. The market for corporate control, the level of agency costs, and corporate collectivism in Japanese mergers. In *Japanese Capital Markets*, ed. by Edwin J. Elton and Martin J. Gruber. New York: Harper and Row.

Sano, Yoshihiro. 1992. U.S.–Japan M&A: Expect more deals. *Tokyo Business Today*, May 1992: 52–53.

Shishido, Zenichi. 1992. Corporate takeovers in Japan. In *Capital Markets and Financial Services in Japan*. Tokyo: Japan Securities Research Institute.

minimum wages   Japan does not have uniform national minimum wages; instead, it has different minimum wages for different prefectures and industries.

Under the minimum wage system set up on the basis of the Minimum Wage Law of 1959, each prefecture has a Minimum Wage Council consisting of public, labor, and mangement representatives. The Council makes recommendations concerning the prefectural minimum wage per day to the chief of the Prefectural Labor Standards Office, who acts on it with the approval of the Ministry of Labor. Thus there are 47 prefectural minimun wages in the economy. In FY 1991, for example, they ranged from ¥4,570 per day in Tokyo, Kanagawa, and Osaka, to ¥4,452 in Aichi, to ¥3,923 in Nagasaki, Miyazaki, and Okinawa. The weighted average of all prefectural minimum wages was ¥3,776 per day in May 1989, ¥3,928 as of March 31, 1990, and ¥4,319 as of March 31, 1992.

In addition there are 392 separate industrial minimum wages that apply to low-paid employees of different trades in different prefectures. The Minimum Wage Councils as well as Prefectural Labor Standards Offices and the Ministry of Labor are involved in the decisons. Within an industry there are dozens of minimun wages because they are determined locally. For example, as shown in table M.2, the foodstuff industry had 12 different cases of minimum wages determined as of March 31, 1992. The weighted average of the industry's minimum wages was ¥4,189.

Thus most low-paid workers have overlapping prefectural and industrial minimum wages applying to them. The higher of the two will be the effective one. The Ministry of Labor is in charge of the overall administration

Table M.2
Average minimum wages by industry (in ¥ per day, as of March 31, 1992)

Industry	Minimum wages	Number of cases
Foodstuff	4,189	12
Textiles	4,531	11
Lumber, woodwork, interior equipment and furniture	4,176	16
Pulp, paper, and paper goods	4,637	7
Publishing and printing	4,558	15
Ceramic and related goods	4,346	24
Machinery and metal processing	4,837	177
Automobile repair	4,305	8
Wholesale and retail	4,489	61
Mining[a]	6,452	3
Others	5,078	8
All industries	4,739	334

Source: Ministry of Labor.
a. Centrally determined.

of the minimum wage system. It makes sure that the minimum wages are revised every year in accordance with changes in wages and prices.

See also **wage structure**.

Address

Central Minimum Wages Council, Ministry of Labor
2-2, Kasumigaseki 1-chome, Chiyoda-ku, Tokyo 100
Tel: (03) 3593−1211

References

Ministry of Labor. 1992. *Handbook of Labor Statistics*.

Ministry of Labor. 1992. *Labour Administration*.

Regional minimum wages. *Japan Economic Journal*, May 20, 1989: 12.

Ministry of Finance   Established in 1870, the Ministry of Finance (MOF) is the most elitist and powerful of all ministries in Japan. In FY 1992 it had a budget of ¥10.47 trillion and a staff of 78,000, both the largest of all ministries (*Nikkei Weekly*, May 30, 1992: 1). The post of the minister is invariably held by an influential person or faction leader of the ruling Liberal Democratic Party and a potential candidate for the position of the prime minister. The power of the Ministry over the economy is exercised by bureaucrats in its various bureaus which are responsible for diverse areas of the economy.

The Budget Bureau of the Ministry is responsible for the national government's budget. The Tax Bureau is concerned with the overall design of the tax structure. The National Tax Administration collects taxes. The Finance Bureau raises nontax revenues and is responsible for government bond issues and the **Fiscal Investment and Loan Program**. The Banking Bureau and the Securities Bureau oversee banking and securities businesses, respectively, and hence influence the nation's monetary policy along with the **Bank of Japan**. Other bureaus deal with customs and tariffs, international finance, local finance, and so on.

Given the Ministry's vast jurisdiction, it is inevitable that some of its bureaus have conflicting interests. For example, the National Tax Administration occasionally objects to the tax changes proposed by the Tax Bureau unless an alternative source of revenue is offered. Critics have also pointed out that the Ministry is seriously understaffed, given its tremendous responsibilities, which makes its decision making very time-consuming and prevents it from responding to changing conditions efficiently.

As is common with all Japanese ministries, MOF officials rely heavily on **administrative guidance** to implement its policies. The private sector generally complies with this guidance. However, the power of the Ministry is not absolute, and it has shown signs of erosion in the last two decades. There are two reasons for this. First, other ministries and government institutions, which have different priorities, also exercise influence over financial policies. For example, the **Ministry of International Trade and Industry** (MITI) controls the Export-Import Bank and the **Japan Development Bank** and has some leverage over foreign exchange. MITI is known to be more concerned with economic expansion, whereas MOF is more concerned with budget balancing. The Bank of Japan shares with the MOF the responsibility for monetary policy. The Bank is known to be more cautious and more interested in macroeconomic stability and in fighting inflation, whereas the MOF tends to be more concerned with the orderly growth of the financial industries and the international impact of Japan's financial policies. Occasionally the minister of finance and the director of the Bank of Japan have openly expressed their policy differences, such as on the appropriate level of the Bank's official discount rate. Where such differences exist, the Bank rather than the MOF is more likely to make the accommodating changes.

Second, **financial liberalization** and the internationalization of Japanese banking and securities businesses have eroded somewhat the power of the MOF. Since 1970 the MOF has lost several of its policy instruments: exchange-rate controls, credit allocation through quotas on bank lending, and interest-rate ceilings on negotiable certificates of deposits (CDs), money market certificates, and large time deposits, and so on, in the late 1980s and early 1990s.

With the revelation, in 1991, of illegal investment-loss compensation made by securities houses to their large clients, the MOF was severely criticized by the public for its failure to prevent such scandals. It interactions with the financial industries were criticized as being more concerned with the interests of the industries rather than those of the public. In addition the **administrative guidance** which the MOF has used as a major means of excercising its regulatory power was criticized as too vague and lacking in "transparency." There was call for the creation of an independent commission similar to the Securities and Exchange Commission in the United States to supervise the securities industry, which will further erode its power. The Ministry has successfully resisted such a call to date and has taken measures to tighten its supervision of the securities industry. The new Securities and Exchange Surveillance Commission, set up in July 1992, is staffed by people from the Ministry.

See also **administrative guidance, Bank of Japan, banking system, financial liberalization, securities companies**.

Address

Ministry of Finance
1-1, Kasumigaseki 3-chome, Chiyoda-ku, Tokyo 100
Tel: (03) 3581–4111

References

Brauchli, Marcus W. 1989. As Japan's economy gains clout, Ministry of Finance struggles. *Wall Street Journal*, Dec. 209: 1, 7.

Chandler, Clay. 1991. Scandal raises questions about system of guidance by Japan's Finance Ministry. *Asian Wall Street Journal Weekly*, July 22: 22.

Japan's men of MOF. *The Economist*, Nov. 28, 1987: 72–73.

Kawakita, Takao. 1991. The Ministry of Finance. Japanese *Economic Studies* 19, No. 4: 3–29.

Tanaka, Naoki. 1991. Proud Finance Ministry has been humbled. *Japan Times* (weekly international edition), Aug. 26–Sept. 1: 11.

Ministry of International Trade and Industry (MITI)   Popularly called *MITI*, the Ministry was established in 1949 through the merger of the Ministry of Commerce and Industry and the Board of Trade. In FY 1992 it had a budget of ¥786 billion and a staff of 12,000, which make it a relatively small ministry in size, smaller than the Ministry of Transport. Its prestige and influence, however, are far greater than its size would indicate. MITI is an important ministry that has been instrumental in guiding Japan's postwar industrialization and export expansion. From its beginning, ministry officials regarded the promotion of international trade as their primary objective. However, industrial expansion, the rationalization of enterprises, and technological improvement were considered to be the prerequisites for trade expansion. These are precisely what have taken place with the Ministry's help.

Through its **industrial policy**, MITI attempted to promote growth industries that would enjoy growing export demand in the world market. At the same time **declining industries** were encouraged to retrench and diversify. Economic incentives such as cheap credit and tax advantages, as well as **administrative guidance**, are used to elicit industry cooperation. In addition Ministry officials have at times deliberately circumvented the **Antimonopoly Law** to assist industries in their industry rationalization and in their development of new technologies.

Until the mid-1960s MITI had adopted restrictive tariff barriers to protect domestic infant industries. It also restricted **foreign direct investment** in Japan until the early 1980s. Since then, however, it has cooperated with Washington in easing the restrictions on foreign investment and in implementing the voluntary export restraints on automobile and steel exports, and so forth. Some **nontariff barriers to trade** have remained, however.

Since the late 1980s and early 1990s, with Japan's persistent trade surplus and mounting foreign pressure to reduce it, MITI has increasingly promoted foreign imports to reduce the trade surplus. In 1992 it started to emphasize the quality of life and consumer interests, in contrast to its past one-sided emphasis on producers' interests. However, with the growing liberalization of of the Japanese economy and internationalization of Japanese corporations, MITI's influence over the economy and companies has also declined.

The wide scope of MITI's power is reflected organizationally in the diverse bureaus that it consists of—International Trade Policy Bureau, International Trade Administration Bureau, Industrial Policy Bureau, Industrial Location and Environmental Protection Bureau, Basic Industry Bureau,

Machine and Information Industries Bureau, and Consumer Goods Industries Bureau.

MITI is advised by a large number (29 in 1992) of councils in its **decision making**. These councils consist of about 50 members who are prominent in their respective fields such as business, academe, government, **labor unions**, **consumer groups**, and the press. Councils are organized either along industry lines to deal with specific industries such as mining, petroleum, and aircraft, or along functional/structural lines to deal with an important aspect of the economy such as industrial structure, industrial technology, international trade insurance, and **small and medium enterprises**. The Industrial Structure Council, which advises MITI on its industrial policy, is considered one of the most important councils.

MITI also has the following specialized agencies in charge of specific aspects of the economy: Agency of Industrial Science and Technology, Agency of Natural Resources and Energy, Patent Office, and Small and Medium Enterprise Agency.

See also **administrative guidance**, **Antimonopoly Law**, **industrial policy**, **trade policy**.

Address

Ministry of International Trade and Industry
3-1, Kasumigaseki 1-chome, Chiyoda-ku, Tokyo 100
Tel: (03) 3501–1511

References

Johnson, Chalmers. 1982. *MITI and the Japanese Miracle*. Stanford: Stanford University Press.

MITI Handbook, 1991. Tokyo: Japan Trade and Industry Publicity.

MITI calls for open markets to benefit consumers. *Nikkei Weekly*, May 16, 1992: 1, 27.

MITI fights to hold influence in new global era. *Japan Economic Journal*, April 1, 1989: 1, 6.

MITI seeking new role for itself in mature economy. *Nikkei Weekly*, May 30, 1992: 1.

Okimoto, Daniel I. 1989. *Between MITI and the Market* Stanford: Stanford University Press.

Mitsubishi Bank   One of Japan's six largest city banks and one of the three major members of the Mitsubishi Group.

See **city banks**, **Mitsubishi Group**.

Mitsubishi Corp.   One of Japan's largest general trading companies and one of the three major members of the Mitsubishi Group.
See **Mitsubishi Group, trading companies**.

Mitsubishi Electric Corp.   A core member of the Mitsubishi Group and a large comprehensive electric machinery producer.
See **defense industry, Mitsubishi Group**.

Mitsubishi Group   The largest and most cohesive bank-centered *kei-retsu*, or business group, in Japan, with a "three-diamonds" (*mitsu bishi*) logo and a prewar *zaibatsu* origin. It consists of some 160 companies in virtually all sectors of the economy with half a million employees. The three most important companies are Mitsubishi Corporation, Mitsubishi Bank, and Mitsubishi Heavy Industries.

The Mitsubishi Group had its origin in the prewar Mitsubishi *zaibatsu*, a large conglomerate that emerged in the 1870s and 1880s. It was founded by Y. Iwasaki and controlled by his family through a holding company. Initially the family business was in shipping, finance, currency exchange, mining, and ship repairs. It expanded into shipbuilding in 1887 with government subsidy as the state-owned Nagasakai shipbuilding yards were transferred to it. In 1917–19 many independent companies including a holding company, Mitsubishi Bank and Mitsubishi Trading Company were created. During the Second World War the group supported the government's war efforts.

After the war the Americans outlawed the holding company and dissolved the Mitsubishi *zaibatsu*. All the group companies became legally independent, but personal ties of company executives remained, which became the basis of the reconstituted postwar Mitsubishi Group. Group members maintain ties through various means. The Kinyokai (The Friday Club) is the monthly forum, held on the second Friday of each month, where the presidents of 30 core companies meet to exchange views. Reportedly they do not make important decisions there that affect the operations of the group companies, although some authors such as Eli (1990: 20) claim that the opposite is true. Through **cross shareholding**, group members maintain financial ties with one another and prevent hostile takeovers. The group bank, Mitsubishi Bank, serves as the main bank for members of the group in extending loans. Because group members are in diverse sectors of the economy, many group companies are often involved together in an industrial project, especially when selling or investing abroad. In this case the general **trading company** Mitsubishi Corporation would be the negotiator with foreigners and the coordinator for the Mitsubishi companies involved.

The business fields in which Mitsubishi companies are active include the following:

Banking: Mitsubishi Bank, Mitsubishi Trust and Banking

Chemicals: Mitsubishi Kasei Corp., Mitsubishi Gas Chemical, Mitsubishi Petrochemical, Mitsubishi Plastics Industries

Construction: Mitsubishi Construction

Electrical/electronics: Mitsubishi Electric.

Food and drink: Kirin Beer

Glass: Asahi Glass

Insurance: Meiji Life Insurance, Tokio Marine and Fire

Machinery: Mitsubishi Kakoki

Mining and metals: Mitsubishi Kinzoku, Mitsubishi Aluminum, Mitsubishi Densen Kogyo

Oil: Mitsubishi Oil

Optics: Nihon

Paper: Mitsubishi Paper

Real estate: Mitsubishi Jisho

Shipbuilding and heavy machinery: Mitsubishi Heavy Industries

Steel: Mitsubishi Seiko

Synthetic fibers and plastics: Mitsubishi Rayon

Trading: Mitsubishi Corp.

Transportation and communication: Nihon Yusen, Mitsubishi Warehouse and Transportation

Vehicles: Mitsubishi Motors

The Mitsubishi Group is traditionally strong in heavy industries and chemicals and relatively weak in computers, communication equipment, and vehicles. With the structural shift of the economy from the former toward the latter, the Mitsubushi Group's challenge is to successfully adjust to the structural changes in order to maintain its leadership role in the economy. The evidence to date indicates that it has done so very well.

See also *keiretsu* **and business groups**, **Mitsui Group**, **Sumitomo Group**.

Addresses

Mitsubishi Bank
7-1, Marunouchi 2-chome, Chiyoda-ku, Tokyo 100
Tel: (03) 3240-1111   Fax: (03) 3240-3350

Mitsubishi Corp.
6-3, Marunouchi 2-chome, Chiyoda-ku, Tokyo 100
Tel: (03) 3210-2121   Fax: (03) 3210-8065

Mitsubishi Heavy Industries
5-1, Marunouchi 2-chome, Chiyoda-ku, Tokyo 100
Tel: (03) 3212-3111   Fax: (03) 3201-4517

References

Mighty Mitsubishi is on the move. *Business Week*, Sept. 24, 1990: 98–107.

Eli, Max. 1990. *Japan Inc.: Global Strategies of Japanese Trading Corporations*. New York: McGraw-Hill. Ch. 2.

Financial *keiretsu* strenghten solidarity. *Tokyo Business Today*. Feb., 1992: 26–30.

Gerlach, Michael L. 1992. *Alliance Capitalism*. Berkeley: University of California Press. Chs. 3–4.

Ito, Takatoshi. 1992. *The Japanese Economy*. Cambridge: MIT Press. Ch. 7.

Odagiri, Hiroyuki. 1992. Growth through Competition, Competition through Growth. Oxford: Clarendon. Ch. 7.

Mitsubishi Heavy Industries   A giant and diversified heavy machinery producer, Japan's top defense contractor and largest shipbuilder, and one of the three major members of the Mitsubishi Group. It is also heavily involved in producing power plants and enviromental-protection equipment.
   See **defense industry, Mitsubishi Group, shipbuilding industry**.

Mitsubishi Motor Co.   Japan's third largest automaker (as of 1992) and a member of the Mitsubishi Group.
   See **automobile industry**.

Mitsui and Co.   A leading general trading company and a key member of the Mitsui Group.
   See **Mitsui Group, trading companies**.

Mitsui Bank   The former name of one of Japan's largest city banks until it merged with Taiyo Kobe Bank on April 1, 1990, to form the Mitsui Taiyo Kobe Bank. The bank was renamed Sakura Bank on April 1, 1992.
   See **city banks**.

Mitsui Group   One of Japan's largest *keiretsu* or business groups with a prewar Mitsui *zaibatsu* origin. The group comprises 76 companies, of which 24 are core companies. In fiscal year 1989 the total transactions of the 76 companies, excluding financial and insurance firms, were about ¥40 trillion, or nearly $300 billion.

As in other postwar corporate groups and unlike the prewar *zaibatsu*, these group members are independent companies. However, various financial ties and business relations such as an interlocking directorate, cross shareholding, joint ventures, and regular executive conferences promote information exchange and help coordinate business activities. The presidents of the 24 core companies meet on the second Thursday of each month in their Second-Thursday Club (Nimoku Kai), while senior executives of the 76 Mitsui companies meet twice a month on Mondays. These meetings serve as a forum for exchange of views and sometimes to mediate disputes and coordinate actions. Reportedly no major decisions affecting group companies are made at these meetings.

Mitsui Group companies are prominent in diverse fields of businesses. The flagship of the group is the Mitsui and Co., a leading general **trading company** whose origin is traced to the merchant house of Mitsui in the early 1600s. The company was established in 1876 as a trading company, shortly after the Meiji Restoration of 1864 and the new government's decision to open the country to foreign trade. The former Mitsui Bank (now Sakura Bank), Japan's first modern commercial bank, was established in 1887 on the foundation of the money lending business of the house of Mitsui. Other businesses in mining, textiles, shipping, and so forth, soon followed. In 1907 a holding company was organized, which controlled 15 major companies and strongly influenced many others (Roberts 1989: 186). This became the prototype of the prewar *zaibatsu*, which was controlled by a family through a holding company.

After World War II all *zaibatsu* in Japan were dissolved under the Allied Command. New postwar corporate groups emerged, however, in the 1950s, and the Mitsui Group was one of them. The postwar Mitsui and Co. was reestablished in 1947. It was fully reorganized in 1957 after a series of **mergers and acquisitions**, which consolidated a number of specialized trading companies established by employees of the prewar Mitsui and Co.

The group's bank, the former Mitsui Bank, was a large **city bank**. On April 1, 1990, it merged with the Taiyo Kobe Bank to become the Mitsui Taiyo Kobe Bank, the second largest bank in Japan in terms of total assets and total deposits. The new bank was renamed Sakura Bank on April 1, 1992.

Important members of the Mitsui Group are prominent in the following fields:

Banking: Sakura Bank, Mitusi Trust and Banking

Cement: Onoda Cement

Commerce: Mitsukoshi (Japan's most prestigeous department store group), Nihon Unisys (computer sale, service, and software)

Chemicals: Mitsui Petrochemical Industries, Mitsui Toatsu Chemicals

Construction: Mitsui Construction

Electrical/electronic equipment: Toshiba Corp.

Food and beverages: Sapporo Breweries, Suntory (beer, wine, etc.)

Insurance: Mitsui Mutual Life Insurance, Mitsui Marine and Fire Insurance (formerly Taisho Marine and Fire Insurance before Aprl 1, 1991)

Machinery: Mitsui Engineering and Shipbuilding, Sanki Engineering

Mining and metals: Mitsui Mining, Mitsui Mining and Smelting

Oil: Mitsui Oil

Paper: Oji Paper

Real estate: Mitsui Real Estate Development

Steel: Japan Steel Works

Synthetic fibers and plastics: Toray Industries

Transportation: Mitsui O.S.K. Lines

Warehousing: Mitsui Warehouse

The major rival of the Mitsui Group is the Mitsubishi Group. They compete in many fields, but they also have different strengths in different fields.
    See also **keiretsu and business groups, Mitsubishi Group, zaibatsu**.

Address

Mitusi and Co.
2-1, Ohtemachi 1-chome, Chiyoda-ku, Tokyo 100
Tel: (03) 3285-1111   Fax: (03) 3285-9800

References

Eli, Max. 1990. *Japan Inc.: Global Strategies of Japanese Trading Corporations*. New York: McGraw-Hill. Ch. 2.

Ito, Takatoshi. 1992. *The Japanese Economy*. Cambridge: MIT Press. Ch. 7.

Gerlach, Michael L. *Alliance Capitalism*. Berkeley: University of California Press. Chs. 3–4.

Odagiri, Hiroyuki. 1992. *Growth through Competition, Competition through Growth*. Oxford: Clarendon. Ch. 7.

Roberts, John G. 1989. *Mitsui: Three Centuries of Japanese Business*, 2d ed. New York: Weatherhill.

Mitsukoshi, Ltd. A top and prestigeous department store and a core member of the Mitsui Group.
See **department stores, Mitsui Group**.

mochiai The cross-holding of stock among publicly traded companies and financial institutions.
See **cross shareholding**.

monetary policy
See **Bank of Japan, financial liberalization, Ministry of Finance, money supply, interest rate structure**.

money market dealers These are companies that specialize in the intermediation of transactions in the short-term **money markets**. Because of their important role, they are directly under the supervision of the **Ministry of Finance**. The **Bank of Japan** also provides guidance for their business activities.

Currently there are six money market dealers, or *tanshi* companies— Tokyo Tanshi, Yamane Tanshi, Ueda Tanshi, Nippon Discount Tanshi, Yagi Tanshi, and Nagoya Tanshi (*tanshi* literally means "short-term loans"). Their operations include (1) **call money market** transactions, (2) bill trading transactions, (3) transactions in government bills, (4) intermediation of foreign exchange trading, (5) intermediation of dollar–call market financing, (6) trading transactions in certificates of deposits, (7) transactions in yen-demonimated bankers' acceptances, and (8) intermediation of interbank deposit transactions. In some of these operations such as transactions in the call funds and CDs, the dealers can either serve as brokers by bringing lenders and borrowers together or trade on own accounts as dealers.

In their operations money market dealers interacts with the Bank of Japan in the following ways: (1) Each dealer maintains a current deposit account at the Bank of Japan for the settlement of call and bill transactions. (2) The dealers utilize exchange transactions between the head office and branches of the Bank of Japan to carry out transactions in call funds and bill trading with financial institutions throughout the country. (3) The Bank of Japan may lend to the dealers for transactions in the call money market and for the purchase of certificates of deposits, or it may lend to **securities finance companies** for their margin transactions through the money market dealers. (4) The Bank of Japan's market operations in private bills and government bills are carried out through the money market dealers. Thus the money market dealers help promote the smooth functioning of the money market, the implementation of the government's monetary policy, and the intergration of the markets in various parts of the country.

As a reflection of the close relations between the six money market dealers and the Bank of Japan, the presidents of five of the six *tanshi* companies are ex-Bank of Japan officials. Also nearly 30% of their board members are former Bank of Japan officials.

The money market dealers have been criticized by large Japanese banks, who are the main borrowers on the money market, for giving preferential treatment to the big lenders. Furthermore the lack of competition among the *tanshi* companies provides no incentives for them to offer discounts on commission fees.

Because of foreign pressure, the Bank of Japan has permitted foreign banks operating in Japan to deal with large Japanese banks directly. In addition the U.S. Treasury Department has requested that the money brokering business be opened to foreign institutions.

See also **money markets**.

References

Mizuno, Yuko. 1989. Money market magnates draw criticisms at home and abroad. *Japan Economic Journal*, Dec. 23: 31–32.

Suzuki, Yoshio, ed. 1987. *The Japanese Financial System*. Oxford: Oxford University Press. Pp. 269–73.

Viner, Aron. 1987. *Inside Japan's Financial Markets*. London: The Economist Publications. Ch. 8.

money markets   Money markets are short-term financial markets in which financial assets of maturity of less than one year are traded. They can be divided into two broad categories: the interbank money market and the open market. The former is larger than the latter. Each in turn is composed of a number of markets, as explained below:

1. *Interbank market*. Lending and borrowing take place among financial institutions. It includes the following:

- **Call-money market**, which is the traditional interbank money market for the transfer of funds from banks with temporary surplus to those with temporary deficit for very short terms (overnight to three weeks). The interest rate on call money has been rather free from direct government or **Bank of Japan** control. The call money market remains the largest interbank market. In 1992 it had an average balance of ¥38.92 trillion.
- Bill market, in which holders of bills that have not matured sell them to buyers at a discount to obtain funds. The bills may be high-grade commercial and industrial bills, trade bills, high-grade promissory notes, and yen-denominated export and import bills. The market is considered to be an extension of the call market. The interest rates on the bill market were controlled by the Bank of Japan until 1975. In 1985 the Bank of Japan also deregulated the bill market, lifting restrictions on the type of financial institutions that could participate in the market. The types of bills traded in the bill market include one-month bills, two-month bills, and over-three-month bills. In 1992 the market had an average balance of of ¥15.01 trillion.
- Dollar-call market, or the Tokyo dollar-call market, in which financial institutions borrow and lend foreign currency funds among themselves for short periods. Started in 1972, it passed the billion dollar level in 1985. The loan period ranges from overnight to over one month. The total value of transactions was $1.21 trillion in 1992.

2. *Open market*. Nonfinancial institutions may participate in the open market. It includes the following:

- *Gensaki* market, the market for the trading of bonds with a repurchase agreement whereby the seller agrees to repurchase the bonds at a specified time at a higher price. Although the transactions involve the buying and selling of securities, they are short-term borrowing and lending in substance because of the repurchase agreement. The repurchase period ranges from one month, two months, to three months. Initially developed in the 1970s to provide nonbank short-term financing for securities houses, it became popular with banks, other financial institutions, and business corporations because it was one of the few financial markets with a market-determined interest rate. However, **securities companies** remain the largest sellers of *gensaki* (i.e., borrowers in the market). In recent years the rates of the *gensaki* and the call markets have moved virtually in tandem. At the end of 1992, the transaction balance was ¥8.85 trillion.
- Certificate of deposit (CD) market. As an increasing number of corporations switched their liquid funds from bank deposits to the more attractive

gensaki instruments, banks lobbied to issue alternative competing instruments. In May 1979 they were permitted to issue negotiable certificates of deposits. A secondary market for trading in these instruments was opened in May 1980. At the end of 1992 the CD balance was ¥16.6 trillion, down from ¥21.1 trillion at the end of 1989.

• Bankers' acceptance (BA) market. Established in June 1985, this is the market for trading in yen-denominated fixed-term bills of exchange, which are issued by companies such as importers and exporters to settle contracts and are guaranteed by foreign exchange banks. The market had a late start because very little of Japanese trade has been in yen.

• Treasury bill market. This market was created in February 1986, following the 1984 recommendations by the Japan–U.S. Yen–Dollar committee that Japan foster a short-term government bond market. Although the market has grown steadily since its establishment, its size remains relatively small. The outstanding amount sold by the Bank of Japan was ¥10.37 trillion at the end of 1992. Japan's treasury bills are issued with low yield to minimize government interest burdens, and almost all are accepted by the Bank of Japan. The latter has sold its treasury bills at market prices. These prices, however, have not affected other money market rates. Thus treasury bill operations as a monetary tool of the Bank of Japan have not been effective.

• **Commercial paper market**. This market was established only in November 1987. Because a commercial paper (CP) is an unsecured promisary note, only corporations and banks with high credit ratings are eligible for issuing it. It is a way to raise low-cost funds. At the end of 1992 the outstanding amounts of commercial paper stood at ¥12.2 trillion, down from ¥15.76 trillion at the end of 1990.

• Euroyen markets. These markets are outside Japan where yen-denominated financial assets (Euroyen deposits, Euroyen CDs, Euroyen loans, etc.) are traded. The markets are located in London, Singapore, Hong Kong, and New York, with London accounting for about 60% of the total trading. The markets are attractive to Japanese financial institutions because they are free from Japanese regulations. As of December 1987 the Euroyen market size was at ¥137.2 billion. The **Tokyo offshore market**, established in December 1986, is a banking market where foreign exchange banks conduct business with nonresidents. It is relatively free from domestic regulations. The value of transactions in the market was $7.02 trillion in 1992.

Transactions in the money markets are dominated by six *tanshi* companies, Japan's **money market dealers**. Presidents of these companies are often ex-Bank of Japan officials. The Bank of Japan buys discount bills, commercial paper, and other financial instruments through the *tanshi* companies in order to adjust money in the market on a daily basis.

See also **call money market, commercial paper market, money market dealers, Tokyo offshore market**.

References

Bank of Japan. 1993. *Economic Statistics Annual. 1992.*

Federation of Bankers Association of Japan. 1989. *The Banking System in Japan.* Tokyo: Zenginkyo. Pp. 108–115.

Suzuki, Yoshio, ed. 1987. *The Japanese Financial System*: Oxford: Oxford University Press. Ch. 4.

Tatewaki, Kazuo. 1991. *Banking and Finance in Japan.* London: Routledge. Ch. 4.

Viner, Aron. 1987. *Inside Japan's Financial Markets.* London: The Economist Publications. Ch. 8.

money supply   Of the various measures of money supply, the **Bank of Japan**, Japan's central bank, focuses on the broad measure of M2 + CD (and sometimes also M3 + CD) in contrast with the United States, which focuses on the narrow measure of M1. M1 is defined as currency in circulation plus demand deposits; M2 equals M1 plus time deposits, while CD stands for certificates of deposit; M3 is M2 plus trust accounts, loan trusts, and **postal savings**.

The Bank of Japan focuses on the broad measure for two reasons. First, it is found that in Japan M2 + CD has a closer relationship with future potential income and expenditure than M1. The latter is more closely correlated with current income and expenditure (Suzuki 1986: 187). Since the Bank of Japan is more concerned with future income and expenditure and their impact on prices, the broad measure is considered more appropriate. Second, it is easier for the Bank of Japan to control M2 + CD than M1. Strict limits exist on the Bank's ability to have short-term control of M1 (Suzuki 1987: 33; author's interview, Bank of Japan, July 16, 1992).

The Bank of Japan does not set a target for money supply, but it announces a quarterly "forecast," which is based on the planned policy actions of the Bank anyway. Thus a forecast differs little from a target except that it implies less policy commitment and can be more easily changed as circumstances change. In fact the actual growth rates of M2 + CD have been very close to the forecasts announced by the Bank of Japan.

Japan's outstanding M2 + CD at year-end was ¥125 trillion in 1975, ¥314.9 trillion in 1985, and ¥515.5 trillion in 1992. The figure for M1 was ¥49.9 trillion in 1975, ¥89.0 trillion in 1985, and ¥136.1 trillion in 1992 (see table M.3). The annual rate of growth of M2 + D averaged 13.1% during 1975–78, declined to less than 10% between 1979 and 1986 (except in 1981), and then rose to an average of 11% during 1987–89. In the early 1990s it declined substantially. Overall, however, the annual growth rates of M2 + CD were relatively even compared with those of M1, which fluctuated greatly and somewhat erratically over the years. The reason for this is that households and corporations can easily shift in their holdings of monetary assets between currency and demand deposits (M1), on the one hand, and time deposits and CDs, on the other hand, all of which are components of M2 + CD. Thus it is easier for the Bank of Japan to control and forecast the growth of the latter. The relatively even growth of M2 + CD has, no doubt, contributed to Japan's low rate of inflation since the mid-1970s.

See also **Bank of Japan, interest rates, money markets.**

References

Bank of Japan. 1993. *Economic Statistics Annual*, 1992.

Grivoyannis, Elias C. 1991. *Current Issues in Monetary Policy in the United States and Japan: The Predictability of Money Demand.* New York: Praeger.

Table M.3
Money supply and growth rates (in ¥ trillions and %)

End of year	M1	Growth rate	M2 + CD	Growth rate
1975	49.9	11.1	125.3	14.5
1980	69.6	−2.0	209.0	7.2
1985	89.0	3.0	314.9	8.7
1986	98.2	10.4	343.9	9.2
1987	103.0	4.8	380.9	10.8
1988	111.8	8.6	419.7	10.2
1989	114.5	2.4	470.0	12.0
1990	119.6	4.5	505.0	7.4
1991	131.0	9.5	516.3	2.3
1992	136.1	3.9	515.3	−0.2

Source: Bank of Japan.

Suzuki, Yoshio. 1986. *Money, Finance, and Macroeconomic Performance in Japan.* New Haven: Yale University Press. Chs. 3, 6, 8.

Suzuki, Yoshio, ed. 1987. *The Japanese Financial System.* Oxford: Oxford University Press. Ch. 6.

Morita, Akio (1921–)   Cofounder and chairman of Sony Corp., known for his international orientation.

See **electronics industry, management practices.**

N

Nagoya and Central Japan   With a population of 2.16 million as of October 1992, Nagoya is the fourth largest city in Japan. It is located approximately at the center of the long Japanese archipelago. It is the capital city of Aichi prefecture and the hub of Japan's third largest industrial region. It is also the business center of Central Japan (*chubu*, which includes Aichi, Gifu, Mie, Nagano, and Shizuoka prefectures) and one of Japan's largest foreign trade ports.

In FY 1989 Nagoya had a gross municipal product of ¥10.87 trillion, or 2.7% of Japan's gross domestic product, which was the third largest among the major cities of the nation. Transportation equipment is the leading industry, followed by general machinery. Aichi prefecture has other centers of industry and commerce, including Toyota city (automobiles), Ichinomiya (textiles), and Seto (ceramics). Central Japan manufactures approximately 50% of all Japanese vehicles. Many automakers—including Toyota, Honda, Mitsubishi, Suzuki, and others—have their corporate headquarters and/or plants located in Central Japan. About 6,000 subcontractors are located in Aichi, Shizuoka, and Mie prefectures. Other industries of Central Japan include machine tools, aerospace, precision instruments, electronic/electric instruments, ceramics, textiles or apparel, steel, petrochemicals and musical instruments. Nagoya handled ¥7.22 trillion exports and imports in 1991, making it the fifth largest port in Japan.

See also **Kansai and Osaka, Tokyo, Yokohama**.

Address

City of Nagoya
1-1 Sannomaru 3-chome, Naka-ku, Nagoya 460-08
Tel: (052) 961-111

References

City of Nagoya. Undated. *Nagoya*.

City of Nagoya. 1991. *Nagoya Statistical Yearbook* (in Japanese).

National Pension
See **pension system**.

National Tax Administration   An agency of the Ministry of Finance in charge of tax collection.
See **Ministry of Finance, tax system**.

National taxes   Taxes levied by the national government, including individual income tax, corporation tax, consumption tax, and inheritance tax.
See **tax system**.

NEC Corp. (Nippon Electric Company)   A large electronics company and Japan's largest producer of semiconductors and personal computers; also a core member of the **Sumitomo Group**.
See **electronics industry**, *keiretsu* **and business groups**.

nemawashi   An informal, pre-decision-making process of discussions in a corporation or organization to facilitate the formation of consensus in subsequent formal decision making.
See **decision making**.

nenko   Seniority-based wage system.
See **corporate personnel practices, permanent employment, wage structure**.

Nihon Keizai Shimbun (Japan Economic Daily)   Japan's oldest and most widely circulated business daily with a circulation of more than three million, published by Nihon Keizai Shimbun, Inc.
See **economic/business research and publications**.

Nihon Keizai Shimbun, Inc.   Japan's leading business publisher. It publishes *Nihon Keizai Shimbun*, Japan's leading business daily. It also compiles the Nikkei Stock Average, a major index of stock prices of the **Tokyo Stock Exchange**.
See **economic/business research and publications, stock price indexes**.

nihonteki keiei   Japanese-style management.
   See **corporate finance, corporate personnel practices, management practices**.

Nikkei commodity futures index
See **commodity markets**.

Nikkei Stock Average   An index of the average price of 225 stocks listed on the first section of the Tokyo Stock Exchange, compiled by Nihon Keizai Shimbun, Inc.
   See **stock price indexes, Tokyo Stock Exchange**.

Nikkei Weekly   An English-language business weekly, available worldwide, published by Nihon Keizai Shimbun, Inc.
   See **economic/business research and publications**.

nikkeijin   Foreigners of Japanese descent. Unlike other foreigners, they are given long-term resident status and can work legally in Japan.
   See **foreign workers in Japan**.

Nikkeiren   Japan Federation of Employers' Associations, a leading business organization.
   See **business organizations**.

Nippon Life Insurance Co.   Japan's largest life insurance company.
   See **insurance companies**.

Nippon Shinpan Co.   Japan's largest consumer credit card company.
   See **credit card industry**.

Nippon Steel   The largest steel producer in Japan and in the world.
   See **steel industry**.

Nippon Telegraph and Telephone (NTT)   Japan's largest telecommunications company and the world's second largest after American Telephone and Telegraph. Privatized in April 1985.
   See **privatization**.

Nissan Motor Co.   Japan's second largest automobile company.
   See **automobile industry**.

Nissho Japan Chamber of Commerce and Industry, a leading business organization.
See **business organizations**.

NKK (Nippon Kokan) Japan's second largest steel company.
See **steel industry**.

Nokyo The nationwide network of agricultural cooperatives and their national federation.
See **agricultural cooperatives**.

Nomura Investment Management Co. Japan's largest investment advisory company and an affiliate of Nomura Securities Co.
See **investment advisory companies**.

Nomura Research Institute Japan's largest private economic research institute or "think tank."
See **economic/business research and publications**.

Nomura Securities Co. Japan's largest securities company.
See **securities companies**.

nonbank financial institutions Japan has some 37,000 nonbank financial institutions, or *nonbanks*, as they are commonly called in recent years. These include credit and finance firms and leasing firms. As much as 95% of their funds come from bank loans. In turn they lend at higher interest rates to medium and small businesses, real estate firms, and so on, which have higher risks. In April 1991, their total outstanding loans were estimated at ¥80 trillion, far exceeding those of regional banks.

The major business areas of nonbanks are given below, along with the outstanding loan balances as of the end of March 1990 in parentheses and the leading companies in each area (*Japan Economic Journal*, May 26, 1990: 36):

1. Consumer credit (¥2.76 trillion): Takefuji, Acom, Promise

2. Business-oriented credit (¥23.81 trillion).

3. Bank-affiliated credit cards (¥0.82 trillion): JCB, Sumitomo Credit Service.

4. Credit sales (¥4.14 trillion): Orient, Nippon Shinpan, Daishinpan.

5. Real estate-related financing (¥3.44 trillion): Nippon Mortgage, Orifund.

6. Leasing (¥9.71 trillion): Japan Leasing, Orix, Showa Leasing.

In the 1980s nonbanks were heavily involved in making real estate loans against the collateral of shares and pieces of property. These have contributed greatly to the speculative rises of land prices of the 1980s, making affordable **housing** beyond the reach of middle-class families in the major metropolitan areas. As stock prices declined in 1990, the portfolios of the nonbanks were put in a precarious situation. Surveys show that more than 60% of the debts of companies that went bankrupt between November 1990 and September 1991 due to land and stock speculation were owed to nonbanks. Consequently many nonbanks are saddled with large bad loans.

Nonbanks are mostly under the jurisdiction of the **Ministry of International Trade and Industry**, but they are also loosely regulated by the **Ministry of Finance**, in contrast to the latter's tight control of the banking institutions. The Money-Lending Regulation Act required them to disclose only their total financial balances. The land price inflation of the late 1980s, however, prompted the Diet to revise the law in May 1991, which now requires nonbanks with financial balances above a certain level to itemize their loans portfolios and provide a description of their real estate loans.

Another regulatory issue involving nonbanks concerns their long-standing request for permission to issue commercial papers (CPs) in the domestic market. Prior to June 1993, only some 450 blue-chip corporations, banks, and securities firms were allowed to issue CPs. Banks were opposed to opening up the CP market lest they lose many principal borrowers as well as their funding cost advantage over nonbanks. Analysts who were in favor of opening up the CP market to nonbanks argued that this would lower the latter's cost of funds and cut their loans to high-risk, high-return businesses such as real estate.

In June 1993 the Ministry of Finance decided to permit nonbanks to issue CPs under strict conditions. Nonbanks are required to receive rating of A-2 or better from at least two credit-rating agencies, and they are not allowed to use the money obtained from CPs to make loans.

See also **consumer credit, credit card industry**.

References

Fujino, Keisuke. 1990. Non-bank finance firms suffering from ever-tightening bank credit. *Japan Economic Journal*, May 26: 36.

Inose, Hijiri. 1991a. Diet bill gives MOF power over non-banks. *Japan Economic Journal*, May 18: 32.

Inose, Hijiri. 1991b. Non-banks taking body blows. *Nikkei Weekly*, Oct. 26: 1.

Japan's "non-bank" financing houses placed under government surveillance. *Japan Economic Review*, Mar. 15, 1991: 5.

Nonbanks come under fire. *Tokyo Business Today*, Dec. 1991: 10.

Sawada, Masaru. 1990. Non-banks left with devastating portfolios as land-price magic proves to be myth. *Japan Economic Journal*, winter suppl.: 17.

nontariff barriers to trade   Policy measures, economic institutions, and business practices that have the effect of discouraging or restricting imports from foreign countries, whether or not such an effect is intended. Thus they complement tariffs in reducing imports. Usually quotas are the most important form of nontariff barriers to trade.

Although Japan's tariffs are no higher than those of other industrialized countries, foreign critics have argued that various types of nontariffs barriers to trade have greatly reduced imports and contributed to the trade imbalance between Japan and its trading partners. The barriers most often cited are the following:

1. *Custom procedures.* The inspection procedure is said to be bureaucratic and time-consuming, and until recently it was very difficult to appeal unfavorable custom rulings.

2. *Restrictive standards and regulations.* For certification purpose, the technical standards adopted are very high, and government regulations are said to be restrictive according to foreign critics. Japanese standards are often written in terms of design criteria rather than performance specifications. This leaves discretionary power for officials to delay or even prohibit entry of foreign goods into the Japanese market even though the products may perform adequately. In addition Japanese officials do not accept foreign test data. This is particularly true with respect to pharmaceuticals. In response, Japanese officials and industry representatives contend that high technical standards have to be maintained because Japanese consumers insist on them and that the Japanese react differently to pharmaceuticals than the Westerners.

3. *Quota restrictions on imports of agricultural products.* Although Japan is a high-cost producer of most agricultural products due to lack of land, it restricts its imports through quotas. Rice is banned completely. Japanese officials cite the importance of self-sufficiency in food, the need for the rural **population** to supplement their incomes through farming, and the importance of preserving traditional values as embodied in farming as the

reasons for such restrictions. Foreign observers have pointed out that it is the inordinate political power of the farmers—political districts were drawn on the basis of immediate postwar population distribution and they have not been revised—that make the restriction of cheaper agricultural imports possible and that the Liberal Democratic Party, Japan's ruling party since 1955, derives much of its support from the rural areas and is simply placing its political interests ahead of the economic interests of the economy and fairness in international trade. There is also the so-called "prior confirmation system," which acts, in effect, like a quota. Under the system imports of specific products such as Korean and Taiwanese silk products and tuna require prior approval by the **Ministry of International Trade and Industry** (Balassa and Noland 1988: 55).

4. *Differences in language, customs, the marketing system, and consumer preferences.* Japan's multilayered **distribution system** is complex and difficult to penetrate. Japanese consumers seem to believe strongly that Japanese products are superior in quality. Japanese language and customs are difficult for foreigners to master. All of these make the cost of doing business in Japan higher. Tokyo's response is that if foreigners are genuinely interested in doing business in Japan, they should make more effort to understand and to overcome these differences.

Komiya and Irie (1990: 84–87) dismiss the alleged nontariff barriers in Japan as "myths" on the ground that conceptually and statistically they are difficult to measure and compare internationally. Subsequently Komiya admits to the existence of nontariff barriers in Japan but argues that they are not unique to Japan as all other countries have them (author's interview, July 7, 1992). Japanese officials and authors generally do not deny that nontariff barriers to trade exist in Japan but regard them as either justified or unimportant. Japan's trading partners think otherwise and regard them as a source of trade imbalance.

See also **rice production and distribution, trade pattern, trade policy.**

References

Balassa, Bela, and Marcus Noland. 1988. *Japan in the World Economy.* Washington: Institutue for International Economics. Ch. 3.

Komiya, Ryutaro, and Kazutomo Irie. 1990. The U.S.–Japan trade problem: An economic analysis from a Japanese viewpoint. In *Japan's Economic Structure: Should It Change?* ed. by Kozo Yamamura. Seattle: Society for Japanese Studies.

Lincoln, Edward J. 1990. *Japan's Unequal Trade*. Washington: Brookings Institution. Ch. 2.

Vogel, David. 1992. Consumer protection and protectionism in Japan. *Journal of Japanese Studies* 18, 1: 119–54.

Norinchukin Bank   The Central Cooperative Bank for Agriculture and Forestry.
   See **agricultural cooperatives, banking system.**

NTT
See **Nippon Telegraph and Telephone, privatization.**

O

official development assistance
See **foreign aid**.

official discount rate   The interest rate that the **Bank of Japan** charges on loans to commerical banks.
   See **Bank of Japan, interest rate structure**.

offshore banking
See **Tokyo offshore market**.

Okura sho   The Ministry of Finance.
   See **Ministry of Finance**.

Orix   Japan's largest leasing company and a nonbank lending institution.
   See **nonbank financial institutions**.

Osaka
See **Kansai and Osaka**.

Osaka Securities Exchange   Japan's second largest stock exchange, located in Osaka.
   See **stock index futures trading, stock index options trading, Tokyo Stock Exchange**.

over-the-counter market   The market in which shares of medium-sized companies are traded. Japan's over-the-counter (OTC) market is relatively small but has grown rapidly since the late 1980s. It is supervised by the Japan Securities Dealers Association but is less organized than the stock exchange. Transactions are executed over the counter of securities' dealers.

Prices are determined through negotiations between a buyer and a seller. Thus prices can vary from one firm to another.

The number of companies listed on the Tokyo OTC market was only 121 in 1980. After the relaxation of standards for the listing in 1983, the number grew to 159 in 1987, 202 in 1988, 275 in 1989, and reached 425 in November 1991, surpassing the number of companies listed on the second section of the **Tokyo Stock Exchange**. The volume of transactions was 477.6 million shares in 1988, which was only 0.17% of the volume of the first section of the Tokyo Stock Exchange and 11.5% of that of its second section. It grew to 1,253.2 million shares in 1990. The market value of its stocks was ¥17.53 trillion on April 25, 1991, whereas the second section of the Tokyo Stock Exchange, where smaller companies are listed, had a total of ¥17.50 trillion.

Various factors account for its recent rapid growth: (1) The relaxation of the public offering rules such as the minimum number of shares to be offered has made it easier for small companies to go public for equity financing. (2) Investors interesed in growth potentials of venture capital investments are attracted to the OTC market because earnings of OTC companies have grown faster in recent years than those of large companies listed on the first section of the Tokyo Stock Exchange. Many of these OTC companies are in service industries, which have grown rapidly in recent years. (3) Some companies believe that the OTC listing will give them good publicity and help the recruiting of university graduates. (4) The Japan Securities Dealers Association has established a nationwide OTC trading system.

However, some problems still plague the OTC market. The computer trading system linking all trading counters was not introduced until October 1991. Traders are mostly limited to the local market, and prices very from place to place. Overall the OTC market is still considered a risky market shunned by major investors.

The market is managed by the Japan Securities Dealers Association. The Nihon Keizai Shimbun, Inc., calculates and publishes the Nikkei OTC average.

See also **stock market, Tokyo Stock Exchange**.

Address

Japan Securities Dealers Association
5-8 Nihonbashi Kayabacho 1-chome, Chuo-ku, Tokyo 103
Tel: (03) 3667-8451

References

Isaacs, Jonathan. 1992. *Japanese Equities Markets*. London: Euromoney Publications. Ch. 6.

Japan Securities Research Institute. 1992. *Securities Market in Japan*, 1992. Pp. 37–39.

Matsuoka, Minoru. 1992. Outline of the Japanese OTC stock market. In *Capital Markets and Financial Services in Japan*. Tokyo: Japan Securities Research Institute.

Mizuno, Yuko. 1991. High-flying start-ups keep trading lively on OTC. *Japan Economic Journal*, May 4: 31.

OTC listings likely to pass TSE 2nd section. *Nikkei Weekly*, Nov. 2, 1991: 14.

P

parallel import system   A new import practice that permits competing importers of foreign products to break the monopoly of the exclusive general import agents.

See **distribution system**.

part-time workers   Officially defined as nonagricultural workers who work less than 35 hours a week.

See **employment pattern, labor force**.

patent system   First established in 1885, way behind England (1623) and the United States (1790), Japan's patent system has grown rapidly. In 1990 it introduced the world's first "paperless" application system.

Japanese companies typically file a large number of patent applications. In 1990 Japan's Patent Office processed 367,590 applications, of which 34,360 were filed by foreigners. Only about 30% of the applications prove to be successful, as compared with 67% in the United States. Japanese companies also send a large number of patent applications abroad, much more than that received from abroad. For example, according to the Patent and Trademark Office of the U.S. Department of Commerce, of the 101,860 patents granted in FY 1991, 21,464 were granted to Japanese individuals and companies.

Aside from the growing inventiveness of the Japanese, the nature of Japan's patent system and the attempts to thwart patent applications by rivals also help explain such large numbers of patent applications. In Japan, as in most European countries, a patent goes to the first person to file an application, not to the first inventor, as in the United States. In addition, as in Europe, the Patent Office automatically makes patent applications public 18 months after they have been filed regardless of whether a patent is ultimately granted. Therefore an inventor cannot exploit his invention as a trade secret in Japan if he fails to receive a patent. If he is granted the patent, however, he can ask for compensation from those who imitated his invention (author's interview, Patent Office, Oct. 18, 1991).

From the Japanese perspective, the first-to-file system is less prone to result in litigations. In addition it fosters the growth of large industry, whereas the first-to-invent system stresses the protection of small entrepreneurial inventors.

The application process consists of two steps. Since 1988 inventors can apply and pay the initial fee (¥14,000) and then decide within seven years whether to complete the application and pay the remaining fee of at least ¥600,000 for the 15 year-term of patent (note: this comes from the escalating annual fees, which are ¥29,000 in the 7–9th year, ¥58,000 in the 10–12th year, and ¥116,000 in the 13–15th year. In some cases the term of patent may be extended to 20 years, with higher annual fees). Although only about 30% of patent applications result in patents, this two-step application process permits and even encourages potential inventors to file patent applications in a defensive move to preempt the first claim from rivals.

Because of the large number of patent applications filed, it usually takes a long time—an average of 32 months in 1990 as compared with 18 months in the United States and 30 months in Europe—for patents to be awarded. In a notorious and, no doubt, exceptional case, it took the Patent Office 29 years (February 1960 to October 1989) to give Texas Instruments its patent on the integrated circuit (*New York Times*, Nov. 22 and 24, 1989). U.S. companies and trade officials have complained that the usual delays are deliberately made to allow Japanese companies to create a competing product while preventing U.S. products from ever reaching Japan. The Japanese authority's response was that the Patent Office was understaffed. From 1980 to 1989, while the number of patent applications nearly doubled, the size of the Patent Office staff declined from 2,367 in 1980 to 2,336 in 1989 as a result of the general government staff reduction. By late 1991 it had risen to 2,396 and is scheduled to increase by 10–20 every year.

Japan also awards hundreds of narrowly defined patents that would be covered in a few broad generic patents in the United States. This practice invites countless challenges, many intended to force the applicant to surrender his technology. Small U.S. firms have complained that they can't afford to defend every Japanese opposition.

Thus the Japanese patent system became an issue in the **Structural Impediments Initiative** (SII) talks between the United States and Japan in

1989–90. U.S. trade officials urged Tokyo to reform these practices that have hurt the U.S. interests. Private-sector advisers to the **Ministry of International Trade and Industry**, which supervises Japan's Patent Office, have also recommended that measures be taken to discourage "patent flooding"—the filing of numerous applications in an attempt to foil rivals —and promote the U.S. practice of awarding broader-coverage patents.

To reduce the delays in screening patent applications, the Japanese Patent Office started outside contracting for some patent inspection work in April 1989. A "paperless" electronic patent application system, the first in the world, was introduced in December 1990. These measures have reduced the average examination period. Top patent applicants in Japan include Hitachi Ltd., Matsushita Electric Industrial Co., NEC Corp., Fujitsu Ltd., and Matsushita Group affiliates.

Patent protection is only one aspect of intellectual property protection. The others are trademarks registration and protection of trade secrets. The Patent Office is in charge of trademarks registration. Trademarks registration in Japan is a slow process; it usually takes 30 months, as compared with one year in the United States. In addition Balassa and Noland (1988: 61) charge that in Japan foreign trademarks may be registered by domestic firms to preempt their subsequent registration by foreign firms that have already used them abroad. In response, the Japanese Patent Office explains that this practice is limited to foreign trademarks that are not well known in Japan (author's interview, Oct. 18, 1991).

See also **Structural Impediments Initiative**.

Addresses

Japan Patent Association
5, Kanda Ogawacho 2-chome, Chiyoda-ku, Tokyo 101
Tel: (03) 3295-8475

Patent Attorneys Association of Japan
4-2, Kasumigaseki 3-chome, Chiyoda-ku, Tokyo 100
Tel: (03) 3581-1211

Patent Office, Ministry of International Trade and Industry
4-3, Kasumigaseki 3-chome, Chiyoda-ku, Tokyo 100
Tel: (03) 3581-1101

References

Akashi, Yoshihiko. 1990. Japan's patenting activity. *Osaka City University Economic Review*, 25: 13–26.

Balassa, Bela, and Marcus Noland. 1988. *Japan in the World Economy.* Washington: Institute for International Economics.

Japanese Patent Office. *Annual Report.*

Japanese Patent Office. 1988. *Guide to Industrial Property in Japan.*

Johnson, Chalmers. 1990. Revisionism, and the future of Japanese-American relations. In *Japan's Economic Structure: Should It Change?* ed. by Kozo Yamamura. Seattle: Society for Japanese Studies.

Matsushita, Mitsuo. 1990. Protection of technology and the liberal trade order: A Japanese view. In *Japan's Economic Structure: Should It Change?*, ed. by Kozo Yamamura. Seattle: Society for Japanese Studies.

Patent War Heating Up. *Tokyo Business Today,* May 1992; 26–31.

Shioya, Yoshio. 1989. Intellectual property rights. In *Japan Economic Almanac, 1989.* Tokyo: Nihon Keizai Shimbun.

Spero, Donald M. 1990. Patent protection or piracy—A CEO views Japan. *Harvard Business Review* 68, 5: 58–67.

Tsuchiya, Hideo. 1989. Mother of invention too prolific for patent office. *Japan Economic Journal,* May 13: 20.

Yoder, Stephen. 1987. Rush to exploit new superconductors makes Japan even more patent-crazy. *Wall Street Journal,* Aug. 27: 18.

pension fund market   Japan's corporate pension fund market was first created in 1966 when the government allowed companies to set up independent employee's pension fund corporations. Since then the market has grown substantially. As of the end of March 1990, a total of 1,406 such corporations deposited ¥19.6 trillion in welfare annuity funds.

Until April 1990, the law restricted the management of pension funds to **trust banks** and life **insurance companies**, which had 70% and 30%, respectively, of the business in 1989. Their investment performance was relatively poor, however, as they earned only 8–9% annual cash return. Since April 1990, the revision of the Employees Insurance Law adopted by the Diet opened the pension fund management market to 143 licensed **investment advisory companies**. Thiry-nine of them are foreign owned, admitted into the market to improve investment performance; the others are subsidiaries of banks and securities houses.

Various regulations, however, have delayed the entry of many investment advisory companies into the market. For example, the minimum fund unit to be managed is fixed at ¥1 billion, and pension funds must be less than a third of an investment advisory company's total funds. Companies affiliated with the **securities companies** have a competitive edge because they have acquired expertise through the management of pension funds entrusted by foreign clients. The most successful ones are the subsidiaries of Japan's four big securities firms (Nomura, Daiwa, Nikko, and Yamaichi). Foreign investment advisory companies' business has remained small to date.

See also **pension system**.

References

Japanese pension funds: Foreigners wait for the goodies. *The Economist*, June 8, 1991: 80–81.

Shida, Tomio. 1989. Pension fund battleground seen as Diet prepares to lift barriers. *Japan Economic Journal*, Dec. 16: 32.

Shida, Tomio. 1990. Pension fund growth mirrors aging nation. *Japan Economic Journal*, May 12: 24.

pension system   Extensively revised in 1986, Japan's pension system consists of the following major plans:

1. *National Pension (kokumin nenkin)*. This is the nonmedical portion of the **social security system**. All people living in Japan between the ages of 20 and 60 are required to join the plan. Its benefits, called the *Basic Pensions*, include (a) the old age pension, payable at age 65, which is based on the period of coverage and is automatically adjusted in accordance with the Consumer Price Indexes, (b) the disability pension, and (c) survivor's pension for dependent spouse and children. The plan is financed by (a) premiums from insured persons who are not affiliated with any other pension plan (self-employed persons, farmers, and nonemployed persons), (b) contributions from pension insurance plans covering employees (see below), and (c) public revenue.

The benefits offered by the National Pension Fund are relatively low—only ¥55,000 a month as of 1990 for those aged 65 or over. Consequently, in April 1991, a second-tier National Pension Fund was introduced by the Ministry of Health and Welfare. The plan is designed for those who are not employed by firms or government offices with other pension plans.

2. *Employees' Pension Insurance (kosei nenkin)*. This provides the second tier of benefits to employees earning wages or salaries. Participation is mandatory for incorporated firms, which establish their own independent Employees' Pension Funds. The funds are managed by **trust banks** and life **insurance companies** under the supervision of the Ministry of Health and Welfare. The benefits, including old age pension (payable at age 60 for men and 55 for women), disability pension, and survivors' pension, are payable

in addition to the Basic Pension under the National Pension. The plan is funded by payroll deductions shared equally by employees and employers (each paid 6.2% of wages as of 1990). As of 1990, the monthly pension benefits, combining Employees' Pension with the National Pension, are about 68% of the retiree's average monthly wages during the period of coverage. As of mid-1990, the Fund was valued at ¥19.6 trillion.

3. *Mutual Aid Associations Pensions (kyosai nenkin)*. Institutions such as the central government, local governments, private schools, and cooperative associations have organized their mutual aid pensions to cover their employees in addition to the National Pension.

As the Japanese population ages, the ratio of pension payments to national income will rise. It is estimated that in the year 2010, premiums will have to be as high as 31% of the average annual wage (or 16.9% of national income) to maintain the current levels of pensions.

See also **pension fund market, social security system**.

Address

Pension Bureau, Ministry of Health and Welfare
2-2, Kasumigaseki 1-chome, Chiyoda-ku, Tokyo 100
Tel: (03) 3503-1711

References

Bronfenbrenner, Martin, and Yasukichi Yasuda. 1987. Economic Welfare. In *The Political Economy of Japan*, vol. 1: *The Domestic Transformation*, ed. by Kozo Yamamura and Yasukichi Yasuba. Stanford: Stanford University Press.

Hiraishi, Nagahisa. 1987. *Social Security*. Tokyo: Japan Institute of Labor.

Isono, Naoyuki. 1990. Insurers lobby for lion's share of new fund. *Japan Economic Journal*, Oct. 13: 30.

Murdo, Pat. 1990. Japan's social security and pension systems face need for new reforms. *JEI Report*, May 25.

Shida, Tomio. 1990. Pension fund growth mirrors aging nation. *Japan Economic Journal*, May 12: 24.

Yamazak, Hiroaki. 1990. The employees' pension system in Japan: past and present. *Annals of the Institute of Social Science*, no. 32: 67–113.

Plaza Accord, 1985   An agreement reached by finance ministers of five major industrialized nations at New York's Plaza Hotel in September 1985 to cooperate by market intervention to bring about a gradual decline in the exchange rate of the U.S. dollar. As a result the yen appreciated rapidly.

See **yen shock, yen–dollar exchange rates**.

political parties   Japan has a multiparty political system, but one party (LDP), the Liberal Democratic Party, has dominated Japanese politics since its founding in 1955, giving Japan nearly 40 years of political stability. It was founded through the merger of the Liberal and the Democratic Parties. Its conservative pro-business orientation has won support from the middle and upper classes; its protective **agricultural policy** has won support from farmers. Its foreign policy is pro-West, although its **trade policies** have created frictions with the West. The LDP was in office from 1955 to August 1993 after it lost a lower house election and is replaced by an eight-party coalition.

The Liberal Democratic Party consists of several factions (*habatsu*), led by senior politicians, contending for power. Factions are groupings of Diet (parliament) members who are bound to a certain group by obligation and background ties. Factions may differ in policy views. Faction leaders are responsible for raising funds for faction members and for securing posts within the party and the cabinet. In return, faction members follow instructions from the leader in intraparty politics. The leader of the dominant faction usually becomes the prime minister, although a less prominent leader can assume the post in the case of deadlock and compromise. Party members gain seniority and leadership roles through repeated reelections to the Diet.

The power of party leaders is limited, however, by the Japanese emphasis on group consensus and fair share, which leads to pragmatic compromises and considerable collective leadership. Posts within the party and the cabinet are distributed according to factional strength. Cabinets are reshuffled frequently to give all party factions their share. In addition powerful career bureaucrats in the ministries are in charge of day-to-day operations of the economy, and thus provide a check on the power of party leaders.

In 1988–89 the Liberal Democratic Party was weakened by corruption scandals and opposition challenges. The Recruit scandal, in which high party officials were exposed for accepting large bribes in the form of Recruit Company's shares, caused the downfall of two short-lived cabinets. The Japanese public's outrage at the extent of the party's corruption, coupled with widespread dissatisfaction at the new **consumption tax** introduced in 1989 by the Liberal Democratic government, caused the party to lose majority control in the upper house of the parliament in a 1989 election (from 142 seats to 109 seats out of 250 seats). The Japanese Socialist Party gained considerable power at its expense. In the lower house, LDP had 293 seats in 1989 and 275 seats in 1990 out of a total of 512 seats (511 seats after December 1992). In a July 1993 election, LDP lost its majority in the lower house for the first time, winning only 227 seats (of which 4 members joined the LDP after the election). Voters' discontent with its continuing corruption scandals is said to be a major reason for this poor result.

Other political parties in Japan include the following:

1. *Social Democratic Party of Japan* (*Japan Socialist Party* before January 1991). Since its reorganization in 1955, this has been Japan's largest and most radical opposition party. Briefly from June 1947 through March 1948, the Socialist Party organized the cabinet. The party has opposed Japan's rearmament and the U.S.–Japan Mutual Security Treaty and advocated closer ties with China and the former Soviet Union. Although it has strong ties with the unions, it has not been able to win much public support before 1989. In the 1989 upper house election, it scored unexpected gains (from 43 seats to 67 seats) because of voters' dissatisfaction with the political corruption of the Liberal Democratic government and the new consumption tax it introduced. Because of the collapse of socialist governments in Eastern Europe in 1990, the party was renamed the Social Democratic Party of Japan in January 1991. However, it has not been able to repeat its election victory. In the July 1992 upper house election, it merely retained its 69 seats (27%). In the July 1993 lower house election, it won only 70 seats (13.7%).

2. *Komeito ("Clean Government Party").* Formed in 1964, it is essentially a religious party, based on Japanese Buddhism. It was founded by Soka Gakkai (Value Creation Society), a lay organization of a sect of Japanese Buddhism, and is supported primarily by the latter's members. Since 1980 it has moderated its initial opposition to Japanese rearmament and the U.S.–Japan Mutual Security Treaty. It won 51 seats in the July 1993 lower house election.

3. *Democratic Socialist Party.* Formed in 1959 as a splinter from the Japan Socialist Party, it is considered one of the centralist parties. It has a more pragmatic approach to the U.S.–Japan Security Treaty and other postwar democratization measures. However it has not had much public support except from right-wing unionists. In July 1993 it won only 15 lower house seats.

4. *Japan Communist Party.* Established in 1922, it was purged during the occupation. In the 1960s it rejected both Chinese and Soviet communist models and moderated its Marxist ideology. In 1976 its party platform supported a multiparty system and continued private ownership, and advocated more independence from the United States in foreign policy. It has substantial support among Japanese intellectuals but is distrusted by both radical and conservative voters. In July 1993 it won only 15 lower house seats.

5. *New parties.* In 1992–93 the LDP's continuing corruption scandals and its failure to introduce political reform led to the formation of new political parties. The *Japan New Party* was founded in May 1992. It calls for the redistribution of powers from the central government to local governments. The *Japan Renewal Party* (Shinseito) was founded in June 1993 by a former LDP minister of finance and 35 other LDP members of the parliament. It stresses the need for political reform. These two parties won 38 and 55 seats, respectively, of the 511 seats in the July 1993 lower house election. This strong showing by the new parties is seen by observers as evidence of Japanese voters' mood for political change, although the ability of the new parties to engineer the change remains to be seen. In August 1933 under the leadership of Morihiro Hosokawa, the founder of the Japan New Party, an eight-party coalition government was organized.

In addition to the above, there are a few other minor parties that lack significant organization and support.

Addresses

Liberal Democratic Party
11-23, Nagatacho 1-chome, Chiyoda-ku, Tokyo 100
Tel: (03) 3581-6211

Social Democratic Party
8-1, Nagatacho 1-chome, Chiyoda-ku, Tokyo 100
Tel: (03) 3580-1171

Komeito Party
8-1, Nagatacho 1-chome, Chiyoda-ku, Tokyo 100
Tel: (03) 3353-0111

References

Curtis, Gerald L. 1988. *The Japanese Way of Politics.* New York: Columbia University Press.

Flanagan, Scott C., et al. 1991. The Japanese Voter. New Haven: Yale University Press.

Hrenenar, Ronald J., ed. 1992. *The Japanese Party System: From One-Party Rule to Coalition Government*. 2d ed. Boulder, CO: Westview.

Kishima, Takako. 1991. *Political Life in Japan*. Princeton: Princeton University Press.

Kyogoku, Jun-ichi. 1987. *The Political Dynamics of Japan*, trans. by Nobutaka Ike. Tokyo: University of Tokyo Press.

population   Japan's population in the postwar period has grown from 84 million in 1950 to 104.7 million in 1970 and 124.4 million in 1992. Because of a declining birth rate, the annual natural rate of increase has declined steadily from 17.2 per thousand in 1950 to 11.8 in 1970 and 3.2 per thousand in 1991 (see table P.1). At the same time life expectancy at birth has risen steadily from 59.6 years for males and 63 years for females in 1950 to 76.1 years for males and 82.1 years for females (or average of 79.1) in 1991, which are the highest in the world. As a result of this slow growth of population and longer life expectancy, the average age of the population has become older. Partly because of its high life expectancy (along with a high literacy rate and high income per capita), Japan is ranked by the United Nations Development Program (1991) as number one in the world in its "human development index."

Table P.2 gives official population projections made by the Ministry of Health and Welfare. The total population is projected to peak around 130 million around the year 2010. It will then start to decline around 2015 and reach 126 million or less after 2025. The percentage of people aged 65 and over in the population will increase steadily from 12.1% in 1990 to 21.3% in 2010 and 25.8% in 2025.

Table P.1
Population size, birth rate, and death rate (in millions; births/deaths in thousands)

Year	Total	Male	Female	Birth rate	Death rate
1950	84.1	41.2	42.9	28.1	10.9
1960	94.3	46.3	48.0	17.2	7.6
1970	104.7	51.4	53.3	18.8	6.9
1980	117.1	57.6	59.5	13.6	6.2
1985	121.0	59.5	61.6	11.9	6.3
1988	122.8	60.4	62.4	10.8	6.5
1989	123.3	60.6	62.7	10.2	6.4
1990	123.6	60.7	62.9	10.0	6.7
1991	124.0	60.9	63.2	9.9	6.7
1992	124.4	61.1	63.4		

Source: Ministry of Health and Welfare.

Table P.2 also gives the projected dependency index of the population. It shows the number of dependents (those aged 0–14 and 65 and above) that each 100 working adults aged 15–64 have to support in the economy. From a dependency index of 43.5 in 1990, the index is projected to rise steadily until it reachs a peak of about 70 in 2025. Then it is projected to decline to the high 60s in 2025. Such high dependency indexes, due primarily to the growing percentage of senior citizens in the population, will imply a heavy burden on the economy in two ways. First, there will be an increasingly tight labor market, since a smaller percentage of the population will be in the working age group. In 1990, 69.7% of the population (86.1 million) was between 15 and 64 in age. It will decline steadily to 67.8% (86.4 million) in 2000, 62.4% (81.3 million) in 2010 and 59.0% (75.8 million) in 2020. Second, there will be a growing demand for all sorts of social services, particularly pension and health care.

Thus Japan's demographic changes in the future will have a profound impact on the economy and serious policy implications for the government.

See also **social security system**.

Address

Council on Population Problems, Ministry of Health and Welfare
2-2. Kasumigaseki 1-chome, Chiyoda-ku, Tokyo 100
Tel: (03) 3503-1711

Table P.2
Population projections

Year	Total (in millions)	Age 0–14 (in %)	Age 15–64 (in %)	Age 65 and above (in %)	Dependency index[a]
1990	123.6	18.2	69.7	12.1	43.5
1991	124.0	17.7	69.8	12.6	43.3
1995	125.5	16.0	69.4	14.5	44.1
2000	127.4	15.2	67.8	17.0	47.5
2005	129.3	15.6	65.2	19.1	53.4
2010	130.4	16.4	62.4	21.3	60.3
2015	130.0	16.3	59.5	24.1	68.1
2020	128.3	15.5	59.0	25.5	69.5
2025	125.8	14.4	59.7	25.8	67.5

Sources: Ministry of Health and Welfare.
a. Dependency index is caculated as (number of people aged 0 to 14 + number of people aged 65 and over)/(number of people aged 15 to 64) × 100.

References

Coleman, Samuel. 1983. *Family Planning in Japanese Society*. Princeton: Princeton University Press.

Hodge, Robert William, and Naohiro Ogawa. 1991. *Fertility Change in Contemporary Japan*. Chicago: University of Chicago Press.

Takayama, Noriyuki. 1992. *The Greying of Japan: An Economic Perspective on Public Pensions*. Tokyo: Kinokuniya.

United Nations Development Program. 1991. *Human Development Report, 1991*. New York: World Bnak/Oxford University Press.

postal savings   Ever since 1875 the Ministry of Posts and Telecommunications has been operating the Postal Banking Service, which includes Postal Money Order and Postal Savings Services. The objective of the Postal Savings Service is to mobilize funds from small savers for social infrastructural **investment**.

The amounts of **savings** that have been deposited with the Postal Savings Service have been very large; sometimes they exceeded the amounts of savings deposited with commercial banks. At the end of 1985 the Postal Savings had an outstanding balance of ¥103 trillion (32.4% of total personal savings), whereas bank savings amounted to ¥100.7 trillion. At the end of 1991 the Postal Savings had an outstanding balance of ¥151.58 trillion (30.2% of total personal savings), whereas commercial banks had ¥208.33 trillion savings deposits.

There are several types of postal savings deposits, including ordinary deposits, fixed-sum deposit certificates, time deposits, and installment deposits. As of March 1990, ¥118.66 trillion, or about 88%, of postal savings deposits were in the form of the fixed-sum desposit certificate (*teigaku chokin*), a high-earning ten-year deposit in which depositors deposit a fixed sum at one time. They can withdraw the money at any post office without penalty after the first six months. However, the longer the money stays in the account (up to ten years), the higher the interest rate becomes, which is compounded semiannually. In December 1991 it was 3.75% for less than one year, 4.25% after one year, 5.35% after two years, and 5.5% after three years. There was a limit of a total of ¥3 million per depositor, but the limit was raised to ¥7 million in January 1990 to accommodate the large amount of money that matured in 1990.

The system offers various advantages to savers. The first is accessibility. Most of the 24,150 branches (as of September 1991) of the post office located throughout Japan offer savings service. Forty percent of all post offices are in the rural areas. Thus the system facilitates household savings, and is traditionally a deposit-taker for small savers, especially in the rural areas. In addition the system offers absolute safety. Formerly the system also offered a tax advantage, but this is no longer the case. Before 1988, interest earnings on postal deposits up to ¥3 million were tax exempt. Since 1988, as part of the **tax reform**, tax exemption is restricted to the disabled, the elderly over 65, and widows. Finally, interest rates on the ten-year fixed-amount postal savings are usually higher than those on bank time deposits.

For these reasons, plus the fact that the Postal Savings Service does not have to pay heavy **corporate taxes**, commercial banks have long viewed postal savings as a competitor for deposits with unfair advantages. However, commercial banks have traditionally concentrated on servicing industries and urban customers, and they had little interest in providing deposit-taking offices in small towns and rural areas.

Postal savings are traditionally allocated by the Trust Fund Bureau of the **Ministry of Finance** to the government's **Fiscal Investment and Loans Program**, which makes loans to public corporations at a low interest rate. With the reform of the tax exemption for small savers (*maruyu*), the postal system is permitted to invest a small percentage of its total deposits in securities, thus providing new competition for commercial banks.

Interest rates for postal savings deposits are decided by a special committee of the Ministry of Posts and Telecommunications, while a separate committee of the Ministry of Finance and the **Bank of Japan** sets other bank and market rates. The former are set at relatively high levels to protect depositors from inflation. This, however, interferes with the government's monetary policy. As a result the Ministry of Finance, the Bank of Japan, and private banks argue that the interest rate–setting mechanisms should be merged. In particular, with the introduction of **financial liberalization**, the Bank of Japan argued in December 1983 that once interest rates are liberalized, uniform market-determined interest rates should apply to similar types of deposits to reflect financial market conditions.

The Ministry of Posts and Telecommunicatins also provides a Postal Life Insurance Plan, and it was authorized a few years ago to begin Postal Pension Plans. The Postal Savings Bureau can also make small consumer loans of up to ¥700,000 for six months, collaterized with postal savings accounts. Commercial banks traditionally are not interested in making small consumer loans.

See also **Fiscal Investment and Loan Program, interest rate structure, *maruyu*, tax reform**.

Address

Postal Savings Bureau, Ministry of Posts and Telecommunications
3-2, Kasumigaseki 1-chome, Chiyoda-ku, Tokyo 100
Tel: (03) 3504-4475   Fax: (03) 3507-8738

References

Bank of Japan. 1993. *Economic Statistics Annual*, 1992.

Iida, Masami. 1990. Banks hoping to lure postal savings deposits. *Japan Economic Journal*, Feb. 24: 5.

Postal Savings Bureau. 1991. *Postal Banking in Japan, 1991*. Tokyo: Ministry of Posts and Telecommunications.

Suzuki, Yoshio, ed. 1987. *The Japanese Financial System*. Oxford: Oxford University Press. Chs. 3–4.

Tatewaki, Kazuo. 1991. *Banking and Finance in Japan*. London: Routledge. Ch. 9.

Viner, James. 1987. *Inside Japan's Financial Markets*. London: The Economist Publications. Ch. 7.

Yokota, Hayato. 1991. Massive money shift alarms banks. *Nikkei Weekly*, Nov. 9: 1.

prepaid cards   A popular way of paying for some goods and services. Prepaid vouchers in the form of magnetic cards can be purchased for set amounts to make telephone calls or to buy train tickets, and so forth. Prepaid telephone cards are commonly used. Prepaid cards should be distinguished from credit cards.
See also **credit card industry**.

price fixing   The fixing of retail prices by the manufacturers, which is a violation of the **Antimonopoly Law**.
See **Antimonopoly Law, pricing practices**.

price indexes and price levels   Japan publishes a number of price indexes, including the consumer price index, wholesale price index, corporate service price index, leisure price index, rural price indexes, and deflators for various national income accounts. The first two are the most important indicators of price levels and inflationary pressure.

The consumer price index (CPI) is published monthly by the Management and Coordination Agency under the Prime Minister's Office, currently with 1990 as the base period. It is based on survey data of 561 items of consumer goods and services, divided into 10 basic categories, each given appropriate weight to reflect its relative importance in the consumer budget. These categories and their weights are foods (31.4%), housing (14.8%), transportation and communications (11.9%), cultural and recreation (11.2%), clothing and footwear (8.6%), fuel, light, and water (5.5%), furniture and household utensils (4.4%), education (4.7%), medical care (3.1%), and others (4.5%). Among these, services constitute 44.2% and commodities 55.8%.

There are regional variations in the CPI. For the **Tokyo** area the **Bank of Japan** publishes a separate series of the CPI in which the weights of the components are different, reflecting the different cost of living in Tokyo. Greater weight are given to foods (39.3%), housing (18.3%), and education (5.6%); transportation and communication, furniture and household utensils, are given less weight. Overall, services constitute 49.5% and goods 50.5%.

The wholesale price index (WPI) is published monthly by the Bank of Japan, currently with 1990 as the base period. It is based on survey data of 1,253 commodities, of which 945 are domestic products for domestic market, 184 are for exports, and 184 are imported products. The industry origin of the products and their weights in the index are manufacturing industry products (90.3%), agricultural, forestry and aquatic products (3.4%), mining products (3.0%), electric power, gas, and water (3.0%), and others (0.3%). These products can also be classified according to the stage of demand and use as follows: raw materials (5.2%), intermediate materials (43.5%), capital goods (15.4%), consumer goods (including consumer durables and nondurables, 24.3%), and exports (11.7%).

The CPI and WPI do not move in synchronization. In general, when exchange rate and oil price changes are the main causes of price changes, as was often the case except in recent years, the WPI tend to lead the CPI in changes. Furthermore the WPI tends to be more sensitive to business fluctuations. Given Japan's complex distribution system, changes in the WPI tend to filter down to the CPI with a lag. However, in recent years with the growing labor shortage, increases in consumer service prices have led those in wholesale prices.

The growing labor shortage and the speculative land and real estate investment boom in the late 1980s have led to rapid increases in the prices of some services in excess of increases in CPI. Land use–related charges such as rents have risen sharply in the large cities, particularly Tokyo. In order to measure and monitor this inflationary pressure, the Bank of Japan introduced a quarterly "corporate service price index" on January 1, 1991. The index includes 74 items, including real estate rent (13.7%), other leasing and renting (10.1%), transportation charges (29.8%), information services (7.3%), communications (7.2%), advertizing fees (6.4%), finance and insurance (6.3%), building maintenance and construction services (13.3%), and judicial and accounting services (3.6%).

Rural price indexes are published by the Ministry of Agriculture, Forestry, and Fisheries. They include the rural consumer price index, the index of selling prices of agricultural products, and the price index of goods used in farm operation and rural livelihood. Thus they are of particular importance to the rural population.

The leisure price index is a new index introduced by the Management and Coordination Agency in August 1991. Although the current consumer price index includes a recreation category, it includes such non-leisure-related items as stationary. The new index excludes educational items but includes travel-related items. It is published monthly along with the consumer price index.

Finally, the deflators for gross domestic products, gross domestic expenditure, gross national expenditure, and so forth, are composite price indexes used to deflate nominal national income and expenditure figures in current prices into real figures in constant base-period prices.

From table P.3 it is clear that Japan's annual price increases in the 1980s and early 1990s were very small by international standards. This was not

Table P.3
Major price indexes (annual average)

Year	CPI	WPI	CSPI	GDP deflators
1980	81.7	110.9		90.0
1981	85.6	112.5		93.4
1982	88.0	114.5		94.9
1983	89.6	111.9		96.3
1984	91.7	111.6		98.5
1985	93.5	110.4	100.0	100.0
1986	94.1	100.3		101.8
1987	94.2	96.5	100.2	101.8
1988	94.9	95.6	101.4	102.2
1989	97.0	98.0	106.0	104.1
1990	100.0	100	110.4	106.3
1991	103.3	99.4	114.1	108.3
1992	105.0	97.8	116.3	

Sources: Bank of Japan, Economic Planning Agency, Management and Coordination Agency.
Note: CPI = consumer price index, WPI = wholesale price index, CSPI = corporate service price index.

the case in the early to mid-1970s when, in the aftermath of the first oil crisis in 1973, CPI rose 11.7% in 1973, 23.2% in 1974, 11.7% in 1975, and 9.4% in 1976.

The slow price increases in the 1980s would have made Japanese prices relatively low by international standards if exchange rates between yen and dollar had remained the same. Unfortunately, the yen rapidly appreciated against the dollar after 1985, making Japanese prices considerably higher than those in other major industrial countries in the late 1980s and early 1990s (when converted at the prevailing exchange rates). For example, the Economic Planning Agency conducted in November 1990 surveys of about 400 consumer goods and services in Tokyo, New York, Hamburg, and London. Against Tokyo's base prices of 100, New York's prices stood at 76, Hamburg's 80, and London's 96. In other words, prices in Tokyo were on average 32% higher than in New York and 25% higher

Table P.4
International comparison of consumer prices (Tokyo = 100, November 1991)

	New York	London	Paris
Overall prices	79	92	86
Japanese-made goods			
VCRs	88	181	166
Cameras	94	133	130
Cars	115	162	156
American-made goods			
Lipsticks	46	43	53
Spark plugs	21	34	50
Photo films	138	178	170
European-made goods			
Watchs	121	95	124
Neckties	61	56	52
Cars	74	149	91
Public utilities			
Electricity	83	90	88
Gas	55	46	65
Food			
Rice	42	90	61
Bread	117	72	127
Beef (shoulder)	29	45	50

Source: Economic Planning Agency.
Note: ¥131 = $1 in November 1991.

than in Hamburg. Japan's prices are particularly high for beef, rice, and gas for cooking and heating. In November 1991 similar surveys of 400 goods and services made by the Economic Planning Agency showed that the price differential narrowed slightly, but Tokyo remained the most expensive city. Against Tokyo's price index of 100, it was 79 in New York, 76 in Hamburg, 92 in London, and 86 in Paris. The Economic Planning Agency attributes the slight decline in price differentials between 1990 and 1991 to the lower inflation in Japan and to government deregulation. Table P.4 summarizes the survey results for different categories of products.

See also **pricing practices, yen–dollar exchange rates**.

References

Bank of Japan. 1993. *Economic Statistics Annual, 1992.*

Corporate service price index: movements and characteristics since 1985. *Bank of Japan Quarterly Bulletin* 1, no. 2, 1993: 51–70.

Fukuda, Shin-ichi, Hiroshi Teruyama, and Hiro Y. Toda. 1991. Inflation and price-wage dispersions in Japan. *Journal of the Japanese and International Economies* 5: 160–88.

Leisure prices get own index. *Nikkei Weekly*, Sept. 7, 1991: 3.

Prices still too high in Japan: EPA. *Nikkei Weekly*, Oct. 19, 1991: 4.

Tokyo most expensive, though less so. *Nikkei Weekly*, June 6, 1992: 3.

pricing practices It is impossible to have a complete picture of pricing practices of diverse private businesses, as these relate to competitive business strategy which business managers are reluctant to talk about. From various reports, however, one can piece together a general picture of pricing practices in some major sectors of the economy:

1. Many analysts suggest that a common pricing rule in manufacturing is reverse cost-plus pricing—that is, firms may first set a competitive selling price that is necessary to secure a certain market share and then strive to cut costs and profit margin to fit that price (Hasegawa 1986). In other words, cost and profit margin are the variables (obviously within some limits), the exact opposite of Western cost-plus pricing. Morita (1992), chairman of Sony Corporation, affirms that this is indeed the case in the consumer **electronics industry**. So does the management of NEC Corp. (author's interview, June 16, 1993). Thus the cost-cutting efforts may be relentless, and large-volume production and sales are needed to help cut costs. Profit margin may be sacrificed in the short run for the sake of market share.

Alternatively, variable cost or marginal cost pricing may be used by some large manufacturing firms. In his discussion of the competitive edge of Japanese business practices over those of the United States, Prestowitz (1988: 180–81) suggests that large Japanese manufacturers regard large interest payments on debt (bank loans being more important than equity capital to Japanese companies) and wages of lifetime employees as fixed costs, costs that have to be paid regardless of the output level. Thus Japanese firms' variable costs are lower than those of American firms, and hence they are willing to accept lower prices as long as the prices are adequate to cover the firms' variable costs. The semiconductors industry is given as an example.

2. In the retail trade it is often observed that Japanese retail prices are usually higher than their counterparts in Western countries. This can be due to a higher markup, higher retail cost, or retail price fixing. Kang (1990) argues that a higher retail markup is reasonable in Japan because of higher rent and more post-sale services such as delivery and repair. In other words, retailing is extremely labor intensive in Japan, and labor is costly in Japan.

The fixing of retail prices of some products such as books and magazines, low-priced cosmetics, records and CDs, and some pharmaceuticals by manufacturers (*saihan*, resale price contract) has been accepted by the Fair Trade Commission as exceptions to the **Antimonopoly Law** as long as free competition and other conditions exist. One reason is to keep numerous small retailers, particularly drug stores, in business. Critics have long argued, however, that illegal price fixing by manufacturers has existed in other industries such as consumer electronics and automobiles. None of them has been prosecuted, however, by the Fair Trade Commission for violating the Antimonopoly Law. It was only in early 1992, after the United States demanded a more rigorous implementation of the Antimonopoly Law following the U.S.–Japan **Structural Impediments Initiative** talks that the Fair Trade Commission announced that fixed prices on 10 medicines and 13 cosmetic products will be abolished as of April 1993. The Commission has also warned *keiretsu* stores in consumer electronics against price fixing.

3. A unique pricing practice—the so-called deferred pricing or post-pricing system (*atogime*)—has existed in the petrochemical and paper industries. The practice allows makers of raw materials or semifinished products to negotiate or finalize their selling prices after the sales contract or delivery is made, or after the prices of the buyers' finished products are

established. For example, in the petrochemical industry, producers of raw materials such as ethyline and polypropyline get their "fair" share of profits by finalizing their prices after their buyers such as the makers of vinyl chloride have fixed the prices of their own products. In the paper industry the practice was introduced in 1977–78 in the aftermath of the 1973 oil crisis. Small producers had difficulties setting prices in the midst of price declines during the recession in 1977 and the subsequent price increases during the economic recovery in 1978. They adopted the practice of "tentative" pricing that gave them the flexibility of renegotiating prices later with industry buyers.

Deferred pricing has brought buyers a mixed blessing. On the one hand, buyers have the right to demand rebates if the prices of their own products subsequently decline. On the other hand, it makes production costs uncertain and account settlements, budgeting, and planning more difficult.

Deferred pricing came under criticism during the U.S.–Japan Structural Impediments Initiative talks because it compounds the difficulties of foreign access to the Japanese market. In the petrochemical industry several ethylene producers have indicated their willingness to abandon it. One reason is the expected competition from South Korean exporters. Large Korean business groups such as Samsung and Hyundai are setting up plants to produce and export ethylene, with Japan as the targeted market. Given this impending competition, Japanese industry would benefit from a faster pricing mechanism that conforms to world standards. Thus analysts in Japan believe that the practice has outlived its usefulness and that it is a matter of time before it is abandoned.

4. In the **construction industry** the practice of *dango* (prebidding consultation) or bid-rigging in public works projects has been uncovered from time to time. It is a way to distribute public works projects among the contractors in which the designated contractor submits the lowest winning bid. *Dango* was brought up by Washington during the U.S.–Japan Structural Impediments Initiative talks as a barrier to entry that has prevented foreign construction firms from entering the Japanese construction market. Because it eliminated price competition, including that from foreign firms, it increased the cost of public works at taxpayers' expense. One estimate puts excess profits from *dango* at 16–33% of the industry's revenues (cited in Johnson 1990: 115).

5. In the **steel industry**, the **Ministry of International Trade and Industry** (MITI) has actively intervened in the pricing process because of the industry's importance. Between 1958 and 1991 MITI attempted to

stabilize steel prices through the so-called list price system (*kokai hanbai sei*, literally, "open sales system"). Under the system the steel company sells a steel product to a designated wholesaler at the "list price" that it had previously reported to MITI. Price stability was considered essential to provide profitability and investment incentives. Because of the practice of list price "discounting" during recessions, analysts disagree on the effectiveness of the system in stabilizing actual market prices.

6. Pricing practices for exports and imports are subjects of much foreign criticism. It has long been observed that Japanese products are often cheaper abroad and do not usually increase proportionally, if at all, when the yen appreciates. On the other hand, imported foreign products are much more expensive in Japan at the prevailing exchange rate. As to high import prices, the higher rent and labor costs mentioned above may explain part of the difference. Another cause has to do with the **distribution system**. The traditional "general import agents" system gives exclusive contracts to some wholesalers or **trading companies** to import brand name products. This has given them the monopoly power to control the distribution and prices of imported goods.

As to the relatively low export prices, which do not rise as much as the appreciation of yen, part of the explanation is that the prices of energy and other raw materials used to produce exports tend to decline as the yen appreciates. Over and above that, however, Johnson (1990: 110) and others have charged that Japanese manufacturers have deliberately set their export prices at lower levels than domestic prices in order to expand their foreign market shares and that they have used their high domestic prices to subsidize exports. Proponents of this view often cite the experience between 1985 and 1988 during which Japanese export prices (calculated in yen) fell relative to domestic wholesale prices.

In an empirical study Marston (1991) estimates that about one-half of the yen's real appreciation between February 1985 and December 1988 was neutralized by Japanese manufacturers by lowering their export prices relative to domestic prices. This type of price discrimination or "pricing-to-market" behavior is possible because the export and domestic markets are separated and have different demand characteristics. Also traditionally cheaper Japanese exports cannot reenter the Japanese market to undercut domestic prices due to government policy and various structural factors, although this has been changing since the late 1980s (Weigand 1989). Marston (1991: 139) expects Japanese pricing-to-market behavior in export to diminish in the future as they diversify their production facilities abroad and can respond to yen appreciation by shifting export production to plants abroad.

7. In the agricultural sector, the price of rice is the most important agricultural price in Japan because of the importance of rice in the Japanese diet and the government's long-standing policy to ban rice imports by subsidizing domestic rice production. The government purchases part of the annual rice output at a price (producer's rice price) set by the government. Since 1960 the price is set annually by the "production cost and income compensation" method, which takes into account the production costs, family labor cost and hired labor cost, and so forth. The precise formula for calculation has been revised from time to time to reflect the supply-demand situation. For the 1990 crop the following factors were taken into account in calculating the price (Nakagawa 1991):

• Family labor cost (28% of price). This is evaluated according to the wages of manufacturing firms with 5 to 999 employees.

• Fertilizer, pesticide, and hired labor cost (50%).

• Interest on capital (4%). Both borrowed and owned capital are included in the calculation at a certain interest rate.

• Rent (21%). Rent on owned land is considered as interest on land asset, evaluated at a certain interest rate.

• Deduction of the price of by-product (− 3%).

See also **construction industry, distribution system, rice production and distribution, steel industry**.

References

Deferred pricing, another practice that outlives its initial usefulness. *Japan Economic Journal,* Apr. 28, 1990: 29.

Hasegawa, Keitaro. 1986. *Japanese-Style Management: An Insider's Analysis.* Tokyo: Kodansha International.

Johnson, Chalmers. 1990. Trade, revisionism, and the future of Japanese–American relations. In *Japan's Economic Structure: Should It Change?* ed. by Kozo Yamamura. Seattle: Society for Japanese Studies.

Kang, T. W. 1990. *Gaishi: The Foreign Company in Japan.* New York: Basic Books. Ch. 1.

Marston, Richard C. 1990. Pricing to market in Japanese manufacturing. *Journal of International Economics* 29 (November): 217–36.

Marston, Richard C. 1991. Price behavior in Japanese and U.S. manufacturing. In *Trade with Japan,* ed. by Paul Krugman. Chicago: University of Chicago Press.

Morita, Akio. 1992. A critical moment for Japanese management? *Japan Echo,* 19, 2: 8–14.

Nakagawa, Hiroshi. 1991. Rice price policy in Japan. Ministry of Agriculture, Forestry, and Fisheries. Mimeographed.

Ohno, Kenichi. 1989. Export pricing behavior of manufacturing: A U.S.–Japan Comparison. *International Monetary Fund Staff Papers* 36, 1 (Mar.): 550–79.

Petrochemical "post-pricing" is headed for the scrapheap. *Japan Economic Journal*, May 26, 1990: 29.

Prestowitz, Clyde V. 1988. *Trading Places*. New York: Basic Books.

Weigand, Robert E. 1989. The gray market comes to Japan. *Columbia Joournal of World Business* 24, 3: 18–23.

Yamawaki, Hideki. 1988. The steel industry. In *Industrial Policy of Japan*, ed. by Ryutaro Komiya, Masahiro Okuno, and Kotaro Suzumura. Tokyo: Academic Press Japan.

prime rates   Interest rates that commercial banks charge on loans and discounts of bills of exceptionally high credit standards.

See **interest rate structure**.

privatization   In 1985 and 1987 three major public corporations— Nippon Telegraph and Telephone, Japan National Railways, and Japan Tobacco—were privatized. The privatization was undertaken to reduce the deficit, provide management flexibility, and improve efficiency. The results to date are mostly favorable, although the process has not been easy and some difficulties remain.

Nippon Telegraph and Telephone (NTT), founded in 1952 as a government company, was privatized in April 1985. It is the world's second largest telecommunications company after American Telephone and Telegraph Co. The government had raised some ¥10 trillion by selling 1.95 million shares each in fiscal 1986 and 1987, and 1.5 million shares in 1988. Additional sales have been delayed repeatedly since fiscal 1989. As of March 1992 the government still holds 65.9% of shares. NTT is the largest private employer in Japan with 250,000 employees in 1992, down from 328,000 in 1979.

NTT's fares for telephone service have been reduced since privatization. Its customer service is said to have been improved. It remains the dominant firm in the telecommunications industry—it had 85.7% of long-distance calls, 89.2% of leased circuits, and 72.5% of car and portable phones in FY 1990. However, increased competition from new common carriers has hurt its profits. To stimulate more competition and efficiency, there are currently three different proposals to reorganize the company, namely to break up the company into (1) regional companies, (2) a long-distance carrier and a company for local calls, and (3) a long-distance carrier and 11 regional companies to supply local services, much like the breakup of AT&T in the United States. The last proposal is said to be the most popular, although no decision has been made yet.

Japan National Railways (JNR), founded in 1949 through the reorganization of a branch of the Ministry of Transportation, ran the state sector of Japan's railway system until it was privatized in April 1987. It excelled in train speed, safety, and punctuality but was plagued by deficit, interference from politicians, and labor strife. In April 1987 it was broken up into six regional Japan Railway companies and one freight company. Its old debt was assumed by a new JNR Accounts Settlement Corp., which also holds all shares of the new companies. Sales of shares to pay for the JNR debt has been delayed because of the stock market's decline.

The former Japan National Railways incurred deficits despite frequent fare increases, whereas the new Japan Railway companies are profitable and have raised fares only once. Because of new managerial flexibility, the companies are diversifying into profitable travel-related services.

The former Japan Tobacco and Salt, a government monopoly, was founded in 1949 through the merger of two government monopolies in tobacco and salt. It was privatized in April 1985 and renamed Japan Tobacco. At the same time the government liberalized the tobacco import and wholesale businesses and opened them to both domestic and foreign firms. However, Japan Tobacco retains a monopoly on domestic production of tobacco products and is required to buy all domestically grown tobacco leaf regardless of quality. Thus privatization has not freed it of government control. All shares are still held by the government but some shares are scheduled to be sold in late 1993. However, because of greater management flexibility and competition from imports, the company is said to be more attentive to customer demand. For example, its product brands have been doubled to 110.

In addition to the above three companies, a state-run hospital in Kagoshima City was sold to a local medical association in October 1989. Finally, there was also the case of government withdrawal of its minority ownership in a special private corporation. In November 1987 the government sold its 34.5% share of Japan Airlines, following the liberalization of Japan's international cargo business and domestic passenger and cargo businesses in 1985.

As to future privatization, the government's housing loan business, the national hospital system, and the postal savings system have been suggested as candidates. However, it is premature to say whether there will be more privatization in the future. The Japanese have a tradition of deference to government authority and are not ideologically opposed to government operation of public service corporations. In addition most of the remaining public corporations are either **government financial institutions** or special-purpose corporations. Both were set up to assist specific sectors of the economy. For this reason they are either unprofitable to operate under private ownership (e.g., Japan Small Business Corporation) or require close contact with various government agencies during the course of their operations (e.g., **Japan Development Bank**). Such public corporations are not likely to be privatized.

See also **railway companies**.

Address

Nippon Telegraph and Telephone Corp.
1-6, Uchisaiwai-cho 1-chome, Chiyoda-ku, Tokyo 100
Tel: (03) 3509-3051

References

Choy, Jon. 1990. Former Japanese public corporations: post-privaization update. *JEI Report*, no. 32A, Aug. 17.

Japanese privatization: Biting the bullet. *The Economist*, Nov. 26, 1988: 9.

NTT no longer acts like a graceful giant. *Tokyo Business Today*, June 1991: 46–48.

Privatization keeps customers satisfied. *Nikkei Weekly*, Mar. 28, 1992: 11.

Privatized rails make headway. *Nikkei Weekly*, Apr. 18, 1992: 1.

property tax   The second largest tax for municipal governments, levied on owners of land, buildings, and other tangible assets.

See **tax system**.

public assistance   A component of Japan's social security system designed to assist the indigent in medical care and living expenses.

See **social security system**.

public bonds   A broad category of bonds that includes government bonds issued by the national government, local bonds, and public corporation bonds.

See **bond market, government bonds**.

public corporations   Aside from government financial institutions, Japan has more than 30 public corporations that are are government-supported, nonfinancial, nonprofit, single-purpose corporations. They receive investment and loans from the government and are financially accountable to the government, but enjoy much operational autonomy. Major public corporations include Employment Promotion Projects Corp., Environmental Pollution Control Service Corp., Housing and Urban Development Corp., Japan Highway Public Corp., Japan National Oil Corp., Japan National Railways Settlement Corp., Overseas Economic Cooperation Fund, Pension Welfare Service Public Corp., Postal Life Insurance & Annuity Welfare Corp., and Social Welfare and Medical Service Corp.

See also **Fiscal Investment and Loan Program, government financial institutions, privatization.**

public finance
See **consumption tax, corporate taxes, Fiscal Investment and Loan Program, government bonds, individual income taxes, taxation system.**

Q

quality control Japanese quality control is characterized by company-wide total quality control and the participation of workers in a large number of quality control circles. Initially taught by American experts, Japanese companies have made quality control an integral part of their production management.

Quality control was first developed by W. A. Shewhart of Bell Laboratories in the United States in the 1930s. It was applied by the U.S. Army for weapons production during World War II. At that time quality control meant *statistical quality control*, which entailed the inspection of product samples and the rejection of the product if the rate of defect exceeds a certain statistical level. In the early 1950s the Japanese learned statistical quality control from visiting American experts. However, that approach was not effective in upgrading the quality of Japanese products because managers felt that quality control was an engineer's job and were indifferent to it.

Feigenbaum (1951) first emphasized companywide participation in total quality control (TQC) instead of statistical quality control by specialists. Visiting American experts as well as Japanese study groups to the United States introduced the new approach to Japan in the late 1950s. But it was Kaoru Ishikawa, Japan's foremost authority on TQC, who was instrumental in popularizing the concept and perfecting the techniques in Japan. He emphasized three main aspects of TQC: (1) Quality control should be extended from the inspection of product to the stages of manufacturing and new product development. In other words, it should start from the early stages of market research and product development and continue through production to final sales. (2) All company units, including top management and all divisions, should be involved in planning and coordinating quality control activities. (3) All workers should participate in quality control through their participation in quality control circles (Ishikawa

1981, 1982, 1985, 1990). Ishikawa emphasized that with TQC, 100% defect-free production can be achieved. His famous slogan, "the next process is your customer," has been used effectively since the 1950s to combat sectionalism in Japanese companies (Ishikawa 1985: 107). The slogan embodies the idea that a defect-free final product comes only from defect-free materials and components, and hence all workers should participate in quality control. Because customers are much venerated in Japan (see **customer sovereignty**), Ishikawa astutely urges workers to think of their fellow workers at the next work process as their valued customers who want to "purchase" defect-free materials and components to produce quality product.

A quality control circle is a small group of workers in the same workshop organized to perform quality control activities, including the improvement of the workplace. It is based on one work unit, such as a section, and consists of a leader and several (average of seven) workers. Members of the group make suggestions for improvement, and they often have the discretion to implement the suggestions themselves. It also serves to promote communication between workers and management.

The first quality control circle was established by Nippon Telegraph and Telephone in 1962 to train foremen on statistical quality control. The idea rapidly spread to other companies for foremen and rank-and-file workers alike in total quality control. In 1965 there were 4,930 quality control circles. In 1985 there were 223,762 (Onglatco 1988: 15–17). According to surveys, quality control circles are more active and effective in large companies than in small ones. This is due to the fact that workers in large companies have a higher level of technical knowledge and skills since most suggestions arising from quality control circles are highly technical.

See also **management practices**.

References

Feigenbaum, Armand V. [1951] 1983. *Quality Control*. New York: McGraw-Hill.

Lu, David. 1987. *Inside Corporate Japan: The Art of Fumble-Free Management*. Cambridge, MA: Productivity Press.

Ishikawa, Kaoru. 1981. *Quality Control, the Japanese Style* (in Japanese). Tokyo: Japanese Union of Scientists and Engineers.

Ishikawa, Kaoru. 1982. *Guide to Quality Control*. Tokyo: Asian Productivity Organization.

Ishikawa, Kaoru. 1985. *What Is Total Quality Control: The Japanese Way*, trans. by David J. Lu. Englewood Cliffs, NJ: Prentice Hall.

Ishikawa, Kaoru. 1990. *Introduction to Quality Control*. Tokyo: 3A Corporation.

Onglatco, Mary Lou Uy. 1988. *Japanese Quality Control Circles: Features, Effects and Problems*. Tokyo: Asian Productivity Organization.

Shea, Gregory P. 1986. Quality circles: The danger of battled change. *Sloan Manaagement Review* 27, 3: 33–46.

quality control circle
See **quality control**.

quality of life
See **GNP, GNP per capita and GDP, health insurance, housing, labor-management relations, population, price indexes and price levels, social security, working hours and stress**.

R

railway companies   Since trains are the main mode of transportation in Japan, the railway network is an integral part of the Japanese society and economy. In the postwar period it has exhibited technical virtuosity, operational punctuality (so much so as to set one's watch by), and some financial problems. Organizationally it has also became complex.

Before its breakup on April 1, 1987, the Japan National Railways (JNR) was Japan's state-run railway system, the mainstay of Japan's railway network that dated back to 1872. It operated 21,000 kilometers of track lines—including the world-famous *shinkansen* ("bullet train") which has been one of the world's fastest and safest trains—and employed 275,000 people. However, because of poor management and interference by politicians, deficits started to appear in 1964, which accumulated to ¥37.5 trillion ($250 billion at ¥150 = $1) by October 1986. The system was also plagued by union unrest. The privatization of JNR became an important part of Prime Minister Yasuhiro Nakasone's domestic program. Other public enterprises privatized by the Nakasone administration included Japan Monopoly Corporation and Nippon Telegraph and Telephone (NTT).

On April 1, 1987, JNR was divided into 11 organizations, including six regional passenger railway companies, one national freight company (Japan Freight Railway Co.), the JNR Accounts Settlement Corp. to settle the ¥25.5 trillion debt, the Railway Technical Research Institute, and a special public company (Shinkansen Holding Corp.) to own and lease the bullet trains to the passenger companies and to support new bullet train construction, with three new subsidiaries—the Railway Technical Research Institute, the Railway Telecommunication Co., and the Railway Information System Co.

The six regional passenger railway companies, making up the so-called JR Group along with the freight company, are East Japan Railway Co. (JR East), Central Japan Railway Co. (JR Central), West Japan Railway Co.

(JR West), Tokai Japan Railway Co. (JR Tokai), Shikoku Japan Railway Co. (JR Shikoku), and Hokkaido Japan Railway Co. (JR Hokkaido). The first three are the largest. The Group is shielded from the debt of JNR by the JNR Accounts Settlement Corp. and exempted from the costs of running the loss-making *shinkansen* service. Thus starting from a clean slate, they began to make profits in 1988.

The debt of JNR was to be repaid by selling JNR land and by selling shares of the new Japan Railway companies. The JNR Accounts Settlement Corp. is responsible for selling the shares and thus to oversee the railway's sale to the private sector. However, as of July 1992 no shares in JR companies have been sold, and only 31% of JNR land had been sold by March 1991. The listing of all JR shares on the securities exchanges has been postponed because of the stock market's decline. In the meantime the old JNR debt has increased and has become an issue in public debate. Taxpayers may eventually have to bear a large portion of the debt burden.

The breakup of JNR has created competition among the six regional JR companies and stimulated them to improve performance, including raising the speed of their "bullet trains" toward 300 kilometers per hour, and thereby competing with airlines for long-distance travel. They have also diversified their operations into new businesses such as marketing their own line of travel products and offering travel-related services. The Railway Technical Research Institute has developed the magnetically levitated (Maglev) train, with commercial development under experiment.

In the private sector proper of the railway network, there are 14 non-JR Group companies, including the Kinki Nippon Railway Co., the Tokyu Corp., and the Hankyu Co. They are all profitable companies and are members of conglomerates. Kinkin Nippon Railway is the largest private railway company in Japan. It forms the Kintetsu Group with more than 160 subsidiaries, including Kintetsu Department Store. It is also engaged in large-scale urban redevelopment in Osaka and in resort development. The Tokyu Group is a large family-controlled conglomerate that was first established in 1922. It has some 350 companies engaged in diverse businesses among which are railways (Tokyu Corp. and Izukyu Corp.), an airline (Japan Air System Co.), railway rolling stock (Tokyu Car Corp.), a department store (Tokyu Department Stores Co.), supermarket chains (Tokyu Store Chain Co.), real estate (Tokyu Land Corp.), and construction (Tokyu Construction Co.). All railway companies are regulated by the Ministry of Transport in fares and timetables.

See also **privatization**.

Addresses

East Japan Railway Co.
6-5, Marunouchi 1-chome, Chiyoda-ku, Tokyo 100
Tel: (03) 3212-4441

Japan Nongovernment Railways Association
6-4, Marunouchi 1-chome, Chiyoda-ku, Tokyo 100
Tel: (03) 3211-1401

Kinki Nippon Railway Co.
1-55, Uehon-machi 6-chome, Tennoji-ku, Osaka 540
Tel: (06) 771-3331   Fax: (06) 775-3468

Tokyu Corp.
26-20, Sakuragaoka-cho, Shibuya-ku, Tokyo 150
Tel: (03) 3434-3171   Fax: (03) 3496-2965

References

Japanese privatisation: Biting the bullet. *The Economist*, Nov. 26, 1988: 89.

Bullet trains shooting to compete with airlines. *Japan Economic Journal*, Mar. 30, 1991: 19.

Former national railways' debt weighs heavily in public debate. *Nikkei Weekly*, Apr. 18, 1992: 8.

Japanese railways: Where rail makes money. *The Economist*, June 11, 1988: 70–71.

Privatized rails make headway. *Nikkei Weekly*, Apr. 18, 1992: 1, 8.

recession cartel (or antirecession cartel)   An arrangement or agreement among firms of an industry facing a severe recession to reduce output by an agreed-upon percentage.
    See **cartels, shipbuilding industry**.

regional banks   Some 130 commercial banks that operate within a specific prefecture.
    See **banking system**.

research and development (R&D)
See **electronics industry, industrial policy**.

retail trade
See **department stores, distribution system, pricing practices**.

rice production and distribution   Rice occupies a special place in the Japanese society and political economy. It is the major staple food in the

Japanese diet, and its cultivation symbolizes the traditional rural way of life. Also, because of the disproportionate political power wielded by farmers, rice production is subsidized by the government and rice import is banned. This has aggravated the trade frictions between Japan and the United States.

Rice consumption has declined as household income increases and the consumption of meat and dairy products increases. Per capita annual consumption of rice was 95.1 kilograms in FY 1970, 78.9 in 1980, 74.6 in FY 1985, and 70.1 in FY 1989.

Rice production has declined slightly over the same period, as shown in table R.1. The decline came about because, since 1969, the Ministry of Agriculture, Forestry, and Fisheries has asked farmers to reduce rice acreage; under the **Staple Food Control Act** of 1942 the Japanese government is formally in charge of all rice production, distribution, and sales.

Since the postwar Land Reform (1945–49), Japanese farms have remained fragmented and small. To prevent the reconsolidation of farmland, joint-stock companies cannot own farmland; agricultural cooperatives can own farmland only if they do the actual farming. Currently the average rice farmer works only 1.65 acres (whereas the typical American farm is 160 times larger).

In the early 1960s the government introduced price support of rice after the Agricultural Basic Law was enacted in 1961 to support agriculture and farm income. A production-cost–parity formula was adopted to determine annual rice purchase prices in order to maintain farm and nonfarm incomes at comparable levels (see **pricing practices**). This resulted in a government purchase price that was as high as four times the world level. The high price induced farmers to maintain a high yield (about 5 tons per hectare) by using a high level of chemical fertilizers. This had led to surplus of rice

Table R.1
Rice production in Japan (unmilled, in million metric tons)

Year	Production	Year	Production
1970	12.7	1985	11.7
1975	13.2	1986	11.6
1980	9.8	1987	10.6
1982	10.3	1988	9.9
1983	10.4	1989	10.3
1984	11.9	1990	10.5
		1991	9.6

Source: Ministry of Agriculture, Forestry, and Fisheries.

supply over demand in some years. To avoid or reduce the surplus, the government introduced rice acreage control in 1969. It entailed subsidy payments to farmers for withdrawing paddy fields from production or diverting their use to nonrice crops.

Currently rice output is distributed in the following ways: (1) About 20–30% of the rice is purchased by the government as government rice through licensed collectors (mainly **agricultural cooperatives**) at the government-determined price. It is then resold to licensed wholesalers and processors at government-determined prices. (2) About 50–60% of the rice is collected by the licensed collectors and sold directly to licensed wholesalers and processors at negotiated prices. (3) About 10–20% is auctioned off by the collectors to wholesalers at the rice exchanges. (4) About 10% is consumed by the farmers themselves or illegally sold by farmers to wholesalers and retailers in the black market (author's interviews, Central Union of Agricultural Cooperatives, Oct. 9, 1991; Ministry of Agriculture, Forestry, and Fisheries, Oct. 3, 1991).

The government's purchase price for the producer (producer's price) is set every year. It is a multiple of the world price. Sometimes it is also higher than the government's selling price, resulting in an additional government deficit. The separation of producer and consumer prices means that there was no "countervailing power" to hold producer prices down. Thus even **labor unions** support high producer prices while they demand low consumer prices (Donnelly 1977: 151). In 1987 government purchase price was cut slightly for the first time in 31 years (see table R.2). Since then it has been cut slightly every year. Both international pressures to end agricultural subsidies and government fiscal retrenchment have contributed

Table R.2
Price of government-controlled rice (in ¥/60 kilograms)

Year	Government purchase price	Government selling price
1983	¥18,266	¥17,033
1984	18,668	17,673
1985	18,668	18,327
1986	18,668	18,598
1987	17,557	18,133
1988	16,644	
1989	16,615	
1990	16,380	

Source: Ministry of Agriculture, Forestry, and Fisheries.

to the price cuts. The producer's price for government-controlled rice is lower than that of non-government-controlled rice, which is of higher quality. For example, the former was ¥16,530 per 60 kilograms in 1991; the latter fluctuated around ¥20,000 in the same year.

As part of the government's control of rice, rice import is banned except in processed forms. Tokyo's rationale for the ban is that self-sufficiency in rice is important for food security purposes. In addition domestic farm groups have long maintained that rice cultivation is part of Japanese culture that should not be given up in favor of imports. A recent argment made by the farm lobby is that rice cultivation preserves the ecological system (Ishikura 1991). Surprisingly, **consumer groups** have not actively supported the lifting of the ban in order to reduce the rice price. The main reason is reportedly the Japanese consumers' demand for "high-quality" rice. Surveys do indicate that consumers believe that foreign rice tastes bad because it is dry and not sticky. Hayami (1988) argues that Japanese consumers have become more tolerant of high rice prices because their food expenditure as a ratio of total expenditure has declined as their incomes rise (also author's interview, July 9, 1992).

In the Uruquay Round of GATT (General Agreement on Tariffs and Trade) negotiations in 1990, Japan refused to give concessions in eliminating its ban on rice imports. It is estimated that without the ban, U.S. rice exports to Japan could amount to $656 million a year (*Wall Street Journal*, Apr. 1, 1991). GATT calls for converting all trade barriers in the agricultural sector to tariffs. The proposal has been hotly debated in Japan. There are indications as of early 1993 that Tokyo will accept tariffication if the Uruquay Round reaches an agreement on world trade in agricultural products.

Besides rice, the government also supports the prices of wheat and barley. Rice farmers who plant alternative crops receive diversion payments.

See also **agricultural cooperatives, agricultural policy, pricing practices, Staple Food Control Act**.

Addresses

Central Union of Agricultural Cooperatives (Zenchu)
8-3, Otemachi 1-chome, Chiyoda-ku, Tokyo 100
Tel: (03) 3245-7565   Fax: (03) 3242-1581

Food Agency, Ministry of Agriculture, Forestry, and Fisheries
2-1, Kasumigaseki 1-chome, Chiyoda-ku, Tokyo 100
Tel: (03) 3502-8111

References

Donnelly, Michael W. 1977. Setting the price of rice: A study in political decisionmaking. In *Policymaking in Contemporary Japan*, ed. by T. J. Pempel. Ithaca: Cornell University Press.

Food Agency. 1991. *Rice and Wheat in Japan.*

Fujiyasu, Minako. 1990. The power politics of rice. *Tokyo Business Today* (Oct.): 26–35.

Hayami, Yujiro. 1988. *Japanese Agriculture under Siege: The Political Economy of Agricultural Policies.* London: Macmillan.

Ishikura, Teruka. 1991. Rice debate goes beyond trade issues. *Nikkei Weekly*, Dec. 28: 6.

Kobayashi, H. 1990. Japan. In *Agricultural Output and Input Pricing*. Tokyo: Asian Productivity Organization.

Ministry of Agriculture, Forestry, and Fisheries. Monthly. *Monthly Statistics of Agriculture, Forestry and Fisheries.*

Moore, Richard M. 1990. *Japanese Agriculture: Patterns of Rural Development.* Boulder, CO: Westview.

Mori, Hiroshi. 1990. Agricultural price policies in Japan. In *Agricultural Output and Input Pricing*. Tokyo: Asian Productivity Organization.

MacKnight, Susan. 1987. Japan, agriculture and the MTN. *JEI Report*, no. 44A, Nov. 20.

ringi system   A formal procedure in decision-making process widely used in large Japanese corporations and government agencies, in which a drafted proposal is circulated among units of the organization for consultation and to seek consensus.
   See **decision making**.

rural price indexes
See **price indexes and price levels**.

S

saihan   Resale price maintenance or the practice of fixing minimum retail prices by manufacturers.
   See **pricing practices**.

Saison Group   A large conglomerate of some 200 firms with the Seibu Department stores as its core company.
   See *keiretsu* **and business groups**.

Sakura Bank   A large city bank, formed in a merger between Mitsui Bank and Taiyo Kobe Bank on April 1, 1990. The new bank was initially named Mitsui Taiyo Kobe Bank until April 1, 1992, when it was renamed Sakura Bank.
   See **city banks**.

samurai **bonds**   Yen-denominated bonds issued in Japan by nonresidents. They were first issued by the Asian Development Bank in 1970 and the World Bank in 1971. In the 1970s the *samurai* bond market was open only to foreign governments, government agencies, and international organizations such as the World Bank and the Asian Development Bank. In the early 1980s it was open to foreign corporations and other nongovernment institutions with a single-A credit rating. Since August 1992, when the Japanese government eased the access to the market for foreigners, foreign government-affiliated bodies with a BB+ or a BBB rating are allowed to issue *samurai* bonds.
   The volume of new issues was ¥915 billion in 1984 and ¥1,115 billion in 1985. In 1986–88 the annual volume of new issues declined rapidly to about half the 1985 level; it rose again to ¥1,101 billion in 1989 and ¥1,203 billion in 1990. The amount outstanding was ¥5,755 in 1990. New

issues declined to only ¥681 billion in 1991, then rose to ¥1,149 in 1992. The amount outstanding was ¥6,499 billion in 1992.

The main reason for the rapid decline in new issues of *samurai* bonds in 1986–88 was the appreciation of the yen after 1985, as continuous appreciation of the yen vis-à-vis the dollar increased the cost of repaying the yen-denominated debt. By 1989 the **yen–dollar exchange rate** had stablized considerably. In an effort to stimulate the market, the **Ministry of Finance** simplified the issuing process on the *samurai* bond market in October 1987. In addition interest rates in Japan remained relatively low, and the yen continued to play an important role in world trade. Consequently in 1989 the volume of new issues started to increase. The dollar's rise in 1989 also contributed to the new surge. U.S. borrowers, including state governments and financial institutions, have become the major issuers of *samurai* bonds. In late 1992 European nations moved to Japan to raise funds because of the European currency crisis and the lower interest rate in Japan. This was also facilitated by the easing, in August 1992, of the rating requirement. As a result the volume of new issuances rose rapidly in late 1992 and early 1993. European government entities such as the National Bank of Hungary and the Turkish government are among the issuers.

The major competing debt instrument of *samurai* bonds is the **Euroyen bonds**, which are yen-denominated bonds issued in the Euromarket. In 1988 the volume of Euroyen bond issues was about four times that of *samurai* bonds. *Samurai* bonds should also be distinguished from the so-called *daimyo* bonds and *shogun* bonds. *Daimyo* bonds are yen-denominated bonds issued in Japan by nonresidents but sold to investors on the Euromarket. *Shogun* bonds are foreign currency-based bonds issed by nonresidents and sold in Japan. The market for the latter is still limited, with only ¥98 billion issued in 1990 and ¥73 billion in 1991.

See also **Euroyen bonds**.

References

Idei, Yas. 1993. *Samurai* market draws riskier issuers. *Nikkei Weekly*, Mar. 15: 16.

Makino, Yo. 1989. *Samurai* bond activity rekindled. *Japan Economic Journal*, Mar. 11: 3.

Japan Securities Research Institute. 1992. *Securities Market in Japan 1992*. Ch. 2.

Tokyo Stock Exchange. 1993. *Tokyo Stock Exchange 1993 Fact Book*.

Sanwa Bank   A large city bank and the core member of the Sanwa Group. See **city banks**.

sarakin   Consumer finance firms or consumer financing for salaried employees; abbreviation of "salaryman *kinyu*" (salaried-men's loans).
See **consumer credit**.

savings   Postwar Japan has maintained a very high saving rate that is unprecedented in Japan and unmatched in the rest of the world. Gross national saving rate in Japan as a percentage of GDP (gross domestic product) was 40.2% in 1970, 31.3% in 1980, and 34.4% in 1990. In comparison, in the United States it was 18% in 1970, 18.4% in 1980, and 14.6% in 1990 (see table S.1). This high saving rate, coupled with the trade surplus in Japan throughout the 1980s, has led to criticisms by foreign countries, particularly the United States, that the Japanese save too much and do not consume and import enough. In response, many Japanese commentators and trade officials have argued that Americans save too little and consume too much.

Japan's high saving rate was necessary for its postwar reconstruction and industrial growth. It has financed a high rate of **investment** that has been near or over 30% of GDP and GNP. It was only after 1976 (with the exception of 1979 and 1980) that the investment rate fell slightly below the saving rate. The excess savings led to large outflows of Japanese savings, which helped to finance the trade deficits of Japan's trading partners, particularly the United States.

Table S.1
Saving and investment rates, Japan and the United States (in % of GDP)

Year	Saving/GDP		Investment/GDP	
	Japan	United States	Japan	United States
1960	32.8	23.2	32.4	18.4
1970	40.2	18.0	39.1	17.9
1975	32.8	17.8	32.8	17.0
1980	31.3	18.4	32.2	18.9
1985	31.1	16.1	28.5	19.2
1986	32.5	15.4	28.1	18.8
1987	32.2	14.8	28.4	17.8
1988	33.3	15.2	30.4	17.4
1989	33.6	15.5	31.5	17.1
1990	34.4	14.6	33.0	16.0
1991	34.5	14.8	32.0	15.3

Source: International Monetary Fund.

While not denying that Japan's saving rate is higher than that of the United States, some economists have pointed out that methodological differences in measuring savings in the two countries have exaggerated the differences. For example, the United States inappropriately counts many durable goods such as furniture as consumer spending, whereas Japan does not. Furthermore, in deducting depreciation from gross savings to calculate net savings, the United States estimates depreciation at replacement cost, whereas Japan uses historical cost. During a period of inflation, replacement cost exceeds historical cost; therefore Japan's method of depreciation overstates its savings by U.S. standards (Horioka 1990: 51–54). Most experts agree, however, that after allowances are made for these differences, Japan's saving rate has consistently exceeded that of the United States by a substantial margin.

National savings are the sum of savings by households, nonfinancial corporations, the government, financial institutions, and private nonprofit organizations. The first three sectors are the most important. As shown in table S.2, households (including unincorporated businesses) had been the largest source of savings in Japan until 1987. Household savings as a ratio of household disposabale income has declined gradually from nearly 23% in 1975 to 14.1% in 1990. Nevertheless, these saving rates have been higher than those of other OECD countries (except Belgium) where a gradual decline has also taken place.

Corporate savings were relatively low in the 1970s, but have been rising as a ratio of GNP since the late 1970s and have become the largest source

Table S.2
Saving rates by sector (in %)

FY	HS/DI	HS/GNP	CS/GNP	GS/GNP
1975	22.8	20.3	7.7	2.3
1980	17.9	16.5	10.9	3.1
1985	15.6	14.5	11.8	4.8
1986	16.1	14.0	12.4	5.3
1987	14.7	13.4	12.9	6.8
1988	14.3	12.8	13.0	8.2
1989	14.6	12.4	13.6	8.6
1990	14.1	12.3	12.6	9.7

Source: Economic Planning Agency.
Note: HS/DI = household savings/disposable income (calendar year basis); HS/GNP = household savings/ GNP (fiscal year). Private unincoporated nonfinancial enterprises are included. CS/GNP = nonfinancial corporations' savings/GNP; GS/GNP = general government savings/GNP.

of savings since 1988. They amount to 10.9% of GNP in 1980, 11.8% in 1985, and 12.6% in 1990. General government savings (including those of the central and local governments) used to be very low but have been rising as a percentage of GNP since the late 1970s. Compared with their respective investment, however, both the corporate and the government sectors have had excess investment over their savings in all years (except 1987–90 for the government); the opposite is true with the households. Thus excess household savings served to finance the excess investment of corporations and the government through the financial institutions. Finally, financial institutions (not shown in table S.2) had little savings before 1984 and have had negative savings since 1985.

The literature on Japanese savings has concentrated on household savings. Analysts have different explanations for the high household savings. Ishikawa and Ueda (1984) regard the semiannual bonuses paid by comnies as buffer incomes that are easily saved because they are lumpy and uncertain, being tied to company performance. Horioka (1984) postulates that households maintain a high saving rate over their life cycle to pay for children's education, **housing**, and bequests. Balassa and Noland (1988) support the "strategic bequest motive" hypothesis. According to this hypothesis, individuals have to maintain a high saving rate for many years for the purchase of houses, which are very expensive in Japan by international standards. After retirement they continue to save and maintain the value of their houses rather than dissave, because they intend to bequest the houses to their heirs in exchange for financial and other assistance while living with them in the same household, as is still common in Japan. The quantitative importance of the bequest motive in increasing the saving rate, however, is disputed by Hayashi, Ito, and Slemrod (1988).

Still other analysts have argued that because of the underdeveloped **social security system**, households have to save for old age support, and that because the Japanese work more hours than workers in other industrial countries, they have less time to shop and consume. Finally, Hayashi, Ito, and Slemrod (1988) contend that government efforts in the postwar period to encourage saving for postwar reconstruction and development have been successful. In particular, until it was reformed in 1988, the *maruyu* system, which exempted interest income from principal of up to 9 million yen per person, is considered to have been effective in promoting household savings. This tax exemption included interest from **postal savings**.

The saving rate as a percentage of GDP or GNP is expected to decline in the future because of the aging of the Japanese **population**. The percentage of the population aged 65 and over was only 12.1% in 1990, but it is expected to rise to 21.3% in 2010 and to reach a plateau of 25.5% in 2020 (see table P.2, **population**). Since the elderly save less than the rest of the population, the overall saving rate will decline.

See also **consumption**, *maruyu*, **postal savings**.

References

Balassa, Bela, and Marcus Noland. 1988. *Japan in the World Economy*. Washington: Institute for International Economics. Ch. 4.

Dekle, Robert, and Lawrence Summers. 1991. Japan's high saving rate reaffirmed. *Bank of Japan Monetary and Economic Studies* 9, 2: 63–78.

Economic Planning Agency. 1992. *Annual Report on National Accounts*.

Horioka, Charles Yuji. 1984. The applicability of the life-cycle hypothesis of saving to Japan. *Kyoto University Economic Review* 54: 31–56.

Horioka, Charles Yuji. 1990. Why is Japan's household saving rate so high? A literature survey. *Journal of the Japanese and International Economies* 4: 49–92.

International Monetary Fund. 1992. *International Financial Statistics Yearbook, 1992*. Washington: IMF.

Ishikawa, Tsuneo, and Kazuo Ueda. 1984. The bonus payment system and Japanese personal savings. In *The Economic Analysis of the Japanese Firm*, ed. by A. Aoki. Amsterdam: Elsevier Science.

Ito, Takatoshi. 1991. The Japanese Economy. Cambridge: MIT Press. Ch. 9.

Management and Coordination Agency. Annual. *Family Saving Survey*.

Takenaka, Heizo. 1991. *Contemporary Japanese Economy and Economic Policy*. Ann Arbor: University of Michigan Press. Chs. 3–4.

Second Association of Regional Banks   National organization of the 65 second-tier regional banks, which were formerly *sogo* banks but converted themselves into regular commercial banks in 1989.

See **banking system**, *sogo* **banks**.

securities companies   Securities companies were established in accordance with the Securities and Exchange Law of 1948 for the underwriting and trading of securities, which banks are not permitted to enter. In addition they play a role in the **investment trust** and the **money market**. In 1992, there were 265 licensed securities companies in Japan, including 49 foreign securities companies, regulated by the **Ministery of Finance**.

Although many securities companies existed in the early postwar period (1,152 in 1949), most of them were small and financially weak and subsequently merged or went out of business. Total paid-in capital of all securities companies was only ¥3 billion in 1949, giving an average capitalization per company of ¥2.6 million. The total increased to ¥1,234 billion at the end of 1990, which gives an average capitalization per company of ¥5.6 billion. This increase reflects the greatly increased volume of business of the securities industry since the late 1970s as Japanese investors with surplus funds sought alternative forms of investment and as corporate borrowers increasingly raised funds in the equity and debt markets.

Securities companies are engaged in the following lines of business:

1. *The stock business.* This is the largest source of revenues. About three-quarters (73% in 1988) of the stock business is in the form of brokerage business to effect stock transactions on behalf of customers. The balance involves dealing in stocks for their own accounts.

2. *The bond business.* Securities companies are engaged in underwriting and distributing new issues of bonds as well as in trading outstanding issues. The bulk of the bond transactions they handle is for their own accounts (self-dealing). However, about 30% of the bond trading is in the form of *gensaki* trading, namely the sale of bonds with a repurchase agreement. With the massive offering of **government bonds** in 1975, the volume of bond transactions has increased rapidly. The internationalization of the securities market also increased the underwriting by securities companies of Japanese corporate bond issues on foreign markets.

3. *Other lines of business.* Securities companies may be involved in aspects of **investment trust** business. They may also be engaged in the transaction of domestic certificates of deposit (CDs), yen-denomiated banker's acceptance, commercial papers (CPs) issued on the domestic market, mortgage-backed securities, and CDs and CPs issued on foreign markets.

The securities industry is dominated by the Big Four—Nomura Securities Co., the world's largest, and Daiwa, Nikko, and Yamaichi Securities Co. Their share of the market, however, has declined over time. In 1980 they had nearly 60% of the market; in the fiscal year ending in March 1991, the four had a 33% market share in stock brokerage in the **Tokyo Stock Exchange**, with Nomura having 9.3%. The Big Four are followed by ten "second-tier" companies: Kokusai, Wako, Okasan, New Japan, Kankaku, Cosmo, Sanyo, Tokyo, Yamatane, and Dai-Ichi. The latter's combined stock brokerage share on the Tokyo Stock Exchange in the year ending in March 1991 was 25%.

Table S.3 shows the revenues and profits of the ten leading securities companies. It is clear that the fall of stock prices that started in 1990

Table S.3
Leading securities companies (FY, in ¥ billions)

Company	Operating revenues			Pretax profits		
	1989	1991	1992	1989	1991	1992
Nomura	986.2	421.8	344.7	488.9	44.1	2.4
Daiwa	660.1	321.1	247.1	313.2	9.3	−7.3
Nikko	601.0	287.9	230.7	260.5	3.1	2.5
Yamaichi	573.5	231.4	188.7	233.7	−36.5	−37.4
Kokusai	215.5	110.5	78.4	76.5	0.2	−17.4
Wako	150.5	69.5	52.2	47.8	−15.7	−22.5
Okasan	121.3	53.4	36.1	31.7	−11.2	−18.5
New Japan	207.2	87.8	69.1	50.1	−44.1	−36.4
Kankaku	180.3	72.0	46.2	44.1	−49.5	−51.0
Cosmo	97.1	40.8	24.5	24.2	−9.5	−17.5

Source: *The Nikkei Weekly*, May 23, 1992, and May 24, 1993.

became a disaster for the industry in 1991–92. Some mid-sized and smaller securities companies were affected even more severely than the big ones.

Although the securities companies are regulated by the Ministry of Finance, the regulation is not as strict as in the United States, and new rules are introduced only when flagrant unethical practices have caused a public outcry and international criticisms. Stock price manipulation is one of those practices. Before 1988 the Big Four periodically promoted selected stock issues or sectors to customers, which made those prices to rise precipitously. The Brady Commission, a U.S. government special body on stock trading, criticized the Big Four's oligopolistic control of the Japanese **stock market** in its 1988 report. As a result the Ministry of Finance imposed in early 1988 an unwritten "30% rule," restricting each securities house to hold its percentage of trading volume in any stock to less than 30% of the stock's total volume each month.

Another unethical practice is the clandestine arrangement made by the big securities firms with their major clients to compensate them for trading losses. This helps to attract big business at the expense of small investors and is in violation of Japan's Securities and Exchange Law. They have done so through the device of shadowy discretionary *eigyo tokkin* accounts set up by securities firms for clients; these accounts are directly managed by the securities houses on a discretionary basis so that funds can be easily moved in and out of them (see **tokkin funds**). It was revealed in mid-1991 that the Big Four paid an estimated ¥120 billion to compensate major clients for stock trading losses from October 1987 to March 1991. Thirty smaller securities firms also paid top clients about ¥20 billion for loss compensation. Such scandals forced the resignation or demotion of senior executives of the Big Four and various penalties imposed by the government. In addition it was revealed that Nomura and Nikko had business dealings with an organized crime syndicate.

Rules against insider trading exist, but it was not until 1990 that the first prosecution of insider trading was filed. Government officials emphasize that the purpose of the rules is to prevent insider trading rather than to punish violators.

In Japan, banking business and securities business are separated by law. Since the late 1980s this separation between banking and securities has been hotly debated. The banks would like to branch out into the securities business, while the securities houses are eager to keep them out. The Ministry of Finance plans to ease the separation by allowing banks to set up securities subsidiaries to underwrite stocks and bonds.

Another policy issue concerns the participation of foreign securities firms in the industry. The slow opening of Japan's securities industry to foreign firms has been one of Washington's complaints about Japan's financial markets. It is charged that foreign securities firms are still excluded from the underwriting businesses and still encounter barriers in entering the business of managing pension funds and investment trusts.

See also **stock market,** *tokkin* **funds, Tokyo Stock Exchange**.

Addresses

Daiwa Securities Co.
6-4, Ohtemachi 2-chome, Chiyoda-ku, Tokyo 100
Tel: (03) 3243-2111

Japan Securities Dealers Association
5-8, Nihonbashi Kayabacho 1-chome, Chuo-ku, Tokyo 103
Tel: (03) 667-8451

Nikko Securities Co.
3-1, Marunouchi 3-chome, Chiyoda-ku, Tokyo 100
Tel: (03) 3283-2211

Nomura Securities Co.
9-1, Nohonbashi 1-chome, Chuo-ku, Tokyo 103
Tel: (03) 3211-1811

Yamaichi Securities Co.
4-1, Yaesy 2-chome, Chuo-ku, Tokyo 104
Tel: (03) 3276-3181

References

Alletzhauser. 1990. *The House of Nomura*. London: Bloomsbury.

Elton, Edwin J., and Martin J. Gruber. 1990. *Japanese Capital Markets*. New York: Harper and Row.

Issacs, Jonathan. 1990. *Japanese Equities Markets*. London: Euromoney Pulications. Ch. 7.

Japan Securities Research Institute. 1992. *Securities Market in Japan*, 1992. Ch. 7.

Suzuki, Yoshio, ed. 1987. *The Japanese Financial System*. Oxford: Oxford University Press. Pp. 260–269.

Tatewaki, Kazuo. 1991. *Banking and Finance in Japan*. London: Routledge. Ch. 8.

Viner, Aron. 1987. *Inside Japan's Financial Markets*. London: The Economist Publications. Ch. 2.

Zielinski, Robert, and Nigel Holloway. 1991. *Unequal Equities: Power and Risk in Japan's Stock Market*. Tokyo: Kodansha International. Ch. 4.

securities finance companies   These are companies that specialize in the financing of securities. Nine such companies were established in 1950, one in each of the cities with securities exchanges, because of the depressed stock market following the dissolution of the *zaibatsu* and the dumping of their stocks on the market. In 1956 they were consolidated into the current three: Japan Securities Finance Company, Osaka Securities Finance Company, and the Chubu Securities Company (located in Nagoya). The last one is by far the smallest of the three. They are supervized by the **Ministry of Finance**.

Their business was initially limited to lending to **securities companies** for margin transactions. In 1960 they began lending to bond dealers for transactions in bonds. Because of the rapid growth of the primary and secondary markets in **government bonds** in the 1980s, the volume of bond dealer financing exceeded that of stock margin transactions in 1982–88. At the end of 1988, for example, the balance of their total loans was ¥2.53 trillion, of which ¥723 billion was for margin transactions and ¥1,230 billion was loans on bonds. The situation was reversed in 1989 and 1990 when loans for margin transactions became more important. At the end of 1990 outstanding loans were ¥2.21 trillion, of which ¥974 billion was for margin transactions and ¥543 billion for bond trading. At the end of 1991 outstanding loans declined to ¥1.87 trillion because of the **stock market** decline, with ¥573 billion and ¥798 billion for margin transactions and bond trading, respectively.

Securities finance companies obtain their funds by borrowing from the **Bank of Japan**, the **city banks**, and the **call money market**. In 1988 they were allowed to raise money by issuing **commercial papers**. At the end of 1990 outstanding call loan borrowings were ¥1,069 billion, and short-term borrowings amounted to ¥767 billion. These fell to ¥871 billion and ¥651 billion, respectively, at the end of 1991.

See also **securities companies**.

Addresses

Japan Securities Finance Compay
2-10, Nihonbashi Kayaba-cho 1-chome, Chuo-ku, Tokyo 103
Tel: (03) 3668-1403

Osaka Securities Finance Company
4-6, Kitahama 2-chome, Chuo-ku, Osaka 541
Tel: (06) 203-1181

References

Bank of Japan. 1992. *Economic Statistics Annual*, 1991.

Federation of Bankers Associations of Japan. 1989. *The Banking System in Japan*. Ch. 1.

Isaccs, Jonathan. 1990. *Japanese Equities Markets*. London: Euromoney Publications. Ch. 5.

Japan Securities Research Institute. 1992. *Securities Market in Japan*, 1992. Ch. 11.

Suzuki, Yoshio, ed. 1987. *The Japanese Financial System*. Oxford: Oxford University Press. Ch. 5.

Tatewaki, Kazuo. 1991. *Banking and Finance in Japan*. London: Routledge. Ch. 7.

securities investment trust management companies   Fund managers of investment trusts.

See **investment trusts**.

seibo   The year-end gift-giving season.

See **gift market**.

Seibu Department Stores, Ltd.   A leading department store chain and the core company of the Saison Group.

See **department stores, *keiretsu* and business groups**.

Seibu Railway Group   A large conglomerate with the Seibu Railway as its core company.

See ***keiretsu* and business groups**.

seikyo   Consumer cooperatives.
See **consumer groups**.

Semiconductor Agreement, 1991   An agreement between Tokyo and Washington, singed on June 4, 1991 and effective from August 1, 1991 for five years, in which Tokyo pledges to promote the share of foreign firms in Japan's chip market to more than 20% by the end of 1992, although the Japanese government does not guarantee that market share. It replaces an earlier five-year accord, which expired on August 1, 1991.

One technical problem with the agreement concerns the calculation of market share. Tokyo and Washington have different formulas for measuring market share. However, the differences reportedly will be narrowed.

To deter possible dumping, Japanese semiconductor companies will collect cost and price data and turn them over to Washington in the event of an antidumping investigation. Also, to prevent chip dumping in third countries, Tokyo and Washington will cooperate with third countries in any GATT action to investigate dumping.

Although Japanese electronics makers pledged to cooperate with the government in implementing the agreement, many have expressed misgivings about the 20% goal. Some questioned the ability of foreign companies to supply such a large amount. Others indicated that a longer period of joint development was needed to install chips in their products. Still others complained that delivery of foreign chips is often unreliable or expressed doubt about the quality of foreign-made chips. In general, Japanese executives do not think that the agreement would do much to restore the U.S. industry's competitiveness.

European Community officials feel that the agreement is discriminatory because it would pressure the Japanese to import more U.S. chips but not the European ones. In the last quarter of 1992 foreign chips attained 20.2% of Japan's semiconductor market, slightly exceeding the target (Nakamae and Clifford 1993).

See also **electronics industry**.

References

Inoue, Yuko. 1991. Firms warily back Japan–U.S. chip accord. *Nikkei Weekly*, June 15: 1, 23.

Nakamae, Hiroshi, and Bill Clifford. 1993. Chip-share precedent worries Tokyo. *Nikkei Weekly*, Mar. 29: 1, 23.

semiconductor industry
See **electronics industry**.

service price index
See **price indexes and price levels**.

shareownership   Financial institutions and business corporations are the largest categories of shareholders in Japan. Before 1972, however, individuals were the largest shareholders.

Table S.4 shows the changes in the patterns of shareownership in the postwar period. It includes only shares of companies listed on any one of the eight stock exchanges in Japan and excludes those traded in the over-the-counter stock market. Important changes include the following: (1) Financial institutions, including all banks and **insurance companies** but excluding **securities companies**, have become the largest shareholders since 1973. (2) Business corporations have more than doubled their share of ownership in the postwar period to become the second largest category. (3) From the largest group of shareowners before 1972, individuals and unincorporated organizations have declined in importance and account for

Table S.4
Shareownership of all listed companies (in %)

	1951	1972	1990	1992
Government and local government	3.1	0.2	0.7	0.6
Financial institutions	12.6	33.9	46.0	44.7
All banks	—	—	22.1	21.8
Investment trusts	—	—	3.7	3.2
Annuity trusts	—	—	0.9	1.0
Life insurance company	—	—	13.1	13.2
Non-life ins. company	—	—	4.1	4.0
Others	—	—	2.1	1.6
Business corporations	13.8	23.6	24.8	24.5
Securities companies	9.2	1.5	2.0	1.5
Individuals and others	61.3	37.2	22.6	23.2
Foreigners	—	3.6	3.9	5.4
Total	100.0	100.0	100.0	100.0

Source: Tokyo Stock Exchange.
Note: (1) On the basis of business years ending on March 31 of each year. (2) "Individuals and others" include unicorporated organizations.

only 23% of shareownership in 1990–92. (4) Government shareownership has been less than 1% since 1954 (not shown in the table). Shareownership by foreigners has increased from 1.2% in 1953 to 5.4% in 1992. It fluctuated in the 4–6% range in the 1980s.

The steady decline of individuals' shareownership is unhealthy for market stability and the diffusion of economic power. In Japan large institutional investors tend to act together in the same direction in the market, thereby causing greater fluctuations than individual investors would (**Tokyo Stock Exchange** briefing, Aug. 7, 1992). There are a few measures that can be taken to encourage individual shareownership. First, the minimum number of shares needed to trade can be reduced; currently it is 1,000 shares, which is high by international standards. Second, raising the dividend–payout ratio will help. The average dividend–payout ratio in Japan is currently slightly less than 30%, which is lower than that of other industrial nations.

As of 1991 Nippon Telegraph and Telepone (NTT) has by far the largest number of individual shareholders (1,619,497), followed by Tokyo Electric Power (609,821) and Nippon Steel (380,933). The revelation in 1991 that securities companies have compensated large companies for investment losses has alienated many individual investors. Hence it can be expected that individuals' share of stock ownership will continue to decline.

Beneath these overall patterns of shareownership are various underlying factors of the economy, including the following business relationships and practices that affect shareownership:

1. Companies that are members of a *keiretsu* or corporate group own each other's shares. The average percentage of a member firm's stock held by other membes has increased over the years for the largest *keiretsu*, from 7–14% in 1963 to 12.2–26.9% in fiscal 1988. In some industrial *keiretsu*, such as the Hitachi Group, the core industrial company of the group typically owns a significant percentage (50% or more in the case of Hitachi) of the shares of other group members.

2. Companies that do business with each other without *keiretsu* ties customarily hold a small amount of each other's stock as a token of goodwill and mutual support. These shares will not be sold as long as the business relationship is maintained.

3. Institutional investors such as trust funds, pension funds, and **insurance companies** tend to hold shares for a long period of time for long-term capital gains. These are considered to be "stable shareholders."

4. Banks and insurance companies often hold shares of their customers in order to promote business with them. They are also valued by the issuing companies as stable shareholders.

5. Between the mid-1980s and 1990, because of the appreciation of the yen and the rising **stock market**, many Japanese manufacturers were heavily engaged in *zaiteku*, or active investment of funds, in the stock market to increase their profits. The fall of the stock market and the recession of the economy since 1991 have dampened such activities.

See also **cross shareholding, Tokyo Stock Exchange**.

References

Choy, Jon. 1991. Patterns and implications of Japanese stockholding. *JEI Report*, Jan. 25.

Isaacs, Jonathan. 1990. *Japanese Equities Markets*. London: Euromoney Publications. Ch. 8.

McDonald, Jack. 1989. The *mochiai* effect: Japanese corporate cross-holdings. *Journal of Portfolio Management* 16, 1: 90−94.

Tokyo Stock Exchange. 1993. *Tokyo Stock Exchange Fact Book*, 1993.

Zielinski, Robert, and Nigel Holloway. 1991. *Unequal Equities: Power and Risk in Japan's Stock Market*. Tokyo: Kodansha International. Chs. 2−3.

Shimizu Corp.   Japan's largest general construction company. See **construction industry**.

shinkansen   The "bullet trains" of the Japan Railway Companies. See **railway companies**.

shinkin banks   Established on the basis of the 1951 *Shinkin* Bank Law, *shinkin* banks, or credit associations, are a special type of financial institution for small- and medium-sized businesses, roughly comparable to savings and loan institutions in the United States. They have their origins in the traditional credit cooperatives and are organized as nonprofit cooperatives or credit associations. Their members are small- and medium-sized enterprises (with no more than 300 employees and capitalization of no more than ¥400 million) and local residents. The number of *shinkin* banks has been declining steadily in the postwar period. There were 435 *shinkin* banks as of December 1992, down from 538 at the end of 1960.

Shinkin banks conduct their business primarily with their members, accepting deposits and installment savings, lending and discounting bills for them. The law permits them to lend to nonmembers up to 20% of their total lending. The maximum loan to a single borrower is set at 20% of the bank's capital or ¥800 million, whichever is smaller. In exchange for these restrictions they are permitted to pay 0.1% more than ordinary banks for fixed-term deposits and 0.25% more for deposits for tax payments and other deposits. Their total assets at year-end were ¥3.7 trillion in 1965, ¥40.9 trillion in 1980, and ¥102.8 trillion in 1991. At the end of 1992 their savings and deposits totaled ¥88.2 trillion, and their loans and discounts totaled ¥65.0 trillion.

As competition in the banking business intensified and interest rate liberalization drove up the cost of funds, some smaller *shinkin* banks merged to increase their scale of operation. Some large ones are expected to join with **city banks** or to transform themselves into ordinary banks.

All *shinkin* banks are members of the Zenshinren Bank, the National Federation of *Shinkin* Banks. Zenshinren is engaged in deposit taking, lending, and funds transfer for members and government and nonprofit organizations. At the end of 1992 it had ¥9.2 trillion in deposits and ¥4.1 trillion in loans. In November 1990 the Federation expressed for the first time its support for mergers among *shinkin* banks.

See also **banking system**.

Address

The National Federation of Shinkin Banks
8-1, Kyobashi 3-chome, Chuo-ku, Tokyo 104
Tel: (03) 3563-4821

References

Bank of Japan. 1993. *Economics Statistics Annual*, 1992.

Federation of Bankers Association of Japan. 1989. *The Banking System in Japan*. Ch. 1.

Interest rate liberalization worries credit associations. *Nikkei Weekly*, Oct. 19, 1991: 16.

Okamoto, Fumio. 1990. *Shinkin* banks offer service in fight against city giants. *Japan Economic Journal*, Mar. 3: 31–32.

Suzuki, Yoshio, ed. 1987. *The Japanese Financial System*. Oxford: Oxford University Press. Ch. 5.

Takagi, Hisao. 1990. Co-ops brace for battle to survive. *Japan Economic Journal*, Nov. 24: 1.

Tatewaki, Kazuo. 1991. *Banking and Finance in Japan*. London: Routledge. Ch. 7.

shinpan **companies**   Credit sales companies.
See **consumer credit**.

shipbuilding industry From a very low level after World War II, Japan's shipbuilding industry developed so rapidly that Japan surpassed Britain in 1956 to become the world's largest shipbuilder. It has remained in that position ever since. However, because the world's demand for new ships slumped after the oil crisis of 1973, the industry went through a long depression in 1974 through 1988. During that period the industry had to adopt measures to restrict industry capacity.

Shipbuilding in Japan is regulated by the Ministry of Transport (MOT). The industry developed very rapidly from the early 1950s through 1973 when world seaborn trade tripled and bulk carriers and crude tankers were needed to transport major commodities such as crude oil, iron ore, coal, and grain. The industry was also assisted with long-term, low-interest loans from the **Japan Development Bank** and the Export-Import Bank of Japan. In 1973 the industry had about one-half (48.6%) of the world's orders for new ships.

In the aftermath of the 1973 oil crisis, new orders fell sharply from a peak of 38 million gross tons in 1973 to 13.3 million tons in 1974 and 3.2 million tons in 1978. Under the MOT's **administrative guidance** the industry began, in 1976, to implement an industrywide reduction in output (28% reduction from peak year output). The Depressed Industries Law of 1978, designed to reduce capacity and balance supply and demand in "structurally depressed industries" or **declining industries**, facilitated further reduction in subsequent years. In 1979 production was limited to 39% of peak-year output. An antirecession **cartel** was also established in 1979 to oversee the reduction. The MOT also assisted qualified smaller shipbuilders to leave the industry with a buy-out program.

The orders for new ships recovered in 1980–81 to 9.8 million gross tons and to 10.7 million gross tons in 1983. It declined rapidly thereafter. A recession cartel was organized in 1987 to reduce industry output. In 1989 new orders rose to 9.7 million gross tons. During the 1980–89 period the MOT continued to regulate production, to prevent price declines, by setting construction goals for individual companies. Nevertheless, competition among companies and from the low-cost Korean shipbuilders led to declining prices of new ships throughout most of the 1980s. New orders climbed to 10.7 million gross tons in 1990 because of a worldwide boom. Japan's world market share has remained at 43–45%. Analysts expect global demand for new tankers to remain at a relatively high level for the next ten years due to the replacement needs for VLCCs (very large crude carriers of more than 200,000 tons) that were built in the 1970s.

Mirroring the long-term decline in the industry, the shipbuilding work force declined from a peak of 361,000 persons (including subcontracted shipbuilders and related industries) at the end of 1974 to 209,000 at the end of 1984 and 126,000 at the end of 1990.

As of 1991 there were 27 shipbuilders, divided into seven groups. In each group shipbuilders often jointly design and produce their orders. The top shipbuilders are the so-called Big Seven: Mitsubishi Heavy Industries, Ishikawajima-Harima Heavy Industries, Mitsui Engineering and Shipbuilding, Hitachi Zosen, Kawasaki Heavy Industries, Nippon Kokan, and Sumitomo Heavy Industries (see table S.5). All of them are capable of building VLCCs. In addition they are all integrated heavy machinery companies that make many other products such as steel structures, "turnkey" plants, and aircraft engines. The diversified nature of their businesses helped to cushion the impact of recession in shipbuilding and enabled them to transfer idled workers from shipbuilding to other lines of business. The "second-tier" shipbuilders are the medium- and small-sized companies that focus more narrowly on shipbuilding and depend on the big ones for technical and financial assistance.

A major change in tanker design and construction is playing a role in the latest demand for new ships. In the wake of the Exxon Valdez oil spill in March 1989, the International Maritime Organization adopted a new ruling in March 1992 to reduce the risk of oil spills. It requires that new tankers larger than 5,000 tons commissioned from July 1993 to be fitted with double hulls and that existing tankers larger than 20,000 tons to be retrofitted when they turn 25 years old. Since double-hull tankers cost about 20% more than the conventional tankers, the new ruling will have important financial implications for the industry.

Table S.5
Leading shipbuilders (FY 1991)

Company	Total sales (in ¥ billion)	Shipbuilding (in %)[a]
Mitsubishi Heavy Industries	2,484.2	14
Ishikawajima-Harima Heavy Industries	811.5	16
Mitui Engineering and Shipbuilding	294.3	32[b]
Hitachi Zosen	312.9	40
Kawasaki Heavy Industries	931.3	8
Sumitomo Heavy Industries	287.3	30[b]

Source: Toyo Keizai, Inc.
a. Share of shipbuilding in total sales.
b. Includes defense-related steel frames, etc.

Japanese shipbuilders are also developing high-tech ships to maintain their competitive edge. For example, Kawasaki Heavy Industries has developed high-speed vessels that can travel at about 80 kilometers per hour. Mitsui Engineering and Shipbuilding has introduced hovercraft for cargo use that may compete with overland truck transportation. Mitsubishi Heavy Industries is constructing luxury passenger liners.

See also **declining industries.**

Addresses

Ishikawajima-Harima Heavy Industries
2-1, Ohtemachi 2-chome, Chiyoda-ku, Tokyo 100
Tel: (03) 3244-5111   Fax: (03) 3244-5139

Kawasaki Heavy Industries
1-18, Nakamachidori 2-chome, Chuo-ku, Kobe 650
Tel: (078) 371-9530   Fax: (078) 371-9568

Mitsubishi Heavy Industries
5-1, Marunouchi 2-chome, Chiyoda-ku, Tokyo 100
Tel: (03) 3212-3111   Fax: (03) 3201-4517

Mitsui Engineering and Shipbuilding
6-4, Tsukiji 5-chome, Chuo-ku, Tokyo 104
Tel: (03) 3544-3131   Fax: (03) 3544-3050

Shipbuilders' Association of Japan
15-16 Toranomon 1-chome, Minato-ku, Tokyo 105
Tel: (03) 3502-2010   Fax: (03) 3502-2816

References

Anderson, Douglas D. 1986. Managing retreat: Disinvestment policy. In *America versus Japan*, ed. by Thomas K. McCraw. Boston: Harvard Business School Press.

Japan Company Handbook, First Section. 1992. Tokyo: Toyo Keizai.

Shipbuilding in Japan, 1990–91. Tokyo: Shipbuilders' Association of Japan.

Shipbuilding. In *Japan Economic Almanac*, various years. Tokyo: Nihon Keizai Shimbun.

Yonezawa, Yoshie. 1988. The shipbuilding industry. In *Industrial Policy of Japan*, ed. by Ryutaro Komiya, Masahiro Okuno, and Kotaro Suzumura. Tokyo: Academic Press Japan.

shitauke   Subcontractor.
See **subcontracting system.**

shogun **bonds**   Bonds issued in Japan in foreign currency, usually the dollar, by nonresidents.
See **bond market,** *samurai* **bonds.**

shohizei   Consumption tax.
See **tax reform, tax system**.

shukko   The practice of transferring employees by large companies to related enterprises for a limited period of time.
See **corporate personnel practices**.

shunto   Spring offensive, Japanese labor unions' annual wage bargaining campaign launched every spring.
See **spring offensive.**

small and medium enterprises   The concept of small and medium enterprises (*chu-sho kigyo*) has its prewar origin in Japan, but its definition has changed over time. Currently, in manufacturing, they are defined by law as those with fewer than 300 employees or less than ¥100 million in capital; in wholesale trade, as those with fewer than 100 employees or less than ¥30 million in capital; and in retail trade and in services, as those with fewer than 50 employees or less than ¥10 million in capital.

This definition is so broad that it covers more than 99% of all enterprises and 81% of employees in 1990. These enterprises include nearly 100% of construction firms, wholesalers and retailers, real estate businesses, and many manufacturing enterprises. Most of these enterprises are relatively small subcontractors for large companies or family-owned businesses in service or trade sectors. It is primarily the small enterprises of this broad category that often face economic difficulties. Small enterprises are defined as those with 20 or less employees in manufacturing and with 5 or fewer employees in commerce and services.

The problems of small enterprises include the following: It is difficult for them to compete with big companies to attract talented managers and skilled workers partly because they pay less. They have more difficulties in obtaining bank loans, they lack the resources for technology and innovation, and they are also the most vulnerable to recessions. The Small and Medium Enterprises Stabilization Law of 1952 was legislated to make it easier for them to form depression **cartels**.

The economic difficulties and the large voting power of the small businesses—Japan's Communist Party tried hard in the 1960s to win their votes—have prompted the ruling Liberal Democratic Party to enact the Small and Medium Enterprise Basic Law in 1963, which provided various measures to assist them: prevention of **bankcruptcies** and aid to disaster victims; promotion of modernization through special subsidized loans and tax provisions; promotion of subcontracting; provision of consultation and guidance, and management training programs; and government procurement from small and medium enterprises.

The Small and Medium Enterprise Agency of the **Ministry of International Trade and Industry** is responsible for coordinating government assistance to small and medium enterprises; it also provides consultation, guidance, and technical assistance to them. Two **government financial institutions** are set up to provide financial assistance to small and medium enterprises—the Small Business Finance Corp. and the Small Business Credit Insurance Corp. The former had outstanding loans of ¥8,322 billion at the end of 1992, while the latter had insured ¥9,921 billion in 1990 and had outstanding loans of ¥435 billion at the end of 1992. Funds from the government's **Fiscal Investment and Loan Program** allocated to purposes related to small and medium enterprises increased from ¥552 billion in fiscal 1970 to ¥3,400 billion in 1980 and ¥4,495 billion in 1991.

The number of bankruptcies among small and medium enterprises has declined since 1985. It was 18,776 in 1985, 12,617 in 1987, and 7,218 in 1989. However, because of the fall of the **stock market** and the recession of the economy in 1991, the number is estimated to have risen to over 11,000.

See also **Fiscal Investment and Loan Program**.

Addresses

Small and Medium Enterprise Agency, MITI
3-1, Kasumigaseki 1-chome, Chiyoda-ku, Tokyo 100
Tel: (03) 3501-1511   Fax: (03) 3501-7805

Small Business Corporation
5-1, Toranomon, 3-chome, Minato-ku, Tokyo 105
Tel: (03) 3433-8811

Small Business Finance Corporation
9-3. Otemachi 1-chome, Chiyoda-ku, Tokyo 100
Tel: (03) 3270-1261

References

Small and Medium Enterprise Agency. 1990. *Outline of the Small and Medium Enterprise Policies of the Japanese Government*. Tokyo: MITI.

Patrick, H., and T. Rohlen. 1987. Small-scale family enterprises. In *The Political Economy of Japan*, vol.1: *The Domestic Transformation*, ed. by K. Yamamura and Y. Yasuba. Stanford: Stanford University Press.

Small and Medium Enterprise Agency. 1992. *White Paper on Small and Medium Enterprises in Japan, 1992*. Tokyo: MITI.

Yokokura, Takashi. 1988. Small and medium enterprises. In *Industrial Policy of Japan*, ed. by R. Komiya, M. Okuno, and K. Suzumura. Tokyo: Academic Press Japan.

social insurance The most important part of Japan's social security system consisting of health insurance, national pension, and employment insurance.

See **employment insurance, health insurance, pension system, social security system**.

social security system Japan's social security system consists of social insurance, public assistance, social welfare services, children's allowances, public health, aid for war victims, and so forth. Social insurance is the most important component of the system. It consists of **health insurance**, national pensions, **employment insurance**, and employment accident compensation insurance. It provides for unforeseen circumstances with funds collected through payments by individuals and employers as well as with public subsidies. In both health insurance and **pension systems**, there are different programs for people of different employment statuses (employees of private firms, government employees, and the self-employed). These are discussed separately in **health insurance** and **pension system**.

Public assistance ("livelihood protection" subsidies) is given to the indigent who cannot support themselves. A minimum amount of livelihood expenses is calculated, which includes basic living expenses, housing, schooling, and medical expenses. Childbirth and funeral expenses are also included where relevant. The difference between this minimum amount and the household's actual income is the amount of assistance to be given. The system is implemented by welfare offices at the city, township, and village levels that ascertain the need and provide counseling and assistance. Thus there is no uniform national standard in implementation. Reportedly there is a feeling of stigma in accepting assistance. In FY 1990 the standard monthly amount of public assistance was ￥82,728 for a household of one elderly (70-year-old woman), ￥119,988 for a household of two elderly (72-year-old man and 67-year-old woman), and ￥162,533 for a fatherless household of three (30-year-old woman, 9- and 4-year-old children). In 1991 an average of 946,000 people per month, or 0.8% of the population, received public assistance, down from the postwar peak of 1,469,000 people in 1984.

Other welfare programs are designed for the elderly, the handicapped, and children with special needs. Among still other programs are a family rehabilitation loan program, a program for the rehabilitation and protection of women (prostitutes), and disaster relief.

The Ministry of Health and Welfare and its Social Insurance Agency are in charge of health insurance, pension, and social insurance, whereas the Ministry of Labor is responsible for employment insurance and employment accident compensation insurance.

See also **employment insurance, health insurance, pension system**.

Address

Ministry of Health and Welfare
2-2, Kasumigaseki 1-chome, Chiyoda-ku, Tokyo 100
Tel: (03) 3503-1711

References

Hiraishi, Nagahisa. 1987. *Social Security*. Tokyo: Japan Institute of Labor.

Ministry of Health and Welfare. 1992. *White Paper on Health and Welfare, 1991* (in Japanese).

Murdo, Pat. 1990. Japan's social security and pension systems face need for new reforms. *JEI Report*, May 25.

Nishida, Yoshiaki. 1990. Reassessment of welfare services and the trend of welfare policy for the disabled. *Annals of the Institute of Social Science* (University of Tokyo), no. 32: 115−54.

Social Insurance Agency. 1989. *Outline of Social Insurance in Japan*.

Soeda, Yoshiya. 1990. The development of the public assistance system in Japan, 1966−83. *Annals of the Institute of Social Science*, no. 32: 31−65.

Tabata, Hirokuni. 1990. The Japanese welfare state: Its structure and transformation. *Annals of the Institute of Social Science*, no. 32: 1−29.

***sogo* banks** Developed from the traditional mutual loan (*mujin*) companies in accordance with the Sogo Bank Law of 1951, *sogo* banks were mutual banks that specialized in financing small- and medium-sized companies until they converted themselves into ordinary banks, or the "new regional banks," in 1989 and became members of the Second Association of Regional Banks.

Sogo banks differed from ordinary banks in that their loans were in principle restricted to small- and medium-sized firms with employees up to 300 persons and a maximum capitalization of ¥100 million and that they were permitted to continue their traditional mutual installment savings and loans business. However, because of the changing needs of their clients, their mutual installment operations had declined since the late 1960s, and they became more similar to ordinary banks, particularly the regional banks. Their banking activities included taking deposits, lending, discounting bills, and transferring funds.

Over the years *sogo* banks had grown about as rapidly as *shinkin* banks, another type of specialized financial institutions for small- and medium-sized firms. Their total assets were ¥3.6 trillion in 1965, ¥7.6 trillion in 1970, and ¥55.5 trillion in 1988. As of 1988 there were 68 *sogo* banks. Their total deposits, including installment savings, were ¥46.2 trillion, and total loans, including mutual installment loans, were ¥38.3 trillion.

In 1989 all 68 *sogo* banks converted themselves into ordinary banks, as was permitted under the Law Concerning Merger and Conversion of Financial Institutions, and the National Association of *Sogo* Banks was changed to the Second Association of Regional Banks.

See also **banking system, *shinkin* banks**.

Address

Second Association of Regional Banks
5, Sanbancho, Chiyoda-ku, Tokyo 102
Tel: (03) 3262-2181

References

Bank of Japan. 1992. *Economic Statistics Annual, 1991*.

The Banking System in Japan. 1989. Tokyo: Federation of Bankers Associations of Japan.

Suzuki, Yoshio, ed. 1987. *The Banking System in Japan*. Oxford: Oxford University Press. Pp. 215–218.

Tatewaki, Kazuo. 1991. *Banking and Finance in Japan*. London: Routledge. Ch. 7.

sogo shosha   General **trading companies**.
See **trading companies**.

Sohyo   The General Council of Trade Unions of Japan, Japan's largest federation of unions before 1987. It merged with the Japan Trade Union Confederation (JTUC-Rengo) in 1989.
See **labor unions**.

sokaiya   Shareholder-extortionist who extort money from companies by threatening to disrupt company's annual shareholders' meetings by revealing company's internal scandals.
See **underworld "businesses."**

Sony Corp.   A leading consumer electronics company known for its innovations and quality prdoucts.
See **electronics industry.**

spring (labor) offensive   This is the common and literal translation of the Japanese term *shunto*. It refers to the unique institutionalized process each spring in which Japanese **labor unions** bargain for annual wage increases. The first *shunto* was organized in 1956. Since then *shunto* has been launched every spring, and it has played an imporant part in Japan's labor movement and wage determination.

Spring is an appropriate time for wage bargaining because April 1 is the beginning of the fiscal year in Japan. April is also the time many companies recruit new workers, following the end of the school year in March, and set up entry-level wages and make adjustments in the wage scales. As early as late fall of the previous year, however, the unions' joint *shunto* coordinating committee would meet and begin to put out tentative demands in the media. Representing employers is the Japan Federation of Employers' Association, or Nikkeiren. It counterbalances unions' initial demand by publicizing the reasons for any wage restraint. It tends to stress the need for Japan to reduce consumer prices rather than to raise wages and insists that wage increases should be based on productivity increases. This type of public airing of positions by the two sides will intensify, invariably with the help of the media and occasionally with the participation of officials. Unions may draw up strike plans, although actual strikes have been relatively few.

By February individual enterprise unions will have put forward their own demands to their management, occasionally with some advice given at the industry or national level. The actual bargaining also takes place at the enterprise level. Historically settlements in a few strategic industries have served as the pattern setters. These were private railway workers (1958–59, 1965, 1968), iron and steel workers (1969–70), autoworkers and shipbuilders (1977), and metal industries' workers (1982–84). In recent years, because of their relative decline, these industries have been replaced by computers, consumer electronics, telecommunications, and transportation industries as the pace setters. The pattern of settlements reached in the private unionized sectors are closely followed by settlements in the public sector. Small nonunionized firms also try to follow the same pattern, with some variations because of the varied conditions of the small firms.

Before the oil crisis of the early 1970s, the rate of wage increases ranged between 9% and 16%. Since then Japanese unions' wage demands have been relatively modest and generally in line with the conditions of the economy. The pay increases unions accepted usually amounted to only 60–70% of their initial demands. For example, in its annual sample survey of 288 firms, the Ministry of Labor found that the unions demanded an average monthly wage increase of ¥15,157 but settled for ¥11,679 in 1980; in 1987, they demanded ¥12,861 but settled for ¥8,275. The average rate of actual wage increase for the sample firms was 6.74% in 1980, 5.03% in 1985, and 5.94% in 1990 (see table S.6). Unions' wage demands have been restrained by fear of inflation and increased Japanese investments in lower-wage countries which have eliminated jobs at home. Since the late 1980s unions have included reduced working hours as part of their *shunto* demands. The actual reduction attained in working hours, however, has been very modest as of 1991, partly because of the labor shortage (see **working hours and stress**).

Dore (1987: 70) attributes the continuing influence and viability of *shunto* to its "containment of the bargaining within a *predictable* procedure, and the heavy involvement of the media in the process." Japan's employers federation, however, has criticized unions' past *shunto* practice of concentrating on nominal wages. It regards Japan's nominal wages, already among

Table S.6
Shunto wage increases (in ¥ per month)

Year	Amount	Percentage
1956	1,063	6.3
1965	3,150	10.6
1975	15,279	13.1
1980	11,679	6.74
1985	10,871	5.03
1988	10,573	4.43
1989	12,747	5.17
1990	15,026	5.94
1991	14,911	5.65

Source: Ministry of Labor.
Note: Figures before 1980 are simple averages of 288 major firms surveyed (160 firms for 1956). After 1980 the figures are weighted by the number of union members.

the highest in the world, as excessive and has suggested multiyear wage bargaining coupled with greater wage differentials for different firms and industries on the basis of productivity. Japan's unions, on the other hand, emphasize the point that Japan's real wage levels and standards of living are still behind those of America and Europe and see *shunto* as the means to raise them. Analysts such as Takanashi et al. (1989) have concluded that multiyear wage bargaining is not likely in the foreseeable future and that *shunto* in its present form will remain intact as long as unions' right to bargain collectively is guaranteed by the law.

Government civil servants do not have the right to bargain over their pay. Employees of public corporations and national enterprises have the right to bargain collectively and participate in the spring offensive. Their pay increases, however, are set by the National Enterprise and Public Corporations Labor Relations Commission in a process of mediation and compulsory arbitration because the managements of public corporations and national enterprises have no powers to negotiate pay increases with unions.

See also **labor-management relations, labor unions, working hours and stress**.

References

Dore, Ronald. 1987. *Taking Japan Seriously*. Stanford: Stanford University Press. Pp. 70–73.

Japan's labor unions work to meet new challenges. *JEI Report*, no. 2A, Jan. 15, 1988.

Koike, Kazuo. 1985. *Understanding Industrial Relations in Modern Japan*, trans. by Mary Saso. London: Macmillan.

Shirai, Taishiro. 1987. Recent trends in collective bargaining in Japan. In *Collective Bargaining in Industrialized Market Economies: A Reappraisal*. Geneva: International Labor Office.

Takanashi, Arikra, et al. 1989. *Shunto Wage Offensive: Historical Overview and Prospects*. Tokyo: Japan Institute of Labor.

stable shareholders   Companies, banks, insurance companies, and so forth, that hold other companies' shares on a long-term basis to maintain business ties or to realize long-term capital gains.

See **corporate finance, cross shareholding, shareownership**.

Staple Food Control Act, 1942   An important legislation passed in 1942 that became the basis of **agricultural policy** in Japan. Aiming to combine self-sufficiency in rice with stable consumer prices, the law authorized the government to buy certain major crops, particularly rice, from the producers at certain prices and sell them to consumers at different prices for different purposes. Government purchase prices of rice paid to producers are to be determined, for the purpose of securing reproduction of rice, by taking into consideration the cost of production, prices, and other economic conditions. Consumer prices of rice are to be determined, for the purpose of stabilizing the consumer's budget, by taking into consideration the cost of living, prices, and other ecoomic conditions. The law also provides for government regulation on the distribution, exports and imports of major food crops.

See also **agricultural policy, rice production and distribution**.

References

Hayami, Yujiro. 1988. *Japanese Agriculture under Siege: The Political Economy of Agricultural Policies*. London: Macmillan.

Moore, Richard M. 1990. *Japanese Agriculture: Patterns of Rural Development*. Boulder, CO: Westview.

Sato, Hideo, and Gunther Schmitt. 1993. The political management of agriculture in Japan and Germany. In *The Politics of Economic Change in Postwar Japan and West Germany*, ed. by Haruhiro Fukui, Peter H. Merkl, Hubertus Müller-Groeling, and Akio Watanabe. New York: St. Martin's Press.

steel industry   The steel industry has been important to Japan's industrialization because steel is an essential industrial material for many other industries such as shipbuilding, automobiles, and machinery. It is also an industry where modern technology and large-scale production are extremely important to cost reduction. In the postwar period the Japanese government has played an important role in fostering the steel industry's growth.

In 1945 the industry had a capacity of only 2 million tons. In 1975 it had a capacity of 150 million tons. This unprecedented rapid rate of expansion was brought about by the government's nurturing and the industry's cooperation. The **Ministry of International Trade and Industry** (MITI), which is responsible for Japan's **industrial policy**, selected steel industry as a priority industry for support because of its intrinsic importance and export potential. In the 1950s it protected the industry from foreign competition but permitted the import of strategic technologies. It also helped to secure strategic supply of loans from **Japan Development Bank** and tax reductions for approved **investment**. Through its **administrative guidance**, it helped the industry to implement orderly expansion so that overcapacity and competitive price cutting would not result from unrestrained expansion and market competition. With the industry's cooperation, MITI throughout the 1960s and 1970s implemented a system of new capacity allocation by which the right to expand capacity was allocated on the basis of a firm's demonstrated efficiency. McCraw and O'Brien (1986: 94) consider this to be the key to the industry's modernization because this led to intense competition among the steel makers to raise productivity in order to earn the right to expand.

Between 1958 and 1991 MITI also actively attempted to influence the industry's output levels and to stabilize steel prices. Price stability is important because investment might otherwise be discouraged for fear of competitive price cutting and declining profits. During the 1958 recession MITI sought to stabilize steel prices by introducing the "list price system" (*kokai hanbai sei*, literally, "open sales system") in which the steelmaker would sell a product to a designated wholesaler at a "list price" that it had previously reported to MITI. The purpose was to ensure that the price met MITI guidelines for price stability. Although the system has been revised subsequently, it was not officially abolished until 1991. Yamawaki (1988: 295–98) considers the system to be ineffective because of competitive price discounting during recessions. Other industry observers contend, however, that during the 1958–91 period, MITI was generally able to influence production and capacity levels of the industry and thus to maintain price stability.

Such blending of government guidance and competition paid off in growth and efficiency. By the mid-1970s Japanese steel companies had become the world's most modern and lowest-cost producers. Crude steel production peaked at 119.3 million metric tons in 1973, while exports of steel products peaked at 37 million tons in 1976 (see table S.7).

Between 1973 and 1990 Japan's annual production of crude steel fluctuated between 100 and 110 million tons, depending on the level of domestic demand. The steep yen appreciation after 1985 reduced production considerably not only because of reduced export but also because of reduced domestic demand from other export industries. Unprecedented layoff of workers occurred in the industry. It also prompted the industry to seek diversification. By the end of 1990, however, domestic demand recovered and so had steel production. Steel production reached 110.3 million tons in 1990 and 109.7 million tons in 1991.

Annual exports of all steel products was over 30 million tons in most of the years between 1974 and 1986. The major export markets have been the United States, China, Taiwan, and South Korea. Since 1987, however, exports have been declining steadily, in part because of new competition

Table S.7
Steel production, exports, and imports (in million metric tons)

Year	Production	Exports	Imports
1960	22.1	2.5	1.2
1965	41.2	9.9	2.7
1970	93.3	18.0	3.2
1973	119.3	25.6	1.9
1976	107.4	37.0	0.9
1980	111.4	30.3	2.4
1985	105.3	33.3	4.5
1988	105.7	23.7	11.1
1989	107.9	20.2	10.9
1990	110.3	17.0	11.7
1991	109.7	18.0	13.8

Source: Japan Iron and Steel Federation.
Note: Figures refer to the production of crude steel and the exports and imports of all steel products.

from South Korea and the yen appreciation. Also the United States has negotiated a voluntary restraint agreement with Japan, which limited Japan's export to the United States to a certain percentage share of the U.S. market. Initially for the period from October 1984 to September 1989, the agreement was extended to March 1992. In January 1993 the U.S. Commerce Department imposed new tariffs on most steel imports from Japan for alleged dumping. The Commerce Department's action was partially upheld when the U.S. International Trade Commission ruled in July 1993 that Japanese exports of corrosion-resistant steel sheet to the United States damaged the U.S. steel industry. Consequently the Commerce Department imposed punitive tariffs of 40.19% on such imports from Japan.

Imports of iron and steel into Japan have increased rapidly since the mid-1980s, from 4.5 million metric tons in 1985 to 13.8 million tons in 1991. South Korea is the major source of imports, followed by Brazil, the former Soviet Union, and China.

In making steel, the industry depends completely on imports for iron ore and coking coal. In 1991 Japan imported 127.2 million tons of iron ore. The major sources of imports are Australia, Brazil, and India. In the same year 64.8 million tons of coking coal were imported, which amounted to 99% of the total consumed. The major sources of imports are Australia, Canada, and the United States.

Table S.8
Leading steel companies (FY 1991; in ¥ billions)

Company	Sales	Pretax Profits
Nippon Steel	2,629.4	100.2
NKK	1,314.8	37.5
Kawasaki Steel	1,208.1	43.1
Sumitomo Metal	1,157.0	40.5
Kobe Steel	1,301.2	47.7

Source: *The Nikkei Weekly*, June 6, 1992: 11.

The industry is dominatd by the "Big Five"—Nippon Steel, NKK (Nippon Kaikan), Kawasaki Steel, Sumitomo Metal Industries, and Kobe Steel. Nippon Steel, the largest steelmaker in Japan and in the world, has about 30% of the domestic market. It is also considered to be the price leader of the industry. It was formed through a merger of two leading steelmakers in 1970. NKK, the second largest, is among the top five steelmakers in the world. Table S.8 gives the sales and pretax profits of the top five steel producers in FY 1991. Although sales of these companies remained at about the same level in fiscal 1991 as in the previous year, profits of all five companies were down substantially from the previous year's levels because of the economy's recession.

Since the mid-1980s the steel industry has faced changes in world and domestic market conditions, and consequently structural changes in the industry have taken place. First, because of rising material and labor costs and competition from the newly industrializing countries, particularly South Korea, all major Japanese steel companies have diversified into new business lines such as machinery, engineering, electronics, communications, and new basic materials. In addition they have established tie-ups with U.S. companies in joint ventures in the United States such as coated sheet steel production for automobiles. This should enable Japanese steel companies to increase production in the United States in the wake of the punitive tariffs imposed in 1993 on exports of corrosion-resistant steel to the United States. Finally, "minimills" have become more important in the industry. These are small steelmakers that use electric furnaces to process scrap or specially processed iron at lower labor cost than large integrated steel mills, which use blast furnace and coke to process iron ore. The latter are being forced to restructure their operations and adopt new technology in order to cut cost.

See also **industrial policy, pricing practices**.

Addresses

Kobe Steel
3-18, Wakinohama-cho, 1-chome, Chuo-ku, Kobe 651
Tel: (078) 261-5111   Fax: (03) 5252-7961

Japan Iron and Steel Federation
9-4, Otemachi 1-chome, Chiyoda-ku, Tokyo 100
Tel: (03) 3279-3611   Fax: (03) 3245-0144

Kawasaki Steel
2-3, Uchi-Saiwaicho 2-chome, Chiyoda-ku, Tokyo 100
Tel: (03) 3597-3111   Fax: (03) 3597-3160

Nippon Steel
6-3, Otemachi 2-chome, Chiyoda-ku, Tokyo 100
Tel: (03) 3242-4111   Fax: (03) 3275-5611

NKK
1-2, Marunouchi 1-chome, Chiyoda-ku, Tokyo 100
Tel: (03) 3212-7111   Fax: (03) 3214-8428

Sumitomo Metal Industries
5-33, Kaitahama 4-chome, Chuo-ku, Osaka 541
Tel: (06) 220-5111   Fax: (06) 223-0563

References

Japan Iron and Steel Federation. 1992. *The Steel Industry of Japan, 1992*. Tokyo.

Klamann, Edmund. 1991. MITI steel cartel fades, yet stable order intact. *Nikkei Weekly*, Aug. 3: 10.

Komatsu, Naoki. 1989. Japan's steel industry is restructuring its way back to profitability. *Tokyo Business Today*, Nov. 1989: 40–45.

McCraw, Thomas K., and Patricia A. O'Brien. 1986. Production and distribution: Competition policy and industry. In American versus Japan, ed. by Thomas K. McCraw. Boston: Harvard Business School Press.

Milbank, Dana. 1993. Japan's big steelmakers feel pinch of minimills, promping a rethinking of the traditional approach. *Asian Wall Street Journal Weekly*, Feb. 8: 24.

Vogel, Ezra F. 1985. *Comeback*. Tokyo: Charles Tuttle. Ch. 2.

Yamawaki, Hideki. 1988. The steel industry. In *Industrial Policy of Japan*, ed. by Ryutaro Komiya, Masahiro Okuno, and Kotaro Suzumura. Tokyo: Academic Press Japan.

stock index futures trading   Introduced in September 1988, stock index futures trading is a form of contract tradindg in which the buyer and seller agree on the delivery of the money based on the difference between a certain numerical value of a stock index contracted between them in advance and that of the acutal stock index on a certain future date.

The two primary stock index futures markets are the **Tokyo Stock Exchange** and the Osaka Securities Exchange. The former trades futures contracts based on the TOPIX index, whereas the latter trades contracts based on the Nikkei Stock Index of 225 stocks. The trading unit of the Tokyo Stock Exchange is ¥10,000 times the TOPIX index, whereas in the Osaka Stock Exchange it is ¥1,000 times the Nikkei index. The method of settlement takes the form of cash payment. Since 1989 the Nikkei futures index has had a larger trading volume in terms of the number of contracts than the TOPIX futures index. The daily average trading volume of the TOPIX index futures was 15,000 and 12,600 contracts in 1989 and 1990, whereas that of the Nikkei index futures was 23,000 and 51,000 contracts in the same years. The daily average trading volume of the TOPIX index futures declined to 6,800 contracts in 1991 and 5,500 contracts in 1992.

The **Ministry of Finance** regulates the stock futures market. In its attempt to avoid the possible amplification of stock price fluctuations due to futures trading, the Ministry limits the rise or fall of the futures contract to 900 points in a day. After that trading must halt, as it did on two occasions in late 1990.

See also **stock index options market, stock market, stock price indexes, Tokyo Stock Exchange**.

References

Apontne, Wayne L. 1991. Future trading thrives. *Japan Times* (weekly international ed.), Nov. 25: 19.

Arai, Tomio, T. Akamatsu and A. Yoshioka. 1993. Stock index futures in Japan: problems and prospects. *NRI Quarterly* 2, 1: 28–57.

Brenner, Menachem, Marti Subrahmanyam, and Jun Uno. 1990. The Japanese stock index futures markets: The early experience. In *Japanese Capital Market*, ed. by Edwin J. Elton and Martin J. Gruber. New York: Harper and Row.

Isaacs, Jonathan. 1990. *Japanese Equities Markets*. London: Euromoney Publications. Ch. 12.

Japan Securities Research Institute. 1992. *Securities Market in Japan*, 1992. Pp. 118–22.

stock index options trading   Stock index options trading is a form of trading in which the buyer pays a certain amount of money to obtain the right or option, not the obligation, to buy a certain amount of stocks on a specific date at a specific price. The trading unit is based on the stock price indexes, such as ¥1,000 times the Nikkei Stock Average for the Nikkei Stock Average options traded at the Osaka Stock Exchange or ¥10,000 times the TOPIX points traded at the **Tokyo Stock Exchange**. If the right is not exercised after a specified time, the option expires. If the option is exercised, either **stock index futures trading** takes effect or cash settlement is made on the basis of the predetermined stock price.

The stock index options trading started in 1989 at the stock exchanges in Tokyo, Osaka, and Nagoya. The options offer investors not only a new investment instrument but also a hedge against the risk of an unfavorable stock price change. Thus they contribute to the stability and expansion of the **stock market** and the stock futures market. One problem, however, is that the minimum trading unit is relatively high, higher than that in the United States, so it is difficult for individual investors to participate in the trading. The trading volume has been modest. The daily average at the Tokyo Stock Exchange declined from 98,073 contracts in 1989 to 197 contracts in 1992.

See also **stock index futures trading, stock market, stock price indexes, Tokyo Stock Exchange**.

References

Isaacs, Jonathan. 1990. *Japanese Equities Markets*. London: Euromoney Publications. Ch. 12.

Koshinaka, Hidefumi. 1989. Investors eager for stock index options debut. *Japan Economic Journal*, June 3.

Japan Securities Research Institute. 1992. *Securities Market in Japan, 1992*. Pp. 122–26.

Tokyo Stock Exchange. 1993. *Tokyo Stock Exchange Fact Book, 1993*.

stock market   A stock market consists of a primary market for new issues and a secondary market for stock trading. The latter in turn consists of trading on the stock exchanges and over-the-counter trading in the offices of **securities companies**. All these components of the market have evolved in Japan with various degrees of maturity.

In the primary market corporate funds are raised through the issuing of new shares or equities of the company. The issues are classified into compensated capital increases and noncompensated capital increases. The former requires subscribers to pay cash for the new shares. In the latter the company issues new shares in an amount equivalent to the legal reserves of its capital or the amount of cash payment that was in excess of its par value during its previous capital increase. In terms of the ownership of the new shares, they can be allocated to current stockholders or sold to general investors in a public offering. In the latter case the company can sell the shares by itself, or through underwriting by a securities company. The price to be paid can be based on the par value of the new shares, the market value, or a level between the two as set by the issuer. Currently the predominant method of issuing new shares is the compensated method in which new shares are sold to the public at market prices. This method is popular because the difference between the market price and the par value may be used as capital reserve to strengthen the capital base of the company.

Secondary stock transactions are divided into trading on the stock exanges and over-the-counter trading in the offices of securities companies. There are eight stock exchanges in Japan—Tokyo, Osaka, Nagoya, Kyoto, Hiroshima, Fukuoka, Niigata, and Sapporo—and the **Tokyo Stock Exchange** is by far the largest of them. Stock exchange trading is limited to members who are securities companies with certain qualifications and to listed stocks that have met certain standards. All securities companies and stock exchanges are given **administrative guidance** by the **Ministry of Finance**, and the Securities Dealers' Association of Japan provides voluntary industry self-regulation. However, Japan does not have an independent regulatory agency comparable to the United States Securities and Exchange Commission to oversee its securities companies and transactions on the stock exchanges. A new Securities and Exchange Surveillance Commission was set up in July 1992 to watch for stock market manipulation. Its independence remains to be seen because its members come mostly from the Ministry of Finance.

The stock market was only a minor source of funds for companies in the high-growth era of the 1950s and 1960s. Bank loans at low interest rates were much more important. After the first oil crisis of 1973, as growth slowed down and interest rates were raised to control inflation, equity financing became cheaper than bank loans and the stock market became increasingly important. Stock exchange trading in Japan grew rapidly between 1985 and late 1989. One major reason is Japan's huge current account surplus which provided financial institutions and corporations with a large amount of capital for financial investment. Other contributing factors are the stronger yen since the Plaza Accord of September 1985, which increased the foreign-exchange risk in investing in overseas securities, and the falling oil prices and declining interest rates in Japan. Finally, some analysts have regarded Japan's stock market as highly speculative, at least during the late 1980s, and open to manipulation by brokers because of lax disclosure requirements (Zielinski and Holloway 1991).

The average price earnings ratio (PER, the price of a share divided by the after-tax earnings per share) of Japanese shares is much higher than in other industrialized economies. For example, in the first section of the Tokyo

Stock Exchange, the average year-end PER was 47.3 in 1986, 58.4 in 1988, 70.6 in 1989, 39.8 in 1990, and 36.7 in 1992. Stockholders are often the company's own banks, insurers, suppliers, and customers. Foreign analysts have regarded such **cross shareholding** as a major cause of the high PER. However, Ueda (1990) attributes the high PER to the declines in risk premium investors require on stocks and to expectations of land price inflation. Zielinski and Holloway (1991: 137) point out that Japanese earnings figures are understated relative to U.S. companies because Japan's accounting rules allow companies to manipulate their earnings by putting profits into reserves, through sales to subsidiaries, and by treating extraordinary gains as recurring income. However, the PER of companies is not as important in Japan as in many other countries. Investors also look at the value of corporate assets, particularly land.

After years of rapid rises in share prices—with a peak of 2,884.8 in TOPIX (Tokyo Stock Price Index) on December 18, 1989, or 38,915.87 in Nikkei Stock Average Index on December 29, 1989—the Tokyo Stock Exchange started to experience a serious decline in early 1990. This was in part a belated correction of the excessively high share prices of the previous years. Tighter credit due largely to the higher official discount rate of the **Bank of Japan** since May 1989 also contributed to the fall in share prices. In addition banks reduced their lending in an effort to meet the 8% capital adequacy ratio which the Bank for International Settlements required by spring 1993. The decline continued through 1990 because of the Iraqi invasion of Kuwait. The total decline in 1990 amounted to an unprecedented 39% in Nikkei Index. Thus the "bubble economy" of the late 1980s—the speculative and inflated wealth in financial assets and land as epitomized by the stock market—is said to have burst in 1990.

To ease the pressure on individual investors to sell stocks bought on credit as stock prices continued to fall, the Ministry of Finance reduced, in February 1990, the purchase margin requirement (the percentage of cash required) from 60% to 50% of a stock's value. By late 1990 it was reduced to 30%. This is the easiest margin term in 25 years.

Changing the margin requirement is only one of the tools that the Ministry of Finance has to influence the stock market. Other tools include its influence on the securities companies to support the market. This has led Schaede (1991) to conclude that Japan's stock market is potentially more stable than that in other countries. On the other hand, insider-trading standards are vague in Japan, and their implementation less rigorous. Until its amendment in 1988 the Securities and Exchange Law of Japan did not even contain provisions that specifically made it unlawful to engage in insider trading (Kanzaki 1992: 20). The first prosecution of insider trading was filed only in 1990, although such practice is believed to be prevalent. Thus Japan's stock market is potentially more open to abuses.

Japan's stock prices remain depressed in 1991–92. It was revealed in mid-1991 that large securities companies had compensated major clients for trading losses at the expense of small investors and that affiliates of two such companies were involved in the speculative stock purchases of an organized crime sydicate. These scandals confirmed the long-standing criticisms of many observers and shook investors' confidence in the stock market. Analysts believe that its recovery and future growth will require a thorough reform of the entire industry, including its relationship with the Ministry of Finance.

Aside from the stock exchanges, shares of some medium-sized companies are traded in the **over-the-counter market**.

See also **bond market, corporate finance, cross shareholding, over-the-counter market, securities companies, shareownership, stock price indexes, Tokyo Stock Exchange**.

Addresses

Securities Dealers Association of Japan
5-8 Nihonbashi Kayabacho 1-chome, Chuo-ku, Tokyo 103
Tel: (03) 3667-8451   Fax: 3666-8009

Osaka Securities Exchange
8-16, Kitahama 1-chome, Chuo-ku, Osaka, Osaka 541
Tel: (06) 226-0058   Fax: (06) 231-2639

Tokyo Stock Exchange
1, Nihonbashi Kabuto-cho 2-chome, Chuo-ku, Tokyo 103
Tel: (03) 3666-0141   Fax: (03) 3639-5016

References

Elton, Edwin J., and Martin J. Gruber, ed. 1990. *Japanese Capital Markets*. New York: Harper and Row.

Isaacs, Jonathan. 1990. *Japanese Equities Markets*. London: Euromoney Publications.

Japan Securities Research Institute. 1992. *Securities Market in Japan, 1992*. Ch. 7.

Kanzaki, Katsuro. 1992. Regulation of insider trading. In *Capital Markets and Financial Services in Japan*. Tokyo: Japan Securites Research Institute.

McDonald, Jack. 1989. The *mochiai* effect: Japanese corporate cross-holdings. *Journal of Portfolio Management* 16, 1: 90–94.

Sakakibara, Shigeki, et al. 1988. *The Japanese Stock Market: Pricing Systems and Accounting Information*. New York: Praeger.

Schaede, Ulrike. 1991. Black Monday in New York, blue Tuesday in Tokyo: The October 1987 crash in Japan. *California Management Review*, 33: 39–57.

Ueda, Kazuo. 1990. Are Japanese stock prices too high? *Journal of the Japanese and International Economies* 4: 351–70.

Viner, Aron. 1989. Inside Japan's Financial Markets. London: The Economist Pulibcations. Ch. 4.

Yamashita, Takeji. 1989. *Japan's Securities Markets: A Practioners' Guide*. Singapore: Butterworths. Chs. 2–5.

Zielinski, Robert and Nigel Hoolway. 1991. *Unequal Equities: Power and Risk in Japan's Stock Market*. Tokyo: Kodansha International.

Ziemba, William T., and Sandra I. Schwartz. 1992. *Invest Japan*. Chicago: Probus. Chs. 1, 7, 8.

stock price indexes   There are two major price indexes of stock prices of the **Tokyo Stock Exchange**: the Nikkei Stock Average and TOPIX, the Tokyo Stock Price Index.

First introduced in 1950, the Nikkei Stock Average, or the Nikkei index, is calculated by Nihon Keizai Shimbun, Inc., publisher of Japan's leading business newspaper. It gives the daily unweighted average of 225 issues selected from some 1,200 stocks listed on the first section of the Tokyo Stock Exchange. When one of the 225 issues included in the calculations suffers an exrights drop from capital increase, an adjustment is made in a coefficient so that continuity between past and present stock price levels can be maintained. However, the index can be misleading and open to manipulation. Trading blocks of shares in just a few small firms in the Nikkei sample can affect the index disproportionately. In addition, because the index was introduced in 1950, it is biased toward the heavy industry.

The 225 stocks included in the Nikkei index were reviewed and revised in early 1992. Nihon Keizai Shimbun plans to revise the content of the 225 stocks every year in the future (communication to the author, Nihon Keizai Shimbun, July 30, 1992).

The TOPIX, introduced in 1969, is a composite index of all stocks listed on the first section of the Tokyo Stock Exchange. It gives the weighted average of all stocks, the weight being the number of listed shares of each stock. It is computed by dividing the current day's total market value by the base day's (January 4, 1968) total market value and multiplying the ratio by 100. To maintain the continuity of the indexes, the base market value is recalculated when there are new listings, delistings, and new share issues. In this way only price movements are reflected by the indexes. TOPIX is computed and published every other minute.

TOPIX is supplemented by subindexes for each of 28 industry groups and for each of three groups (large, medium, and small in terms of the number of listed shares) by which companies listed on the first section are classified. These subindexes are calculated in the same way and published six times a day.

A new Nikkei stock price index, used mainly by professionals, has been introduced. The broader Nikkei Stock Average (500) or Nikkei 500 was introduced in 1982. It includes 500 stocks from the first section of the Tokyo Stock Exchange and hence gives a broader picture of the market.

See also **Tokyo Stock Exchange**.

References

Elton, Edwin J., and Martin J. Gruber, eds. 1990. *Japanese Capital Markets*. New York: Harper and Row.

Isaacs, Jonathan. 1990. *Japanese Equities Market*. London: Euromoney Publications. Ch. 3.

Japan Securities Research Institute. 1992. *Securities Market in Japan*, 1992. Ch 3.

Takeuchi, Satoshi. 1990. Accuracy of Nikkei average in tracking market questioned. *Japan Economic Journal*, Jan. 20: 32.

Tokyo Stock Exchange. 1993. *Tokyo Stock Exchange Fact Book, 1993*.

Ziemba, William T., and Sandra L. Schwartz. 1992. *Invest Japan*. Chicago: Probus. Ch. 2.

Structural Impediments Initiative (SII)   Negotiations between Washington and Tokyo in 1989–90 on ways to remove Japanese barriers to free trade in order to improve American access to the Japanese market and to reduce the trade imbalance between the two countries.

The impediments to free trade in Japan are perceived by Washington to be embedded in the structure of the Japanese economy. The initiative was made by the Bush administration to ask Tokyo to remove the impediments to head off protectionist legislation being contemplated by Congress. The initiative was proposed in mid-1989, and SII talks with Japanese trade officials were conducted from June 1989 through spring 1990. A joint final report was issued in June 1990, with recommendations for both governments. It also provides for follow-up meetings to review the progress made in implementing the recommendations.

The six categories of Japanese structural impediments criticized by American negotiators are as follows:

1. *Japanese **saving** and **investment** patterns*. Excessive savings limit consumption and imports. Public investment is too low relative to savings.

2. *Land use pattern*. Inefficient land use and high land prices restrict the supply of **housing** and land for buildings in metropolitan areas.

3. ***Distribution system***. The **Large Retail Store Law** restricts the establishment of large stores in favor of existing small retailers who are less likely to carry imports. The existing complicated distribution system discourages foreign firms to sell in Japan.

4. *Exclusionary business practices*. Practices such as price **cartels**, supply restraint cartels, market allocations, and bid-rigging violate the **Antimonopoly Law** and restrict fair and free competition and imports. Government delays in patent examinations hurt foreign firms.

5. ***Keiretsu** relationships*. Certain aspects of *keiretsu* relationships, including **cross shareholding** and exclusive supplier-manufacturer-distributor relationships, promote preferential intragroup business, inhibit **foreign direct investment** in Japan, and give rise to anticompetitive business practices.

6. *Price mechanisms*. Price differentials between domestic and overseas markets are large and unreasonable due to government regulation of the domestic market and weak enforcement of the Antimonopoly Law.

These six areas do not exhaust all issues of trade disputes between the two countries. For example, the issue of Japan's ban on rice import is not included because it was turned over to the **Uruguay Round** of GATT negotiations.

The following structural impediments in the United States were brought up in the SII talks and in the final report. However, since they are not the real focus of SII, observers consider them to be a mere "face-saving" device for Japanese officials to agree to reductions in Japan's own structural impediments.

1. Excessive government deficits and deficient saving rates.

2. Low corporate investment activities and supply capacity.

3. Shortsighted corporate behavior that is not conducive to the productivity of U.S. workers and the competitiveness of U.S. corporations.

4. Government regulations on both exports and imports that discourage international trade and competition.

5. Insufficient research and development.

6. Ineffective export promotion.

7. Inadequate work force education and training.

Both governments pledge to carry out a number of recommendations to reduce their respective structural impediments. For example, the Japanese government has agreed, in principle, to adopt measures to achieve the following: to increase public investment, especially in social overhead capital; to rationalize land prices and to promote further supply of housing and land for buildings in metropolitan areas; to relax the implementation of the Large Retail Store Law; to accelerate measures to facilitate imports; to enhance the Antimonopoly Law and its enforcement; to ensure greater transparency and fairness in **administrative guidance**; to strengthen monitoring by the Fair Trade Commission of transactions among *keiretsu* firms; to speed up patent examinations; to conduct joint price surveys with the U.S. government to promote a competitive market, and so on.

The SII talks and the final accord have elicited varied responses in both Japan and the United States. First, Japanese **consumer groups** have not particularly welcomed the proposed liberalization of Japan's market, even though it would benefit consumers in the form of lower prices. Many government officials and scholars have criticized the U.S. demands on Japan. They have two major arguments: (1) Many of the structural issues such as *keiretsu* and pricing mechanisms cannot be controlled or managed by the Japanese government. (2) Japan–U.S. trade imbalance is primarily the result of macroeconomic policy such as large U.S. government deficit and low savings, and not of Japan's structural factors. Changing the latter therefore would not necessarily help the trade imbalance (Komiya and Irie 1990).

Keiretsu or business groups are clearly the worst of Japan's structural impediments in Washington's view. In response, Imai (1990a, b) has reiterated that Japan's *keiretsu* are rational, evolving organizations that have engaged in market competition and that there is no clear evidence that they impede entry into business or discriminate against foreign firms in their transactions. Nakatani (1990) contends that the *keiretsu* system has been effective and resilient as the pillar of Japanese-style capitalism, but he agrees that it has been exclusionary and is therefore not accepted by the international community. He suggests that the government offer *keiretsu* groups incentives to welcome foreign companies to join them so that the international community will accept them without attempting to weaken them.

In the United States, MIT economist Dornbusch (1989) criticizes U.S. efforts to open Japan's market via SII as misguided. He distinguishes two issues—U.S. external imbalance and market access in Japan—and argues that the U.S. external imbalance requires macroeconomic adjustment at home, while access to Japan's market is best attained through a result-oriented **trade policy**. This trade policy would set multiyear targets for import growth, with an automatic, across-the-board tariff surcharge if performance is inadequate. Feldstein, a former chairman of the President's Council of Economic Advisers, criticizes the U.S. efforts to push up Japanese public works in order to reduce trade imbalance as ill-advised. He argues that Japan should neither raise nor lower its domestic infrastructural investment artificially in order to manipulate its trade surplus and that any country's decision on such investment should be based on the value of such investment to its people and not on its impact on the current account balance (interview in *Japan Economic Journal*, Aug. 11. 1990).

Johnson (1990) contends that the structural impediments have been indeed unique and important aspects of Japan in its rise as a state-fostered mercantile power, not a market-oriented free trader, but he doubts that the SII accord will be implemented at all becuase the opposition parties in Japan control the Upper House of the Diet and can block implementing legislation. He argues that postwar Japan has a history of agreeing to U.S. demands when the political pressure is great but failing to deliver its promises afterward.

Tyson (1991) argues that unfair trading practices and structural impediments to Japan's market do exist in Japan, but these are not the only cause of Japan's trade surplus. She suggests managed trade through negotiations at detailed sectoral level as the short-term answer and harmonization of policy practices and rules, while recognizing some differences in policy practices as the long-term solution.

See also *keiretsu* **and business groups, cross shareholding, distribution system, patent system**.

References

Dornbusch, Rudiger. Misguided efforts won't open Japan's market. *Japan Economic Journal*, Dec. 16, 1989: 9.

Imai, Ken'ichi. 1990a. The ligitimacy of Japan's corporate groups. *Japan Echo* 17, 3: 23–28.

Imai, Ken'ichi. 1990b. Japanese business groups and the structural impediments Initiative. In *Japan's Economic Structure: Should It Change?* ed. by Kozo Yamamura. Seattle: Society for Japanese Studies.

Johnson, Chalmers. 1990. Trade, revisionism, and the future of Japanese–American relations. In *Japan's Economic Structure: Should It Change?* ed. by Kozo Yamamura. Seattle: Society for Japanese Studies.

Komiya, Ryutaro, and Kazutomo Irie. 1990. The U.S.–Japan trade problem: An economic analysis from a Japanese viewpoint. In *Japan's Economic Structure: Should It Change?* ed. by Kozo Yamamura. Seattle: Society for Japanese Studies.

Nakatani, Iwao. 1990. Opening up fortress Japan. *Japan Echo* 17, 3: 8–11.

Sheard, Paul. 1991. The economics of Japanese corporate organization and the "Structural Impediments" debate: A critical reveiw. *Japanese Economic Studies* 19, 4: 30–78.

Tyson, Laura D'Andrea. 1991. Managing trade by rules and outcomes. *California Management Review* 34, 1: 115–143.

Utagawa, Reizo. 1991. The U.S. structural impediments initiative (SII): Implications for Japan. In *Japan and the United States: Troubled Partners in a Changing World*. Cambridge, MA: Institute for Foreign Policy Analysis.

Yamamura, Kozo. 1990. Will Japan's economic structure change? Confessions of a former optimist. In *Japan's Economic Structure: Should It Change?* ed. by Kozo Yamamura. Seattle: Society for Japanese Studies.

subcontracting system   Subcontracting is widespread and very important in Japanese manufacturing industries. The subcontractees are typically large manufactureres. The subcontractors are typically small- or medium-sized enterprises; a large majority of them have fewer than 20 employees. They produce parts or undertake a particular processing for a number of "parent" companies. By contrast, large U.S. manufacturing companies tend to make more "in-house" parts themselves.

The **automobile industry** in particular is highly dependent on subcontractors. From the car makers to their subsidiaries and independent parts makers, each has its own subcontractors, with the result that there is a hierarchy of primary, secondary, and tertiary subcontractors. The relationship between subcontractee and subcontractor is close and cooperative. They often share facilities and technical know-know. Japanese automakers are said to purchase about 70% of their parts from subcontractors, whereas the "buy ratio" for American automakers is said to be about 30%.

Because of the disparity in economic power between the large corporations and their subcontractors, abuses by the former such as late payments have occurred. To minimize them, the Subcontractors' Protection Law was enacted in 1956. It prohibits unfair practices such as late payment (over 60 days) for subcontracted work, refusal to accept subcontracted products, and compulsory purchase of materials from subcontractees. The Fair Trade Commission and the Small and Medium Enterprise Agency of the **Ministry of International Trade and Industry** (MITI) are empowered to implement the law.

From the perspective of large corporations, subcontracting offers them various advantages: (1) Since the small- and medium-sized enterprises have lower wages, it is economical to have simple labor-intensive parts produced by them. (2) It frees the large companies from numerous peripheral tasks and permits them to concentrate on the major production processes and the final assembly, thereby reaping the benefit of greater division of labor. (3) Japanese subcontractors are reputed to be reliable and produce high-quality parts. (4) In times of recession large corporations can cut back on their subcontracted work. This gives them flexibility in production while retaining their permanent employees. In other words, the subcontractors serve as buffers during recession for the large corporations.

From the point of view of subcontractors, the system enables them to concentrate on their specialized lines of business while enjoying stable business relations with large corporations during normal times. However, in a business downturn, they are likely to have reduced orders and have to bear the brunt of business adjustment. Consequently, in order to protect themselves, subcontractors have begun to diversify and to have a number of subcontractees. Traditionally it was not rare for small parts makers to rely on a single customer for 80–90% of their sales. By the late 1980s it was felt that a single customer's share should not exceedd 30%. Furthermore, since 1982–83 when the economy experienced slower growth, a growing number of them have grouped together to form cooperatives for mutual help. In a cooperative, members can acquire orders for other member companies as well as for themselves. If an order is too large for a subcontractor, it can be shared by other members. Some cooperatives also help members to branch out into new business lines.

According to surveys conducted by MITI, the number of small manufacturing subconstractors declined from 465,369 at the end of 1981 to 378,046 at the end of 1987 (*Nikkei Weekly*, Apr. 4, 1992: 1). The chronic labor shortage and the soaring cost of starting up manufacturing units are said to be the reasons for the decline. If the trend continues, large corporations have to either rely more on overseas suppliers or increase in-house production of parts, as some companies have already started doing.

As the government agency in charge of assisting **small and medium enterprises**, the Small and Medium Enterprise Agency of MITI has been providing assistance to qualified subcontractors in setting up new businesses or acquiring new skills.

See also **customer sovereignty, small and medium enterprises**.

Address

Small and Medium Enterprise Agency
3-1, Kasumigaseki 1-chome, Chiyoda-ku, Tokyo 100
Tel: (03) 3501-1511

References

Asanuma, Banri, and Tatsuya Kikutani. 1992. Risk absorption in Japanese subcontracting: A microeconometric study of the automobile industry. *Journal of the Japanese and International Economics* 6, 1: 1–29.

Klaman, Edmund. 1991. Lowly subcontractors begin to assert technological might. *Japan Economic Journal*, Mar. 30: 1.

McMillan, John. 1990. Managing suppliers: Incentive systems in Japanese and U.S. industry. *California Management Review* 32, 4: 38–55.

Oishi, Nobuyuki. 1992. Subcontractor attrition eroding economic base. *Nikkei Weekly*, Apr. 4: 1, 23.

Patchell, Gerald. 1992. Shinchintaisha: Japanese small business revitalization. *Business and the Contemporary World* 4, 2: 50–61.

Sakai, Kuniyasu. 1990. The feudal world of Japanese manufacturing. *Harvard Business Review* 68, 6: 38–49.

Subcontractors join up to win order. *Japan Economic Journal*, Jan. 30, 1988: 5.

Uekusa, Masu. 1987. Industrial organization. In *The Political Economy of Japan*, vol. 1: *The Domestic Transformation*, ed. by Kozo Yamamura and Yasukichi Yasuba. Stanford: Stanford University Press. Pp. 499–506.

Sumitomo Bank   One of Japan's largest city banks and a core member of the Sumitomo Group.
　　See **city banks, Sumitomo Group**.

Sumitomo Corp.   A leading general trading company and a core member of the **Sumitomo Group**.
　　See **trading companies, Sumitomo Group**.

Sumitomo Group   Along with the **Mitsubishi Group** and the **Mitsui Group**, the **Sumitomo Group** has a prewar *zaibatsu* origin. Smaller than the other two, the Sumitomo Group is considered to be more tightly organized than the Mitsui Group. It consists of more than 130 companies, with 20 core companies whose presidents meet regularly in the White Water Club (Hakusui Kai). The three most important companies are traditionally Sumitomo Bank, Sumitomo Metal Industries, and Sumitomo Chemical Co. Since the 1970s, Sumitomo Corp., NEC Corp., and Sumitomo Electric have also gained prominence.

　　The origin of the group goes back to the early seventeenth century when the Sumitomo family went into retail business and copper refining. During the Meiji period many more companies were founded, but copper, heavy industry, and chemicals were its strong fields. Before the Second

World War, 239 companies belonged to the Sumitomo *zaibatsu*. An Osaka-based holding company controlled the group.

Although the *zaibatsu* was dissolved after the war, the group reemerged without a holding company and the Sumitomo family ties. Member companies are active in the following fields:

Banking: Sumitomo Bank, Sumitomo Trust & Banking

Cement: Sumitomo Cement

Chemicals: Sumitomo Chemical, Sumitomo Bakelite

Construction: Sumitomo Construction

Electrical/Electronics: Sumitomo Electric Industries, NEC Corp.

Food and Beverages: Asahi Breweries

Glass: Nippon Sheet Glass

Insurance: Sumitomo Life Insurance, Sumitomo Marine & Fire Insurance

Machinery: Sumitomo Heavy Industries

Metals: Sumitomo Metal Industries, Nippon Stainless Steel, Sumitomo Light Metal Industries

Mining: Sumitomo Coal Mining, Sumitomo Metal Mining

Real Estate: Sumitomo Realty & Development

Rubber: Sumitomo Rubber Industries

Trading: Sumitomo Corp.

See also **keiretsu and business groups, Mitsubishi Group, Mitsui Group**.

Addresses

Sumitomo Bank
4-6-5, Kitahama, Chuo-ku, Osaka 541
Tel: (06) 227-2111   Fax: (03) 3282-8480

Sumitomo Chemical Co.
4-5-33, Kitahoma, Chuo-ku, Osaka 541
Tel: (06) 220-3891   Fax: (06) 220-3347

Sumitomo Corp.
5-15, Kitahama, Chuo-ku, Osaka 541
Tel: (03) 3217-6997

Sumitomo Metal Industries
5-33, Kitahama 4-chome, Chuo-ku, Osaka 541
Tel: (06) 220-5111   Fax: (06) 223-0563

References

Eli, Max. 1990. *Japan Inc.: Global Strategies of Japanese Trading Corporations*. New York: McGraw-Hill. Ch. 2.

Gerlach, Michael L. 1992. *Alliance Capitalism*. Berkeley: University of California Press. Chs. 3–4.

Ito, Takatoshi. 1992. *The Japanese Economy*. Cambridge: MIT Press. Ch. 7.

Sumitomo Corporation. *The Sumitomo Group*. (No date).

Odagiri, Hiroyuki. 1992. *Growth through Competition, Competition through Growth*. Oxford: Clarendon. Ch. 7.

T

tanshi **companies**   Japan's six short-term credit brokers or money market dealers.
  See **money markets, money market dealers**.

tariffs
See **trade policy**.

tatene   Manufacturers' suggested or "list" prices.
  See **pricing practices**.

tax reform   Japan's postwar tax system was initially designed by American economist Carl Shoup in 1949 during the occupation. It was a system based on comprehensive income tax in which all categories of income are added together and are subject to the same tax rate. Shoup had also called for the elimination of preferential tax treatment given to special interests or strategic industries. However, Japanese officials preferred tax benefits to subsidies to promote strategic industries; they felt that tax preferences would be more effective because they are given only after an enterprise has followed government suggestions, whereas subsidies are paid in advance. Consequently preferential tax provisions proliferated in the Japanese **tax system**, making the system highly inequitable.

  The greatest inequity of the tax system was that virtually all of the wage earner's income was subject to taxation, whereas many expenses could be deducted from business or agricultural income. Dividends and capital gains on stocks were almost tax free. To encourage **savings**, interest earnings from various types of savings within certain limits were tax exempt.

  Attempts at tax reform were made repeatedly over the years. They culminated in the 1988 tax reform with the following major changes: (1) A new 3% **consumption tax** was introduced in 1989 to broaden the tax base.

Eight excise taxes were eliminated. (2) **Individual income tax** and corporate income tax were simplified, and the tax rates reduced. (3) To plug the old loopholes in the income tax, a flat 26% (20% national and 6% local) capital gains tax was introduced. Tax exemption for interest income from various types of privileged savings—small-saver *maruyu* savings, **postal savings**, national and local bonds, savings for the formation of employee's assets, and postal installment savings for **housing**—was eliminated and replaced by a flat rate of 20% withheld at the source. (4) The burden of the inheritance tax was reduced. The minimum taxable inheritance was raised to a basic minimum of ¥40 million plus ¥8 million per statutory heir. The top rate was reduced from 75% to 70%.

Hatta (1992) considers the latest tax reform to be regressive. According to his calculation, it benefits the higher income groups more than the lower ones.

See also **consumption tax, corporate taxes, individual income tax, *maruyu*, postal savings system, tax system.**

References

Hashimoto, Kyoji, et al. 1990. Japan's tax reform: Its effects on the tax burden. *Japanese Economic Studies* 19, 1: 31−60.

Hatta, Tatsuo. 1992. The Nakasone-Takeshita tax reform: A critical evaluation. *American Economic Review* 82, 2: 231−36.

Ishi, Hiromitsu. 1989. *The Japanese Tax System*. Oxford: Oxford University Press.

Kaizuka, Keimei. 1992. The Shoup tax system and the postwar development of the Japanese economy. *American Economic Review* 82, 2: 221−25.

Noguchi, Yukio. 1987. Public finance. In *The Political Economy of Japan*, vol. 1: *The Domestic Transformation*, ed. by Kozo Yamamura and Yasukichi Yasuba. Stanford: Stanford University Press.

Noguchi, Yukio. 1992. The changing Japanese economy and the need for a fundamental shift in the tax system. *American Economic Review* 82, 2: 226−30.

tax system   Japan's taxes can be divided into national taxes levied by the national government and local taxes levied by the prefectural and municipal governments. In total the former is about twice as large as the latter. For example, in FY 1991 total national tax revenue (including stamp revenue) was ¥65.22 trillion, whereas total local tax revenue was ¥32.68 trillion. In FY 1992 the figures were ¥60.50 trillion and ¥35.07 trillion, respectively. However, part of the tax revenue collected by the national government is allocated to local governments.

Taxes can also be divided into direct and indirect taxes. The former are levied directly on individuals and corporations, while the latter are levied indirectly as consumption tax, excise tax or charged as fees. For both national and local taxes, direct taxes are much more important as sources of revenues.

The structure of national taxes is given in table T.1. **Individual income tax** (called "income tax" in Japan) is the largest national tax, accounting for 41.9% of total national tax revenue in FY 1992. Corporate income tax (called "corporate tax" or "corporation tax" in Japan) is the second largest national tax, accounting for 24.8% of total national revenue in FY 1992. Other national taxes are inheritance tax, liquor tax, gasoline tax, **consumption tax** (or commodity tax before April 1, 1989), and stamp revenue. In the 1988 **tax reform**, the rates for individual and corporate income taxes and the inheritance tax were cut; eight excise taxes (commodity tax, sugar tax, travel tax, electricity tax, gas tax, etc.) were eliminated, while the consumption tax was introduced. The latter has become the third largest national tax.

Local taxes are the major source of revenue for local governments. They consist of prefectural taxes levied by the 47 prefectures (which include **Tokyo** Metropolis) and municipal taxes levied by 3,239 municipalities (656 cities, 1,998 towns, and 585 villages as of April 1, 1991). Other sources of revenue are taxes collected by the national government and transferred to local governments (called "local transfer tax"), national government grants (called "local grant tax"), and subsidies for specific uses

Table T.1
National taxes (FY; in ¥ trillions)

	1980	1985	1990	1991	1992
Total	28.37	39.15	60.82	65.22	60.50
Income tax	10.80	15.44	24.35	25.74	25.35
Corporate tax	8.92	12.02	18.64	19.27	14.98
Inheritance tax	0.44	1.06	1.86	2.05	2.72
Consumption tax[a]	1.04	1.53	4.87	4.94	4.97
Liquor tax	1.42	1.93	1.91	2.00	2.03
Tobacco tax	—	0.88	0.96	0.99	1.01
Gasoline tax	1.55	1.56	1.42	1.50	1.58
Custom duties	0.65	0.64	0.86	0.85	0.88
Stamp revenue	0.84	1.41	2.03	2.15	1.67

Source: Ministry of Finance.
a. Introduced in FY 1989. Figures for 1980 and 1985 are for the commodity tax.

(education, social welfare, public works, transportation, and regional development, etc.) and public bonds. The sizes of these sources of local revenues in FY 1991 are given in table T.2.

The structure of local taxes is given in table T.3. The tax base and rates of major local taxes are legislated by the Diet and are the same in all prefectures and municipalities. The most important local taxes are explained below:

1. Inhabitant taxes are a form of local income tax levied on individuals and corporations. The prefectural inhabitant tax has two rates (2% and 4%) on the income of individuals, and one rate for corporations (5% of their national corporate taxes). The municipal inhabitant tax is the most important municipal tax and has a more complicated structure, including a per capita tax on individuals and corporations and progressive rates on individual and corporate income.

2. The enterprise tax, also called a "business tax," is the most important prefectural tax. It is collected from both individuals (unincorporated businesses) and corporations on the basis of net income, not on sales or turnover. Its tax rates are progressive, with a ceiling of 12% as of 1991.

3. Municipal property tax is the second largest tax for municipal governments. It is levied on owners of land, buildings, and other tangible assets. According to Ishi (1989: 249), the assessed value of property for tax purpose tends to be only a fraction of its market value, and great disparity exists among property assessments of equal value. This has created sentiments of unfairness among taxpayers and among different communities.

4. Special-purpose taxes include a number of minor taxes such as the automobile acquisition tax, the gas oil delivery tax, and the hunting tax at the

Table T.2
Sources of local revenues (FY 1991; in ¥ trillions)

	Amount	Percentage of total
Local taxes	32.68	46.1
Local transfer tax	1.77	2.5
Local grant tax	14.84	20.9
National subsidy	10.68	15.1
Public bonds	5.61	7.9
Miscellaneous	5.30	7.5
Total	67.14	100.0

Source: Ministry of Finance.

prefectural level and the bathing tax, the establishment tax, and the city planning tax at the municipal level. Unlike "regular taxes," these are earmarked for specific uses.

The Tax Bureau of the **Ministry of Finance** is responsible for tax policy on the basis of recommendations made by the Tax Commission. The National Tax Administration Agency is in charge of tax administration. The Ministry of Home Affairs oversees local taxation.

See also **consumption tax, corporate taxes, individual income taxes, tax reform**.

Addresses

Local Tax Bureau, Ministry of Home Affairs
1-2, Kasumigaseki 2-chome, Chiyoda-ku, Tokyo 100
Tel: (03) 3581-5311

National Tax Administration Agency
1-1, Kasumigaseki 3-chome, Chiyoda-ku, Tokyo 100
Tel: (03) 3581-4161

Tax Bureau, Ministry of Finance
1-1, Kasumigaseki 3-chome, Chiyoda-ku, Tokyo 100
Tel: (03) 3581-4111

Table T.3
Local taxes (FY; in ¥ trillions)

	1985	1990	1991
Prefectural taxes: total	10.20	14.34	15.27
Prefectural inhabitant tax	2.95	4.12	4.95
Enterprise tax	3.94	6.47	6.40
Real property acquisiton tax	0.43	0.65	0.61
Prefectural Tobacco excise tax	0.31	0.35	0.36
Automobile tax	1.04	1.20	1.26
Special-purpose taxes[a]	0.90	1.33	1.44
Municipal taxes: total	13.11	16.45	17.40
Municipal inhabitant tax	6.65	8.52	8.80
Property tax	4.17	5.89	6.43
Municipal tobacco excise tax	0.55	0.61	0.63
Special-purpose taxes[a]	0.93	1.23	1.32
Total local taxes	23.32	30.79	32.68

Source: Ministry of Finance.
a. Include a number of minor taxes earmarked for specific uses.

References

Aoki, Torao. 1986. The national taxation system. In *Public Finance in Japan*, ed. by Tokue Shibata. Tokyo: Tokyo University Press.

Gomi, Yuji. 1992. *Guide to Japanese Taxes, 1991–92*. Tokyo: Zaikei shohosha.

Ishi, Hiromitsu. 1989. *The Japanese Tax System*. Oxford: Oxford University Press.

Ishihara, Nobuo. 1986. The local public finance system. In *Public Finance in Japan*, ed. by Tokue Shibata. Tokyo: Tokyo University Press.

Kuboi, Takashi. 1990. *Business Practices and Taxation in Japan*, 3d. ed. Tokyo: Japan Times.

Ministry of Finance. 1992. *An Outline of Japanese Taxes, 1991*.

Ministry of Finance. 1992. *Financial Statistics of Japan, 1991*.

Noguchi, Yukio. 1992. The changing Japanese economy and the need for a fundamental shift in the tax system. *American Economic Review* 82, 2: 226–30.

Ogura, Seiritsu, and Naoyuki Yoshino. 1988. The tax system and the fiscal investment and loan program. In *Industrial Policy of* Japan, ed. by Ryutaro Komiya, Masahiro Okuno, and Kotaro Suzumura. Tokyo: Academic Press Japan.

Saito, Tadashi. 1991. Local governments in Japan: National and international aspects. *JEI Report*, no. 41A, Nov. 1: 1–12.

teigaku chokin   Fixed-sum postal savings deposits with a ten-year term, popular with small savers because of its high interest rate.
   See **postal savings**.

tenzoku   Long-term transfer of employees to a subsidiary.
   See **corporate personnel practices**.

tokkin funds   A special type of **investment trust** funds with tax advantages for investors. *Tokkin* is the abbreviation of *tokutei kinsen shintaku*, which is translated literally as "specified money trust." It is a type of trust fund held at **trust banks** in which institutional investors give specific instruction for management. *Tokkin* funds are, in theory, managed by both investors and **investment advisory companies** for investment in stocks. They were popular in the 1980s with companies, commercial banks, and **insurance companies** because they are anonymous and pay out dividends that are tax free or taxed at relatively low rates. These funds grew rapidly in the 1980s. Partly as a result of the investment of these funds, trading volume on the **Tokyo Stock Exchange** increased very rapidly in the late 1980s.

Tokkin funds were an important source of profits for insurance companies in the late 1980s. The **Ministry of Finance** limited their investment in *tokkin* funds to 5% of their total assets until September 1990, when it was raised to 7%. The bad fall in the Tokyo Stock Exchange in 1990 prompted the increase in order to induce the insurance companies to keep their huge funds in the **stock market**. In the wake of the **securities companies'** scandals in 1991 and the depressed stock market, many trust fund investors have redeemed their monies because of the worsened prospects for returns. At the end of March 1993, the outstanding value of *tokkin* at trust banks was estimated at ¥18.92 trillion.

Eigyo tokkin funds are a shadowy version of *tokkin* funds. In pursuit of higher return, investors have the funds managed directly by the institutional sales departments of securities companies on a discretionary basis. Since the insitutional sales departments of securities companies are not authorized to act as investment advisers, such accounts are surreptitious in nature. They charge no fees and are not registered with the Ministry of Finance. Such discretionary accounts enabled securities companies to easily move money in and out of clients' accounts. Some of these funds were used as an investment trust, and some to finance illegal activities such as supporting the share prices of companies who put up money in these *eigyo tokkin* funds. It is estimated that a total of ¥5 trillion was invested in *eigyo tokkin* accounts in 1989, with ¥2 trillion of them managed by the four leading securities companies (Nomura, Daiwa, Nikko, and Yamaichi).

To attract funds to these *eigyo tokkin* accounts, it was common, prior to 1991, for securities companies to promise investors guaranteed returns, although such a practice is illegal. In 1991 it was revealed that securities companies have widely used these accounts as a vehicle for compensating clients for investment losses, often without the latter's knowledge. Because these scandals have outraged the public and intensified foreign criticisms of Japanese business practices, the Ministry of Finance and the Japan Securities Dealers' Association have acted to tighten rules on the management of *tokkin* funds. The Ministry is unwilling, however, to see the erosion of its own power by the establishment of an independent regulatory body like the U.S. Securities and Exchange Commission to oversee the securities industry, as many commentators have suggested. Analysts contend that until such an independent body is established, abuses will occur again.

See also **securities companies**.

References

Isaccs, Jonathan. 1990. *Japanese Equities Markets*. London: Euromoney Publications. Ch. 8.

Nagano, Kenji. 1991. Push seen for new rules of integrity. *Nikkei Weekly*, July 6: 4.

Tightened tokkin fund rules to curb abuses. *Japan Economic Journal*, Feb. 17, 1990: 31.

Tatewaki, Kazuo. 1991. *Banking and Finance in Japan*. London: Routledge. Ch. 8.

Tomomatsu, Hidetaka. 1991. Exposure of coziness chills securities industry. *Nikkei Weekly*, July 6: 1, 4.

Viner, Aron. 1987. *Inside Japan's Financial Markets*. London: The Economist Publications. Ch. 9.

Tokyo   Tokyo is Japan's capital, its largest city, and the hub of its largest industrial region, Kanto. The Metropolis of Tokyo is a vast self-governing unit consisting of 23 special wards, 26 cities, 7 towns, and 8 villages, with a **population** of 11.86 million people in 1990 (8.13 million for the 23 wards in 1992). It is also the nation's third largest port. With the rapid development of the Japanese economy and financial system, Tokyo has also become one of the financial centers of the world.

In FY 1990 Tokyo produced ¥83.25 trillion of gross municipal product, which was by far the largest among the nation's large cities. Tokyo' gross municipal product as a share of Japan's gross national product has grown from 16.7% in FY 1975 to 17.7% in FY 1985 and 19.2% in FY 1990. In 1990 it led the nation's major cities in the production of general machinery (¥1.09 trillion), metal and nonmetal products (¥1.18 trillion), and foodstuffs (¥744 billion) and was second among the cities in the production of electric machinery, chemicals, and petroleum. The **Tokyo Stock Exchange** is by far the largest in the nation, having 87% of the total stock trading volume on all eight stock exchanges in the nation in 1991. As the nation's third largest port behind **Yokohama** and Narita International Airport, it handled 11.8% of Japan's exports and imports in FY 1991. Tokyo also has some of Japan's most prestigeous universities. The University of Tokyo is considered to be the top university of the nation.

The great concentration of population, corporate headquarters, and government ministries and agencies has produced overcrowding, traffic congestion, and high prices of land, **housing**, and many goods and services. Nevertheless, Tokyo's well-developed urban subway network along with the connecting suburban railways make it possible for a large number of people to commute to work from the outlying areas into Tokyo. It is estimated that the commuters increase Tokyo's day population by as much as 30%.

To relieve the concentration of population, the government announced in 1985 the Capital Redevelopment Plan to develop core business cities elsewhere such as Yokohama and Kawasaki and to encourage the relocation of business and government agencies there. In 1989 it was decided to move 79 government offices and agencies from Tokyo to Yokohama. However, the plan is yet to be implemented and the prospect is not clear.

The Kanto region comprises Tokyo and six other prefectures: Ibaraki, Tochigi, Gumma, Saitama, Chiba, and Kanagawa (which includes Yokohama). This is Japan's largest industrial region. In FY 1989 it produced more than 37% of Japan's GNP. It had a population of 38.5 million in 1990, which amounted to 31% of Japan's total population.

See also **housing, Kansai and Osaka, land uses and policies, Nagoya and Central Japan, Yokohama**.

Address

Tokyo Metropolitan Government
8-1 Nishi-Shinjuku 2-chome, Shinjuku-ku, Tokyo 163
Tel: (03) 5321-1111   Fax: (03) 5388-1329

References

Economic Planning Agency. 1992. *Annual Report on Prefectural Accounts* (in Japanese).

Tokyo-to Bunka Shinkokai. 1991. *Living in Tokyo: Guide to Foreign Students*. Tokyo: Tokyo Metropolitan Culture Foundation.

Waley, Paul. 1991. *Tokyo: City of Streets*. New York: Weatherhill.

Tokyo Commodity Exchange for Industry (TOCOM)   Japan's largest commodity exchange and the world's leading platinum exchange.
See **commodity markets**.

Tokyo Grain Exchange
See **commodity markets**.

Tokyo International Financial Futures Exchange (TIFFE)
See **financial futures market**.

Tokyo offshore market   Officially called the Japan offshore market, this is the banking market, established in December 1986, in which banks conduct banking business with nonresidents (foreign corporations, foreign governments, international institutions, and overseas branches of foreign exchange banks). The market is free from government regulation of interest rates, reserve requirements on deposits, and deposit insurance. It is exempt from withholding tax; that is, interest repatriated by nonresidents is not taxed at the source. Nor are the transactions restricted to any currency. However, residents are prohibited from the market, and there are limits on the inflow of funds from the offshore acounts into domestic accounts.

The Tokyo offshore market was set up to serve as a center for the world's transactions in yen and thus promote the international business of Japan's banking institutions and the internationalization of yen. From $1.38 trillion in 1986, the transaction level increased to $7.02 trillion in 1992. The amount outstanding was $625 billion at the end of 1992. Market participants have complained about the rigid separation of offshore accounts from domestic accounts, calling for deregulation.

See also **money markets**.

References

Federation of Bankers Association of Japan. 1989. *The Banking System in Japan*. Ch. 6.

Hanabuchi, Satoshi. 1990. Offshore banking grows dramatically after government reforms. *Japan Economic Journal*, summer suppl.: 17.

Suzuki, Yoshio, ed. 1987. *The Japanese Financial System*. Oxford: Oxford University Press. P. 127.

Tatewaki, Kazuo. 1991. *Banking and Finance in Japan*. London: Routledge. Ch. 5.

Viner, Aron. 1987. *Inside Japan's Financial Markets*. London: The Economist Publications. Ch. 7.

Tokyo over-the-counter market
See **over-the-counter market**.

Tokyo Stock Exchange   Japan has eight stock exchanges and the Tokyo Stock Exchange is by far the largest of them. As shown in table T.4, it had 87% and 86% respectively of total stock trading volume and value on all stock exchanges in 1989, which declined to 80.4% and 74.7%, respectively, in 1992. During the **stock market** boom of the late 1980s, Tokyo Stock Exchange surpassed the New York Stock Exchange in stock market value and trading value to become the world's largest ($4.26 trillion in market value versus $2.9 trillion for New York Stock Exchange at the end of 1989). By the end of 1991, however, its market value had declined to $3.02 trillion, compared with $3.71 trillion for the New York Stock Exchange.

Table T.4
Stock exchanges and stock trading

Stock exchange	1989		1992	
	Volume[a]	Value[b]	Volume[a]	Value[b]
Tokyo	222,599	332,617	66,408	60,110
Osaka	25,096	41,679	12,069	15,575
Nagoya	7,263	10,395	3,300	3,876
Kyoto	331	443	225	322
Hiroshima	189	235	110	136
Fukuoka	267	330	139	129
Niigata	397	475	163	178
Sapporo	151	221	149	129
Total	256,296	386,395	82,563	80,456

Source: Tokyo Stock Exchange.
Note: Trading in foreign stocks is not included.
a. In millions of shares.
b. In ¥ billions.

The Tokyo Stock Exchange was founded initially in 1878 as part of the Meiji government's modernization program. From 1943 to 1947 all of Japan's stock exchanges were merged into a single Japan Securities Exchange. The Tokyo Stock Exchange in its present form was established in 1949.

At its peak in 1988 the average daily stock trading on the Tokyo Stock Exchange exceeded one billion shares. In 1991 it was 380 million shares. Trading is limited to listed securities. The Exchange is divided into two sections for domestic stocks—the first section for large companies and the second section for medium-sized companies and newly listed companies. There is a foreign section for foreign stocks. At the end of 1992 stocks of 1,229 companies are assigned to the first section, and those of 422 companies to the second section. Stocks of 119 foreign companies are listed in the foreign section.

A company applying for listing on the Tokyo Stock Exchange is screened by both the Exchange and the **Ministry of Finance**. The securities traded are divided broadly into stocks and bonds. The Exchange was not open to foreign stocks until 1973, and it was only in December 1985 that six foreign securities companies, including Merrill Lynch, Morgan Stanley & Co., and Goldman, Sacks & Co., were approved as traders on the Exchange. As of March 31, 1993, there were 124 members in the Exchange, including 24 foreign security firms.

Two **stock prices indexes** are commonly used for the Tokyo Stock Exchange—the Nikkei Stock Average and TOPIX, the Tokyo Stock Price Index. The former gives an unweighted average of 225 selected issues listed on the first section of the Exchange. The TOPIX is based on the weighted average of all stocks listed on the first section of the Exchange.

Japan does not have an independent regulatory agency comparable to the U.S. Securities and Exchange Commission to oversee its **securities companies** and activities on the securities exchanges. Instead, the Ministry of Finance gives securities companies and stock exchanges **administrative guidance** and the Securities Dealers' Association of Japan provides voluntary industry restraints. In July 1922 a new Securities and Exchange Surveillance Commission was established to watch for stock market manipulation. Since its members come from the Ministry of Finance, its independence remains to be seen.

See also **shareownership, stock market, stock price indexes**.

Addresses

Tokyo Stock Exchange
1, Nihonbashi Kabuto 2-chome, Chuo-ku, Tokyo 103
Tel: (03) 3666-0141   Fax: (03) 3639-5016

Tokyo Stock Exchange New York Research Office
45 Broadway, New York, NY 1006
Tel: (212) 363–2350

References

Elton, Edwin J., and Martin J. Gruber, ed. 1990. *Japanese Capital Markets*. New York: Harper and Row.

Isaccs, Jonathan. 1990. *Japanese Equities Markets*. London: Euromoney Publications.

Tatewaki, Kazuo. 1991. *Banking and Finance in Japan*. London: Routledge. Ch. 6.

Tokyo Stock Exchange. 1993. *Tokyo Stock Exchange Fact Book, 1993*.

Viner, Aron. 1987. *Inside Japan's Financial Markets*. London: The Economist Publications. Ch. 3.

Zielinski, Robert, and Nogel Holloway. 1991. *Unequal Equities*. Tokyo: Kodansha International.

Tokyo University   Japan's most prestigeous university.

See **economic/business research and publications, education system**.

Tokyu Group   A large family-controlled conglomerate of some 300 companies, including Tokyu Corp., a railway company, Tokyu Department Store, and Tokyu Store Chain Co.
See **railway companies**.

TOPIX   Tokyo Stock Price Index.
See **stock price indexes**.

toshi gingo (*togin*)   City banks, Japan's large commercial banks with headquarters in major metropolitan areas.
See **banking system, city banks**.

Toshiba Corp.   A leading electronics manufacturer and core member of the Mitsui group.
See **electronics industry, Mitsui Group**.

total quality control   Quality control in product design and manufacturing in which all employees and management participate.
See **quality control**.

Toyo Keizai Shinposha   A major business publisher.
See **economic/business research and publications**.

Toyota Group   An industrial group comprising Toyota Motor Co. and its major suppliers, including Nippondenso, Toyoda Machine Works, Aisin Seiki Co., Toyoda Auto Body Co., Toyoda Automatic Loom Works Ltd., and Kanto Auto Works Ltd.
See **automobile industry,** *keiretsu* **and business groups, subcontracting**.

Toyota Motor Corp.   Japan's largest automobile producer and industrial corporation, and the world's third largest automobile company as of 1991 in terms of sales and assets.
See **automobile industry,** *keiretsu* **and business groups**.

Toyota production system
See **just-in-time system**.

trade pattern   Japan's international trade pattern can be discussed in terms of its product composition, trading partners, and export-import imbalance.

Japan exports are dominated by manufactured products, particularly machinery and equipment, although the most important product groups in terms of competitiveness and world market shares have changed significantly over time. In the 1950s unskilled labor-intensive products such as textiles, apparel, rubber and plastic products, leather and leather products were important. The major export products were textiles, steel, and vessels in the 1960s, automobiles, steel, and chemicals in the 1970s and 1980s. Since the late 1980s high-tech equipment and electronics have become increasingly important, although automobiles, chemicals, and steel remain dominant. Automobiles remain the largest category of export products, amounting to more than 18% of total exports (see table T.5).

Japan's imports are dominated by fuels, foodstuffs, metal ores, and other raw materials. Because of its lack of natural resources, Japan depends heavily on imports for some primary products essential for consumption and industrial production. It imports about half of its caloric intake of food and about 30% of its total food value. It imports about all of its crude petroleum, iron ore, lead ore, bauxite, wool and cotton, and about 75% of its coal and zinc ore. On the other hand, the imports of machinery and equipment are relatively low (about 16% of total).

Because of the need to import fuels, foodstuffs, and raw materials, Japan has to export manufactured products to earn the necessary foreign exchanges. However, there is one complication. The developing countries and the Middle East from which Japan imports raw materials and energy

Table T.5
Japan's exports by commodity (in $ billion, custom clearance basis)

	1968	1973	1983	1990	1991
Foodstuffs	0.4	0.8	1.4	1.6	1.8
Textiles	2.0	3.3	6.6	7.2	7.9
Chemicals	0.8	2.1	6.9	15.9	17.5
Metals	2.3	6.8	18.4	19.5	21.1
Iron-steel products	1.7	5.3	12.8	12.5	13.6
Machinery and Equipment	5.7	20.4	99.6	215.1	236.6
Motor vehicles	0.7	3.6	26.1	51.0	54.8
ICs	—	—	—	7.6	8.2
Vessels	1.1	3.8	6.0	5.6	6.7
Precision instruments	0.4	1.0	5.4	11.6	12.9
Others	1.8	3.5	14.0	27.6	29.5
Total	13.0	36.9	146.9	286.9	314.5

Source: Japan Tariff Association.

do not have the population or income levels to buy sufficient manufactured goods from Japan to balance the bilateral trade. The oil export countries in particular run a large trade surplus with Japan. To offset these import deficits, Japan must run export surpluses with other countries. However, the export surpluses with other industrial countries in the 1980s have become excessive, far more than necessary to pay for imports, thereby becoming a source of friction with the West.

Japan's trade surplus was only $2.1 billion in 1980, but it rapidly increased to $20 billion in 1981, $56 billion in 1985, and to a peak of $96.4 billion in 1987 before it started to decline. In 1991 it was $77.8 billion. The large imbalance between Japan's exports and imports has been attributed by Western analysts to various factors that limit imports into Japan such as governmental **nontariff barriers to trade**, *keiretsu* (business groups), the exclusionary business practices that make Japanese firms favor doing business with other related Japanese firms, the trading practices of the **trading companies**, the high **savings** by Japanese households, and the **distribution system** with its numerous small retail stores. The attitude of the consumers is also considered to have played a role. For example, Lincoln (1990: 80) criticizes the "gullible public" who has limited exposure to foreign products in Japan, and who had accepted the "need" to protect small, weak Japanese firms from international competition, and the "myth" of overall Japanese superiority in the 1980s.

Table T.6
Japan's imports by commodity (in $ billions)

	1968	1973	1983	1990	1991
Foodstuffs	1.9	6.0	14.9	31.6	34.5
Textile materials	1.0	2.2	2.1	2.6	2.5
Textiles	0.2	1.7	3.0	12.8	13.7
Metal ores and scrap	1.6	4.0	6.5	9.1	8.8
Other raw materials	2.3	6.0	9.6	16.7	15.9
Mineral fuels	2.7	8.3	58.9	56.7	54.8
Coal	0.5	1.4	4.9	6.2	6.4
Petroleum	1.7	6.0	40.1	31.6	30.2
Chemicals	0.7	1.9	7.2	16.0	17.4
Machinery and equipment	1.3	3.5	10.4	40.9	42.9
Others	1.4	4.7	13.8	48.3	46.7
Total	13.0	38.3	126.4	234.8	236.7

Source: Japan Tariff Association.

In response, Ryutaro Komiya of the Research Institute of the **Ministry of International Trade and Industry** disputes Lincoln's point and argues that, on the contrary, Japanese consumers tend to regard imported foreign consumer goods as prestigious luxuries (author's interview, July 7, 1992). Various Japanese authors and officials have also criticized the inability or unwillingness of Western firms to learn and adapt to the Japanese market and institutions and to strive to satisfy the demand of the Japanese consumers. American automakers' failure to change the driver's seat to the right in their cars exported to Japan is often given as an example.

In terms of trading partners, the United States has remained Japan's largest trading partner throughout the postwar period, although its importance has declined somewhat in the 1980s because of the growing importance of other countries. In addition, the United States is more important as a market for Japan's exports (29.1% in 1991) than as a source of its imports (22.5% in 1991). Consequently there is substantial export surplus in Japan's trade with the United States ($38.2 billion in 1991). Japan's trade surplus vis-à-vis the United States was only $7 billion in 1979 but increased steadily to a peak of $52.1 billion in 1987 before it started to decline. This pattern of export surplus is true with virtually all other industrial countries except Canada and Australia, which supply foodstuffs and raw materials to Japan. Japan also has export surplus with the newly industrializing economies of South Korea, Taiwan, Hong Kong, and Singapore and the developing countries in Southeast Asia, Latin America, and Africa.

Among the developing countries, China is Japan's largest trading partner, followed by Indonesia. Japan had trade surplus with China until 1988 when import deficit started to emerge. Japan has import deficit with Indonesia, Malaysia, Saudi Arabia and United Arab Emirates because of the imports of raw materials and fuels.

In the analytical literature on Japan's trade pattern, an issue of particular interest to American economists has been the apparent low level of manufactured goods imported by Japan. For example, in 1990 Japan imported $117.5 billion of manufactured goods, slightly less than what Italy imported ($123.2 billion) in the same year despite the much larger size of the Japanese market and national income. These imports amounted to 50.9% of Japan's total imports in 1990, which was the lowest manufactured import ratio among the industrial countries (in the United States, it was 78.6%; Germany, 76.9%; Italy, 71.0%). The ratio in Japan was 22.8% in 1980, 31% in 1985, and 50.4% in 1989, all much lower than the corresponding ratios in the other industrial countries. The question is: Are these low levels

Table T.7
Japan's trade by region and country (1991; in $ billions)

	Exports	Imports	Balance
Developed countries	176.3	116.9	60.1
United States	91.5	53.3	38.2
European Community	59.2	31.8	27.4
Australia	6.5	13.0	−6.5
Developing countries	125.6	100.7	24.9
Latin America	12.8	9.8	3.0
Asia	96.2	58.8	37.4
Newly industrializing economies in Asia	66.9	27.3	39.6
Middle East	12.3	29.3	−17.0
Africa	3.6	1.9	1.7
Communist countries	11.9	19.1	−7.2
U.S.S.R.	2.1	3.3	−1.2
China	8.6	14.2	−5.6

Source: Ministry of Finance.

of manufactured goods the result of market forces at work or are they the result of government trade policy and/or other structural barriers to imports?

Balassa and Noland (1988: 239–54), Lawrence (1987), and Lincoln (1990: 18–25) have argued that Japan's imports of manufactured goods are lower than what one would expect, given its high income and industrial structure. Saxonhouse (1989) disagrees and maintains that Japan's specific factor endowments can adequately explain Japan's composition of imports. Grossman (1990) also argues that factor endowment explains Japan's trade pattern but does so in a dynamic setting of R&D and innovation. Lawrence (1991) further argues that the low level of manufactured imports is more pronounced in industries in which keiretsu-related firms are dominant. However, the validity of his methodology is challenged by Saxonhouse (1991). Adding to the debate, several Japanese economists have contended that American criticism of Japan's trade policy is unjustified because the U.S.– Japan trade imbalance is either due to the loss of international competitiveness of American firms or due to the strength of Japanese firms at home ("natural market barriers") and abroad, and not due to Japan's import barriers (cited in Lincoln, 1990: 25–29). Komiya and Irie (1990) express the view widely held by Japanese officials that the U.S. trade deficits are macro problems stemming from government deficits and low domestic savings, and that Japan is one of the most open countries among OECD members. Thus there is no consensus among economists on the issue.

See also **trade policies**.

Addresses

Japan External Trade Organization (JETRO)
2-5, Toranomon 2-chome, Minato-ku, Tokyo 105
Tel: (03) 3582-5511

JETRO, New York
44th Floor, McGraw-Hill Bldg, 1221 Avenue of the Americas
New York, NY 10020-1060
Tel: (212): 997-0400

Ministry of International Trade and Industry
3-1, Kasumigaseki 1-chome, Chiyoda-ku, Tokyo 100
Tel: (03) 3501-1511

References

Balassa, Bela, and Marcus Noland. 1988. *Japan in the World Economy*. Washington: Institute for International Economics. Chs. 2–3.

Grossman, Gene M. 1990. Explaining Japan's innovation and trade: A model of quality competition and dynamic comparative advantage. *Bank of Japan Monetary and Economic Studies 8*, 2: 75–99.

Komiya, Ryutaro. 1990. *The Japanese Economy: Trade, Industry, and Government*. Tokyo: University of Tokyo Press. Ch. 1.

Komiya, Ryutaro, and Kazutomo Irie. 1990. The U.S.–Japan trade problem: An economic analysis from a Japanese viewpoint. In *Japan Economic Structure: Should It Change?* ed. by Kozo Yamamura. Seattle: Society for Japanese Studies.

Lawrence, Robert Z. 1987. Imports in Japan: Closed markets or minds? *Brookings Papers on Economic Activity*, no. 2: 517–48.

Lawrence, Robert Z. 1991. Efficient or exclusionist? The import behavior of Japanese corporate groups. *Brookings Papers on Economic Activity*, no. 1: 311–30.

Lincoln, Edward. 1990. *Japan's Unequal Trade*. Washington: Brookings Institution.

Ministry of International Trade and Industry. Annual. *White Paper on International Trade*.

Sato, Ryuzo, and Julianne Nelson, eds. 1989. *Beyond Trade Friction: Japan–U.S. Economic Relations*. Cambridge: Cambridge University Press.

Saxonhouse, Gary R. 1989. Differentiated products, economies of scale and access to the Japanese market. In *Trade Policies for International competitiveness*, ed. by Robert C. Feenstra. Chicago: University of Chicago Press.

Saxonhouse, Gary R. 1991. Efficient or exclusionist? The import behavior of Japanese corporate groups. Comments and discussion. *Brookings Papers on Economic Activity*, no. 1: 331–36.

trade policy   The underlying premises of Japan's trade policy in the early postwar period were (1) Japan is a resource-poor country that has to import most of its natural resources, (2) it has to pay for these imports by the export of manufactured goods, and (3) it can best do so by protecting and promoting its manufacturing industries. On the basis of these premises, an import-restricting and an industry- and export-promoting trade strategy was adopted in the 1950s. The ministry that is in charge of trade policy is the **Ministry of International Trade and Industry** (MITI). In fact the name of the Ministry itself is indicative of the close link between industry and trade to policymakers. In the separate area of agricultural products, import restriction, including total ban of rice import, has been adopted for domestic political reasons.

The protection and promotion of domestic industries was accomplished by keeping the domestic market from cheaper imports and **foreign direct investment** in Japan, and by giving incentives to domestic industries to raise productivity in order to be internationally competitive. Import restrictions were achieved by means of tariffs and **nontariff barriers to trade**. Tariffs were high in the early postwar period but had been successively reduced since the mid-1960s as Japan joined GATT and OECD. Currently tariff rates on nonagricultural products are generally no higher than their counterparts in the United States and the European Community. However, tariff rates remain high on fresh and processed agricultural products, alcoholic beverages, and wood products, for example. Nontariff barriers to trade remain numerous and restrictive. These include quotas on agricultural and fishery products, and stringent testing and certification requirements, and custom procedures. Restrictions on foreign direct investment in Japan have been gradually liberalized due to U.S. pressure.

To give domestic industries incentives to raise productivity and become internationally competitive, MITI has used **industrial policy** and **administrative guidance**. The purpose is to promote industries that are considered to have good growth prospects in the world market. MITI's policy measures are carefully crafted to raise productivity through industry rationalization, R&D, investment, and so forth, without fostering complacency and high costs. The **steel industry** in the 1960s and 1970s is the best example in which MITI's trade and industrial policies led to intense competition among domestic producers to raise productivity in order to qualify for capacity expansion. As a result Japan's steel industry became the world's largest and a major export industry in the 1970s. However, MITI's industrial policy has not always been effective, especially since the 1970s, and the protected and promoted industries have not always become efficient. The petrochemical industry is an example.

Until the mid-1960s when Japan joined the OECD and GATT, the government provided tax and monetary incentives to industries to expand exports. By the late 1970s Japan had became a major trading power and exporter of manufactured goods. However, throughout the 1970s and 1980s Japan's rapid expansion in some export products such as textiles, steel, electronics, and automobiles had caused growing protectionism in the West, and Tokyo's policy concern became increasingly the protection of its export markets. To ensure Japan's foreign market access and to forestall unilateral trade restrictions on its exports, MITI has been pragmatic in negotiating agreements on managed trade. These include the following: voluntary export restraints (VERs) on textile exports to the United States in the 1970s; VERs on the exports of steel, automobiles, color televisions, and semiconductors to the United States since 1981; VERs on automobile exports to the European Community from 1991 until the end of 1999. There was also the 1985 Plaza Accord to let the yen appreciate against the dollar in order to help reduce the U.S. trade deficit with Japan.

Since the mid-1980s, as Japan's trade surplus reached new heights (peak of $96.4 billion in 1987), Tokyo has, after some hard bargaining, increasingly accepted the U.S. demand to help increase the imports of certain products. These include the **Beef-Citrus Quota Agreement** (1988) with the United States to replace quotas with tariffs on beef and citrus imports and the **Semiconductor Agreement** (1991) with the United States to increase American firms' semiconductor market share in Japan. There was also the broad-ranging **Structural Impediments Initiative** agreement (1990) with the United States, concluded despite much domestic opposition, to reduce business practices that are said to impede imports. The effectiveness of these agreements in promoting imports remains to be seen, however. For example, Okimoto argues that it is easier for MITI to ask Japanese companies to restrain exports than to increase imports; the main reason is that administrative guidance is less effective in high-tech sectors with rapidly changing technologies and industrial structures (cited in *Japan Econoic Journal*, Feb. 17, 1990: A1).

As part of the new policy concern to reduce trade friction with the West, MITI has also encouraged Japanese companies, particularly automakers, to increase **direct overseas investment** and production, on the one hand, and to increase imports of foreign parts, on the other hand.

In the separate area of agricultural imports, the ban on rice imports is caused by political pressure from organized farmers and has been a major irritant in U.S.–Japan trade relations. The issue is related to world agricultural trade being discussed in the ongoing **Uruguay Round** of GATT negotiations. Since the United States and the European Community reached an agreement on agricultural issues in late 1992, Tokyo is reportedly willing to replace the import ban with high tariffs on rice import. The tariffs will be reduced gradually over a number of years. No final agreement has been reached yet as of July 1993.

See also **trade pattern, yen–dollar exchange rate**.

Address

Ministry of International Trade and Industry
3-1, Kasumigaseki 1-chome, Chiyoda-ku, Tokyo 100
Tel: (03) 3501-1511

References

Balassa, Bela, and Narcus Noland. 1988. *Japan in the World Economy*. Washington: Institute for International Economics. Ch. 3.

Komiya, Ryutaro. 1990. *The Japanese Economy: Trade, Industry, and Government*. Tokyo: University of Tokyo Press. Ch. 1.

Komiya, Ryutaro, and Kazutomo Irie. 1990. The U.S.–Japan trade problem: An economic analysis from a Japanese viewpoint. In *Japan's Economic Structure: Should It Change?* ed. by Kozo Yamamura. Seattle: Society for Japanese Studies.

Lincoln, Edward. 1990. *Japan's Unequal Trade*. Washington: Brookings Instituton.

Prestowitz, Clyde V., Jr. 1987. U.S.–Japan trade friction: creating a new relationship. *California Management Review* 24, 2: 9–19.

Sato, Ryuzo, and John A. Rizzo. 1988. *Unkept Promises, Unclear Consequences: U.S. Economic Policy and the Japanese Response*. Cambridge: Cambridge University Press.

Sato, Ryuzo, and Julianne Nelson, eds. 1989. *Beyond Trade Friction: Japan–U.S. Economic Relations*. Cambridge: Cambridge University Press.

Shiraishi, Takashi. 1989. *Japan's Trade Policies: 1945 to the Present Day*. London: Athlone.

trademark registration
See **patent system**.

trading companies   Unique to Japan, these companies are engaged in the marketing of products and other related services both in and outside of Japan. There are over 1,700 trading companies in Japan. Traditionally they are the main exporters and importers of the economy, although their shares of these businesses have declined since the early 1970s because of the structural changes in the economy. In 1991 they handled 43% of Japan's total exports and 76% of total imports, down from 69% and 81%, respectively, in 1971.

About 16 of these companies are called *sogo shosha* (i.e., general trading companies). They deal with a wide range of products from raw materials to finished products and operate in many foreign countries. The industry is dominated by the six or nine largest general trading companies— Mitsubishi Corp., Sumitomo Corp., Mitsui & Co., Itochu Corp. (C. Itoh & Co.), Marubeni Corp., Nissho-Iwai Corp., Toyo Menka (Tomen), Nichimen Corp., and Kanematsu-Gosho. Of these, Itochu Corp. has had the largest sales in recent years, whereas Mitsubishi Corp. has been the most profitable one (see table T.8). Each of the top six is a core member of Japan's six financial **keiretsu**. In FY 1990 the top six alone had combined sales of ¥107.8 trillion, which declined to ¥99.8 trillion in FY 1991 and ¥92.5 trillion in FY 1992 because of recession in the economy. In FY 1990 the top nine had combined sales of ¥126.6 trillion, of which ¥53.7 trillion or 42.4% was in domestic sales, ¥15.4 trillion was in exports, and ¥23.1 trillion in imports.

Sogo shosha's traditional businesses have been in the low margin handling of bulk commodities such as crude oil, chemicals, metals, and machinery. The Big Nine alone typically handle more than half of Japan's imports (67% in 1987 and 56% in 1990). They have also performed the exporting function for small manufacturers who are too small to engage in the export business themselves, and they have provided credit to small- and medium-sized companies. They serve as "quasi banks," since they borrow from banks and lend to corporations, especially those inside their *keiretsu* groups.

Table T.8
Leading trading companies (in ¥ billions)

Company	FY 1990		FY 1992	
	Sales	Profits[a]	Sales	Profits[a]
Mitsubishi Corp.	17,421.4	94.3	14,996.5	75.6
Sumitomo Corp.	19,212.6	77.2	16,530.3	41.0
Mitsui and Co.	18,234.1	66.1	15,495.9	59.2
Itochu Corp.[b]	20,596.0	54.4	18,529.3	49.8
Marubeni Corp.	19,015.6	54.8	16,863.7	37.4
Nissho Iwai Corp.	13,343.2	24.5	10,149.6	15.5

Source: *Nikkei Weekly*, May 30, 1992 and May 24, 1993.
a. Pretax profits.
b. Better known in the West as C. Itoh and Co. before that name was dropped in October 1992.

The large trading companies are also the first Japanese firms in the postwar period to make **direct overseas investments**. Often they assisted small Japanese firms to establish manufacturing facilities abroad by forming joint ventures with them and with local interests. They serve as general contractors for overseas development construction projects. They are also engaged in third-country trade where both the buyer and seller are non-Japanese. With the opening of the markets in Eastern Europe and the former Soviet Union, large trading companies are among the first to set up joint ventures there. During April 1989–September 1989, the sales of the nine major trading companies consisted of domestic sales (41.2%), third-country sales (22.2%), imports (21.2%), and exports (15.4%). During April 1991–March 1992 the corresponding figures were 44.3%, 25.8%, 16.8%, and 13.1% (Japan Foreign Trade Council).

The strength of the general trading companies lies in their worldwide network of communications and business ties, its marketing expertise, financial resources, and their economies of scale. They are particularly adept in arranging complex package deals that involve simultaneously exporting, importing, and financing, such as counter-purchase trade with the (former) communist countries and the Third World countries. The largest six trading companies are members of the six financial *keiretsu* groups and can draw on the expertise of other companies of their respective groups in their business dealings. Yoshino and Lifson (1986) stress that *sogo shosha* perform a unique function of combining the flexibility of the market with the advantage of integrated planning for their clients, while the latter retain their freedom of choice and independence.

Since the 1970s, as capital shortage became capital surplus in Japan, the financing function of the trading companies became less important. Most Japanese companies have also become more internationalized, selling their products through their own marketing departments. These have resulted in losses in the 1980s for many trading companies, especially the medium-sized ones. The telecommunications revolution has also produced many products that are new to them. The trading companies thus see diversification into new products or activities as crucial to their future vitality. For example, most of the leading trading companies are said to have set up special departments in recent years to advise clients on **mergers and acquisitions**. But the initial investment costs of starting new business lines are high for medium-sized trading companies. Consequently mergers may be a practical solution for them, as some have already opted to do.

See also *keiretsu* **and business groups, Mitsui Group, Mitsubishi Group, Sumitomo Group**.

Addresses

Itochu Corp.
1-3, Kyutaro-machi 4-chome, Chuo-ku, Osaka
Tel: (06) 241-2121   Fax: (03) 3497-7915

Marubeni Corp.
5-7, Honmachi 2-chome, Chuo-ku, Osaka 541-88
Tel: (06) 266-2111   Fax: (03) 3282-2331

Mitsui and Co.
2-1, Ohtemachi 1-chome, Chiyoda-ku, Tokyo 100
Tel: (03) 3285-1111   Fax: (03) 3285-9819

Mitsubishi Corp.
6-3, Marunouchi 2-chome, Chiyoda-ku, Tokyo 100
Tel: (03) 3210-2121   Fax: (03) 3210-8051

Nissho Iwai Corp.
5-8, Imabashi 2-chome, Chuo-ku, Osaka 541
Tel: (06) 209-2111   Fax: (03) 3588-4919

Sumitomo Corp.
5-15, Kitahama, Chuo-ku, Osaka 541
Tel: (03) 220-6000   Fax: (03) 3217-6997

References

Choy, Jon. 1988. Japan's Sogo Shosha: Back to the Future? *JEI Report*, no. 34A, Sept. 2.

Eli, Max. 1990. *Global Strategies of Japanese Trading Corporations*. New York: McGraw-Hill.

Kim, W. Chan. 1986. Global diffusion of the general trading company concept. *Sloan Management Review* 27, 4: 35–43.

Market evolution saps trading house power. *Japan Economic Journal*, Mar. 16, 1991: 14.

Sogo shosha: Sales department of Japan, Inc. *Tokyo Business Today*, Apr. 1986: 50–55.

Sumiya, Fumio. 1993. Trading titans: Agile enough to thrive? *Nikkei Weekly*, July 26: 1.

Yonekawa, Shin'ichi, and Hideki Yoshihara, eds. 1987. *Business History of General Trading Companies*. Tokyo: University of Tokyo Press. Chs. 1–3.

Yoshino, M. Y., and Thomas Lifson. 1986. *The Invisible Link: Japan's Sogo Shosha and the Organization of Trade*. Cambridge: MIT Press.

treasury bill market   One of the short-term money markets open to both financial and nonfinancial institutions, in which short-term government treasury bills are traded to lend and borrow money.

See **money markets**.

trust banks Trust banks are financial institutions that are engaged in both a trust business and banking operations and are required by law to maintain separate trust and banking accounts. In the trust business, they manage various types of assets (money, pension, securities, real estate, etc.) as trustees for their clients. In the banking business, they accept deposits, mainly demand deposits from large corporations and lend for working capital. Lending in the trust accounts is primarily long-term loans for plant and equipment.

There are seven trust banks in Japan—Mitsubishi, Sumitomo, Mitsui, Yasuda, Toyo, Chuo, and Nippon—with a total of 436 branches as of September 1992. Six of them were converted from prewar trust companies in 1948. All seven concentrate on trust business. One **city bank** (Daiwa Bank) and two regional banks (Bank of Ryukyu and Bank of Okinawa) also operate a trust business, but banking operations are their major business area. Several foreign banks are also engaged in the trust business.

In the trust business, arrangements are made under which assets belonging to an individual or a company are placed in the custody of the trustee who, depending on the type of trust, manages them for the benefits of the owner or a third party. There are many types of trusts in Japan, including money trusts, pension trusts, loan trusts, securities investment trusts, employees' property formation benefit trusts, and land trusts. In a land trust the landowner entrusts the land to the trust bank, which raises funds, builds an income-producing structure such as an office building or a shopping mall, finds tenants and manages the building or sells it, and pays the trust owner the earnings from the operation. The trust bank usually receives between 5% and 10% of the rental income. After the contract period—usually 20 years—expires, the property owners get back

Table T.9
Deposits of trust banks (May 31, 1993)

Bank	Deposits (in ¥ trillions)
Mitsubishi Trust and Banking	28.82
Sumitomo Trust and Banking	28.78
Mitsui Trust and Banking	27.36
Yasuda Trust and Banking	22.18
Toyo Trust and Banking	18.47
Chuo Trust and Banking	10.95
Nippon Trust and Banking	3.55
Total	140.10

Source: Federation of Bankers' Association of Japan.

full property rights and rental revenue or trust dividends. Land trusts were popular in the late 1980s because of the real estate inflation.

Table T.9 gives the total deposits (combining banking and trust accounts) of the seven trust banks.

Addresses

Mitsui Trust and Banking
1-1, Nihonbashi-muromachi 2-chome, Chuo-ku, Tokyo
Tel: (03) 3270-9511

Mitsubishi Trust and Banking
4-5, Marunouchi 1-chome, Chiyoda-ku, Tokyo
Tel: (03) 3212-1211

Sumitomo Trust and Banking
5-33, Kitahama 4-chome, Osaka-shi, Osaka
Tel: (06) 220-2121

Yasuda Trust and Banking
2-1, Yaesu 1-chome, Chuo-ku, Tokyo
Tel: (03) 3278-8111

References

Bank of Japan. 1993. *Economic Statistics Annual, 1992.*

Suzuki, Yoshio, ed. 1987. *The Japanese Financial System.* Oxford: Oxford University Press. Ch. 5.

Tatewaki, Kazuo. 1991. *Banking and Finance in Japan.* London: Routledge. Ch. 7.

Trust Fund Bureau   A bureau of the **Ministry of Finance**. Postal savings and public pensions are deposited with the bureau and used in the **Fiscal Investment and Loan Program.**

See **Fiscal Investment and Loan Program.**

tsusansho (tsusan sangyo sho)   The **Ministry of International Trade and Industry** (MITI).

See **Ministry of International Trade and Industry.**

U

underworld "businesses"   Japan has low crime rates by international standards. However, organized crime and its associated underworld "businesses" are present in some sectors of the economy.

Japan's National Police Agency estimates that the nation has a total of 3,490 mobster organizations and 56,600 gang members or *yakuza* at the end of 1992. Their annual income was estimated by the agency to be ¥1.3 trillion in both 1988 and 1989, although observers believe that the actual income was as high as ten times the official figure. The largest source of income was dealing in drugs, accounting for 34.8% of the total income in 1989. In addition the gangsters are active in gambling and bookmaking (16.9%), business-protection (8.7%), mediation of disputes (7.3%), credit collection, violence against companies, prostitution, and so on. All these illegal activities accounted for more than 80% of their income in 1989.

Gangsters are also involved in legitimate businesses such as money lending, construction, and real estate, which accounted for 10% of their total income in 1988 and 19.7% in 1989. However, even in these legitimate businesses, the gangsters resort to shady practices and profit from the power of their gangs. For example, indirectly through their ties with many finance companies, their loan sharking exacts high interest rates from the desperate borrowers, and late payments or defaults are dealt with harshly. The gangsters also control the day-labor market in construction.

Some gangsters have been involved in stock market manipulation with funding from securities firms. In 1991 it was revealed that affiliates of Japan's two leading securities firms, Nomura Securities Co. and Nikko Securities Co., were involved in gangster's speculative stock purchases. The crime syndicates were also compensated by the securities houses for investment losses.

There is a "traditionalist" side to *yakuza* that is said to appeal to some nostalgic Japanese. Japanese gangs are highly organized, and the gangsters are said to have a moral code of their own with extraordinary emphasis on seniority and loyalty, which evokes the ancient *samurai* (warrior) tradition.

Another type of unethical "business," uniquely Japanese, is practiced by extortionists who are usually tied to the gangsters. Called *sokaiya*, these extortionists are self-styled shareholders'-rights advocates who exhort money from companies by threatening to disrupt shareholders' meetings by revealing company's internal scandals. They buy a minimum amount of a company's shares to get into shareholders' meetings. Once paid off by the companies, however, they intimidate other shareholders instead. In their peak in the 1970s, *sokaiya* were paid more than ¥10 billion annually. The revision of the Commercial Law in 1982 made such payments illegal and drove *sokaiya* underground. In their efforts to minimize possible disruption by these exhortionists, many companies hold their annual shareholder meetings on the same day and try to speed up meeting proceedings. Some companies reportedly finish their meetings in less than 30 minutes!

A new law became effective in March 1992 that will enable Japanese police to deal with the crime syndicates more effectively. The syndicates may face prosecution if they are found to have engaged in any of 11 types of racketeering.

See also **business ethics**.

Address

National Police Agency
1-2, Kasumigaseki 2-chome, Chiyoda-ku, Tokyo 100
Tel: (03) 3581-0141

References

Corporate courage needed to fight "Mafia capitalism." *Nikkei Weekly*, July 13, 1991: 6.

Hirao, Sachiko. 1991. Despite new law, *yakuza* groups find way into firms, capital. *Japan Times*, May 20–26: 8.

Idei, Yas. 1991. Corporate chiefs ready to face strong-arm *sokaiya*. *Japan Economic Journal*, May 4: 6.

Itoh, Yoshiaki. 1993. Anti-gang law wracks mob ranks. *Nikkei Weekly*, Mar. 22: 1, 23.

Japan's gangsters: Honourable mob. *The Economist*, Jan. 27, 1990: 19–22.

Kanabayashi, Masayoshi, and Marcus W. Brauchli. 1991. Japanese gangsters' expanding role in the economy worries law-enforcement, government officials. *Asian Wall Street Journal Weekly*, June 10: 11.

Kaplan, David E., and Alec Dubro. 1986. *Yakuza*. Reading, MA: Addison-Wesley.

unemployment   Unemployed persons in Japan are defined as those who have no jobs, do not do any work, but are able and willing to work and have made efforts to find a job. Unemployment as a ratio of the labor force in postwar Japan has been consistently much lower than that in other industrialized countries. Table U.1 shows the unemployment rate in Japan, the United States, Germany and Britain in selective years.

The official unemployment statistics require some qualification, however. The figures for Japan understate the real extent of unemployment because workers temporarily released from work by companies with partial pay during a recession are not included in the statistics; yet these workers are not really working, although they are not laid off in the Western sense. In addition many "discouraged," disabled persons are not actively seeking work because of the discrimination against them and the great difficulties they encounter in getting to the workplace. Similarly unemployment figures for the United States do not include many "discouraged" workers

Table U.1
International comparison of unemployment rates (in %)

Year	Japan	United States	Germany, F.R.	Britain
1975	1.9 (1.0)[a]	8.3	4.7	4.1
1980	2.0 (1.1)	7.0	3.8	3.8
1985	2.6 (1.6)	7.1	9.3	11.9
1988	2.5 (1.6)	5.4	8.7	5.4
1989	2.3 (1.4)	5.2	7.9	6.3
1990	2.1 (1.3)	5.5	7.2	5.9
1991	2.1 (1.4)	6.7	6.3	8.1

Source: International Labor Organization.
a. The number in parentheses indicates the number of unemployed in millions.

Table U.2
Unemployment rate by age and sex (in %)

Age	1980		1991	
	Male	Female	Male	Female
All ages	2.0	2.0	2.0	2.2
15–24	4.0	3.2	4.7	4.2
25–39	1.7	2.5	1.6	2.9
40–54	1.3	1.3	1.1	1.5
55+	3.4	0.9	2.5	1.2

Source: Management and Coordination Agency.

who do not bother to look for work because of the futility of such attempts. Nevertheless, it is clear that real Japanese unemployment has been lower than that of other countries.

Table U.2 gives the unemployment rate by age and sex. It can be seen that the unemployment rate of males aged 15–24 is double that of the national rate; it is also high for females of that age group. The rate for males aged 55 and over is also relatively high but is surprisingly low for their female counterparts. Presumably older women who have to work are willing to do low-paying menial work such as cleaning and vending that are shunned by younger workers.

Unemployed persons receive unemployment benefits if they have been covered by **employment insurance**. The amount and duration of benefits depend on the wage level while employed, age (longer for older unemployed), the period of employment insurance, and the nature of employment status (regular, part-time, or seasonal).

See also **employment discrimination, employment insurance**.

References

Institute of Labor. 1992. *Japanese Working Life Profile, 1991–92.*

International Labor Organization. *Bulletin of Labor Statistics.* Various years.

Management and Coordination Agency. Annual. *Labor Force Survey.*

unemployment insurance
See **employment insurance**.

universities
See **economic/business research and publications, education system**.

Uruguay Round   Started in September 1986, this is the eighth round of multilateral trade negotiations conducted under the auspices of the General Agreement on Tariffs and Trade (GATT). World agricultural trade liberalization was one of the main issues. It exerted pressure on Japan to lift the rice import ban and replace it with tarrifs on rice imports.

See also **rice production and distribution, trade policy**.

V

venture capital industry Japan's entrepreneurs or start-up companies face a number of obstacles to growth. One of them is the small size of the venture capital industry. The others, which stem from the structure of the economy, are the dominance of large established corporations in R&D spending and in manufacturing expertise; the complicated distribution network that favors brand names and personal contacts; the prestige and traditional **lifetime employment** system of large companies, and the growing labor shortage that make it difficult for small businesses to recruit experienced managers and workers. These structural factors increase the risks of start-up venture companies and hence reduce the willingness of venture capitalists to invest in them.

There are two sources of funds to finance new business ventures independent of affiliation with an established large company. The first and relatively minor source is the three semipublic small business development companies jointly established by the government (the Small Business Finance Corporation) and the private sector. These companies are Tokyo Small Business Development Co., Osaka Small Business Development Co., and Nagoya Small Business Development Co. They provide **investment** consultation and may subscribe to the newly issued stocks of qualified small businesses. However, their funds are very limited.

Private venture capital companies constitute the second and a larger source of funds. There were 100 such companies in 1990, established and funded by banks, **securities companies**, and **insurance companies**. The largest by far of these is Japan Associated Finance Co., founded by Nomura Securities Co. in 1973. The second largest is Nippon Investment Finance Co., founded by Daiwa Securities Co. in 1982. In 1982–85, following the computarization of Japanese businesses and homes and the development of new high-technology industries, these venture capital companies were active in financing innovative start-up firms. However, many of the new high-tech firms failed in 1985–87, causing losses to the venture capitalists. Consequently venture capital companies have scaled down their investments and shifted their loans to the service sector, since the Japanese economy itself is becoming more service oriented. In addition some of the venture capital companies have invested in the newly industrializing economies of East Asia, particularly Hong Kong and Taiwan with their numerous small and innovative companies.

In the late 1980s and early 1990s Japan's venture capital industry underwent a period of new growth. Their number increased from 80 at the end of 1985 to 100 in mid-1990. One favorable factor was the development of the **over-the-counter** (OTC) **market**. Following the liberalization of the OTC market rules such as the public offering of shares, more medium-sized companies became interested in listing their shares on the market. Japanese investors saw growth potential in some of these companies. As a result the OTC market grew rapidly in the late 1980s and early 1990s, and its trading volume was not affected by the fall in the **Tokyo Stock Exchange** in 1990. Since venture capital companies assist unlisted firms for public offering of their shares in the OTC market, they have stepped up their business operations. At a time when the separation between the securities business and the banking business is being reduced by **financial liberalization**, both securities companies and banks are safeguarding their future businesses by various means, including the promotion of the venture capital business of their subsidiaries.

Because Japan's venture capital companies are set up by securities companies and banks, they have been criticized by analysts for favoring low-risk, established mid-sized businesses over developing firms, and for striving to develop new clients for their parent company's main business rather than to promote innovative venture businesses. It is even said that there is no true venture capital industry in Japan.

See also **over-the-counter market**.

References

Borton, James W. 1991. *Venture Japan: How Growing companies Worldwide Can Tap into the Japanese Venture Capital Markets.* Chicago: Probus.

Choy, Jon. 1988. Update on Japan's venture capital industry: Problems and promises. *JEI Report*, July 29.

Clark, Rodney. 1987. *Venture Capital in Britain, America and Japan.* London: Croom Helm. Ch. 3.

Ikegami, Teruhiko. 1990. Rivals challenge industry giant JAFCO. *Japan Economic Journal*, July 28: 27.

Suzuki, Yoshio, ed. 1987. *The Japanese Financial System*. Oxford: Oxford University Press. Pp. 254–56.

Venture capital business finally emerging. *Japan Economic Journal*, July 21, 1990: 22.

VLSI Research Cooperative Very Large-Scale Integrated Circuit Research Cooperative, a government-guided research cooperative of five major computer companies between 1976 and 1980.

See **electronics industry, industry policy.**

voluntary export restraint (VER) Requests made by Washington to Tokyo, and also to some newly industrializing economies, to "voluntarily" restrict exports of certain products (textiles, automobiles, machine tools, steel, etc.) for a certain period of time to prevent sharp increases in these imports.

See **automobile industry, trade policy.**

W

wage structure The wages an employee receives in Japan depend on several factors—age, sex, education, job status, nature of industry, size of establishment, and so on. These factors affect both the starting wage level and subsequent annual wage increases; they affect both the regular monthly contractual wages and the biannual bonuses.

Most Japanese employees are recruited right after graduation from high school, junior college, or university, and work continually for one company until retirement or for a substantial number of years. These are the standard or regular employees who are the concern of most government statistics and who receive much more wages and benefits than nonregular employees.

Standard employees' starting wages are determined by the educational level and sex. High school graduates are usually the production workers; university graduates are the candidates for managerial positions. Female graduates are recruited for clerical-track positions, whereas male graduates are recruited for career-track positions. In subsequent years wages will increase every year with age or seniority. This is the *nenko*, or seniority-based, wage system which still prevails in most companies, although in some companies it is modified or outweighed by merit or performance. However, the annual increase will be different for different workers, depending on sex, education, job status, and so forth. The **spring offensive** is the ritualized procedure through which unions launch their demand for annual wage increases for negotiation with employers.

Employees' wage earnings include the monthly contractual wages and biannual bonuses, given in June–July and December, that are based on company profits. Individual employee's bonuses also vary with seniority, education, and job status.

Table W.1 shows the average contractual earnings of standard employees by age and sex. It shows that at age 50–54, female employee's wages

Table W.1
Contractual earnings of standard employees by age and sex (in ¥1,000 per month; June 1990)

Age	Years of service	Contractual earnings		Female/male ratio (%)
		Female	Male	
18–19	0	131	143	915
20–24	3–4	155	174	89.2
25–29	5–9	180	219	82.5
30–34	10–14	210	269	78.1
35–39	15–19	236	323	73.2
40–44	20–24	258	369	70.0
45–49	25–29	300	421	71.1
50–54	30–	318	443	71.8

Source: Ministry of Labor.
Note: Included are companies with 1,000 employees or more.

Table W.2
Earnings of standard employees by age and education (male, 1990 in ¥1,000)

Age	Senior high school graduates		University graduates	
	Wages/month	Bonuses/year	Wages/month	Bonuses/year
18	151.6	11.7	—	—
22	184.0	754.0	188.8	34.0
30	255.5	1,161.2	276.2	1,391.6
40	355.7	1,905.1	435.5	2,459.1
50	493.4	2,661.9	599.4	3,737.7
53	521.8	2,894.1	645.3	4,219.4
60	352.9	2,130.1	616.7	2,547.6

Source: Ministry of Labor.

in 1990 were 2.4 times those of 18- to 19-year-old females. For males the ratio was 3.1 times. It also shows that, at the same age and with the same seniority, a man always makes more than a woman. Furthermore the differentials between male and female earnings increase with age due to limited opportunities for promotion for most women in their clerical-track positions.

The role of education as well as age can be seen in table W.2. In 1991 an average male high school graduate starting work at age 18 made ¥151,600 a month with small bonuses. A university graduate starting work at age 22 made about the same amount as a high school graduate with 4 years of seniority, but with less bonuses. Two years later (not shown in table W.2),

Table W.3
Indexes of employee earnings by sector (1990 = 100; standard employees)

	1980	1985	1991
All industries	70.4	84.6	100.3
Mining	72.1	87.2	104.5
Construction	63.1	77.8	103.4
Manufacturing	68.4	83.3	100.3
Transport and communication	68.6	82.8	103.1
Wholesale and retail trade	75.4	85.2	103.8
Finance and insurance	67.2	87.6	101.4
Real Estate	62.8	74.8	100.0
Services	74.8	88.1	103.6

Source: Ministry of Labor,

the university graduate would earn more salary and bonuses as well. Because the high school graduate is likely to be a production worker and the university graduate a management-track candidate, the differences in regular wages and bonuses continued to widen with the increase in ages. At age 53 the earnings of both reach their peak. At age 60 both persons are likely to have retired from the original company and are working at a subsidiary at reduced pay. The university-educated executive continued to draw high pay but reduced bonuses. It should be added that graduates of two-year junior colleges are likely to earn significantly less than university graduates because the former are predominantly women in clerical positions.

An employee's earnings are affected by his (her) position or job status, although this is correlated with age and education. For example, in 1991, a company director made an average of ¥592,800 in monthly regular salary and ¥3,270,300 in annual bonuses; a section chief made ¥475,700 and ¥2,547,400, and a chief clerk ¥403,500 and ¥1,802,600 for monthly regular wages and annual bonuses, respectively.

Finally, employee earnings vary from industry to industry. The ranking of industries in their employee earnings also changes over time, reflecting structural changes of the economy and of the labor market. Table W.3 shows the indexes of earnings (contractual earnings plus bonuses) of standard or regular employees in various sectors. It can be seen that wholesale and retail trade and services have remained high-paying sectors between 1980 and 1991. On the other hand, construction was low paying in 1980 but had become a high-paying sector by 1991. It should be added that the earnings of nonregular employees are much lower and are not included in the statistics.

Analytically some economists have debated the nature of bonuses of Japanese companies. Freeman and Weitzman (1987) regard them as profit sharing and hence a source of wage flexibility for companies. Others regard them as relatively rigid or as deferred wage payment (cited in Aoki, 1988: 176–78). The debate is inconclusive.

See also **minimum wages**.

References

Aoki, Masahiko. 1988. *Information, Incentives, and Bargaining in the Japanese Economy.* Cambridge: Cambridge University Press.

Freedman, R., and M. Weitzman. 1987. Bonuses and employment in Japan. *Journal of the Japanese and International Economies,* 1: 168–94.

Institute of Labor. 1992. *Japanese Working Life Profile, 1991–92.*

Management and Coordination Agency. Annual. *Labour Force Survey.*

Ministry of Labor. Annual. *Basic Survey on Wage Structure.*

warrant bonds　Also referred to as *equity-warrant bonds,* these are a special type of corporate bond with equity warrants attached to them to lower the interest cost of corporate borrowing. The warrants are certificates that give investors the right to buy a fixed amount of new shares of the issuing company at a predetermined price (called *exercise price*) for a relatively long period such as four years. If the stock price goes up during that period, investors can buy the shares at the lower exercise price, thereby making a profit. In return for this option, investors accept a lower interest rate on the bond. Warrants can also be detached from the bonds by the securities firm that underwrite them and traded on the secondary market. In 1990 their value was said to be about 20% of the face value of the warrant bond issued by Japanese corporations on the Euromarket. Thus if the equity-purchase warrants are not exercised because of falling stock prices, investors stand to lose this amount.

Warrant bonds can be denominated in yen or in a foreign currency, mostly the dollar or Swiss franc. The Eurodollar warrant bond is traded in the Euromarket, primarily London. First introduced in 1981, the volume of Eurodollar bonds issued by Japanese corporations on the Euromarket grew rapidly in the late 1980s. In 1986, when domestic sales of warrants were first permitted in Japan, Japanese companies floated $9 billion worth of Eurodollar bonds with warrants attached. In 1988 the total volume was $14.7 billion. In the first nine months of 1989, it was over $50 billion.

Eurodollar warrant bonds appealed to Japanese corporate borrowers be-cause they offer a relatively low-cost way of raising money under largely unregulated conditions. They were also popular with Japanese investors as a way to particiapte in the domestic equity market because of booming stock prices. In the late 1980s most (70–80% in 1989) of the bonds issued by Japanese borrowers on the Euromarket were bought by Japanese inves-tors, mostly institutions. However, with the slump in Japan's stock prices since 1990, the market dwindled; many warrants expired unexercised and became worthless. Some major **securities companies** reportedly have repurchased equity warrants near expiration to cover the losses of their major clients.

Domestic offering of warrant bonds of the detachable type began in December 1985. However, the offerings dwindled to zero in fiscal year 1987 and 1988 and then rose to ¥915 billion in 1989. They were ¥395 billion and ¥382 billion in FY 1990 and 1991.

Japan's Big Four securities firms—Nomura, Daiwa, Nikko, and Yamaichi Securities—dominate the underwriting of these bonds issued by Japanese corporations on the Euromarket. The share of foreign securities firms is very small, although they serve as the leading comanagers of Eurobonds. The Big Four also dominate the secondary market for interbank warrant trading in Tokyo. One reason given by Japanese executives for preferring the Big Four to underwrite their warrant bond issues is that the latter's influence in Tokyo helps prevent stock prices from plunging when shares are sold after investors exercise their warrant to buy company stock.

Eurodollar warrants are high-return securities detached from the Euro-dollar warrant bonds. Securities houses bring about 80% of them into Japan to sell mostly to individual investors. Warrants are not listed on the **Tokyo Stock Exchange**; they are traded over the counter to small investors. They are high-risk securities because there is little public information on the financial conditions of most of the companies that issue the warrant bonds. In addition prices for the same warrant can vary greatly from dealer to dealer because there is no system linking over-the-counter brokers. Finally, their prices fluctuate much more than stock prices.

See also **bond market**.

References

Bubble's burst deflates market for convertibles, warrant bonds. *Japan Economic Journal*, winter suppl., 1990: 6–8.

Japan's equity-warrant bonanza. *The Economist*, Dec. 9, 1989: 85.

Senner, Madis. 1989. *Japanese Euroderivatives*. London: Euromoney Publications.

Shida, Tomio. 1989. Big Four tighten grip on Eurobond market. *Japan Economic Journal*, July 29: 2.

welfare programs
See **social security system**.

wholesale trade
See **distribution system**.

wholesale price index
See **price indexes, and price levels**.

window guidance   Guidelines given by the Bank of Japan to commercial banks concerning the appropriate levels of their loans. It was officially discontinued in June 1991.
    See **Bank of Japan**.

women in the labor force   Despite the constitutional guarantee of sexual equality (Article 14), the equal pay provisions of the Labor Standards Law, and the ratification of the **Equal Employment Opportunity Law** in 1986, Japanese women still lag behind their male counterparts in employment, wages, and promotion opportunities. Nevertheless, women's participation in the **labor force** has increased, and the number of management positions held by women has increased over the years, although the rate of increase is relatively slow.
    Of Japan's labor force, women constituted 31.8% in 1965, 34.1% in 1980, and 39.9% in 1990. This steady increase is due in part to the growing labor shortage in the economy, particularly in the 1980s. Yet the bulk of the female workers are concentrated in low-paying clerical jobs that require little training. For example, in 1990 34.4% of female employees were clerical and related workers, 20.6% were craftswomen and production workers, and 12.5% were sales workers; only 13.8% were professional and technical workers. In addition a large percentage of female workers are part-time employees who work 35 hours or less a week with low pay and few benefits. These part-timers as a percentage of total female employees have increased from 12.2% in 1970 to 19.3% in 1980 and 27.3% in 1990. They tend to work in the wholesale and retail trade (34.2% in 1990) and other services (28.5%) in predominantly small-scale establishments with 1–29 employees.

Traditional family values, still strong in Japan, give women the primary responsibility for childcare and housework. In addition, day-care facilities are far from adequate for working women with young children. As a result women tend to interrupt their careers for marriage and child rearing after five to 10 years of working. This reduces the average female employee's seniority as well as the employer's willingness to invest money in training female workers. In 1990 the average years of employee service was 7.3 years for women as compared with 12.4 years for men. After 10–15 years of absence from the labor market, a woman may return to work, but usually she has to restart at a low pay and often as a part-time worker. The part-time employment status gives her the flexibility needed to continue her role as the homemaker.

Given all these cultural, social, and economic factors, it is not surprising that few Japanese women hold management positions. A survey shows that in 1989 only 1.29% of managers were women. Another survey, conducted in 1986, shows that only 23% of the respondents were willing to work for a woman. A poll taken in 1991 by *Nihon Keizai Shimbun*, Japan's leading business newspaper, shows that 78% of women who hold management positions are either section chiefs or deputy section chiefs, the lowest of managerial positions.

Women's earnings lag behind those of men with the same seniority, not only because they start up with a lower base pay but also because their salary increases are slower—they have less opportunities for promotion in their predominantly female clerical track as compared with the male-dominated general track from which management candidates are selected. As a result women's earnings as a percentage of those of men of the same age decline with age. For example, according to the Ministry of Labor's survey statistics for June 1990, the average contractual earnings of standard female employees aged 18–19 were 91.7% of those of male employees of the same age. The ratio declined to 78.1% at age 30–34, and 71.1% at age 45–49 (see table W.1, **wage structure**). Similarly as of June 1991, a 20-year-old regular female production worker with senior high school education received 94% of the contractual wages of her male counterpart. The ratio declined to 77% at age 30 and 68% at age 50. Note that the figures are for regular employees who were hired immediately after graduation and who have worked continually for the same enterprise. For women who interrupted their career to raise children before returning to work, their earnings would be much less than those given for their ages.

In a large scale five-nation survey of working women conducted in June 1990 by *Nikkei Woman*, a Nihon Keizai Shimbun, Inc., publication, it was found that one-third of the Japanese women surveyed voiced disatisfaction with their jobs, compared with 14–16% in the other four countries (United States, Germany, Australia, and Brazil). Only 32% said that they found their work interesting and fulfilling.

Interestingly, an increasing number of Western companies with offices in Japan, unencumbered by the heavy weight of tradition, are hiring more educated Japanese women, especially those who have studied in the West, for managerial positions. Reflecting on this trend, Lansing and Ready (1988) have argued that this makes good business sense for foreign employers while contributing to worthy social changes in Japan.

In the future the role of women in the labor force is likely to increase further, partly because of the aging of the labor force and the labor shortage. The continuing diversification of the Japanese economy, including the growing importance of the service sector, will also provide new job opportunities for women.

See also **employment pattern, Equal Employment Opportunity Law, labor force, labor laws, wage structure**.

Address

Women's Bureau, Ministry of Labor
2-2, Kasumigaseki 1-chome, Chiyoda-ku, Tokyo 100
Tel: (03) 3593-1211

References

Hill, M. Ann. 1990. Women in the Japanese labor force. In *Japan's Economic Challenge.* Washington: Government Printing Office.

Japan Institute of Labor. 1990. *Women Workers in Japan.* Tokyo.

Lansing, Paul, and Kathryn Ready. 1988. Hiring women managers in Japan: An alternative for foreign employers. *California Management Review* 30, 3: 112–27.

Lo, Jeannie. 1990. *Office Ladies, Factory Women: Life and Work at a Japanese Company.* Armonk, NY; M.E. Sharpe, Inc.

Maki, Omori. 1993. Gender and the labor market. *Journal of Japanese Studies* 19, 1, winter: 79–102.

Ministry of Labor. 1989. *White Paper on Women Workers.*

Murdo, Pat. 1991. Women in Japan's work world see slow change from labor shortage, Equal Employment Law. *JEI Report,* no. 33A, Aug. 30.

Prime Minister's Office. 1990. *Japanese Women Today.*

Saso, Mary. 1990. *Women in the Japanese Workplace.* London: Hilary Shipman.

working hours and stress   Japanese workers work more hours per year than those in other industrial countries. According to the Ministry of Labor, Japanese workers averaged 2,159 hours on the job in 1990, about 170 hours more than the average for Americans and the British and 500 hours more than that for Germans and the French. The Japanese regular workweek was 48 hours over 6 days until April 1989 when the Labor Standard Law was revised to cut statutory working hours from 48 to 46 hours.

Long working hours in Japan have led to the Western criticism that the Japanese overwork and underconsume, thereby contributing to Japan's trade imbalance. Many Japanese, especially government officials, have taken the criticism seriously and have tried to do something about it. As early as 1984 the government proposed to cut the workweek to 45 hours over 5 days and to increase paid holidays from 6 days to 10 days a year. In 1987 it suggested that the country adopt a twice-monthly five-day workweek system; the other two weeks would still have five and half days. In 1988 it proposed that that the country have a five-day 40-hour workweek or 1,800-hour workyear by March 1993. By 1992 it is commonly accepted in Japan that to be truly modern and affluent, Japanese citizens must have the time as well as the means to enjoy the fruits of their labor. Starting on May 2, 1992, about 500,000 national government employees work five days a week.

The actual pace of reduction in working hours in the private sector, however, has been far short of these proposals and it varies greatly among industries. Financial institutions first started closing one Saturday each month in August 1983. In August 1986 they started closing two Saturdays each month. Beginning in January 1989, banks and stock exchanges are closed on Saturdays; government offices are closed two Saturdays a month. According to the Ministry of Labor's survey of firms with 30 or more regular workers, the number of hours worked per month averaged 186.6 in 1970, 175.7 in 1980, 175.8 in 1985, 174.0 in 1989, and 171.0 in 1990. Finance and insurance have the shortest working hours (148.4 hours per month in 1990), while mining, construction, transportation, and communication have the longest (over 185 hours per month in 1990).

Long working hours, however, do not necessarily mean high labor productivity per hour worked; on the contrary, they may lower it. For example, observers have noted that some Japanese office workers may put in long hours but may also spend much time reading newspapers or have little to do. Studies by the Ministry of Labor and several scholars including Jorgenson and Kuroda (1990) indicate that labor productivity (output per working hour) is lower in Japan than in several other industrialized countries, particularly the United States, although the gap has been narrowing.

The causes of continuing long working hours in Japan are said to be both cultural and economic. Culturally, Sullivan (1992) argues, the Japanese regard hard work as an end in itself, something expected of all good, moral citizens, and workers strive to live up to that expectation. In contrast, Americans are said to regard work as a means to life's other goals, including more leisure. Seward and Van Zandt (1985) postulate that the Japanese work ethic is rooted in Japan's Zen Buddism that exhorts hard work. This is reminiscent of Berger (1986) who views the postwar economic success of East Asian capitalism in terms of secularized Buddism and Confucianism.

Economically, various analysts have attributed the continuing long working hours in the 1980s mostly to the continued economic expansion, the growing labor shortage, and the high **housing** costs of the late 1980s. Despite their high incomes Japanese workers have to work long hours, including overtime, to pay for high housing loans and to save for retirement. **Labor unions** were intially against the proposed work-hour reduction for fear of pay cuts. They changed their positions, however, by the late 1980s. In 1991 and 1992 the Japan Trade Union Confederation (Rengo) included reduction in working hours as part of its **spring offensive** (*shunto*) wage bargaining demands. It has also announced the target of cutting annual work hours to 1800 by March 1994. As to employers, although many of them would like to cut overtime labor cost, many small labor-intensive companies were reluctant or unable to do so because they could not afford automation and also feared that competitors would not cut hours.

Official statistics on working hours do not include the unpaid overtime worked by employees at many companies, particularly the banks. Nor do they reflect the stress that comes from such long working hours and other corporate demands that employees are obligated to comply with as part of the socially expected "work ethic." There is a special term, *karoshi*, that means literally death from overwork. The word has become part of the Japanese common vocabulary since the early 1980s, suggesting a widespread awareness of the phenomenon. Although the phenomenon is not unique to the Japanese, it is believed to be more prevalent among Japanese employees than among their counterparts elsewhere. Reliable statistics are lacking, however, because companies invariably deny its existence in order to avoid bad publicity and the legal and financial implications.

One particularly stressful demand of corporate life is related to job transfers to other cities for male office workers, often without the family accompaning them, lest the children's schooling for competitive examinations be disrupted. Because of all of these, many male office workers are said to suffer from alienation from their own families. Okifuji's (1990) portrayal of "men who can't go home" is a poignant reminder of the high human toll of the exacting corporate life in Japan, of which long working hours are merely one manifestation.

See also **wage structure**.

References

Berger, Peter. 1986. *The Capitalist Revolution*. New York: Basic Books.

Daimon, Sayuri. 1991. "Karoshi" phenonmenon spreading to female work force. *Japan Times* (weekly international ed.), Sept. 3–Oct. 6: 7.

Jorgenson, Dale W., and Masahiro Kuroda. 1990. Productivity and international competitiveness in Japan and the United States, 1960-1985. In *Productivity in the U.S. and Japan*, ed. by C. R. Hulten. Chicago: University of Chicago Press.

Ministry of Labor. Annual. *Yearbook of Labor Statistics*.

National Defense Counsel for Victims of Karoshi. 1990. *Karoshi: When the "Corporate Warrior" Dies*. Tokyo: Madosha.

Okifuji, Noriko. 1990. Men who can't go home. *Japan Echo* 17, special issue: 48–52.

Saito, Tadashi. 1992. Quality of life in Japan: Is it affluent or not? *JEI Report*, no. 22A, June 12.

Seward, Jack, and Howard Van Zandt. 1985. *Japan: The Hungary Guest—Japanese Business Ethics vs. Those of the U.S.* Tokyo: Lotus Press. Ch. 5.

Sullivan, Jeremiah. 1992. Japanese management philosophies: From the vacuous to the brilliant. *California Management Review* 34, 2 (winter): 66–87.

Takahashi, Hideo. 1990. The long workweek in Japan: Difficult to reduce. *JEI Report*, Mar. 16.

Y

yakuza   Japan's gangsters or members of organized-crime syndicate.
See **underworld "businesses."**

yen-denominated foreign bonds   Bonds issued in Japan in yen by nonresident institutions such as international agencies, foreign governments, and foreign private corporations. Popularly called *samurai* **bonds**.
See *samurai* **bonds**.

yen–dollar currency futures   Contracts to trade yen and dollars at a given exchange rate on a specific future date.
See **financial futures market**.

yen–dollar exchange rates   The yen–dollar exchange rate, the most important of the yen's exchange rates against major foreign currencies, has changed substantially in the postwar era. Government intervention in the value of the yen against the dollar has generally been passive since the end of the fixed exchange rate system in 1973. It is neither a policy of free floating exchange rate nor that of complete manipulation.

The exchange rate was first fixed by the American Occupation authorities in 1949 at 360 yen to the dollar. It remained unchanged until 1971 when it was changed to 308 yen. However, these rates are the "basic rates" set by the **Ministry of Finance**. In the Tokyo foreign exchange market there are other types of yen–dollar exchange rates that better reflect the supply and demand conditions for the dollar and that can differ substantially from the basic rates. The first is the interbank rate, the rate at which dollar is traded between banks for spot exchanges (spot rate) or for forward exchanges (forward rate). It accounts for the bulk of the foreign exchange transactions. The second is the customer's rate, which includes TT (telegraphic transfer) selling and buying rates for spot and forward exchange transactions between banks and customers. Prior to September 1990 there were also the foreign exchange banks' TT buying and selling rates for transactions between foreign exchange banks. Table Y.1 gives the monthly closing average of interbank spot rate along with the lowest and highest rate per dollar of the year.

In early 1973, with the "dollar crisis," Japan abandoned the system of fixed exchange rates and allowed the yen to float. The yen appreciated in 1970–73 as it first emerged as a major international currency. In 1974–75 it fell to around 300 against the dollar because of the first oil crisis. It appreciated again in 1975–78 as the Japanese economy recovered from the oil crisis. However, Japan's trade deficit in 1979 because of the second oil crisis caused the yen to decline in 1979 and early 1980.

Between 1981 and 1984 the yen generally fell because of the increase in Japanese capital outflow due to high interest rates in the United States and the liberalization of foreign exchange laws in Japan in December 1980. Then it rose rapidly in value from about 250 yen to the dollar in 1984 to slightly above 200 yen in 1985 and 128 yen per dollar in 1987. The rise was precipitated by the Plaza Accord of September 1985 in which the finance ministers of five major industrial countries agreed to cooperate by market intervention to ensure a gradual depreciation of the dollar. The yen

Table Y.1
Yen–dollar exchange rates (interbank spot rate in ¥ per $, monthly closing average)

	Interbank rate	Lowest	Highest
1970	357.65	357.40	359.84
1975	305.15	284.90	307.00
1980	203.00	202.95	264.00
1981	219.90	198.70	247.40
1982	242.49	217.70	278.50
1983	234.34	227.20	247.80
1984	247.96	220.00	251.70
1985	202.75	199.80	263.65
1986	162.13	152.55	203.30
1987	128.25	121.85	159.20
1988	123.63	120.45	136.80
1989	143.62	123.80	151.35
1990	133.72	130.30	137.10
1991	128.07	125.10	130.15
1992	126.62	—	—

Source: Bank of Japan.

reached a historical high of 120.45 yen to the dollar on January 4, 1988. It then fell and fluctuated between the 125–150 range during 1989–91 before it rose to between 125 and 130 yen per dollar in the first half of 1992.

Yen appreciation is called *endaka* in Japan. The *endaka* after 1985 created one of the most severe recessions in Japan, commonly referred to as the **yen shock**. The **steel industry** was among the most severely affected industries.

The strong yen has also affected Japan's trade with the United States and other countries. The nature and extent of the effect, however, is a matter of debate by analysts. Some believe that *endaka* has made Japan more open to the other Asian economies and has promoted division of labor and integration in Asia, creating an emerging "yen block" (*The Economist*, July 15, 1989). Corker (1989) estimates that, by late 1987, Japan had exported 19% less and imported 10% more than what it would have done without the yen appreciation since 1985. Corker (1991: 9) further concludes that Japanese trade flows have responded "in a remarkably flexible way to the economic environment of the late 1980s."

Because a substantial trade imbalance between Japan and the United States remained in the late 1980s, other analysts have either criticized the inappropriateness of using exchange rate adjustment to solve the imbalance or criticized Japan's economic structure and corporate behavior in limiting the improvement in the Japan–U.S. imbalance. In the first approach, some Japanese commentators have suggested that the yen–dollar exchange rate may have to go as low as 100 yen to the dollar before the Japan–U.S. trade imbalance can be eliminated, and that rate would have grave consequences for the Japanese economy. Even at the rate of about 128 yen to the dollar in 1987, McKinnon (1987) considered the yen to be grossly overvalued, thereby imposing undue deflationary pressure on Japan and leading to growing demand for protection to insulate domestic markets from the unpredictable fluctuations in the international economy. An exchange rate below that would drive the two currencies farther away from purchasing-power parity (i.e., the rate at which a dollar would buy the same basket of goods and service in the United States as a dollar's equivalent in yen would buy in Japan). McKinnon argues that what is needed is not yen appreciation but macroeconomic adjustment in the United States such as reducing the fiscal deficit. Similarly Komiya and Irie (1990) prescribe macroeconomic adjustments in the United States to solve the trade imbalance because they regard U.S. budget deficits and the low saving rate to be the root cause of U.S. trade deficit.

The second approach concentrates on Japan's structural factors and corporate behavior in explaining the presumed limited efficacy of yen appreciation in reducing trade imbalance. For example, some analysts have argued that yen appreciation has not raised Japanese export prices proportionally for the following reasons: (1) It has spurred cost cutting in export industries. (2) The cost of material imports declines with a stronger yen or a cheaper dollar. (3) Some manufacturers have reduced export prices relative to domestic prices (Marston 1991). (4) It has stimulated Japanese manufacturers' **direct overseas investment** and production.

On the effect of yen appreciation on Japanese imports, Petri (1991) contends that the effect has been dampened by the structural factors of the Japanese market such as the high distribution margins and the preference of Japanese businesses and government to buy from other Japanese suppliers. The same focus on the structural factors of the Japanese economy as the cause of trade imbalance underlied the U.S.–Japan **Structural Impediments Initiative** talks in which Washington requested Japanese reforms in many structural aspects of the economy such as the **distribution system**, *keiretsu* groups and "excessive" saving because they are believed to have impeded imports into Japan.

See also **Structural Impediments Initiative, trade policy, yen shock**.

References

Corker, Robert. 1989. External adjustment and the strong yen: Recent Japanese experience. *International Monetary Fund Staff Papers* 36, 2: 464–93.

Corker, Robert. 1991. The changing nature of Japanese trade. *Finance and Development*, June: 6–9.

Hamada, Koichi and Hugh T. Patrick. 1988. Japan and the international monetary regime. In *The Political Economy of Japan*, vol. 2: *The Changing International Context*, ed. by T. Inoguchi and Daniel Okimoto. Stanford: Stanford University Press.

Komiya, Ryutaro, and Kazutomoto Irie. 1990. The U.S.–Japan trade problem: An economic analysis from a Japanese viewpoint. In *Japan's Economic Structure: Should It Change?* ed. by Kozo Yamamura. Seattle: Society for Japanese Studies.

Komiya, Ryutaro, and Miyako Suda. 1991. *Japan's Foreign Exchange Policy: 1971–1982*. North Sydney: Allen and Unwin.

Marston, Richard C. 1991. Price behavior in Japanese and U.S. Manufacturing. In *Trade with Japan*, ed. by Paul Krugman. Chicago: University of Chicago Press.

McKinnon, Ronald I. 1987. Currency protectionism: Parity lost. *Wall Street Journal*, Feb. 2.

Petri, Peter A. 1991. Market structure, comparative advantage, and Japanese trade under the strong yen. In *Trade with Japan*, ed. by Paul Krugman. Chicago: University of Chicago Press.

yen in international transactions   The role of the yen in international trade and finance is relatively small compared with that of the U.S. dollar and German mark. It was used in only 39.4% of Japan's exports and 15.6% of its imports in 1991. In 1980 only 29.4% of exports and 2.4% of imports were in yen. Only 9.1% of the official holdings of foreign exchange of all countries was in the yen in 1990, compared with 56.4% for the dollar and 19.7% for the German mark. The figure in 1980 was 4.4% for yen, 68.6% for dollar, and 14.9% for German mark.

The factors that would promote the international use of the yen are (1) Japan's sizable share of world exports, (2) Japan's role as the world's largest net creditor nation since 1985, and (3) Japan's low rate of inflation, which is among the lowest in the developed countries.

However, in order for foreigners to hold financial instruments denominated in the yen for liquidity and investment and to pay for imports, the access to such instruments must be relatively free from controls, and much import must be denominated in the yen. This is not the case. Japan lacks well-developed short-term financial markets that would satisfy foreigners' need for liquid and safe financial instruments. Its treasury bill and **commercial paper markets** are not well developed, and retrictions exist on some Euroyen investments. These factors reduced the yen's ability to serve as a medium of exchange in international financial markets and as a reserve currency for official holdings of foreign exchange.

The bulk of Japan's foreign trade is denominated in foreign currencies, not in the yen, thus reducing the yen's use as an international unit of account and medium of exchange. In particular, only a small percentrage of Japan's trade with North American is denominated in the yen (16.4% of exports and 10.2% of imports in 1989). One reason for this is that the bankers' acceptance market in Japan is not well developed, which makes it difficult for Japanese firms to obtain trade financing in yen. Japanese banks not only lend abroad in foreign currencies to take advantage of higher yields abroad, they also borrow overseas in foreign currencies to make foreign currency loans to domestic firms (**impact loans**) to take advantage of the less stringent regulations on such loans. In addition Japanese exporters reportedly have sought to denominate their exports in foreign currencies in order to maintain their export market shares in spite of the appreciation of the yen and reduced profit margins. Imports are denominated mainly in the currencies of other developed countries.

Nevertheless, since 1987 the share of Japan's foreign trade denominated in the yen has grown. The percentage of Japan's exports denominated in the yen was 33.4% in 1987, 34.7% in 1989, and 39.4% in 1991. Analysts expect the trend to continue and cite exporters' attempt to reduce exchange risk as the main reason. The percentage of imports denominated in the yen was 10.6% in 1987, 14.1% in 1989, and 15.6% in 1991. Japanese officials worry that this growing trend for Japanese companies to settle their foreign trade in yen instead of dollars will make it more difficult to cut the nation's trade surplus through exchange-rate manipulation.

See also **financial liberalization, yen–dollar exchange rates**.

References

Inose, Hijiri. 1992. In trade, yen gains on dollar. *Nikkei Weekly*, Feb. 15: 1, 10.

International Monetary Fund. Annual. *IMF Annual Report*.

Tavlas, George S. and Yuzuru Ozeki. 1991a. The internationalization of the yen. *Finance and Development*, June: 2–5.

Tavlas, George S., and Yuzuru Ozeki. 1991b. The Japanese yen as an international currency. *IMF working paper*, no. 91/2.

yen shock   The severe recession that stemmed from the large appreciation of the yen vis-à-vis the U.S. dollar since September 1985.

In 1978 there was a small yen shock (*yen shoku*) due to the rise in the value of the yen. **Bankruptcies** among the small- and medium-sized businesses increased. By and large, however, the Japanese economy withstood the shock and was not appreciably damaged by it.

Since the Plaza Accord of September 1985 when the world's leading central banks agreed to further the dollar's decline, the value of the yen in relation to the dollar increased by more than 60% by April 1987. The short-term adverse impact on Japanese exports was severe. Bankcruptcies more than doubled in 1986. The industries hardest hit are the export-oriented electronics, steel, and automobile. The **steel industry** had to resort to unprecedented massive layoffs as well as production cutbacks. While the Japanese industries were going through the difficulties, their competitors in South Korea, Taiwan, Hong Kong, benefited from the shock as their exports became relatively cheaper.

The shock has prompted Japanese industries and government officials to reexamine their production and trade strategies. Some firms, such as the electronics giant Matsushita Industrial, have decided to increase their production of lower-value labor-intensive products or components in Southeast Asian countries where labor cost is much cheaper. Still other firms have decided to increase automation and concentrate on higer-value models. Other firms have decided to diversify to reduce the impact of high yen.

Government officials have stressed the desirability of reorienting Japanese industries from the export market to the domestic market. The yen shock illustrates vividly the vulnerability of Japanese industries because of their export dependence.

See also **yen—dollar exchange rates**.

References

Kanabayashi, Masayoshi, and Bernard Wysochki, Jr. 1986. Yen's rapid rise against the U.S. dollar shakes Japan's export-oriented industry. *Wall Street Journal*, Feb. 5.

McKinnon, Ronald I. 1987. Currency protectionism: Parity lost. *Wall Street Journal*, Feb. 2.

Nishikawa, Hiroshika. 1990. Influence of exchange rate fluctuations on Japan's manufacturing industry—Empirical analysis 1980–88. *Bank of Japan Monetary and Economic Studies 8*, 1: 79–134.

Wysocki, Bernard Jr. 1987. Battling a high yen, many Japanese firms shift work overseas. *Wall Street Journal*, Feb. 27: 1, 10.

Yokohama   Located on the western shore of Tokyo Bay in Kanagawa prefecture just 30 kilometers south of **Tokyo**, Yokohama is Japan's largest port and second largest city in terms of population (3.27 million as of October 1992). It was opened to world trade in 1859, after the Friendship and Commercial Treaty between Japan and the United States was signed in 1858. It also has much manufacturing industry. Currently there is a massive urban development project (*Minato Mirai* 21) under way to develop its waterfront area into an international business center (author's interview, Yokohama City Hall, July 23, 1992).

In FY 1989 Yokohama had a gross municipal product of ¥9.35 trillion, or 2.3% of Japan's gross domestic product, the fourth among the major cities behind Tokyo, Osaka, and Nagoya. Its residents produced, however, 3% of Japan's gross national product in the same year, because many of them commute to work in Tokyo. Yokohama's major industries are electrical machinery and general machinery. In 1990 it produced ¥1.77 trillion of electrical machinery and ¥950 billion of general machinery, which placed Yokohama as the first and the second, respectively, in these industries among the major cities. Manufacturing output constituted 23% of total output, followed by services (19%).

Yokohama has been Japan's leading foreign trade port since the mid-1960s. In 1990 it handled 13% of Japan's foreign trade. Its waterfront development projects, a showcase of urban development in Japan, is expected to attract more foreign as well as domestic businesses.

In the Capital Redevelopment Plan announced by the Japanese government in 1985 to reduce the concentration of business and government agencies in Tokyo, Yokohama is to be developed as a core business city for relocating some companies and government agencies. In 1989 the government decided to move 79 officies and agencies to Yokohama. As of 1992, 16 of them were planning such a move. Yokohama's future development will be enhanced by such relocation.

See also **Nagoya and Central Japan, Kansai and Osaka, Tokyo.**

Address

City of Yokohama
1-1, Minato-cho, Naka-ku, Yokohama 231
Tel: (045) 671-2655   Fax: (045) 663-3415

Reference

City of Yokohama. 1992. *Yokohama: Facts and Figures, 1992.*